James Dunkerley was born in the Thames valley in
1953. He studied at the universities of York and
Oxford and was subsequently Research Fellow in
Latin American Studies at the universities of London and Liverpool. He now works for the Latin
American Bureau, London. The author of *The
Long War: Dictatorship and Revolution in El Salvador* (Junction Books 1982) and *Los Orígenes del
Poder Militar* (La Paz 1984), he is currently preparing a detailed historical survey of the Bolivian revolution of 1952 and, with Jenny Pearce, a survey of
the contemporary crisis in Central America.

James Dunkerley

Verso

Rebellion in the Veins

Political Struggle in Bolivia,
1952–82

British Library
Cataloguing in Publication Data

Dunkerley, James
    Rebellion in the veins.
      1. Bolivia — Politics and government, 1952 —
      I. Title
      984′.052   F3326

ISBN 0 86091 089 X
      0 86091 794 O Pbk

Verso Editions
15 Greek Street London W1

Filmset in Baskerville by
Red Lion Setters, London

Printed in Great Britain by
The Thetford Press
Thetford, Norfolk

To Ana María

Ñoqayllapi Tukukuchum
kinsantin múndoj rigornin:
wajcha kaywan, sapan kaywan,
Rúnaj wasinpi kausaywan.

Contents

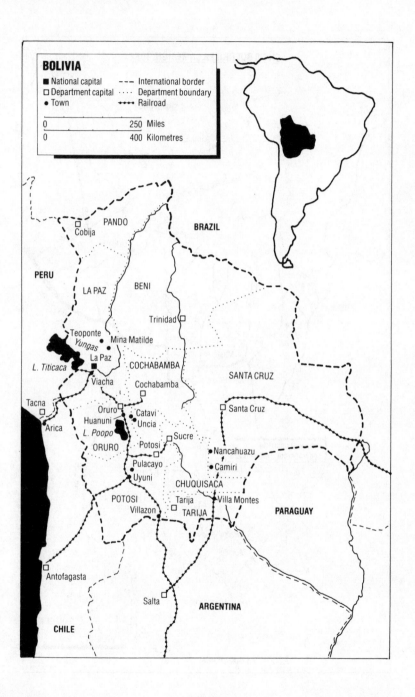

BOLIVIA

■ National capital   --- International border
□ Department capital   ····· Department boundary
● Town   ●●●● Railroad

| 0 | | 250 | Miles |
| 0 | | 400 | Kilometres |

PANDO

BRAZIL

Cobija

PERU

LA PAZ

BENI

Trinidad

Teoponte
Yungas
Mina Matilde

L. Titicaca
La Paz

COCHABAMBA

Viacha

SANTA CRUZ

Cochabamba

Tacna

Oruro
Catavi
Santa Cruz

Arica

Huanuni
Uncia

L. Poopo

ORURO

Potosi
Sucre

Nancahuazu

Pulacayo

Camiri

Uyuni

CHUQUISACA

POTOSI

Tarija
Villa Montes

Villazon

TARIJA

PARAGUAY

Antofagasta

Salta

ARGENTINA

CHILE

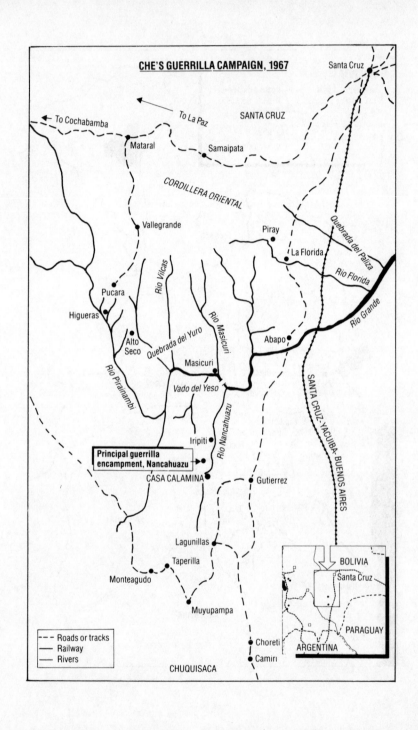

CHE'S GUERRILLA CAMPAIGN, 1967

Foreword

Bolivia is a country with a reputation. Not so long ago it was for Ché Guevara, for whose death its citizens are on occasions held to be collectively responsible. More recently it has been for cocaine. But in general it is for political disorder. Readers of serious newspapers may retain in the back of their minds the fact that the country has experienced a large number of military coups; they will not, in all probability, recall the exact number, but it is very high. Yet, Guevara was an intruder, an Argentine arriving from Cuba to fight an international revolution. The fact that he did not understand Bolivia played an important part in determining that he died there. In recent years production of cocaine has indeed flourished in the east of the country, but while a great many peasant farmers are involved in the cultivation of the coca leaf from which the drug is obtained, the small number of traffickers in cocaine have become a cosmopolitan breed, in no sense representative of the nation as a whole and capable of influencing its government only for a very short period.

The question of Bolivia's political instability is more profound. Even inside Latin America the country's politics are frequently treated with a certain indulgence as a cacophonous provincial struggle between pompous officers and surly indian workers locked into some indigenous teleology that denies the Andean state even a modicum of order and has deprived the nation of considerable opportunities for material progress. Behind such an image one can perceive traces of racism and a rather crude geo-political determinism: a country situated away from the sea in the bleak fastnesses of the Andes and overwhelmingly populated by indians does not make for mature and pacific government. Perhaps it was for this reason that someone once described Ecuador, which has a similar population but more order, as 'Bolivia on valium'. The newspapers trot out the mathematics of disorder — all of it fifth-hand and incorrect — but do not pose the question that if disorder is so prevalent might it not be order itself? Could there not be a system in the chaos? Should it not be understood less as interruption than as continuity?

Such questions are not pursued because, on the face of things, Bolivia is not a very important country. Although its debt is high, so is that of almost every Latin American state, and the $3.8 billion owed to the banks by Bolivia does not even begin to compare with the $90 billion debt on Brazil's books, threatening to plunge the international financial system into chaos. Bolivia has not smuggled its way into international recognition by dint of prowess at football. It won the Latin American championship for the first and only time early in the 60s, provoking celebrations of such magnitude that there was a momentary lapse in the operation of both state and civil society; but even the most ardent fan will, when pressed, admit that this may have been marginally affected by the fact that foreign teams were obliged to play for ninety minutes at an altitude of 12,000 feet. The clubs of La Paz, Oruro and Potosí rarely lose the home legs of international fixtures; an alarmingly palid Zico summed up the situation after Brazil went down to a listless defeat in 1982: 'It is suicide to play football in Bolivia'. Neither does the country have outstanding territorial claims against metropolitan states; its principal dispute is with Chile, which in 1880 took possession of Bolivia's coastal lands, thereby sealing it off from the sea and, apparently, the rest of the world.

We need no intricate conspiracy theory involving lesser mortals who are not citizens of the republic to sustain the view that history has connived at Bolivia's marginalisation. Between 200 and 500 A.D. Tiwanaku was established as the major religious centre for a large swathe of an Andean population that upheld one of the most advanced 'illiterate civilisations' in world history. Its dominance lasted until 1000. Only partially subdued by the Inca empire, the area that is today Bolivia was for a period of 150 years the source of incomparable wealth for the Spanish empire. Potosí became one of the largest and richest cities in the Americas, the site of a vast productive enterprise involving not just forced labour but also highly sophisticated wage systems, complex engineering works, and industrial relations no less charged or intractable than those in many contemporary centres of monopoly capitalism. In 1800, when this system was on the verge of collapse, the population of Bolivia was larger than that of any other region of South America except Brazil, and over five times greater than that of Argentina. Even in 1850, when the first phase of European immigration was in sight, Bolivia had twice as many people as Argentina, and its population of 2.1 million easily overhauled that of 1.4 million in Chile.

The era of Anglo Saxon empires changed all this. Bolivia became the world's leading producer of tin, but in a manner that neither propelled internal development nor drew the country out of its isolation. It has remained a backward economy, a society inextricably bound up with the exigencies of forging an existence in the most difficult of physical conditions and still deeply enmeshed in an ancient autochthonous culture. There have, of course, been important changes and the imprint of foreign intrusion is not hard to find. The urban middle class is, like its hemispheric peers, considerably better dressed than that in Europe, consumes a healthy ration of beer brewed by German immigrants, and is very familiar with the exchange rate of the US dollar. If it were to be characterised by a social distinctiveness other than its small size and relative poverty, it would perhaps be that it is uncommonly well-mannered. This parochial peculiarity is matched by other minor anomalies that are markedly less indigenous. The stamp of the British presence in the opening decades of the century has been left in the mines through the continued usage of words such as 'winch', 'block-caving', and 'sink and float', all of which are an integral part of the vocabulary of a proletariat that is, far from coincidentally, amongst the most militant in the world. The football league features teams like 'The Strongest' and 'Blooming', 'Always Ready' being relegated at the end of the 1981 season. A major source of finance for the emerging Amazonian department of the Beni is known, for reasons which are not entirely local in their origin, as BIG Beni – *Banco Industrial y Ganadero del Beni*. There are, of course, the more familiar stigmata of imperialism in garish Coca Cola signs, the large and offensive buildings of North American banks, and an inordinately large number of Japanese cars. Bolivia is, therefore, an occupied country, but its occupation has been remarkably uneven as a result of a singular but largely ignored history.

The revolution of April 1952, *la Revolución Nacional*, remains one of the most under-studied of the post-World War Two political revolutions. There are two English language books in print that consider it with more than passing reference; even in Spanish its bibliography cannot compare with that of the revolutions in Mexico, Cuba, Nicaragua or even El Salvador. Like many other national liberation struggles waged in the aftermath of the war it failed to achieve its objectives yet for a while it was an event that matched the scope of the Mexican revolution before it, concentrating the attention of the

Americas if not the world. Today it continues to have a special interest for sympathisers of Trotskyism, who identify in Bolivia one of the strongest contingents of their movement but otherwise some knowledge of 1952 and what followed it is the exclusive preserve of a handful of academics who are marginalised less by their intellectual attributes than by the fact that they have chosen to focus them in this area. The revolution was a long time – two Bolivian generations – ago, but it is still the central feature of the country's political history. At a time when Latin America is once again the scene of critical political conflicts that are in some respects comparable to the Bolivian experience, the events of 1952 and their legacy should be reclaimed for political as well as historical purposes.

In endeavouring to provide some foundation for such a retrieval I have adopted a straightforward chronological and narrative approach. I am conscious that this has to no small degree constrained the manner in which I have depicted an essentially alien land and society, where, for example, a 'valley' is frequently not a graduated depression in the landscape but a narrow, barely accessible gorge between steep peaks, a land where over a quarter of all vehicles are lorries, only a fiftieth of all roads are paved, and communications are qualitatively worse than, say, in Chile or Argentina. It is not difficult to see that such factors have important political effects and need to be incorporated into our vision of public confusion. Similarly, I have not dwelt on the subtle but critical differences between the family unit in Bolivia and that in modern Europe or North America, explained at length the particular importance of 'Level 411' in the Siglo XX mine, or attempted to unravel the specific connotations of 'Lechingrado' or 'Lechín's tree', to which Alejandro Orfila, the general secretary of the Organisation of American States, was obliged to walk in order to converse with the legendary leader of the COB. Perhaps most important of all, the present survey desists from extended discussion of life in the countryside and those features of the social organization of Bolivia's indigenous peoples which would normally be considered the province of anthropologists. The existence if not the full character of these features should emerge from a text that has the simple purpose of providing a panoramic view of a political history that is sufficiently complex and unknown to require consideration in measured stages. A chronological depiction does, of course, carry with it a plethora of problems, not least of which is the imposition of linear order on phenomena that need to be deconstructed and analysed with respect to their synchronic characteristics as well as their historical development. Nonetheless, the need to know 'what has happened' exists at various levels, and if this version is pitched uncomfortably close to the track along which the freight train of Whig history trundles happily to and fro, it is to be hoped that it provides at least some basic elements for the construction of a fuller and richer discussion.

Although they frequently did not share my naive estimation of the possibilities and ramifications of harnessing the results of historical research to a polemical survey of contemporary politics, a great many people have contributed in a more or less direct way to this book. Most have assisted by encouraging preparation of a separate, more academic study of 1952, the results of which were partly siphoned off to provide the basis for the present text. My chief debt is without doubt to Laurence Whitehead, who, in addition to motivating fruitful discussions on Bolivia over many years, has ignored the central tenet of academic practice by making generous loans of original material and his own varied and incisive writings. These have been pillaged extensively but the source is, I think, attributed in each case. I have also been aided with enthusiasm, humour, and constant efficiency in the face of often appalling conditions by the staff of the library of the Universidad Mayor de San Andrés, La Paz. To its director, the distinguished historian Alberto Crespo Rodas, and his assistants Luis Verástegui and Jenny Peñaranda, my thanks. The text has also benefited a great deal from discussions with two politicians who have played an important part in the writing of their country's history: Guillermo Lora (POR) and José Luis Roca (PDC). For reasons of space it has not been possible to include the results of a modest oral history project on 1952 which was undertaken in 1981 and 1982 and funded by the Social Science Research Council (New York), the Nuffield Foundation, and the British Academy. However, many of the testimonies that were recorded have exercised a strong influence on sections of the text. Of those who participated, I should like to make a special note of gratitude to the following: Daniel Saravia; Víctor López; Filemón Escóbar; Sinforoso Cabrera; Colonel Arsenio González; René Ruíz González; and Alfonsina Paredes. Very special thanks go to Zelma Aguilar and Penelope Woolcock, who were largely responsible for the success of the project and imposed their own stamp upon it. I am also grateful to Wilbert Van Miert, who sent me press cuttings when I was out of the country, and Rolando Morales Anaya, who kept me apace with the complexities of the contemporary economy. Alberto and Chela Aguilar were, as always, in the front line, dispensing affection, domestic support, and occasional protection from the consequences of my erratic behaviour. At my other home Bill Schwarz has passed judgement on the acceptability of all anecdotes, suffered aimless monologues well past midnight, and adroitly quizzed dubious passages into shape. Thanks to him this book has in no sense resulted in the oppression, repression or depression of the household that produced it. Finally, I have been sustained throughout by the independent love of Dylan and Penny, whose affection extended to reading a draft. It is a long list, but none of its members can be brought to task for the errors or idiocies that the curious reader may dig out; these will be mine alone.

1.
BACKGROUND
TO REVOLT

Late in the afternoon of Tuesday 8 April 1952 a rather corpulent senior army officer left the front entrance of the presidential Palacio Quemado and hurriedly made his way through the cobbled streets of La Paz to the nearby offices of the Dirección General de Policías. A bystander braving the sharp autumnal chill on the benches of the Plaza Murillo to observe the comings and goings of dignatories would not, in all probability, have expressed much surprise. Although La Paz had no television and its papers kept the photographic content of their editions to an absolute minimum, General Antonio Seleme Vargas was well known to *paceños* as a more than usually active and voluble minister of government in the junta of General Hugo Ballivián. It was Seleme who was responsible for making the regime's constant accusations against the *Movimiento Nacionalista Revolucionario* (MNR) for planning a rebellion and 'entering into alliance with the communists'; under his direction police chief Donato Millán had his men search bread queues for subversive literature and engage in frequent round-ups of union militants and left-wingers. In recent weeks the minister's *carabineros* had been particularly emphatic in breaking up large popular demonstrations demanding supplies of bread, meat and sugar, which, with inflation running at over 65 per cent, were the objects of keen speculation and rarely to be found in the markets.

That a busy senior member of the cabinet should visit the palace at the end of a working day was eminently unremarkable. That he should depart without an escort might perhaps have stirred the curiosity of those cognisant of military protocol; but there were few observers that afternoon, which showed no signs of unusual political activity or crisis. The city was recovering from the damage caused by very heavy late summer rains and preparing for Easter weekend. Despite a recent increase in cinema prices there were the usual long queues; the Cine Princesa was registering particularly good audiences for 'Amor o Pecado?' ('The Astonished Heart'), starring Noel Coward, Celia Johnson and Margaret Leighton. The attention of the press had been diverted from rumours of another *golpe* (coup) by a heated exchange of views on the price of Bolivian tin between the producers and a Texan senator by the name of Lyndon B. Johnson. The economic situation was exceedingly poor and the junta had finally been obliged to promise fresh elections by the end of the year, but there was little evidence of either an imminent collapse of the regime or an upturn in the activity of the MNR.

The manifestly nervous Seleme knew otherwise. After over thirty years of largely undistinguished service as an artillery officer in which he had fought one international and one civil war and maintained his commission through 14 changes of government, the 48-year old *cochabambino* of Arab extraction must have been aware that he had embarked upon the most critical week in his public life. Although – to the great surprise of the president's adjutant – the meeting with Ballivián had ended with warm *abrazos* and protestations of loyalty and admiration on both sides, it had also confirmed Seleme's dismissal from the cabinet. Indeed, the most surprising feature of the encounter was that the ex-minister did leave the Quemado alone and not under arrest since the president and the majority of his colleagues were convinced that Seleme was preparing a coup. The day before this accusation had been made at a cabinet meeting by the young minister of labour, Colonel Sergio Sánchez, a man who Seleme knew to have high ambitions of his own and whose nickname of '*peroncito*' betrayed a proclivity for populist gestures that sat uneasily within the stern authoritarian policies of the regime. Sánchez had been both correct and unnervingly precise in his timing. The previous day Seleme had gone to the house of an MNR militant, Raúl Canedo Reyes, and sworn loyalty to the party, an oath that was preserved for posterity by a discreetly hidden tape-recorder. While the general was holding his final discussion with the president the MNR's *Comité Revolucionario* had collected at the Canedo house under the chairmanship of Hernán Siles Zuazo to finalise plans for a rising of which Seleme would be military chief and which would elevate him to the presidency until new elections were held in October.

Seleme's dismissal meant that the plans for the rising had to be brought forward since the support of his 2,000 policemen was crucial to the capture of the capital. Hence the speed with which the general made his way to the police headquarters where he appraised Millán and Colonel César Aliaga of his plans. These caused the consternation of the former, who was compelled to release a group of *movimientistas* his men had apprehended when they were taking up position, but relieved the latter, whom the MNR had recruited separately as a justifiable safeguard against the fickle tendencies of his commander. Seleme then made off to see Siles in an effort to persuade him to bring the *Falange Socialista Boliviana* (FSB) into the rising. In the event, last-minute talks with the FSB resulted only in acrimony and news of the coup reaching the army commander, General Humberto Torres Ortiz, who rapidly left his home to assemble a force from the principal garrisons stationed in the *altiplano* (Andean plain). Ballivián also prudently chose not to sleep at the palace that night. This meant that Seleme was unable to negotiate an early surrender or talk his colleagues into a switch of allegiances, a move of which he had high hopes since Torres Ortiz had himself held discussions with the MNR and was not expected to fall in behind Ballivián. However, this state of affairs also facilitated the comparatively easy occupation of the city centre from midnight onwards by the *carabineros* and armed units of the MNR. At 6 a.m. on the 9th. the state-controlled Radio Illimani went on the air to announce that the revolution had triumphed.

The MNR was experienced in such actions and had prepared the ground well, grooming officers in key positions, especially in the police. Amongst those who had promised support was Captain Israel Tellez, commander of the arsenal at Orkojahuira; but when Tellez was finally able to coax the key to the strongroom out of a reluctant warrant officer the rebels discovered only 80 weapons and a limited amount of ammunition. Obligatory military service ensured that the capital did not lack men who knew how to shoot straight, and there were numerous private stores of rifles and pistols as a result of many petty clashes with the military over recent years, but the failure to secure at an early stage a stock of heavy weapons was a distinct setback. For Seleme it became decisive when he received confirmation that Torres Ortiz would not discuss terms, had established headquarters at the airforce base of El Alto on the crest of the vast crater in which La Paz nestles, and was gathering nine regiments with a total of 8,000 men to put into effect a long-standing contingency plan for sealing off the city and isolating an insurrection. At 3 p.m. the rebels came under attack from the Lanza regiment, moving out from the principal barracks in Miraflores, and a contingent of cadets, advancing up from the Colegio Militar to take the affluent neighbourhood of Sopacachi. An hour later Torres Ortiz felt sufficiently confident to have planes drop leaflets demanding unconditional surrender before 6 p.m. although a small group of factory workers had managed to hold off the cadets while the *carabineros* were still containing the advance of the Lanza. This, however, failed to lift Seleme out of his deepening pessimism, and after discussions with fellow insurgent officers he went on Radio Illimani at 7 p.m. to announce that he was handing leadership of the rebellion over to the civilians. The general then scuttled off with Millán to the security of the Chilean embassy.

Seleme proved to be correct in his belief that the revolt would now lead to an outright confrontation with the military and that the rebels were too low on ammunition to have more than an outside chance of success. But he deserted his own cause too soon. Over the following two days the fierce fighting in and around La Paz transformed a traditional *golpe de estado* into a popular insurrection.[1] By mid-afternoon on Friday the 11th. the armed forces had been categorically defeated, thrown into flight or won to the revolutionary cause. When General Torres Ortiz met the new leader of the insurrection, Hernán Siles, at the village of Laja to sign a formal document of surrender it was not the dissident *carabineros* who held control of the capital but hastily-formed units of factory workers, MNR militants, townsfolk and miners, now heavily armed and making demands for the complete dismantling of the military apparatus, nationalisation and workers' control of the mines, an agrarian revolution, and the formation of popular militias.

Within hours of the fall of the Ballivián junta it was plain that the old order had been emphatically overthrown and that the MNR regime which was to replace it would depend heavily on the support of armed workers whose expectations went much further than allowed for in the party's ill-defined reformist programme. Under the conditions of the Cold War, the McCarthy crusade, and the escalating campaigns against the regimes of Arbenz in Guatemala and Mossadegh in Iran as well as the Korean War it was unsurprising that the April revolution excited so much attention in the rest of the hemisphere and produced alarm in Washington at the prospect of a 'communist takeover' in a state that lay at the heart of South America, bordering on five other countries including Perón's Argentina.

It is not difficult to find evidence as to why such an event might have occurred. Bolivia was notoriously backward. Its gross domestic product (GDP) was a meagre $118.6 per capita, making it the poorest country in the hemisphere with the sole exception of Haiti.[2] Over 72 per cent of the economically active population worked in agriculture, which in 1950 accounted for cultivation of less than two per cent of land area with annual production valued at only $117 million, which was still 33 per cent of GDP. Manufacturing industry employed only four per cent of all workers and contributed less than nine per cent of GDP. Mining, on the other hand, employed 3.2 per cent of the active population and produced 25 per cent of GDP. A country the same size as France, Italy and West Germany combined possessed a population of 2.7 million, of which just 22 per cent lived in settlements of over 2,000 people, its capital city being only 267,000 strong, well ahead of the second largest town Cochabamba, which had a population of 80,000. Only 31 per cent of Bolivia's population was literate; eight per cent had completed secondary education. In 1950 there were 3,700 registered students in the country's five universities which issued 132 degrees in that year. Bolivia had fewer schools than Paraguay; its total budget was little larger than that of Argentina's smallest province, Santa Fé. Nearly three children in ten died in the first year of life and the life expectancy at one year fell well short of fifty. There were 706 doctors in the republic, less than half the national stock of lawyers.

These indices of structural underdevelopment were matched by those for recent economic performance, underscoring the extreme fragility of the system which the military junta had been charged with defending. The cost of living index in 1951 had risen to 5,041 from a base of 100 in 1931, the exchange rate of the *boliviano* falling from

30.14 to the dollar in 1938 to 176.11. Over 18 per cent of imports to an overwhelmingly agricultural country were foodstuffs while both the tonnage and value of tin exports — the mainstay of the economy — were the lowest in over a decade, permitting the government to spend no more than $30 a head in its budget.[3]

The Rule of the Rosca

However eloquent these statistics might be, they do not explain the particular nature of the Bolivian economic crisis or how this came to culminate in the April insurrection. The central feature was, in fact, less the sheer backwardness of the country than the manner in which it was structured through combined and uneven development, a common phenomenon in backward capitalist countries, in which a relatively advanced, export-oriented capitalist sector — in this case tin mining — coexisted and inter-related with an archaic, stagnant and predominantly provincial organisation of agriculture. The imbalances and tensions caused by this structure were further heightened and directly politicised by the fact that control of the strategically vital tin industry lay in the hands of a tiny oligarchy which wielded such enormous influence over the state's fiscal affairs and exercised a corresponding political power that it fully justified its title of *superestado minero* (mining superstate). By the 1940s the omnipotence of this group was under severe challenge, in part as a result of the inherent dangers of reliance upon the export of a single commodity in a generally unfavourable international market and in part as a result of domestic pressures. These derived from both a radicalisation of the mining proletariat and a wider political movement that fused nationalist, democratic and reformist elements into a broad anti-oligarchic mandate. The strength and popularity of this movement may in one sense be explained by the fact that the disparities in wealth and power nurtured under the regime of the great mineowners were so great that they were bound in time to expose it to an irresistible offensive, but the manner in which this finally took place was more complex than a simple, populist and Machiavellian analysis will allow.

The power of the tin companies was indisputable: three family firms controlled eighty per cent of an industry that accounted for eighty per cent of national exports and provided the state with its only secure tax base and input of foreign exchange. Before 1941 these companies produced up to a quarter of the world's tin and never less than 15 per cent; during the war their share rose to 49 per cent. In 1945 the 'big three' produced 35,000 fine tons of ore when no other enterprise in Bolivia had an output of over 400 tons.[4] The Rosca (literally, small kernel), to use its more popular title, had established a presence in the international market that evoked analogies with the colonial silver boom, when the mines around Potosí pumped huge quantities of the metal into the seventeenth century European market, fuelled a long-term inflationary spiral and transformed a bleak provincial village into a city of over 160,000 people, one of the largest and most active commercial centres in the Americas and by the early nineteenth century the source of nearly half the global monetary stock.[5] In 1950 the population of Potosí was barely 40,000 and its former glory signalled only by an inordinately large number of colonial churches, the pockmarked and exhausted hill that towered behind the town, and the still unspoilt charm of nearby Sucre, the garden city that provided legal and ecclesiastical administration during the colony and which, despite its backwardness, remains Bolivia's legal capital.

Tin was in many respects built on the infrastructure of silver to carry into the twentieth century Bolivia's dependence upon mining. It was not the colonial silver industry it replaced but a 'second phase' that took place in the last half of the nineteenth century, brought the first railways to the country, displaced the chaotic rule of the military caudillos, and established links with Anglo-Chilean capital that were to buttress a southern agro-mining elite that held direct political power but was in many aspects similar to the oligarchy of tin which succeeded it. The hegemony of the silver mineowners did not last for long; it was not until the 1870s that it had ensured a firm policy of free trade and only after the loss of Bolivia's seaboard to Chile in the War of the Pacific (1879-83) that it was able to secure undisputed political power. By this stage the extended and very costly process of rehabilitating the flooded and long-unused mineshafts inherited at independence (1825) had reached its peak, the Huanchaca mine being the world's second largest in terms of production after Broken Hill, with a peak annual output of 130,000 kilos valued at six million pesos. However, within a decade the general shift of the leading economies to the gold standard placed the industry's future in grave doubt.[6] Its decline was rapid and irreversible: in 1895 the revenue from silver exports was still 17 times greater than that of tin, but by 1902 only ten per cent greater, and in 1908 tin accounted for 66 per cent of export income against silver's share of only 17 per cent.

Only one leading silver firm survived the crash intact, that of the Aramayo family, which had made a practice of diversifying production from a comparatively early stage. The expansion of the new mineral, dynamised by massive rearmament in the metropolitan states of Europe and the introduction of canned foods both there and in the US, prompted the rise of a new generation of capitalists who at first had to enter into high-risk ventures with Anglo-Chilean capital in order to compete with the high-quality, low-cost shallow deposits dredged in Malaya and Indonesia (later Nigeria and the Congo as well). Most of Bolivia's deposits were, in contrast, set deep in hard rock and soon proved to be of rapidly diminishing richness, falling from an average content of 6.65 per cent in 1925 to 0.98 per cent in 1970. Yet their early excavation was greatly facilitated by the fact that tin is generally found in similar geological conditions to silver and could initially be exploited using the existing infrastructure.

Perhaps the most remarkable feature of the growth of the Bolivian tin industry was that the exigencies of high-bulk transport over some of the world's most difficult terrain, the need to ensure ever-increasing recapitalisation in order to locate, extract and undertake rudimentary treatment (concentration) of progressively poorer and deeper veins of ore, and the growing necessity of integrating the excavation process with international smelting and marketing facilities favoured not foreign entrepreneurs but native capitalists. Having benefited from early infusions of external capital, the domestic entrepreneurs were able to use their local knowledge and influence as well as substantial initial revenues and exceedingly low rates of tax to break free from high dividend-paying associations, reinvest heavily and buy out British and Chilean operators working either on a small scale or under counter-productive pressure from their shareholders. The pattern of development and control thus operated against the normal tendency but nevertheless made it obligatory for the Bolivian Rosca to become international capitalists as well as local monopolists.

The largest and most renowned enterprise was that owned by Simon Patiño, who by the 1920s controlled forty per cent of national production, and on the eve of the revolution was responsible for ten per cent

of world tin output. The Patiño company was the backbone of the
Rosca, developing into a powerful multinational corporation on the
basis of the rich deposits in its principal mining centre Siglo XX-Catavi,
large sections of which were bought off Chilean and British operators
who lacked the disposable capital, local expertise and legal and coercive
resources to develop their properties to the full. Patiño had started in
1896 with a cheap four-hectare site near the present complex, working its rich and shallow veins with a small crew in initially bad financial conditions. By 1906 he was able to set up his own bank, the Banco
Mercantil, with capital of £1 million, twice the sum held by the country's five other banks and greater than the total revenue of the state,
which imposed a meagre four per cent export tax on tin.[7] By 1924
Patiño had wrested control of the entire Llallagua site (the Siglo XX
mine and the Catavi concentration plant) from Chilean interests,
constructed a private $5 million railway from nearby Uncía to Macha-
camarca (on the main Oruro to Chile line), acquired the mines of Col-
quechaca, Kami, Colavi and Oploca and was registering an annual
revenue of $3 million after tax. However, when the regime of the
Republican Party increased export taxes from 7.5 per cent to nearly
15 per cent the following year, Patiño felt obliged to take a step already
dictated by the scale of his operations and moved his headquarters to
Delaware, reducing his exposure to fiscal and political pressures as
well as providing himself with a secure base from which to administer
international operations. (Delaware was chosen because it is a state
with particularly lax company law; in fact, Patiño himself spent most
of his time in Paris, closer to his European interests). By buying heavily into Malayan interests and purchasing important processing plants
throughout the world, the most strategic of which was the Williams
Harvey foundry at Bootle, the corporation obtained control over the
entire production process, a quarter of the world's pre-war smelting
capacity and, as a consequence, a substantial influence in the setting
of the world price. On Patiño's death in 1947 his company was registering profits of 31 per cent of capital value and controlled over a hundred subsidiaries world-wide; his own personal wealth was valued at
£70 million by Fortune magazine.[8]

This process of internationalisation took place on a much more
modest scale in the case of the other two companies, which both
depended on Patiño's European smelting plants. The *Compagnie
Aramayo de Mines de Bolivie S.A.*, registered in Switzerland in 1915

but quoted on the London Stock Exchange from 1906, concentrated its operations in the old silver zones around Potosí (Chorolque; Tasna; Telamayu; Animas) although it also bought the *paceño* pits of Caracoles and Viloco (where it began to develop wolfram) and the northern gold field of Tipuani.[9] From the 1920s the Aramayo share of national production rested at a steady seven per cent, with annual production rising to 3,000 fine tons in the 1940s. By this stage, however, the long-established and somewhat cautious enterprise was experiencing commercial and political pressures to no less a degree than its larger rival. It contested official estimates of its assets, challenged government-sponsored wage settlements (although it was usually more generous than Patiño) and ran a virulent campaign against increased fiscal impositions, particularly the requirement that a varying percentage of foreign exchange earnings be lodged with the state-owned Banco Central, permanently short of hard currency. There is little doubt that Patiño was able to reduce the effects of this obligation more easily than Aramayo, but it is equally clear that the latter had also adopted a policy of decapitalisation by the 1940s, demonstrated in the declaration of average dividend payments of 10.7 per cent over 15 years and reinvestment of only $5 million in the same period. Between 1940 and 1948 Aramayo registered profits of Bs.643 million and paid taxes of Bs.98 million. Significantly, the company resisted all efforts to establish a foundry in Bolivia; despite the fact that it gained no special advantage and incurred massive transport costs in using Patiño's British facilities, it was not prepared to countenance the enormous political and financial risks of concentrating the production process within national boundaries.[10]

The last major company to be established was that of Mauricio Hochschild, a Jewish immigrant from Austria who started out as a metals broker but by the early 1920s was acquiring valuable mines as many of his independent clients went bankrupt during the post-World War One recession. Hochschild's first major acquisition was the *Compañía Unificada del Cerro de Potosí*, soon followed by the important Oruro pits of San José and Colquiri. With these properties Hochschild overtook Aramayo to control a quarter of national production of tin as well as significant quantities of silver, copper and other metals. In 1948 the group's profits exceeded £700,000.

With such formidable resources the tin barons exercised substantial political power although none sought high office, generally preferring to lobby from abroad as ambassadors while their lawyers and advisors served in cabinets of varying political complexion. From the 1930s the Rosca found itself out of sympathy with many and openly opposed to a number of the country's transient regimes; it was at times compelled to resort to extreme measures in order to obtain acceptable operating conditions. However, since Aramayo owned *La Razón*, Hochschild had a controlling interest in *Ultima Hora*, and Patiño possessed a large share in *El Diario*, the companies were able to draw on the power of the press to complement the influence of their men in government, the reserves of their banks, and their close contacts with key consuming nations. They were, therefore, deeply immersed in the indigenous ruling class and integrated into its state apparatus. This allowed them to consolidate their advantages over competitors although, by the same token, it also made them a clear target for opposition.

One important factor in the weakening of this ruling class and the generation of a severe crisis on the eve of the revolution lay beyond the Rosca's control: the radical alteration of the structure of the world market caused by World War Two. By dint of prescient cartelisation and common acceptance of reduced quotas and revenues the companies had survived the 1929 crash and the recession that followed without succumbing to a retreat before US capital as was occurring in many Latin American countries. However, the outbreak of war in Europe and Asia compelled a major realignment, for not only were Malayan deposits now in the hands of the Japanese but the Atlantic shipping lanes were also too vulnerable for smelting at Bootle to be continued despite Patiño's early hopes. By late 1942 Bolivia was the only major supplier of tin to the Allies and — of most immediate importance — it was obliged to deal exclusively with the US, which possessed virtually no tin of its own. (Alaska produced forty tons a year between 1900 and 1940). The US government built a huge smelting plant at Texas City near Houston and imposed a great deal of political pressure on the particularly pliant regime of General Peñaranda to obtain a low price for ore as part of the Allied war effort. The official New York price index for tin stood static between 1941 and 1945 but the real price actually fell during these years, progressively depriving the Bolivian state of vital tax revenues and reversing the upward trend of the companies' profit margins. (That of Patiño had risen from £80,000 in 1939 to £1.4 million in 1942 but dropped back to £300,000 in 1946). In order to minimise the effect in the short-term and meet the very great demand the Rosca maximised production, increased its labour force by forty per cent and had doubled 1938 production within four years.[11] At the end of the war, therefore, substantial deposits of tin had been mined at decreasing profit with the result that the pits were in commercial terms over-manned and badly undercapitalised. The companies' response to this situation inside the country was to gener-ate serious political problems, but the international ramifications were no less severe since the US now possessed the world's largest smelt-ing capacity and massive buffer stocks of tin, enabling it to 'nurse' the international price in much the same way as a major producer but without many of the concomitant risks.

The full implications of this state of affairs were not immediately apparent since prices rose steadily if modestly in the post-war years and by 1950 they had reattained their 1935 level. However, the out-break of the Korean war renewed demand in conditions of open com-petition; the price of £600 a ton in June 1950 rose vertiginously to £1,600 in February 1951. The rapid inflation generated inside the US and the political unacceptability of financing the war effort with increased taxes added great weight to the lobby for a sale of buffer stocks to reduce the price and ease the crisis. By June 1951 Washing-ton was selling at £900 a ton tin it had bought from Bolivia at between £200 and £400 during the mid-40s. The Bolivian producers had lost a critical market advantage and, with their profit margins in manifest danger, joined forces with the Ballivián junta to negotiate an increase to £1,200. However, the US Reconstruction Finance Corporation (RFC) was under extreme pressure from domestic forces to force the price right down through buffer sales. The figurehead of this campaign was Lyn-don B. Johnson, who protected the interests of his constituency in forth-right terms: 'the tin producers appear more concerned about the prospect of future unsaleable tin surpluses than with the spectre of Communist aggression'.[12]

The RFC maintained its position and was little impressed by the Bolivians' drastic resort to halting all tin exports for nine months. Although the junta was losing revenue, it could not withstand the political consequences of an early climb-down, while the companies justifiably feared that, should the Malayan insurgency fail, the end of the Korean War would push prices lower still and cripple their opera-tions. (In the event prices fell steadily until 1958 and only retrieved the average 1951 level in 1964 as a result of another war, that in

Vietnam). The Rosca's few options were narrowed still further when Washington signed an agreement with the British government at a price above that offered to the Bolivians, raising another spectre — that of a complete monopoly of Malayan and US-owned tin.

Although in negotiating with the Ballivián government the US was dealing with a regime that was not only 'friendly' but had also come to power through a coup to stop a democratically-elected government assuming office because it was 'communist-backed', Washington failed to perceive the impact of its effective boycott or to comprehend why negotiations had become so bitter. This only became clear a few weeks after the tin barons finally started to move towards the US terms in March 1952. Unsurprisingly, the first reaction to the April revolution in the US was to criticise the RFC's tactics, but in the long-term the power derived from Washington's tin stocks was to be of critical importance in controlling political developments inside Bolivia.

These international factors undoubtedly played an important part in prompting the final removal of the Rosca and the collapse of the *ancien regime* over which it had presided with decreasing assurance for half a century, but they were matched by the more immediate challenge presented by the companies' own workers, who in the decade prior to 1952 had acquired unprecedented organisational strength and a commitment to radical politics.

The size of the mining proletariat was very small compared to the population working in the countryside; at its peak during the expansionary war years it was only 53,000 strong, a figure that was never equalled after 1952. Yet this sector possessed an economic and political influence out of all proportion to its size by virtue of the strategic importance of the industry. Moreover, Bolivian miners lived and worked in conditions that were — and continue to be — far more onerous than those which are generally considered crucial to determining the particular bonds of solidarity and radicalism of miners throughout the world. We will return to this subject later but it is worth noting here that, with very few exceptions, Bolivian camps are located in very high, infertile and isolated regions of the Andes with extremely harsh climatic conditions and only the most rudimentary form of communications; virtually all basic supplies must be shipped in over long distances and steep mountain ranges, in some cases to camps well above the snow-line. They are bleak and dangerous industrial outposts populated by communities entirely dependent upon their employer for power, housing, food and medical care as well as work.

When the US Board of Economic Warfare set about negotiating a contract with the Rosca it sent a commission to inspect conditions in the mines before writing labour clauses into the final agreement. The Magruder Commission (1943) was considered an outrageous intervention by Patiño, not least because it added to the already substantial literature itemising conditions in his mines. Amongst its many criticisms, the Commission noted 'the total absence of free association and collective bargaining', that, 'the real wages of mineworkers have declined in spite of substantial increases of cash wages', that there was no minimum wage, and that mining communities as a whole had a nutritional intake which was of a 'level well below standards commonly accepted for good health . . . dangerously low'.[13] According to MNR, only three per cent of Patiño's workers earned more than a dollar a day in 1943. In October 1946 the *sindicato* (trade union) at Catavi was presenting demands for a minimum adult male wage of the equivalent of 32 cents a day.[14] At the same camp Patiño had, according to the union, provided only 3,869 one-room, one-window and unplumbed houses for a total of 7,500 miners, who had an average of three children each.[15] Although the shafts of the mines are not as endangered by gas as are coal seams, they lack the most minimal safety standards and are maintained in extremely precarious fashion, leading to a high number of accidents. Often standing waist-high in water, faceworkers are subjected to an intense heat that makes the wearing of the few protective face-masks available extremely difficult after only a few minutes' work. As a result the incidence of silicosis has always been high. In 1945 the chief medical officer at the central hospital at Oruro found that the average age of those with third degree silicosis was 32, with a median 4.5 years spent at the face.[16]

Under such conditions the major camps had developed into centres of militant syndicalism supervised by nearby military garrisons. Yet, largely because of their isolation, the mines had not been greatly affected by the doctrines of anarchism and anarcho-syndicalism that swept into Bolivia from Argentina and Chile in the first decades of the century. This was to make them accessible to other political currents in the 40s, but it did not signify any lack of radicalism or reduce the level of social conflict, which in many cases during the pre-war era led to open fighting and the direct intervention of the army. The first

The mine at Potosí

Above Inside Siglo XX. *Below* Mine worker at Poopó, near Oruro

Photograph: Jenny Matthews/Format

major instance of this occurred in 1923 when the military put down a strike in Uncía (a town five miles from Siglo XX) by killing eight workers and wounding a dozen more. In December 1942 this scenario was repeated on a larger scale. After a year in which Patiño had increased his revenue by 84 per cent, inflation had reached thirty per cent, and the company's real (sterling) wage bill had increased by less than five per cent, workers at Catavi went on strike in demand for wage increases of between twenty and seventy per cent. The company made a few efforts at negotiation and prevailed upon the regime of General Peñaranda to send in troops. There was no armed resistance but 35 people were killed—including a number of women who traditionally headed protest marches—in an unusually vicious attack by the local garrison.[17]

These were the most notable cases, attracting attention throughout the country and generating acrimonious political debate, but there were many other instances of violent repression, with several camps being subjected to virtual states of siege from the early 1940s. As the Association of Medium Mineowners noted towards the end of the decade, 'every day the repression or punishment of leaders of illegal strikes becomes more and more necessary'.[18] In his memoirs René López Murillo recalls that as a young lieutenant stationed at Catavi in the late 40s he received—in addition to his army pay—700 *bolivianos* in cash, Bs.1,500 in housing allowances, 200 Derby cigarettes, free entry to the cinema and cheap rates at the *pulpería* (truck store) every month from the Patiño company; his men received lesser amounts to ensure their compliance with the firm's directives and to blunt the impact of the miners' radio station, which urged them to join their brothers and 'become soldiers in the class struggle'.[19] Nevertheless, the US embassy joined Patiño in expressing unhappiness at the 'unsatisfactory deportment of the local police' at Siglo XX during the civil war of 1949, forwarding and supporting a letter written by D.C. Derringer Jnr., Patiño's local manager, in which he urged, 'that American technical police experts be sent to Bolivia to train an elite guard'. It is of some significance that the embassy thought that the company would pay for such services, reflecting its relationship with the formal state.[20]

By this stage the embassy that had so emphatically backed the Magruder report was describing the miners as 'notoriously radical', and warning that some groups were 'known to be participating in military drills', offering 'an exceptionally fertile field for the development of

Soviet Communism'.[21] What had occurred in the interim was that the mining proletariat had formed a national union federation, headed by men close to the MNR but also friendly to the Trotskyist *Partido Obrero Revolucionario* (POR), whose leaders had drawn up the federation's programme, committing it on paper to the abolition of capitalism and the establishment of the dictatorship of the proletariat. One less exciting but more immediate result was that by 1946 Patiño's wage bill had risen by more than fifty per cent over that of 1941, and he was now presented with stiff resistance to the lay-offs made necessary by the decline of demand in the post-war period.

The establishment of the *Federación Sindical de Trabajadores Mineros de Bolivia* (FSTMB) at a congress attended by some thirty delegates in June 1944 at Patiño's Huanuni mine was very much the initiative of the MNR, which was at the time a junior partner in the reformist regime of Major Gualberto Villarroel (1943-46). Although the party's sponsorship was to be of critical importance after 1952, at the time it reflected neither the distinct orientation towards the labour movement nor any firm ideological control over it. Indeed, the important Siglo XX union had been formed earlier on the initiative of two middle-class followers of the pro-Moscow *Partido de la Izquierda Revolucionaria* (PIR), the Ruíz González brothers. Moreover, although the MNR had gained sympathy in the mines through its effective parliamentary attacks against the Peñaranda government (1940-43) for the Catavi massacre, and had capitalised on this when the PIR adopted the disastrous policy of joining the traditional parties to oppose the 'nazi-fascist' MNR and 'totalitarian' Villarroel, its fall from power in 1946 deprived it of the patronage to support its invectives against the Rosca. Over the following six years of retreat and clandestinity the MNR increased its contact with the miners and gained the affiliation of key union leaders — particularly the artful and charismatic Juan Lechín Oquendo (executive secretary of the FSTMB) and Mario Torres Calleja (general secretary) — but it never dedicated itself to working with the rank and file nor captured complete control. This was in part because the miners were distrustful of tight party links and closely attached to the idea of union independence, but it also reflected the influence of the POR, which not only inveighed against the tin barons with as much zeal as the MNR but also possessed an infinitely more coherent and radical programme which its militants defended in the camps themselves.

In November 1946, four months after the fall of the Villarroel-MNR regime, the FSTMB held an extraordinary congress at the southern mine of Pulacayo under conditions of rising repression and a strong right wing backlash. Attending the congress were two of the POR's youngest and most active militants, Guillermo Lora (a delegate for Siglo XX) and Fernando Bravo (acting, remarkably, as a correspondent for *El Diario*). Despite a good deal of confusion abetted by Lechín's doubts and prevarications, Lora and Bravo were finally able not only to write the executive secretary's extremely radical speech but also to gain support for an extensive political resolution which has since been constantly derided by parties of almost every political persuasion but remains despite its age a central programmatic reference-point for the Bolivian miners and, by extension, the working class as a whole. The Thesis of Pulacayo was, in essence, an application of Trotsky's 1938 Transitional Programme to Bolivian conditions and with special reference to trade-union objectives. It defined Bolivia as a backward capitalist country, identified the proletariat as the only truly revolutionary class, called for an alliance under its leadership with peasants, artisans and the petty bourgeoisie, denounced Stalinism and the Rosca in equal measure, warned against the dangers in believing in 'worker ministers' appointed to bourgeois governments, demanded a sliding scale of wages, occupation of the mines and a central trade-union confederation, and emphasised that the union movement could only have any lasting impact if it developed into a working-class offensive against capitalism.[22] Ironically, the platform might have disappeared into obscurity had Patiño not undertaken the left's propaganda tasks for them and had the entire Thesis reprinted in *El Diario* as a warning of where the FSTMB was going.

While many took much of the Thesis as self-evident and others considered its strategic line as too academic to merit prolonged debate, it was the resolution's emphasis on tactical demands and methods that gained it general acceptance even from those who were far from sympathetic to Trotskyism. In future even MNR members of the FSTMB would recognise the validity of many sections of the Thesis, a fact that by no means necessarily strengthened the POR, which lacked the organisational capacity to turn the miners' radical syndicalism and general sympathy towards it into direct political support. The overall result was that in the years prior to the April revolution when the mining proletariat was held at bay by repression it developed a strong

radical orientation that was in many respects circumscribed by econo-
mism but also threatened to break beyond it to head an independent
working-class political initiative. The contradictions in this relationship were to be a constant feature of the miners' actions over the thirty
years that followed the revolution.

Decay in the Countryside

The Thesis of Pulacayo opened with the words, 'Bolivia is a backward
capitalist country. Qualitatively speaking, capitalist exploitation pre-
dominates over the other diverse economic formations which are to be
found in the country and which are a legacy from the past.' Nowhere
in the economy was the weight of the past more evident or more detri-
mental to its overall performance than in agriculture, the organisation of which abounded in feudal residues. If mining was Bolivia's
most capital-intensive, modern and dynamic sector and linked the
country directly to the world economy, agriculture certainly predominated in terms of employment, determining the economic rhythm
and socio-political pattern of life throughout most of the national
territory. As we have seen, over seventy per cent of the economically-
active population worked in this sector, the great majority settled in
the arid highland provinces of the *altiplano* or the more fertile Cochabamba valley system; the malaria-ridden east and north of the country was extremely sparsely-settled although these regions (Santa Cruz;
Beni; Pando) accounted for the bulk of Bolivia's landmass.

In precise and local terms the forms in which land was owned and
cultivated were varied and complex, combining sundry systems of
emphyteusis (perpetual right to lands owned by another, or a heredit-
ary lease), usufruct (right to temporary possession and use of lands
owned by another), communal cultivation, and the traditional European system of freehold ownership. However, the balance of power
and property in the countryside was in general both very clear and
grossly imbalanced, being based on a latifundia (large estate) system
established during the colony and expanded during the nineteenth
and twentieth centuries to the detriment of the communal lands surviving from the pre-conquest era. This system of concentrated private
ownership of immense estates both sustained the backwardness and
structural inequalities of Bolivian agriculture and served to maintain

a tradition of economic and social oppression of the indigenous masses that was not unlike a combination of serfdom and apartheid.

Table One demonstrates very clearly the scale of concentration of land in large estates as well as indicating the inefficiency with which they were run, although the low fertility of land on the *altiplano* should be borne in mind in this connection.

Table 1

Ownership of Land, 1950

Size of Property (Hectares)	No. Properties	Total Owned (Hectares)	Total Exploited (Hectares)	Exploited as % of Owned
Less than 5	51,198	73,877	40,028	54.2
5 to 50	19,503	278,459	86,378	31.0
50 to 200	5,014	478,291	76,090	15.9
200 to 1,000	4,033	1,805,408	134,790	7.4
1,000 to 5,000	4,000	8,724,776	167,006	1.9
5,000 to 10,000	797	5,146,334	55,365	1.0
Over 10,000	615	16,233,954	85,850	0.5
Total	85,160	32,741,096	645,506	

Source: *Censo Nacional Agropecuario, 1950*

Amongst the 615 estates which controlled approximately half the country's farmland but were responsible for only 13 per cent of total cultivation was one reported to be over 6½ million hectares in size while fifty per cent of the rural population held 0.13 per cent of cultivated land, necessarily subjecting it to intense exploitation. It was estimated that in 1938 eight *hacendados* (hacienda owners) owned a tenth of all cultivated land.[23] The high level of imports of foodstuffs and the fact that less than six per cent of cultivated lands were farmed with machinery — imports of agricultural machinery were valued at less than $6 million over the decade before the revolution — highlight the inefficiency of this form of rural organisation in a country which possessed the natural resources to be a net exporter of agricultural goods. Indeed, it is difficult to deny the strength of the argument that the hacienda had developed less as a unit to utilise land or optimise production than to control labour, a tendency which would not have tempered expansionary pressures on the *comunidades*, eighty per cent of which were located in the populous departments of La Paz and Oruro, and many of which encompassed rich lands around Lake Titicaca.[24]

Between independence and 1950 the number of communities dropped from around 11,000 to 3,799, holding slightly over seven million hectares in nominally collective ownership, which in practice was subjected to a system of indigenous hierarchy accepted and fully exploited by both Spanish and republican authorities as the only practical means of maintaining rural peace, guaranteeing the once vital head tax, and providing a renewable supply of labour for the mines. Although greatly reduced in size and membership, the number of surviving communities in 1950 reflects at least a degree of success in resisting the encroachments of the latifundia which had been sanctioned by the statutes of 1866, 1879 and 1884 in an endeavour to capitalise the market for land if not to incorporate the majority of the rural population within the market economy. Yet, according to the 1950 census, *comunarios* of various types were heavily outnumbered by the 259,000 heads of family who owned no land either individually or collectively. This sector of the population also dwarfed the 16,000 tenant farmers of all description, ninety per cent of whom possessed less than 35 hectares each.[25]

In economic terms the 'dual economy' of the hacienda and the *comunidad* was more apparent than real for the communities did sell an appreciable portion of their surplus and were not entirely rooted in subsistence agriculture. Equally, the low level of hacienda production, the limited local market, and the predominance of labour rent as the principal form of peasant employment and land tenure ensured that progress towards commercial farming in this sector was marginal. There were, of course, some regional exceptions, particularly the pastoral economies in Tarija and parts of Santa Cruz and Beni, and the traditional grain lands of Cochabamba, which had few communities, more than an average number of tenants and generally smaller properties. These exceptions did not, however, alter the general picture of the mass of rural labourers having the use of a plot of land on a hacienda either by giving the owner a large share of its produce or by working on the fields of the main estate for at least three and sometimes five days a week with their own seed, tools and means of transport, thereby remaining marginalised from the money economy.

The use of the terms 'feudal' and 'serfdom' with respect to labour on the manorial estates is not purely impressionistic for although in a rigorous sense these practices belonged to a long-superseded mode of production with its own distinctive economic limits and socio-political superstructure, a number of important features remained intact well into twentieth-century Bolivia. Central amongst these was the obligation of the labourer and his family to render free service to the landlord, a practice known as *pongueaje* for men and *mitanaje* for women. Usually this obligation was for two weeks a year, forcing workers to rely upon the support of their family on the plot or spend valuable cash in finding a replacement. A description of *pongueaje* in Cochabamba, written in 1949, reveals the extent of these servile obligations to the owner of the demesne:

'The *pongo* must bring his own food, even though he has a right to the leftovers from the master's table. So when he goes to fulfil his obligation, he takes with him an earthenware or copper cooking pot, quite covered in soot, a faggot of kindling wood and a sack of llama turds for fuel, and some supplies of food.

The *pongo* is given a spot in the great house for his quarters, some alleyway near the mangers and pigsties, and here he builds a fire to prepare his soup, boil up his corn-grits or toast his corn. But like a watch-dog he must sleep in the lobby ready to open the door for the master's children and for the master himself if he is a night-bird and likes to spend his time at the club or in a tavern.

His work occupies him from dawn until far into the night, and amongst his labours are the following: to help in the kitchen, to look after the harness and mind the poultry. He must sweep out the rooms, the courtyards, clean the stables and pigsties and do the garden. The traditional colonial estate house is a little world, a kind of Noah's ark with every kind of animal in it. The *pongo* is builder, messenger, nanny and brewer of *chicha* (corn beer). He fills in the gaps in the phalanx of servants during the day. And at night he has other tasks to complete the dark rosary of his obligations: spinning, weaving, husking corn, *mukeo* (chewing corn for *chicha*, fermented with saliva) and, of course, minding the doorway'.[26]

The practice of *pongueaje* was formally outlawed in 1945 by the Villarroel regime, but it remained in force for another seven years with landlords often including the number of available *pongos* in advertisements for the sale of their property. The *hacendado* possessed almost complete authority over the life of his or her *colonos*, with the power to administer whippings, remove land and privileges, settle disputes and even impose decisions about their private life. In this the landlord was usually supported by the local priests, whose need for tithes from parishioners, who persisted with their own religious customs while generally accepting the ceremonies of Christian faith, helped to bond an impressive circuit of local control. Twenty five years before the revolution the US ambassador referred to the country's million 'pure indians' as 'slaves', remarking that, 'there appears to be a general understanding between the landlords and the Church that contact with no Catholic priest except those who speak the native language is permitted, to prevent the latter from learning Spanish, which attainment usually causes him to flee the farm and find work in the cities.'[27]

If this was — on occasions — the case, it certainly did little to encourage a liberal attitude on the part of the *hacendados* towards their charges, whom they held in paternal contempt as some species of subhuman. In the 1930s local landowners opposed the purchase of rundown convent lands in Cochabamba by a peasant cooperative because the native labourers were 'lazy, liars, deceitful, and nobody can trust them'.[28] Ten years later *Los Tiempos*, Cochabamba's leading daily paper, launched a series of intemperate attacks against Villarroel's abolition of *pongueaje*, describing the president as an 'irresponsible demagogue who is unleashing and agitating the Indian hordes and threatening to destroy civilized Bolivians and their property'.[29] In 1949 the *Sociedad Rural Boliviana* published a pamphlet defending its 'spiritual orientation' to social relations in the countryside because, 'in Bolivia 15 per cent of the inhabitants of certain cities live in the Twentieth Century, the indians of the *altiplano* live in the Sixteenth Century and those that populate the Amazonian region still live in a pre-historic era. As a result, it is impossible to apply European theories to all of America, as Marxists vainly imagine'.[30]

Such attitudes were underpinned by a social system that up until the eve of the revolution prohibited the entry of '*indios*' into certain central streets and plazas of La Paz and freely printed in its newspapers photographs of captured peasant 'criminals' stripped of their lower clothing and placed in irons.[31]

One of the most consistent features of this regime was its entrenched racism. Almost without exception, rural workers were '*indios*', a term loaded with disparagement until it was repossessed with provocative pride in the 1970s by the growing movement for the political independence of Bolivia's native peoples, a movement which at its extreme rejects the alternative term of '*campesino*' (literally, countryman) as often imprecise and a euphemism that occludes the issues of race and nationality.

The division of society into social classes was closely paralleled by divisions of race, determined in large part by mother-tongue and physiognomy but also by occupation and dress, enabling a substantial minority of the population to be considered *mestizo* or *cholo* (of mixed blood) because it had urban residence or contacts, a command of Spanish, and dressed in European costume. The term 'white' was even more prone to manipulation and only infrequently corresponded to Caucasian stock rather than membership of the ruling class and aspirations to an association with Hispanic or European heritage. In many cases it was employed simply to confer distinction from the indigenous masses and paper over the high level of miscegenation evident even in the uppermost echelons of society. Bolivia, like the *Audiencia de Charcas* before it, was a Creole construction based on the firm suppression of the Aymara, Quechua and Guaraní nations and the negation of the ancient kingdoms of Kollasuyu and Tawantinsuyu. Yet, a quarter of a century after the foundation of the republic probably less than twenty per cent of the population was conversant in Spanish, with a very much smaller group having it as their mother-tongue. In 1950 a million people spoke only Quechua, 664,000 only Aymara, and Spanish remained a minority language although it was used by the majority of those who were bilingual. Even in 1976 over one fifth of the population had no Spanish whatsoever.[32]

One permanent and deep-seated fear of the landlord class was that this besieged ethnic and cultural identity might fuse with discontent over lack of land to overcome the peasantry's structural atomisation, generally conservative outlook and proclivity for patronage, and trigger off a series of rural revolts. Although this possibility was frequently exaggerated for political ends, the fear was not without foundation. Oral traditions had preserved the example of Tupaj Katari, who in 1781 had led the highland provinces in a rebellion against colonial and Creole rule and, in alliance with Tupaj Amaru's Cuzco rising, had displaced imperial authority over a region that stretched as far south as Salta for a number of months. The popular memory of Katari certainly incubated a millennarian vision but it also gave impetus to a number of less extensive movements: those of 1866-71, in defence of the *comunidades*, and 1898-1900, which broke out after a decade of unrest and in the midst of a 'white' civil war in which one side felt sufficiently threatened to mobilise and arm the '*indios*' in its defence, a move which was rare in the extreme and loudly condemned.

Discontent in the countryside was usually provoked by specific complaints, had limited aims and parochial limits — despite the surprisingly high level of mobility of those carrying goods or seeking seasonal work — but it was none the less dangerous for that. Following the popular rising of Zarate 'El Temible' Willka in 1899, the rapid buildup and professionalisation of the army was directed primarily towards the repression of the very peasantry which populated its lower ranks. In 1914 the British ambassador confidently dismissed any possibility of a successful indigenous rebellion, employing only marginally more derision than that which he and his colleagues reserved for the Bolivian ruling class, 'In these days . . . any attempt at revolt is doomed to failure, and the Indian dream of the restoration of the Inca dynasty, if indeed it has ever existed in their dull, drink-sodden brains, will speedily vanish before a volley of Mauser bullets . . . '.[33] Such a response did, in fact, become the norm, but it was very seldom if ever provoked by genuinely restorationist movements rather than discrete outbreaks of exasperation at abusive practices by landlords, *corregidores* (local police chiefs and executive officers) or majordomos. In March 1921 the *comunarios* of Jesús de Machaca killed a number of local dignatories and their *corregidor* after he had left a prisoner to die of starvation in the lock-up whilst away on a ten-day visit to La Paz. The army replied by killing several hundred *campesinos*, burning houses and destroying crops before seventy 'ringleaders' were sent to jail in the capital. The incumbent president, the *mestizo* Bautista Saavedra, was not expected to demonstrate any lenience since, when acting as a defence lawyer for Willka twenty years earlier, he had referred to 'blood-thirsty orangutans', 'the profound perversion of Aymara moral sensibilities', and a 'morally atrophied race, degenerating into dehumanisation . . . '.[34] Similarly radical repression was meted out in 1927, when the newly-constructed railway from Potosí to Sucre rapidly increased the value of local lands and accelerated hacienda pressure on the communities, which began to mobilise in the departments of Potosí and Chuquisaca.

The British ambassador (different man, same response) reported 12,000 to be 'on the warpath', but 'a hundred or two . . . were shot down and order was restored', adding in mitigation that the indians 'are most savage if aroused' and 'revert to cannibalism and devour their fallen enemies'.[35] The report received by Washington was equally risible insofar as it passed on the accusation that the revolt had been sparked off by the execution of Sacco and Vanzetti in the US, but it also contained one alarming feature, the confirmed presence of 'communist agitators' in the region. In this case it was the brothers Luis and Tristán Marof, early and energetic radical militants who were not, as the government claimed, in active correspondence with Bukharin but were fluent in Quechua and Aymara and constantly jailed for their rabble-rousing activities in town and country alike.[36] Over the following decades the hidden hand of communist agitation was discovered to be behind almost every instance of rural unrest, but far more important than this was the dislocation of hundreds of thousands of *campesinos* from the multiple constraints of their parochial existence by recruitment into the army to fight against Paraguay in the Chaco War (1932-35).

The Rise of Mass Politics

In the 1930s the regimes of the liberal free-trade oligarchies established in the second half of the nineteenth century entered severe economic and political crisis throughout Latin America, giving rise to new forms of political domination in order to contain an effective expansion of the political nation and combat the influence of radical currents of thought. In the main it was the military that undertook this task since its institutional character gave it both the coercive and ideological means to fill the breach, albeit often only temporarily. This was a decade full of Bonapartist projects, political fluidity and experimentation as well as economic reorganisation. Certainly a good deal of the accumulated power of the hacienda and the accretions of formal democracy remained unscathed but there was a closure of certain established forms of government in many countries, evident from Cárdenas's consolidation of a reformist state bureaucracy in Mexico to Getulio Vargas's semi-corporativist movement in Brazil and the emergence of the Popular Front government in Chile.

This general tendency found an echo in Bolivia. Over the twenty years before the revolution the oligarchy came under increasing attack from various sectors, which on a number of occasions exercised formal political power. The old order was constantly challenged and progressively weakened but it managed to retain its grip through sheer economic might and increasing resort to dictatorship and repression.

The economic origins of this extended crisis were firmly situated in the world slump. Despite the tin barons' dexterous management of production quotas and their ability to revive prices within the space of three years, Bolivian public finance was thrown into total disarray and small businesses suffered bankruptcy on an unprecedented scale. Even for the relatively resourceful and sophisticated small mining companies the impact was severe: membership of the *Asociación de Industriales Mineros* fell from 47 companies in 1924 to 16 in 1932. In 1931 the *boliviano* ceased to be a convertible currency and the government suspended payments on a public debt equal to almost fifty per cent of export earnings. The cost of living rose from a base of 100 in 1931 to 1,011 a decade later and 5,041 in 1951; the germ of inflation was firmly implanted into the economic system. Unemployment also increased quickly and substantially although no precise figures were recorded. Thus, while the large enterprises rode the crisis comparatively well, small companies went to the wall, the middle class lost much of its earning power and savings and the working class was badly hit by the loss of jobs and a sharp fall in real wages. The economy of the Rosca was shown in no uncertain terms to be both vulnerable and exceedingly partial in its favours; it would never retrieve the peaks of the 1920s or reassemble the political alliances that had served it so well in the opening decades of the century.[37] However, in political and social terms this crisis was to be overshadowed by another which so profoundly affected the nation that it wrenched the fabric of old Bolivia apart.

The Chaco War has been identified by the MNR and many writers on modern Bolivian political history as the single most important cause of the 1952 revolution. In many respects this argument has weight but it tends to diminish the influence of subsequent political developments which, while they often stemmed either directly or indirectly from the experience of the war, were also determined by other factors both nationally and internationally. Nonetheless, the war undoubtedly played a central role in opening a new epoch.

On the surface the three years of fighting between Bolivia and Paraguay over possession of the huge tracts of inaccessible bushland that comprised the Chaco Boreal represented simply another defeat for Bolivia in a string of border wars that had deprived the state of over half the territory inherited at independence. The war was fought hundreds of miles from the main centres of population and this served to place even greater pressure on the nation's rudimentary logistical resources and greatly disorientate and debilitate hundreds of thousands of recruits shipped from the *altiplano* and the valleys to the southern lowlands that were alternately scorched dry and drenched in sudden, violent downpours; many more were killed by illness and thirst than by Paraguayan bullets. In all, some 250,000 men were sent to the front, a very high proportion of all those aged between 17 and fifty in a population of barely two million. Of these troops, over 50,000 were killed and 20,000 were captured, some spending up to four years in insalubrious camps where they developed an abiding hatred of their senior commanders and political masters as well as an intense nationalism. The war, therefore, touched most sectors of Bolivian society, and almost without exception its effect was to generate discontent with the terrible conditions at the front, the manifest incompetence of the high command, and the rigidity and 'cowardice' of a government that had provoked the conflict in the first place and then presided over an almost uninterrupted series of defeats, replacing commanders at regular intervals, failing to provide adequate supplies or take any initiative that would bring the troops back from the 'green hell' where they were easily outmanoeuvred by the Guaraní, more accustomed to such terrain and conditions.

After the first year of the war, when it had become clear what military service entailed, many peasant communities resisted conscription and had to be press-ganged. The overwhelming majority of the foot-soldiers were Aymara and Quechua *campesinos* for whom this nightmare provided their first extended contact with urban folk, an introduction to the notion of Bolivia as a nation, and talk of politics as well as the ability to use a firearm and pick up a smattering of Spanish. For the middle-class youth drafted in as NCOs and subalterns it had a similarly severe impact; not only did they perceive and bear the consequences of the incompetence and self-seeking ways of their seniors, but they also shared the conditions of the front-line troops, learnt of life in the *campo* and the mines, and were obliged to reflect upon the political system which had led them into such an unmitigated disaster. An entire generation was dislocated by the experience of the war. Of those who returned from the army with positive political opinions the great majority had acquired a vibrant nationalism. Only a tiny proportion of leftist militants were demobbed; a minority had remained true to their pacifism and gone into exile, many more were shot at the front for their beliefs.[38]

Even before the final defeat and the highly dangerous task of demobilisation the army had come to the centre of the political arena, replacing President Salamanca with his vice-president in November 1934. After the final truce it was compelled to adopt a still higher profile in order to defend its corporate identity and place firm limits on radical currents that were emerging inside as well as outside its ranks. Following a short general strike in 1936, the high command overthrew President Tejada Sorzano to open a decade of military rule, the first time serving officers had governed — with one short exception in 1930-31 — since 1880.

The post-war period witnessed an outburst of popular sentiment that is so integral to political crisis but so difficult for political science to capture. In this case it was a very specifically determined sense of communal betrayal, shared suffering, a manichaean vision of cowardice and heroism, a generational divide and ideological displacement compounded by the collective trauma of defeat in war. These often intangible elements combined to erode liberal hegemony and its broader sense of an order of things, providing the cultural matrix within which new nationalist and radical political ideas took shape.

Tejada Sorzano's fall, significantly prompted by a combination of trade-union and military power, saw the opening of a period of populist army rule that has since been dubbed 'military socialism'. The regimes of Colonels David Toro (1936-37) and Germán Busch (1937-39) were in practice marked by a lack of cohesion and direction, which drove them on an erratic course from the proto-fascist declaration of obligatory syndicalisation to the nationalisation of Standard Oil (1937) and the lodging of all foreign exchange earnings with the Banco Central, and back to the dissolution of a leftist-dominated congress and the declaration of a full dictatorship (1939). Nevertheless, these regimes maintained a consistently populist and nationalist temper which undoubtedly sapped the force and initiative of leftist groups agitating amongst the workers and veterans but also worked to the overall detriment of the Rosca, whose managers were constantly attempting to hold back impulsive young officers from taking ill-considered measures. This Bonapartism laid down a blueprint for future developments in its efforts to bestow military rule with a popular and national character, its concentration upon developing the resources and apparatus of the state, an authoritarian patronage of sectors of the workers' movement, and the support given to the reformist convention of 1938. The assembly produced a good deal of verbose and acidic debate but out of it came a new labour code that limited the working day and established basic social security and a constitution that sanctified property only insofar as it had a social function. Thus, while 'military socialism' finally buckled under pressure from the tin barons and their allies, it showed them to be politically vulnerable and cast them as the antithesis of a nationalism now enshrined in the experience of the Chaco.

When the young and unstable war hero Germán Busch blew out his brains in August 1939 as a final gesture of exasperation at his inability to harness the big companies or control the parties of the left he ended one of the most dynamic and confused periods of Bolivian political life. Opposing forces had tried to exercise influence through the same government, which survived less out of any internal political logic than by virtue of the fact that it represented the 'good and healthy' element of a defeated army and was backed by the veterans. With Busch's death a predominantly Chaco-determined politics came to an end. The interregnum that followed demonstrated that this see-sawing caesarism had been partially successful insofar as the left remained deeply divided and disorganised. The regimes of Generals Carlos Quintanilla (1939-40) and Enrique Peñaranda (1940-43), backed by a hurriedly-constructed alliance of the traditional parties known as the *Concordancia*, reimposed the mandate of the Rosca without great difficulty. Toro's nationalisation was qualified with the payment of generous compensation and Busch's measures were either reversed, in the case of foreign exchange directives, or left to collect dust on the statute book, in the case of the labour code and many clauses of the constitution.

This easy restitution of the old order underscored the nebulous nature of the post-bellum political forces, many of which were a good deal less radical than their rejigged titles suggested. However, if the feverish activity of Toro and Busch had succeeded in delaying the development of new political currents, Peñaranda's unimaginative regime had the effect of speeding up their emergence. The parties that were consolidated in this period were to have a remarkably long life and many of their leaders would still be at the centre of political affairs a full forty years later. Over the decades that followed the rule of the colonels would prove to be less important in itself than as a critical watershed out of which a new mass politics was born.

The two forces that most clearly manifested the nationalist and corporativist influences of the 1930s were the MNR and the FSB, both of which initially looked to Europe for direction. The Falange was founded in Chile in 1937 in the image of its Spanish namesake. For many years the party remained a marginal force and was simply one of a fluid set of tiny fascist groups proselytising in the universities. Its founder and leader, Oscar Unzaga de la Vega, was an excitable but skilled speaker who gradually made himself the focus of young officers and students who were unimpressed by the tedium of economic programmes or the minutiae of social policy but flourished on the conspiratorial existence of secret cells and the heady sentiments of the party's 1941 'Decalogue', an 'authentically youthful creation' which proclaimed, 'Under the auspices of Organisation, Justice and Solidarity the New Bolivian State will be an integral organism which, based on a nation's desire to exist, will subordinate personal interests, and those of groups and classes, to the supreme interest of *bolivianidad* . . . individuals will participate in the organic unity of the State through a corporate regime in which everyone will undertake their functions in accordance with the quality and specialisation of their work.'[39] There were only marginal alterations in the substance and tenor of the party's ideology over the following forty years. Whilst it generally represented a useful collaborator in conspiracy and could always be counted upon to muster a number of sympathetic officers and bands of extremist students for demonstrations and terrorist activity, it rarely came to exercise leadership over the traditionalist right and entered government for the first time in 1971.

In its early stages the MNR was not so distinct from the FSB. The sympathising journalists who worked on *La Calle* in the 30s and early 40s were certainly more sophisticated and creative, developing a potent and highly popular brand of invective against the Rosca, but their nationalism was fundamentally little less mystical than that of the falangists. However, the driving force of the MNR came from the oratorical skills and parliamentary propaganda of a cluster of young men who were veterans of the Chaco and had developed their corporativist sympathies in a broad anti-oligarchic and anti-imperialist direction. Figures such as Víctor Paz Estenssoro, Hernán Siles Zuazo, Walter Guevara Arze, Germán Monroy Block, Carlos Montenegro and Augusto Céspedes were all university-educated, in or on the edges of the professional elite, and had played some part in the 'socialist' experiments of the 1930s. In 1941 they came together to form the MNR on a programme that was not dissimilar to that of the German nazi party. An early document shows the combination of these strains. 'We denounce as anti-national any possible relation between international political parties and the manoeuvres of judaism, between the liberal democratic system and the secret organisations . . . We demand the absolute prohibition of the intervention of foreign shareholders or capital in newspapers, magazines and other publications . . . '[40] The intellectuals of the MNR possessed a clear sense of history which led them to demand from an early stage the 'economic liberation and sovereignty of the Bolivian people', but they had no coherent programme for this bar invectives against capital which was foreign; they neither explicitly threatened the nationalisation of the mines nor promised an agrarian reform. A few hundred strong, the party looked principally to a military alliance since its anti-imperialist line was understood by many in the working class to be but one aspect of a predominantly fascist orientation. Certainly the US embassy held this view, constantly linking the MNR with Perón, and describing it in 1946 as, 'typically totalitarian of the Nazi-fascist type, being bitterly anti-semetic (sic) and many of its prominent leaders being Nazi sympathizers. While in power it exercised tyrannical methods in suppressing opposition'.[41]

The party that most consistently and vehemently supported this critique was the pro-Moscow PIR, founded in 1940 by a group centred on the *cochabambino* intellectuals José Antonio Arze and Ricardo Anaya. Having spent the period of the Chaco exiled in Santiago, these figures were greatly influenced by the Chilean communist party's policy of a 'popular front with democratic parties of the bourgeoisie', a line that was forcefully underwritten on an international scale after the German invasion of the Soviet Union. Despite the fact that it had no formal attachments with the Kremlin, the PIR was a highly orthodox party, producing a stream of literature on Marxist theory and the socio-economic development of Bolivia, which, it argued, required a stage of bourgeois democracy, the eradication of feudalism, and a massive development of the forces of production before a socialist revolution could be launched.[42] It was the PIR that drew together the major leftist currents of the 1930s. In the 1940 presidential elections Arze polled remarkably well against Peñaranda; the party outnumbered the MNR in congress and its following in the universities and unions was considerably greater. For the first few years of its existence the PIR appeared to have remedied the long-standing absence of a local communist party and seemed to be making great progress towards forming the first mass party of the left in the country's history.

In this it was constantly opposed by the POR, established in 1935 by Tristán Marof and José Aguirre Gainsbourg but splitting soon afterwards over Marof's insistence on a broad populist orientation. Aguirre may properly be called the father of Bolivia's longstanding and robust Trotskyist tradition but his early death in a fairground accident left the movement without any obvious leader. Although Tomás Warqui (Oscar Barrientos) and Miguel Nuñez kept the party alive, it remained a very small nucleus of worker intellectuals and student activists until 1946, by which time both the POR and the MNR were beginning to benefit in terms of numbers and influence from the degeneration of the very much larger PIR.[43]

This shift in the balance of forces occurred during and in the period immediately following the Villarroel regime, founded on a coup which ousted the genial incompetent Peñaranda in December 1943. The new military regime was of a very different character to its predecessor. Planned and staffed by young officers of the secret RADEPA lodge (*Razón de Patria*), it represented a more emphatically nationalist and authoritarian response to the post-Chaco climate than had either Toro or Busch, and was constantly obliged by US pressure to camouflage the sympathy of many *radepistas* for the Axis powers and justify its backing of and from the military regime in Argentina, where Perón was now established as a highly influential leader. Unskilled in politics and civil administration, the lodge sought a civilian ally and, having been rejected by the PIR, fixed upon the MNR, with which it had much common ideological ground. The PIR quickly moved to form a bloc with the traditionalist right and the US embassy on the basis of the new regime's 'dictatorship' and 'rejection of democracy'.

The central problem for the PIR and the constant concern of the

Rosca was less the intermittent brutality or necessarily dwindling fascist motifs of the regime than its successful policy of gaining the backing of important sectors of the working class and peasantry. Villarroel declared that he was not an enemy of the rich 'but more a friend of the poor'; he allowed his MNR ministers to increase fiscal pressures on the tin companies through the Banco Central, applied the Busch labour code, supported higher wage awards, attached himself closely to the establishment of the FSTMB, formally abolished *pongueaje* and presided over the country's first *Congreso Indigenal* of assorted *campesino* representatives (1945). All of this took place in an uneven and strictly limited fashion. The MNR economists led by Víctor Paz did not reflate the economy; instead they brought inflation down and increased reserves with orthodox policies. The *radepistas* continued to control public order with strong-arm tactics and undeniably persecuted members of the PIR as well as executing a number of conservative leaders. The encouragement of the peasant movement never went past formal declarations; the 1945 congress was effectively forced upon the regime and, as we have seen, conditions in the countryside remained extremely backward. Trade-union freedoms were greatly expanded but still observed in a highly partisan way, in much the same way as in Perón's Argentina. Moreover, Washington possessed a trump in its control over tin sales and was able to force the resignation of a number of MNR ministers, restrict the regime's foreign policy, and prohibit it from launching a concerted offensive against the Rosca, which continued to control the press and the commanding heights of the economy.[44]

In the final instance it was this factor, combined with the inherent contradictions and natural limits of the political form that this emphatic but disorganised reformist endeavour took, that led to its downfall. The PIR's still impressive industrial base in the towns and substantial backing from the middle class allied to the tin companies' ideological apparatus and the formidable 'democratic' pressures exerted by Washington strengthened a popular urban movement against the regime's authoritarian style. By July 1946 the military, already divided along generational lines by RADEPA, had ceased to be a viable repressive force, all the leading papers were in opposition, and key sectors of the middle class were pressing for wage increases that the state could not meet. In a remarkable, perhaps unique, political conjuncture, the traditional right and the orthodox left combined to lead a popular insurrection that bore the indelible stamp of the international moment when the confused but resolute president was dragged from the palace and lynched in the manner of Mussolini.[45]

Eye-witnesses recount that when Villarroel and his aides were hoisted on the lamp-posts in the Plaza Murillo an unseasonal thunderstorm broke out, impressing the superstitious in the mob. Some more secular participants, principally rank and file militants of the PIR, were also ruminating on the course the rebellion had followed. Although it had generated a mass following in the towns, this proved to be distinctly ephemeral, and in the countryside and mines the revolution was met with passive opposition and discontent from the start. Within six months its true social content was laid bare; it was to be the last instance of popular backing for a right wing movement, all but destroyed the PIR, and left a deep scar on the political memory of the left. Villarroel had become a martyr for nationalism and his overthrow a damning indictment of political opportunism, however prettily it was theorised.[46]

The revolution of July 1946 opened a political phase that became known as the '*sexenio*', a six year interlude of conservative rule and increasing repression between the makeshift military-sponsored reforms of Villarroel and the April insurrection. In the first instance popular support for the rebellion and the international context required that democratic form be scrupulously observed; power was held by the head of the supreme court until relatively free elections early in 1947, the MNR was effectively banned but the POR-FSTMB *Bloque Minero* contested the poll and won half a dozen seats. However, by the end of the year domestic conflict and the onset of the Cold War made this small but vocal opposition unacceptable, particularly since it was helping to open up fissures in the ruling alliance.

Although the peasantry did not rally to defend Villarroel, it displayed active discontent throughout 1947 on a scale not seen since the turn of the century. Yet, while the MNR and to some extent the POR had begun to make a number of contacts with *campesino* leaders, and political literature occasionally appeared in the countryside, the former opposed any policy of mobilising the rural masses while the latter lacked the resources to make an efficient job of it.[47] There was by no means any unified movement, still less a clear notion of political direction, but the landlords' refusal to adhere to the Villarroel decrees and their determination to stamp out 'subversion' increased tension considerably. In the mines the failure to defend the fallen regime heralded a measured retreat, but the new Hertzog government could not immediately ban the FSTMB or exile its leadership, particularly whilst *piristas* held the labour ministry. However, in January 1947 the PIR entered into armed conflict with the miners of Potosí, hitherto the party's stronghold, and the resulting massacre effectively finished it off as a force within organised labour, a process which in some respects had been underway since well before 1946 because the breaking of the Hitler-Stalin pact had led the PIR, like many other communist formations in Latin America, to reduce radical demands in order to aid the Allied war effort. One result was the fortification of the POR and MNR, which continued to cultivate the FSTMB leaders on the basis of its patronage under Villarroel and close contact with Lechín. Another was the weakening of the PIR at a national level which opened it up to attacks from the right. Within a year it was forced into opposition, no longer a 'democratic ally' but a 'pro-Soviet communist force'. Inside the workers' movement little attention was paid to attacks of this nature for the PIR was already tarnished by its close association with a Patiño-led Rosca offensive in September 1947 against high manning levels. This took the form of a highly successful 'white massacre': collective redundancy and re-employment on individual contracts and at lower wages. In this manner the militants who had founded the union were purged and labour costs dramatically reduced. Strikes broke out but lacked leadership and were repressed with determination, the most bloody instance occurring in May 1949 in Siglo XX.

There were certain qualifications to this picture of resolute political entrenchment. Hertzog refused to wipe many of Villarroel's reforms from the statute book, continued to pressure the Rosca for taxes, and persisted in allowing the PIR to operate; but after some 18 months of uncertainty, effectively ended by Patiño's offensive, the central forces in Bolivian society were clearly entering a process of complete polarisation. The MNR showed great resilience in staging propaganda actions, attempting local risings, and chipping away at the unsteady unity of the army, which had been traumatised by the strongly anti-militarist content of the 1946 revolution and was greatly debilitated by the extensive purge of *radepistas*.[48] Building on the memory of Villarroel, progressively excising its more fascist characteristics, entering into tactical alliances with the POR, recruiting junior army officers and deepening its relationship with the outlawed leadership of the

FSTMB, the MNR began to build up an appreciable movement whilst reaping all the benefits from its persecution by the regime. Indeed, illegal status helped to subordinate substantial divisions over policy and preserve an alliance of the 'pure' nationalists — who contrived to hold on to their quasi-fascist beliefs, relished the underground struggle and possessed few hard programmatic positions — the 'pragmatic centre' in exile — which, led by Paz and Guevara, attempted to develop a reformist orientation that would address the central social issues — and the 'left' — almost exclusively centred on the labour leaders, and influenced by the POR and the Chilean left, with which it had close contact in exile. All these groups interpreted in their own way the 'multi-class', 'reformist', 'nationalist' and 'democratic' aspirations that were the principal motifs of a formation which lacked a programme but possessed an impressive organisation.

In August 1949 the MNR attempted to realise its accumulated political assets in an insurrection which failed miserably in La Paz but gained momentary control of most other important centres. However, the party's internal leadership still relied on a conspiratorial approach and placed too much confidence in its allies in the military as well as suffering from the earlier defeat of the miners' strike in its refusal to mobilise the peasantry. The rising failed to accumulate popular support and was quashed with brutality and efficiency. This loss of initiative appeared to be confirmed when, in mid-1950, the schoolteachers, to the fore in the 1946 campaign against Villarroel, led a general strike in the towns, creating an insurrectionary situation in La Paz but again suffering harsh suppression, which reached its peak in the blanket bombardment of the working-class quarter of Villa Victoria. However unpopular it might have been, the regime still had the advantage of superior force, full US backing and a formal democratic mandate.[49]

It was on the last point that matters finally turned. In May 1951 the government of Mamerto Urriolagoitia, the former vice-president who had ousted Hertzog from office in 1949 on the grounds of 'ill health' when he failed to take a stringent line on repression, was obliged to hold elections. Given the MNR's failure to capitalise on the intermittent offensives of the weakened labour movement over the previous five years and in view of the international importance of holding an open poll, the party was allowed to stand candidates, although its leaders were prohibited from returning to the country. Such was the confidence of the ruling class that three right wing candidates entered the lists while the left, excluding the PIR, joined forces behind the MNR. In the event, even on the official count the MNR won a clear plurality with Víctor Paz and Hernán Siles as its candidates. Fighting from exile and clandestinity, the MNR had succeeded in transforming its campaign into one for full democracy as well as against the power of the Rosca and the anachronistic relations in the countryside.

Hoist by his own petard, Urriolagoitia took what proved to be a disastrous step for the Bolivian ruling class in what has entered popular parlance as the '*mamertazo*'. Alleging, not without some foundation but on the basis of forged documents, that an informal alliance existed between the MNR and the newly-formed *Partido Comunista de Bolivia* (PCB), established in 1950 by the dissident youth wing of the PIR, the president pronounced the election result a danger to democracy and handed power to the armed forces. The existing high command, already lacking confidence in many of their officers, passed the republic's highest office over to General Ballivián and quickly assigned themselves diplomatic posts abroad. This final desperate manoeuvre lasted just under a year.

The MNR's victory in 1951 provided the element that proved fatal for the *ancien regime*. The junta could only legitimise itself on anticommunist grounds, yet the PIR was a spent force and the MNR seen as authentically nationalist, closely attached to the reforms of 1943-46, and largely exonerated in the public eye from the excesses of the Villarroel period by the greater repression that had followed it. The party's campaign for democratic rights was now at one with that of the miners, the professional middle sectors and urban workers who had successively been repressed and had their living standards cut. It also had the implicit backing of other opposition parties excluding the FSB, and, in the last instance, it had succeeded in eroding the dependability of the repressive state apparatus. It had, in sum, optimised the contradictions in the status quo; the party's rise to power possessed an air of predictability. However, neither the form the April revolution took nor the extent of popular mobilisation that followed it could have easily been foreseen, and these proved to be critical in determining the course Bolivian history would take over the following thirty years.

Foto Lucio Flores.

2.
THE NATIONAL REVOLUTION

In purely military terms the odds in April 1952 were heavily against the rebels although it should be borne in mind that a conscript army often has only a marginal advantage when pitted against armed civilians, many of whom have military training and are more resolute than strictly commanded and nervous young recruits. This factor was certainly important on the night of the 10th, when a full moon cancelled out the advantage gained by the army in cutting the capital's electricity supply. As the troops moved in file down from El Alto and up from Miraflores and San Jorge they found themselves outmanoeuvred by factory workers who were familiar with the terrain, organised in guerrilla groups, and acting largely on their own initiative. The army officers reacted erratically, some ordering their men to hold tight formation, others making precipitate retreats or simply disappearing. Despite the superiority of their firepower many conscripts willingly surrendered to people who had been urging them not to shoot at their own families and friends or destroy the city, a threat that was taken seriously when the artillery was ordered to bombard the centre from the heights but succeeded only in wrecking houses in the workers' quarters. Whole groups of rank and file soldiers reversed

Popular militia, 1952

their forage caps—the traditional sign of having changed sides—
under the insults, pleading and even angry blows of the *cholas*, working women whose familiar authority frequently overcame the residual
fear of the officer class.

Despite such setbacks, many of which stemmed from the resolutely
popular character of the rebellion, Torres Ortiz still possessed sufficient resources to keep La Paz under siege and whittle down the insurrection at the end of the first day of fighting. However, the army's
position became untenable when, early on the 11th, it found its lines
of retreat cut off by a strong detachment of miners from the nearby
Milluni camp which took the railway line to Oruro, captured a munitions train, and launched a flanking attack on the El Alto base. This
situation was made worse by the news that the revolution had
triumphed in Oruro, where General Jorge Blacutt had at first miscon-
strued the nature of the rising and offered to collaborate with Manuel
Barrau of the MNR only later to reverse his stance, order the machine-
gunning of the large crowd collecting in the main plaza, and provoke
a swift and exceedingly violent assault on the barracks which drove
the troops out of the city. Casualties in Oruro reached 90 dead and
250 wounded; in La Paz some 400 died, but in Cochabamba, where
the revolution amounted to little more than the assumption of authority by MNR leader Walter Guevara Arze, there was no fighting of any
consequence. Elsewhere in the country party militants took over barracks and prefectures peacefully, often with the help of the *carabineros*. Following Torres Ortiz's surrender and flight to the Chilean
border resistance crumbled very quickly. La Paz was strewn with cast-
off uniforms and thousands of discarded weapons, quickly collected
by a populace that was to employ them in its own defence intermittently over the next two decades. Many officers went underground
and only surfaced to re-enter civilian life as unobtrusively as possible,
marking the end of a military generation. Others either fell prisoner
or stayed at their posts to await an outcome that looked decidedly
bleak. Amongst these were two young sub-lieutenants captured on the
11th, Alberto Natusch Busch and Luis García Meza, men who years
later were to make their mark on the course of Bolivian political life in
an unmistakably military manner. Yet at the time it seemed that the
country's military apparatus would be swept away for good by a movement that had no precise political direction and was backed by
heterogeneous forces in a broad alliance but was liable to outstrip its

initial leadership, possibly along the lines of the Russian or Chinese revolutions.

Establishing a New Regime

Whatever the broad political expectations of the *paceño* working class on Good Friday 1952, one thing was demonstrably clear: it fully supported the MNR's rise to power. Through its record in opposition, victory in the 1951 poll, and initiation of the insurrection the MNR had established a deep-seated legitimacy; there was no question that it would take formal power with an unprecedented popular mandate. Thus, the leader of the rising, Hernán Siles Zuazo, was sworn in immediately as provisional president pending the return of party chief Víctor Paz Estenssoro from exile in Buenos Aires. Siles appointed an interim cabinet drawn largely from the internal MNR leadership and generally cautious in character. Colonel Aliaga was made interior minister as a sign that the alliance with the *carabineros* would be maintained; but Lechín was appointed minister of mines, soon to be joined by Germán Butrón in the labour ministry and the *cruceño* Ñuflo Chávez, minister of peasant affairs, as representatives of the working class in the regime. In the first instance this appeared to be no more than a discrete and precautionary move; working-class ministers had been appointed before, and these men were leading party members. However, their presence very quickly came to be seen by the unions as an obligatory representation of the workers' movement.

Siles was a founder of the MNR and had frequently contributed to the scurrilous *La Calle*, but he was also of good *chuquisaqueño* stock, the son of President Hernando Siles (1926-30), and had served in parliament several times over the previous 15 years. Nearly 40 years old, he had spent much of the *sexenio* in exile or clandestinity and was acknowledged as the driving-force of the internal sector of the party, of which he was *sub-jefe*. Thin, short-sighted, adorned with an unprepossessing pencil moustache, and of a rather mild personal disposition, Siles was known as '*el conejo*' (the rabbit) and scarcely fitted the image of a populist caudillo, but he was better attuned to this role than to that of an intellectual and never displayed the mental prowess of Paz or Walter Guevara. Although initially more attached to the rightists in the party than these figures, Siles was also deeply pragmatic, skillful in political manoeuvre and a fine public speaker, qualities that were to enable him to assume the presidency of the republic for a third time 31 years after he first held the post and 44 years after he first entered congress. Siles's first speech after taking power was both a clarification and a warning:

> 'I ask for effort and calm. Let us have no excesses. We are too poor to be destroyed any more. . . . We are not going to repeat what happened on 21 July (1946) since we don't want to destroy, but to build a new Bolivia. We offer you only honest work and sacrifice, but (this will be) a government of structural transformation in the economic, political and social fields. We are going to work so that the Bolivian economy belongs to Bolivians and not to exploiters who live abroad. We are going to incorporate the *campesinos* into the Bolivian economy and national life so that they are no longer the objects of derision. We will also increase national production and diversify it. . . . This is a completely democratic movement supported by the great majority of the Bolivian people, with no relation to foreign parties, least of all the Communist Party. . . . Viva la Revolución! Gloria a Villarroel! Viva Bolivia!'[1]

It was, of course, far too early to make concrete announcements or pre-empt any decision of the *jefe*, but Siles stressed the importance of several themes that were soon established at the centre of party doctrine: that the MNR was not drawn from nor defended the interests of any one social class but was rather a bloc of three classes — the workers, peasants, and middle class; that class contradictions were subordinate to those between the nation and its enemies, any attempt at the creation of a communist society in the capitalist sphere of the world being utterly futile; and that since it contained a number of divergent currents the MNR was obliged to respect its outer tendencies but also to maintain a balance between them. As later expressed by José Fellmann Velarde, this meant that, 'the victory of the rightist faction in the party would signify a victory for the Rosca, while that of the left would, by the same token, be a triumph for communism.'[2]

On the 15th Víctor Paz arrived at El Alto airport. He was greeted by a crowd of sixty thousand, carrying placards which proclaimed 'El MNR es el Pueblo', 'Nacionalización de las Minas', 'Reforma Agraria', 'Villarroel Mártir — Estenssoro Salvador', and 'Bienvenido Padre de los Pobres'. Such was the press that it took the cavalcade a full half hour to move the half block between the cathedral and the presidential palace. The scene was one of joyous chaos and high expectation. This was scarcely abated by Paz opening his speech with the shout 'Jaccha t'anta uthjani' (there will be much bread), but when he returned to his mother tongue the new president was more sober. He began by reminding the crowd that it was an alliance of the Rosca and the communists that had defeated Villarroel and that any nationalisation of the mines would first have to be carefully studied by a commission. There were few idle promises: 'When we possess the necessary resources the government will ensure the improvement of the life of the collectivity'. He demanded 'no violence, no vengeance', but was interrupted by the crowd, which evidently had not kept apace with ideological shifts inside the MNR when it shouted 'Down with the Jews!'. 'There are no racial distinctions in this revolution', replied Paz, 'the crooks will be brought to justice, be they Jews, foreigners or Bolivians'.[3] At his inauguration the next day Paz added little to these sentiments except to emphasise that, 'this is not an anti-capitalist government precisely because of the seriousness of our task, which is in no sense demagogic. We want to ensure progress for the majority; we take on this task and assume responsibility for it because Bolivia is extraordinarily rich but it needs capital.'[4]

This cautious approach barely distinguished the new regime from its predecessors and it was not new to Paz. He was neither a man of action nor a refurbished revolutionary. Perhaps his most bombastic moment had been the damning indictment of the Catavi massacre made in congress in 1943, but even this, for all its force, had leant heavily on the legalistic logic and measured irony that were an integral part of the local tradition of parliamentary rhetoric. At that stage Paz was undoubtedly a fervent nationalist and not above employing certain Marxist categories. Yet his formidable reputation as an intellectual was based principally on long experience in financial administration, a background that had nurtured a deep awareness of the practical problems of bringing about social change as well as a fundamentally managerial approach to politics. Paz was less an ideologue than an intelligent and pragmatic politician in the populist mould but of firmly conservative sensibilities. One of the very few natives of the somewhat pacific southern department of Tarija to impose their stamp on national political life, he came from a respected landowning family. Born in 1907, Paz was by 1932 serving as legal advisor to the budgetary commission, fought in the Chaco as an NCO, and after the war rose quickly to a senior position in the finance ministry. Very brief spells working for Patiño and as minister of economy for Peñaranda interrupted a career as university professor and parliamentary deputy from 1938 to 1946; thereafter he lived off a private income, writing political tracts from exile in Uruguay and Argentina. His large mouth and high forehead earned him the nickname of '*el mono*' (the monkey) but even in the working class where he has long since forfeited much of the popularity bestowed upon him in 1952 he is still referred to with a degree of reverence as 'el Doctor Paz'. What he lacked in terms of populist touch he made up for in the image of a responsible and capable statesman, ever willing to mediate and always distanced from the endemic corruption and violence of Bolivian politics. This image was sustained for a remarkably long time and even when it had become irredeemably tarnished Paz's almost legendary skill as a political broker enabled him to act as virtual king-maker as late as 1980.

These skills were required immediately since the day after Paz was sworn in as president a meeting took place to form what was rapidly to become the single most powerful body in Bolivian public life, the *Central Obrera Boliviana* (COB). Since its establishment on 17 April 1952 the COB has developed into one of the most militant trade union confederations in the world. It has the distinction of being the only Latin American confederation that possesses authority over an entire workers' movement, it has remained independent of all international affiliations, and — despite numerous reiterations of its rejection of party connections — plays a central and explicit role in national politics, paralleled only by that of the military. The COB's independence and the radicalism of its rank and file have frequently been placed in jeopardy by the actions of its leadership, and it has often retreated into a narrow syndicalism, but it continues to retain a quite remarkable degree of support from the working class.

The birth of the COB was in many respects the most natural result of the revolution. The Thesis of Pulacayo had called for such a body, and throughout the *sexenio*, particularly during the 1950 general strike, rapidly-organised coordination committees had been formed in an effort to unify the unions, many of which were still young or backward but manifested an increasingly coherent and radical political disposition. The consolidation of the FSTMB and the collapse of the divisive politics of the PIR, which went so far as to dissolve itself several months after the revolution, strengthened this tendency, but until the conditions of repression were removed it proved impossible to bring it to realisation. In 1952, as in 1982, it was the strategically important miners' union that provided the backbone of the COB. Juan Lechín Oquendo became its executive secretary, a post which he has never since lost despite numerous challenges, deep political entanglements and a surfeit of transparent errors and misguided actions which only the most resolute opportunists make and survive.

Yet, despite a notoriously uneven record 'Don Juan' remains a true folk hero with a constituency, grudging or otherwise, deeper and broader than that ever possessed by his peers Paz and Siles, with whom he shared a political affiliation more out of necessity than choice. Born in the northern mining town of Corocoro in 1914, Lechín is of Lebanese extraction and middle-class parents, never having worked down the pits. He came to a prominent position in the labour movement late in the day, having served in the Chaco and gained a following as a star goalkeeper in the camp team at Catavi where he was employed as a clerk. Lechín's schoolboy contact with Siles, his popularity and easy-going manner made him a key figure in the MNR's contact work in the mines during the 40s. Yet, his reputation would have been distinctly less durable and radical were it not for the advice and support he received from the POR in the early days. This gave his speeches a radical edge, enabled him to acquire a more acute perspective in analysing tactical situations, and kept him to organisational tasks he would otherwise have forsaken. Lechín was never a revolutionary militant; reading bored him, he felt uncomfortable with theory and genially despised the puritanical lifestyle of the *porista* militants. Moreover, he sought a political alliance that would give more than programmatic orientation; like the pit leaders grouped around him, he wanted to restore the political conditions that had led to the establishment of the FSTMB. He therefore forsook his dalliance with Trotskyism and returned to the MNR, but always giving priority to his syndicalist position, which remained the principal source of his authority and prestige.[5]

The meeting on the 17th was attended by Lechín and Butrón, the first and only genuine 'worker ministers', Mario Torres and Melquíades Luna for the FSTMB, and two representatives each from the main unions (factory workers; railwaymen; bank workers; private sector employees; construction workers; peasants). Many did not yet have a firm political affiliation but all the major currents on the left were represented and much of the preparatory work was undertaken by the POR representatives, Edwin Moller, Miguel Alandia and José Zegada. The following day Lechín announced to the press that the COB would require the new government to rescind all anti-worker legislation, respect the COB's independence, implement nationalisation of the mines and railways, sponsor an 'agrarian revolution', diversify the economy and work to improve the lot of wage-earners.[6]

The COB's first statement also called for a congress to be held at the earliest opportunity but in fact this did not take place until 1954, which was the source of considerable discontent in its ranks. In the interim the leadership operated on an ad hoc basis, thrashing out policy and tactics in well-publicised meetings in which Lechín and his pro-MNR followers held the upper hand but were constantly challenged to take a harder line principally by the POR but also on occasions by the PCB. The result of this process undoubtedly favoured the MNR but it also yielded a programme and set of statutes that were well to the left of the party leadership.

After an initial period of discontent with the idea of formal representation in the government because the worker ministers frequently failed to report back or request a clear mandate, the system gained acceptance from a majority. In August 1952 Luna sponsored a FSTMB motion calling for Lechín's resignation from the cabinet, the Siglo XX union sending a telegram that noted the 'proven interference, sabotage and depreciation' of his actions by right-wing elements, putting the independence and prestige of the miners' union in peril.[7] This suspicion of the dangers of what the COB called *cogobierno* was never to disappear, being sustained not only by the POR's critique of participation in a petty-bourgeois regime but also by a basic syndicalist disquiet at official entanglements and the resulting compromises. However, in the first months of the revolution this distrust was overcome with the argument that *cogobierno* was the most efficacious means of securing union demands and halting the regime's retreat from popular policies: 'the worker ministers presented the most serious obstacle to any counter-revolutionary efforts within the state apparatus'.[8] The ministers remained, and their number was eventually increased to five although at no stage were they appointed by the unions and neither did they seek a direct mandate from the COB or subject themselves to powers of recall, allowing the MNR to reap considerable benefit from their presence whilst avoiding any formal recognition of 'joint-government'.

This was an obligatory move; even Guillermo Lora, who strenuously opposed formal participation, pointed out that 'for the majority of the masses, the COB was their only leader and their only government'.[9] Whatever demands the COB made and whoever exercised influence within it, the MNR was forced to accept its legitimacy and mass following, and compelled to win its leadership to the government's cause. In the event, it registered much success in this, but the process entailed making a number of central concessions and engaging in a series of acute conflicts.

The MNR left was almost without exception drawn from the COB. Moreover, the pressure it put on the party leadership was increased by the fact that it had the support of non-party elements in its campaign to 'deepen the revolution'. Although it was still in the process of consolidation, the young PCB was well represented in the COB, supporting the strategy of a national liberation front comprised of parties from various classes. It criticised the MNR for rejecting this with its thesis of 'one party which represents all classes at once', but kept political attacks to a minimum and adopted a strategy of backing the MNR's labour left, which it considered 'healthy, conscious and valiant'.[10] As a result it proved difficult for the government to launch an offensive specifically against the PCB without attacking an ally of one of its key sources of support; it therefore directed its invectives against 'communists' in general during the first phase. Equally, the MNR leaders in the COB were still close to the POR and eager to win its militants to their cause. In this context we should bear in mind that the Trotskyists had amassed considerable sympathy over the *sexenio* and although they were from an early stage highly critical of the MNR regime, they made no call for an immediate workers' government, demanding instead a radicalisation of proposed reforms, the defence of the regime against imperialism and the revolutionary education of the masses.[11]

However, simple acquiescence in this situation on the part of the MNR leadership soon proved insufficient. In September the COB, under strong pressure from the left, published a draft programmatic platform in its paper *Rebelión*, edited by the *porista* Edwin Moller. This statement was intended to allay the fears about *cogobierno* and issue a challenge to the MNR right. It opened by clarifying the position of the worker ministers,

'The aim should not be to place a worker in a capitalist cabinet, conserving the economic order untouched, but to take all the power for the working class and change the capitalist structure for one that meets the needs of the people. . . . Against speculation and the manipulation of exchange rates the workers and the COB demand the total monopoly of commerce by the state. . . . The COB plans the occupation of the factories and mines by the workers as the only means of preventing the sabotage of the revolution. . . . Nationalisation without compensation and under workers' control. The workers will accept no other form. . . . the Bolivian people cannot be put under the obligation of heavy indemnities. . . . The destiny of the revolution is intimately tied to the destiny of private property which can only be resolved by the revolutionary action of the masses. . . . The national congress of workers is a step towards obtaining a workers' parliament which will transcend the democratic bourgeois juridical framework and open the road to a government of workers and peasants.'[12]

This was too much for the government; it was nothing less than a slightly diluted version of Pulacayo. The MNR's central body, the *Comité Político Nacional* (CPN), immediately condemned it and reminded the COB leaders that it alone possessed the authority to issue political statements on behalf of the party, thereby raising the question of discipline and forcing Butrón to make a hasty retreat and emphasise that the document was only a draft and not official COB policy.[13] However, the Trotskysant phrases of the *proyecto* succeeded in drawing the party's right into the fray, which seems to have been Lechín's intention all along. On 18 September the periodical *En Marcha*, controlled by the right but speaking in the name of the entire party, launched an unbridled attack on

a declaration of principles that are openly Communist and in the name of the COB, a fact that is grave for the country and the future of the national revolution. The MNR, therefore, is obliged to declare that . . . it is in essence a national party and thus against international communism . . . that the noted programme of the COB is contrary to all nationalist sentiment . . . that ninety per cent of the workers are nationalist and belong to the MNR; on the other hand, the leaders of the COB are mainly international

Communists, from the POR, PIR and PCB. ... The MNR believes that the country should develop a spirit of enterprise amongst Bolivians and also foreign capital. ... Consequently it does not accept the wish of the COB to suppress commerce and private enterprise. ... That contrary to destroying the army as the leaders of the COB demand, the MNR sees the need to reorganise a national army. That the leaders of the COB are ... attempting to develop an anti-Bolivian policy in favour of Russian-Soviet imperialism.[14]

The breach that had been papered over for five months was now in the open for all to see. It posed a sharp challenge to the MNR leadership, which was obliged to mediate between these forces whilst it was itself strongly anti-communist and under insistent pressure from a clear right-wing majority on the party's national committee. Although Siles was now moving closer to Paz's policy of neutralising both extremes through extended negotiation, he himself was on record as stating that the MNR was the last bulwark against communism in Bolivia, and he could scarcely allow the COB to pursue its present line, on this occasion siding with the provocative authors of the *En Marcha* attack.[15]

The first major clashes over concrete policy concerned the military question. In April the army had been all but destroyed. While the *carabineros* still remained intact they were greatly outnumbered by the heavily-armed popular militias formed in the factories, mines and countryside as well as by MNR militants in the towns. At the May Day celebrations most of the forty thousand COB contingent that marched noisily past the presidential palace were carrying weapons and many held placards demanding the complete abolition of the army. Throughout May Oruro was under the total control of the popular militia, which threw out a succession of army and police officers sent to administer the city's forces. Only a top-level delegation headed by Foreign Minister Walter Guevara was eventually able to persuade the belligerent civilian troops to accept an army officer as their commander, with the guarantee that he would be answerable to locally elected bodies.[16] In La Paz itself the police issued a plaintive communiqué stating that it had four hundred men on the street at any one time and hoped that the *milicianos* might collaborate with them in protecting the peace.[17] There was little that the police could do; for months after the revolution the La Paz nights were full of the sounds of shooting as various armed groups imposed their own law and order. It soon became clear that there were two types of militia, those derived from the MNR's *grupos de honor* and answerable to the party leadership, and those based on the workplace, largely independent of the MNR, and linked through the local union to the COB. These Lechín hoped would replace the army completely. Speaking at Huanuni at the end of May, he proclaimed that 'the disappearance of the army was a great triumph in that it saw the end of a force created by the people to defend its sovereignty but which then passed into the service of the Rosca. . . . We must not permit the reorganisation of the army. What better army than the people? In order to rid ourselves forever of massacres we must state once and a hundred times that we do not want an army. (Remember) it was one of the Rosca's lawyers who once said, "there is no general who can resist a cannonade of a million *pesos bolivianos*".'[18] Although he recognised that it would be no easy task to dismantle or even curb the militias, Paz openly opposed Lechín from the start. While the Colegio Militar was closed down, annual conscription to the ranks was only delayed and the president authorised the opening of a new airforce college in Santa Cruz only seven weeks after the revolution; amongst its first intake was the young Juan Pereda Asbún, a future military president who would come to power through a coup. The day after the opening a US military mission arrived in La Paz to visit the run-down and understaffed ministry of defence, headed by an ex-RADEPA officer hurriedly promoted to general. Amongst the visitors was a certain airforce captain named Fox, who would too play a critical role in organising a right-wing military coup.[19] However, Paz was confident that the nationalists in the armed forces could be depended upon to revive the spirit of Busch and Villarroel. Many in the officer corps were purged, but substantial numbers were kept on the rolls at low rates of pay, obliged to swear loyalty to the party and dedicate themselves to 'productive activity', primarily engineering. In September Paz declared himself convinced that the army had been weaned away from its old attitudes towards 'new technical and productive concepts', but this was not all: 'the army is a factor in external security but it must also take a stand against any internal disturbance that might take place because internal security is not simply secured at the border but vice-versa . . . '. At the same time the chief of staff (*Jefe de Estado Mayor General*—JEMG), Lieutenant Colonel Delfín

Cataldi, affirmed that, 'the mentality of the nationalist officer is fully identified with the true sentiment of the National Revolution: against the Rosca and against Communism'.[20] Within weeks Paz announced that the Colegio would be reopened the following year with an intake drawn largely from the 'popular classes', thereby guaranteeing generations of nationalist officers for the future. This caused uproar in the COB but Lechín himself was eventually to sign the necessary decree. Paz made it plain that the military question was one of principle on which he would not concede, and after several days of fierce exchanges and great tension the COB finally held back from an all-out challenge on the issue. Military spending was almost halved, numbers cut, equipment withheld and troops quartered well away from the mines and the city centres to be engaged largely in road building. The official armed forces were in extremely poor shape and no match for the militias, but despite the crushing blow of their defeat they had survived.

The issue of the army highlighted the cautious reformism of the MNR leadership. Its first major measure was not taken until late July and was concerned neither with altering property relations nor with instituting new forms of popular power but introducing a fundamental reform of the democratic system in granting universal suffrage. By suppressing the traditional qualification of being male and literate for membership of the formal political nation — a qualification which meant that it won the 1951 election with the support of 2.6 per cent of the population — the MNR increased the electorate in one move from around two hundred thousand to over a million; in effect, it had enfranchised the *campesinado*. Some 13 Latin American countries had already given women the same voting status as men, but this change had generally taken place in the 1930s and 1940s, and states such as Brazil, Chile and Peru continued to prohibit illiterates from political participation into the 1970s; the MNR's measure was relatively neither as innovative nor as overdue as might at first appear to the European mind.[21] Enfranchisement was an obligatory move, but its full social and political ramifications remained open without much wider change since peasant votes were highly vulnerable to local pressure and could feasibly be harnessed to a conservative backlash. Such complementary action in the shape of an agrarian reform was not, in fact, to be taken for another year.

This graduated character of the changes implemented by the MNR government was also reflected in a remarkable lack of rupture in cultural life and political style. The word '*compañero*', borrowed from the unions, found a firm place in the popular vocabulary, and Paz's triumphant V-sign became a central feature of the party's limited iconology, these being adopted to counter the '*camarada*' and clenched fist of the traditional left. '*Campesino*' also made its way into the lexicon and joined the more formal '*indígena*' to displace '*indio*'. However, on the streets social comportment was little changed; there was no alteration in modes of dress — even of the tie-removing variety evident after July 1946 — or major adjustment of the staid etiquette of the urban middle class. Ponchos and *lluchus* (a knitted hat with earflaps) were donned with manifest self-consciousness by political leaders at meetings in the countryside but otherwise remained firmly on the supplicant side of official desks. There was still little interest in indigenous music in the towns (the boom in *música folklórica* was not to occur until the 1960s under the leadership of the great *tupiceño* guitarist Alfredo Domínguez and the ever-active master of the *charango*, Ernesto Cavour); the MNR contented itself with expropriating a number of *huaynos* and traditional *cuecas* onto which a partisan lyric was imposed, as in the case of the party's anthem, Gastón Velasco's 'Siempre'.

Neither was there any sudden renaissance in literature or the arts. The social novel of the Chaco continued to be written in substantial quantities but threw up very few gems: the best examples of the genre, such as Augusto Céspedes's *Sangre de Mestizos* or Jesús Lara's semi-fictional *Repete*, were pre-revolutionary. This was also true, as argued in a forceful but sensitive essay by Guillermo Lora, for the less prolific lineage of the mining novel, the most important of which still remains *Socavones de Angustia*, written by Fernando Ramírez Velarde about events in 1929 and published in 1947.[22] Although Bolivia's most celebrated novel remains Nataniel Aguirre's *Juan de la Rosa* (1885), the country's equally unimpressive record in fostering good poets did alter somewhat in the post-revolutionary epoch, but it was well over a decade before the likes of Oscar Alfaro, Oscar Cerruto and the young Pedro Shimose were to receive proper acclaim for their verse, while the results of Jesús Lara's life-long dedication to collecting and translating Quechua tales and poems were inspected much less widely than they were respected. Moreover, Alfaro and Lara were rare examples of writers who took an abiding interest in social change or revolutionary politics. Painting, on the other hand, did register a more immediate impact, largely because of the direct political use that could be made of the work of a small group of talented muralists who had moved beyond a picturesque but static *indigenismo*. The figureheads of this movement were Walter Solón Romero, whose fine set of prints 'Don Quijote en el Exilio' (1981) testifies to a change in medium but no diminution in either political commitment or pictorial force, and the veteran POR militant Miguel Alandia Pantoja, whose work bore the stylistic influence of Orozco rather than that of the more radical Rivera. Today an appreciation of Alandia's swirling figures in indict-ment of the Rosca and celebration of the people's struggle is virtually impossible since they are limited to adorning the covers of the books of his life-long friend and political mentor, Lora; the anti-militarist mural commissioned by Víctor Paz for the presidential palace and completed in 1953 was hacked to bits by General Barrientos's minions in 1964, that on the western face of the COB headquarters was removed before the building was razed on the orders of Colonel Arce Gómez in September 1980, and the internal decoration of the Villarroel mauso-leum remains out of public bounds.[23]

In other areas Bolivia was too backward and the revolution too early to exploit to the full its symbolic and propaganda potential let alone dynamise creative effort. In June 1952 an enterprising salesman from the Pye television company, a certain Mr Albert Rose, arrived in La Paz and declared that the country could have a television system within the year; in the event it was to take fifteen. Nor was there any revolutionary cinema. Only one poor documentary was made in the immediate aftermath of the April rising, and over the thirty years since there has been no film on it, fictional or otherwise, in contrast to the cases of Mexico, Cuba, Nicaragua and even El Salvador. By the mid-1950s Bolivia had two hundred cinemas but these depended on an unhealthy diet of cheap Mexican thrillers and sub-titled American movies that had already done the rounds in Lima or Buenos Aires. It was to be the next generation of revolutionaries that would make recourse to celluloid but even they were for a long time effectively rep-resented by just one man, Jorge Sanjinés, whose *Yawar Mallku* (Blood of the Condor), *El Coraje del Pueblo* and *Fuera de Aquí* are amongst the best of modern Latin American political film. It is doubtful that even had the resources been available the MNR would have made a very good job of it judging by the extraordinarily dreary and sycophantic content of the official newspaper *La Nación*, which was a good deal less informative than *La Razón*, the standard-bearer of the Rosca silenced for good after the insurrection. The country's best political journalism and most pithy comment was not to be found in any MNR periodical but in the leftist weeklies like *El Pueblo*, edited by the redoubtable Fernando Siñani. The party leadership had outgrown the frivolities of *La Calle* while recruits to the youth wing had little experience of that adversity which generates independent and imaginative political literature.

In one area, however, the MNR did make some change. From the onset of the *sexenio* it had been compelled to make increasing use of its women militants, and on occasions they came right to the fore of activity, especially in propaganda actions. During and after the insurrection the 'Barzolas' (named after María Barzola, a woman killed in the Catavi massacre of 1942) were renowned for their vigorous and sometimes violent imposition of the party line amongst the popular sectors. Lidia Gueiler Tejada was the *de facto* leader of this movement, playing a prominent part in the April insurrection, becoming Paz's secretary and then joining the leadership of the left wing along with her husband Edwin Moller.[24] Gueiler's role was certainly remarkable and equally surely represented the party's adroit exploitation of her good looks and boundless energy in an unambiguously *machista* society where one such woman can inspire admiration rather than induce repudiation. Gueiler was the only woman to impose her stamp on the upper echelons of the MNR, as head of its 'feminine' rather than feminist section; the wives of the other top dignataries continued to dedicate themselves to the traditional rite of good works and supporting their spouses at formal occasions. Nevertheless, the MNR was obliged to recognise both the debt to its women workers and the latent power of a sex that was now enfranchised, in all possibility formed the majority of the labour force, was entering the professional occupations in still small but growing numbers, and exercised total dominance in the urban market place. The social controls on women remained severe, especially in the household, but they now had to be treated as a legitimate constituency beyond the traditional celebration of wife and mother. Needless to say, there was manifest tokenism in the constant reference to the 'men and women of the MNR', but this was part of the discernible move towards adopting the language and motifs of a modern politics that was conceived in terms of the nation as a whole and respected the importance of the consumer if not consumerism as a means of incorporation. However, the party's power did not derive from these factors and neither did it make great efforts to construct its legitimacy around them, preferring to keep them subordinate and complementary to its economic reforms, which were centred on the nationalisation of the holdings of the tin barons and the agrarian reform.

Nationalisation of the Mines

The problem of the large mining companies took first place on the revolutionary agenda. Since its inception the MNR had tried to extend state control to this sector by fiscal means, and after 1946 was drawn ever closer to the FSTMB's demand for outright nationalisation. However, in April 1952 the party was by no means in full accord with the union's position, which insisted on workers' control (*control obrero*) and no compensation. The MNR leadership was also very anxious to avoid any friction with the US and a boycott of tin of the type that had proved so damaging to the junta. The need to tighten up the foreign reserves and fiscal position was, nonetheless, overwhelming: reserves were less than $30 million and, according to the official records, the personal tax returns of the Patiño family in 1951 amounted to a mere $415.[25] Accordingly, the regime's first move was to require that tin exports be processed by the state-controlled Banco Minero and all foreign exchange earnings be converted at the Banco Central. At the same time Paz appointed Víctor Andrade as ambassador to Washington, a post he had held under Villarroel. Andrade was a relative latecomer to the party, connected with its right wing and, as an ex-employee of Nelson Rockefeller's International Basic Economy Corporation in Guayaquil, Ecuador, a great deal more sympathetic to US interests than to those of the 'crypto-communists' he saw lurking behind the leaders of the COB. In later years he proclaimed that he would be prepared to work for the CIA (of which he had been widely accused) rather than see Bolivia 'go communist', but in 1952 his task was to assuage the fears of Eisenhower and the State Department about a nationalisation that the MNR was obliged to implement in one form or another. This task entailed a number of discussions with the US president's brother, Milton, who was later dispatched to assess the position in Bolivia, and games of golf with Eisenhower himself at the Burning Tree Club, an activity which reflected Andrade's success in cultivating favour in the upper reaches of the US government.[26]

Washington was, of course, hard to convince. A new Republican administration, headed by a soldier and whole-heartedly pledged to the ethos of free enterprise in a world over which it possessed unprecedented dominance, known to be destabilising the reformist regime in Guatemala, immersed in the Korean war and the McCarthyite anti-communist crusade, and already deeply unhappy about the state of its relations with the Bolivian tin industry, presented a formidable obstacle. Moreover, Andrade was faced with the problem that Mossadegh's nationalisation of the oil companies in Iran was blowing up into a major political crisis. However, the ambassador received much support from Paz, who within days of returning to Bolivia declared that 'the nationalisation of the mines is not a rigid or general proposition', and that in order for it to work serious preliminary study would be needed, especially in order to retain the services of foreign technicians.[27] This was picked up immediately in the US; two days later *American Metals Market* noted,

'the declarations emanating from La Paz have been contradictory and disconcerting for the foreign observer. On his arrival from Buenos Aires, the new president, Víctor Paz Estenssoro, declared that nationalisation would be the subject of investigation but that there would be no precipitate moves on the tin industry in this respect. This declaration might have been considered too soft by the extremist radicals who figure in some number in the ranks of the *Movimiento*. But for capital, wherever it comes from, 'nationalisation' has alarming implications, a fact the president appears to have recognised and attempted to placate when, the next day, he gave assurances that his party is not 'anti-capitalist' and recognises the urgent need that Bolivia has for foreign capital. . . . We hope that events show the disquieting implications have been premature.'[28]

These comments were given prominence in the Bolivian press, and although they were designed to avert any kind of nationalisation, Paz responded by continually emphasising the need for 'tranquil study' of the problem and the dangerous implications of the fact that 20 per cent of Patiño's shareholders were North American. This response paid off; early in May *Time* described Paz as 'an expert in balancing the budget . . . he is not a Mossadegh when it comes to finances'. The magazine also noted that Paz was prepared to sell tin at $1.21 a pound, which even the junta had refused to do. Lechín, on the other hand, 'has worked with Trotskyists and even speaks, after a fashion, like a Marxist, snarling that he and his workers are independent of the government. He wants the nationalisation to be effected quickly. The preparation of a report by the commission should take no longer than 30 days.'[29]

Lechín's position on this question was again very different to that of Paz. At the May Day march he gave clear warning of the attitudes of the FSTMB and the COB:

'The Revolution is not over. Only the opportunists and bureaucrats can think that with the taking of the Palacio Quemado its course has been run. The Revolution has only just begun and with the sacrifice of our martyrs we must construct it on the base of an organised and conscious proletariat, the only guarantee of saving it from the Rosca and the counter-revolutionary sabotage of opportunism. . . . We are here to demand, orientate and defend. So long as we don't nationalise the mines so that the capital of Bolivians stays with Bolivians; so long as we don't execute an agrarian reform so that the lands cultivated by Bolivians belong to them; so long as we don't get rid of the speculators and give the people bread, and while we fail to build up our organisation and develop our political consciousness, the Rosca will destroy our Revolution. We are the only guarantee against the counter-revolutionary coup which the oligarchy is planning. We demand that the government realise our programme. Those who are against our programme are against Bolivia because our programme is the programme of the exploited of Bolivia.'[30]

This was strong stuff but it soon proved to be somewhat divergent from Lechín's practice, a disparity between words and deeds that was to be a consistent feature of the COB leader's erratic career. On 13 May the government announced the establishment of a commission to study the prospects for nationalisation; Lechín and Torres were shortly afterwards coopted onto it. There was to be no immediate expropriation, and the issues of compensation and *control obrero* were effectively made *sub judice*, the subject of back-room bargaining. Lora, who called for the immediate occupation of the mines,

identified this move as prompting the first and possibly the most critical down-turn in popular mobilisation.[31] In retrospect it is clear that a
key component of the revolution was in the process of being manager-
ialised, but at the time it took the form of a political vacuum; the pace
of change was perceived to have been braked and would henceforth
be the subject of administrative negotiation. The popular response
was not very tangible. If the notion of compensation was anathema,
control obrero remained a nebulous concept to many. Moreover,
nothing had been decided. There was a notable lack of agitation and
debate over the ensuing months; the issue appeared in some sense
both critical and resolved.

For the regime this delay was crucial. It enabled the full demands of
the COB to be held at bay whilst the party leaders could instruct those of
the union movement as to the complexities and political ramifications
of nationalisation. They were not persuaded but successfully cajoled
into discussion and an effective truce in the public arena. In the event,
the commission's work lasted not one month but five. It was only at the
end of October that the COB, already knowing the outcome, returned to
its original demands in a long and detailed open letter to Paz, enumer-
ating the reasons why compensation would represent a continuation of
the exploitative tradition of the Rosca and critically impair the nation's
finances, and why any expropriation would not achieve its objectives
without a fundamental change in the social relations in the mines. The
comments on compensation were most vehement, but the COB's position on *control obrero* was also outlined with some strength:

> 'In this respect, *compañero Presidente*, we wish it to be made
> plain that our position is, on the one hand, to avoid demagogic
> campaigns by irresponsible elements, and, on the other, to show
> to the timid and those who ignore the level of political maturity
> attained by the workers of Bolivia that they are sufficiently devel-
> oped to know their own capacity. We desire that the mechanism
> of *control obrero* be established in a direct form, that is, through
> workers' delegates or representatives. We request that this should
> be made effective in the planning of production, in documenta-
> tion and accounting practices, in the provisioning and adminis-
> tration of the stores and *pulperías* and, most importantly, in the
> investment of the surplus-value resulting from this activity.'[32]

This late intervention achieved a compromise although it was one that before too long was discerned as highly disadvantageous to the FSTMB. On 31 October Paz and Lechín went to Siglo XX — Catavi, the site of the most concerted opposition to the Rosca and the largest congregation of miners, and signed the nationalisation decree amidst the noise of exploding dynamite and generous volleys from the local militia. The celebrations were prolonged and joyous; Bolivia had achieved her 'economic independence' and the revolutionary regime had fulfilled its principal nationalist mandate.

By the terms of the decree and its complementary measures the already established *Corporación Minera de Bolivia* (Comibol) took possession of all holdings in the country previously controlled by Patiño, Hochschild and Aramayo — 163 mines operated by 13 companies with a total production of 27,000 metric tons (four times greater than that of the remaining private sector) and a workforce of 29,000. However, compensation was to be paid, eventually to the extent of $27 million, more than two-thirds of the country's foreign exchange reserves at the time. The FSTMB had only two representatives (rather than delegates) on Comibol's board of seven, but the system of *control obrero* was to be allowed, albeit only a full year after the decree and again in the form of individual representatives rather than in a collective form or through delegates subjected to the power of recall.

In Washington the question of compensation was seen at the time as far more important than some subsidiary arrangement about workers' representation. Andrade knew this and responded accordingly:

> '1) My government subscribes wholeheartedly to the principles of democracy; 2) the nationalisation of the properties of the Patiño, Hochschild and Aramayo groups represented a special one. Nationalisation of private property is not the policy of Bolivia; 3) nationalisation of the tin mines did not mean confiscation of the property. We intend to pay the former owners every cent that is due to them; 4) the government of Bolivia realises the part which private capital can contribute toward the development of its resources and hopes to attract that private capital.'[33]

Despite reservations this line was eventually accepted. The Eisenhower administration had already recognised the Paz Estenssoro government and, in a rare manifestation of political perspicacity, identified it as essentially friendly and anti-communist in character. There were indeed some rumblings from Patiño's US shareholders,

but after Aramayo and Hochschild had failed in their efforts to persuade the Chilean courts to confiscate cargos of tin lying on the dock-
side at Arica there was no open campaign by the Rosca to boycott
Comibol. Nationalisation prompted the exodus of 170 of some 200
foreign engineers and technicians, but by January 1953 a Williams
Harvey team was in La Paz to negotiate a new contract on behalf of
the Patiño-owned foundry. They agreed to take 50 per cent of Comibol's output, underlining the great dependence of the state corporation on foreign firms, in this case one it had just replaced at the point
of extraction.

Thus, with US neutrality, the companies' grudging acquiescence in
nationalisation, and a tacit truce between the regime and the FSTMB,
the commercial future of Comibol appeared reasonably solid. A year
after nationalisation the government published a set of commemorat-
ive speeches in which it was maintained that 'the mines have been
administered in irreproachable form . . . social conflicts have disappeared. Now that *control obrero* is established, it is the underground workers who maintain the rhythm of production . . .'. Víctor
Paz pointedly made no reference to workers' control but began his
eulogy by praising the foreign *técnicos* who had stayed behind.
Lechín, on the other hand, suggested that 'we can now say we control
our own destiny', chanced a quick quote from Adam Smith, and
stressed that workers' control in Comibol was unique in the world and
identified the workers completely with their work.[34]

The reality, sadly but predictably, was at odds with this vision
although in some important respects the organisation of Bolivia's
mines was transformed. First, whatever the internal realignments,
Comibol's position in the world market was no better and in some
aspects discernibly worse than that of the Rosca before it. The change-
over certainly unsettled markets for a while but the price of tin was
anyway on an emphatic downward trend; it did not rise between 1952
and 1961 and only reattained its 1951 level in 1964. Moreover, it was
within three months of nationalisation that price levels took their big-
gest dip: from $1.20 to $0.80 per pound. The RFC made a small spot
purchase in January 1953 but was not to buy again until July. Comibol's exports rose somewhat in 1953 but thereafter they fell steadily; in
1958 earnings from tin were less than half those in 1952.

Secondly, Comibol itself offered no viable solution to this deterior-
ating position. From the start the corporation at the centre of the

Bolivian economy proved to be an inefficient entity, the scene of end-less political conflicts and the object of consistent mismanagement and progressive bureaucratisation. This is not the place to concern ourselves with the full details but a few points should be registered. The most important of these from a purely commercial viewpoint was the problem of reviving an infrastructure that was badly undercapit-alised and possessed rapidly diminishing resources. At first sight this task would seem to have been made unrealistic by the demands of labour since the power of the FSTMB plainly required that all those fired for union and political activity be reinstated immediately. In four years Comibol's labour force rose from 29,000 to 36,000 and $8 million was paid out in 'redundancy pay' as a bonus for re-employment by the state. However, the rank and file effectively accepted the argu-ment that Comibol could not afford to increase basic wages; it there-fore held back from making long overdue claims and continued to work under conditions very similar to those that had prevailed under the Rosca.

Thus, in a period of rampant inflation the effective price freeze on a range of basic commodities in the *pulperías* took on a critical impor-tance for workers whose real wage fell by 42.5 per cent between 1950 and 1955.[35] Both René Ruíz González and Walter Gómez, who have made close studies of Comibol, point to an actual decline in labour costs from 38 per cent in 1952 to 35 per cent in 1958, rising again only when union power was greatly curtailed (the increase being due less to labour militancy than the aggregate effects of undercapitalisation). According to Gómez, Comibol's labour costs per worker were $86 per month in 1952, dropped to $42 in 1956, and never rose above $70 before 1970.[36] Some US economists suggest that wages rose substan-tially on the basis of the rise of *pulpería* subsidies, and argue, on the basis of reduced exports of ore, that productivity dropped off extremely sharply.[37] Productivity certainly did fall but if we base our calculation on production per face worker we find that an output of 3.91 fine tons per man in 1952 rose to 4.5 in 1956 and fell only to 3.6 in 1958 despite constantly falling ore content, an acute shortage of equipment and the maintenance of inefficient methods from extraction to initial con-centration. Moreover, taking the level of total crude ore extracted at Siglo XX, we find that an average shift in 1955 produced 1.31 tons against 1.22 tons in 1950 with overall excavation rising from 1.05 mil-lion tons to 1.45 million. This, plus the fact that in 1960 it took ten

Table 2

The State of Central Comibol Mines, 1956 (a)

Mine	Profitability	Estimated Life (Yrs)	Tin Content % (b) 1950	1960	Pulpería Subsidy ($ per ton 1956)	Production (c) Cost ($ per lb.)
Colquiri	+	16	2.02	0.68	2.74	1.54
Huanuni	+	8	1.90	0.97	3.52	1.18
Catavi	+	10	1.20	0.68	2.21	1.62
Chorolque	−	3-4	1.80	1.94	2.05	0.69
Potosí (Unificada)	+	4	1.72	1.10	5.91	1.27
Caracoles	−	3	2.00	0.94	3.89	0.87
Viloco	+	2-3			3.89	1.06
Oploca	+	1-2				
Siete Suyos	−	'None'				1.59
San José	−	'None'			19.07	1.32
Santa Fé	−	'None'				
Morococala	−				4.41	1.79

Notes:

a. All data except columns three and four is derived from the Ford, Bacon and Davis Report (1956). All these pits continue to operate in 1983, demonstrating the value of improvements in smelting techniques for low grade ores as well as the authors' underestimation of the capacity of faceworkers and engineers to locate new veins and reorganise the exploitation of those already discovered.

b. Where no figures are given data is not readily available.

c. The average market price for a pound of tin in 1956 was $0.98; overall profitability is not based on tin alone although in all mines, except Viloco, it is by far the largest earner.

metres advance to produce a ton of ore against only one metre in 1950, goes a very long way to qualifying the image of indiscipline and laziness conjured up either out of political interest or from misconceived calculation.[38]

Much of Comibol's overemployment and inefficiency was centred not down the pits but on the surface, the percentage of interior workers on the total payroll dropping from 82 per cent in 1952 to 52 per cent in 1959. By 1967 nearly a third of the corporation's 22,250 employees had desk jobs, and of the 14,700 manual workers only 7,600 worked at the face, the rest being employed in undermechanised and ill-organised transport and processing activities on the surface.[39] Comibol was the principal victim of the MNR's capitulation to the demand for 'jobs for the boys'; its administration became grossly overstaffed and correspondingly inept. Up to 1964 it possessed no dependable assessment of its income, and even in 1970 it had no single system of accounting. In 1963 Comibol's projected production level was miscalculated by a margin of over 30 per cent after having been altered three times in the course of the year. Consultants brought in to assess its operations were consistently critical, noting substantial administrative shortcomings in a whole range of activities from the lack of a clear decision-making process to simple sabotage and theft.[40] Combined with the poor quality of the ores this contributed greatly to the corporation's losses, which had reached $13 million in 1960 when production costs were still above market prices. However, Comibol's early lack of profitability was perhaps most critically determined by the MNR's overall economic policy which was designed less to revive the tin industry than to spur on diversification particularly in favour of the oil industry. The regime's principal mechanism for this was the use of a number of different exchange rates, and it obliged Comibol to sell its dollars to the Banco Central at rates considerably below those on the free market (for example, at Bs. 230 against Bs.683 to the dollar in 1953 and Bs.570 against Bs.2,979 in 1955). If the corporation had been allowed to sell dollars at the free market rate it would have made a profit of $103.8 million up to 1955 instead of a loss of Bs.10.2 billion.[41] In 1956 Comibol contributed $30 million to the *Corporación Boliviana de Fomento* (CBF) and $10 million to the state oil company *Yacimientos Petrolíferos Fiscales de Bolivia* (YPFB) when, according to the US firm Ford, Bacon and Davis, it needed only $2.25 million to rectify its own structural problems. Under the MNR over $100 million was transferred from Comibol to YPFB. In theory diversification was correct and highly desirable but in practice it was grossly mismanaged.

In organisational terms nationalisation greatly strengthened the FSTMB and the COB. The office of *control obrero* was vested with substantial managerial authority and effective powers of veto over many issues at camp level. This caused considerable difficulties for Comibol's managers, who were by no means always able or willing to reach an amicable entente with the *controles*, who, despite the fact that they operated individually, could not afford to clash too often with a rank and file which elected them in open assemblies. In the smaller, less militant camps conflict could be contained to specific minor issues, but in Siglo XX – Catavi, ever the focus of discontent in this period, the *Controles* soon came to play a dominant role in highly-charged negotiations not only between the workforce and the management but also between the *sindicato* and the less powerful but government-backed *Comando Especial* of the MNR. Significantly, the most important holders of the office at Siglo and Catavi were not MNR members; at the Siglo pit the bombastic and highly popular communist leader Federico Escóbar retained the job from 1955 to 1963, reflecting the continued authority of the PCB in the local union notwithstanding numerous attacks from the MNR and the more erratic influence of the POR. At Catavi the post was held for several years by Sinforoso Cabrera, who resisted pressure to join the MNR and maintained his sympathies for the POR although he was not a militant of the party. In general, however, the post of *control obrero* became increasingly bureaucratised – Mario Torres received Bs.90,000 as chief *control obrero* when rank and file pay was Bs.4,000 – and as relations between the FSTMB and the MNR worsened the plant unions were forced to resort to traditional methods of direct mass action against a management over which they had no formal control.

Yet, early in 1953 this development was anticipated by very few people and the preponderance of the COB was sufficiently great to provoke a sharp political crisis. This took two forms: a purging of the extreme right of the MNR and a concerted campaign against the influence of the POR; in both instances the centrist MNR leadership won important gains.

After the violent exchanges of September 1952 it was clear that the MNR's traditionalist right could not remain subdued for long. The level of mass mobilisation, the independence and strength of the militias, the 'arrogance' of the COB, and Paz's apparent willingness to cede to many of its demands strengthened the conservatives' view that the national revolution was becoming one with a markedly communist direction. Early in January 1953 this group, which included some like Alfredo Candia, Luis Peñaloza and Hugo Roberts who held senior positions in government and party, joined with the JEMG Colonel Cataldi to attempt a coup in order 'to free the president from communist influence'. The attempt was badly organised and suppressed by the *carabineros* even before the militias had taken to the streets. The rebels were only a minority of the party leadership and did not include many who themselves held substantial reservations about the direction of the government, but their action marked an important watershed. While he had engaged — sometimes very vehemently — with the COB, Paz was now perceived as the target of the right and although he dealt with the dissidents very leniently, his popularity increased markedly, giving him greater scope with which to tackle the left. This, allied to the fact that the revolutionary process was shown to be extremely vulnerable, strengthened Paz's hand in requiring the COB leadership to fall into line and curb the power of non-party elements in its organisation.

By early 1953 the MNR was extremely confident of its political ability to contain the FSB and 'oligarchic reaction'. The party's newly-established *Instituto de Capacitación Política* was now fleshing out policy and producing publications to support its attacks on the other parties. That dedicated to the FSB — soon publicly opposed to the MNR's revolution — exhibited untempered derision of a political current that, 'after many years of sterile and vegetative activity dedicated to pure *anti-pirismo*, a party with which it had contested hegemony in the bars of Cochabamba', had failed to support the rebel cause in the 1949 civil war, the general strike of 1950, the democratic slate in the 1951 election, the April rising in 1952 and even its own ideological soul-mates in January 1953.[42] The MNR vigorously repudiated FSB claims to have a monopoly on Catholic policies in the public arena; this, it asserted, was simply a veil for fascism while the government itself was in every regard closer to the central doctrines of the Christian faith.

The threat posed by the POR was more immediately serious since it allegedly controlled at least half of the COB's 13-person central committee, a subject of much press invective early in 1953. While the MNR

turned over responsibility for an ideological and theoretical denunciation of Trotskyism to Carlos Velarde, who attacked it as pro-imperialist
because it 'derided the peasantry . . . middle class and national bourgeoisie', Paz leaned heavily on Lechín to reduce its members at the
top of the COB.[43] This was helped by the PCB's deep-seated opposition
to the POR. In Siglo XX the communist union secretary, Gabriel Por-
cel, waged a campaign against Lora's younger brother César, and
made no move when he was jailed for a year on a charge trumped up by
the local MNR comando. In the COB itself the most vehement attacks
against the Trotskyists came from the communist student delegate Sergio Almaraz. The party was forced onto the defensive and although it
would be some time before it was thrown into crisis, the months after
January 1953 marked a decline in its influence.[44] Nevertheless, these
months proved to be no less taxing for the government party for,
having successfully negotiated the hurdle of nationalisation, it was
confronted with widespread discontent in the countryside and the
overbearing need to implement an agrarian reform.

Agrarian Reform

The MNR's position on agrarian reform was broadly similar to its
approach to nationalisation; the subject as such had not appeared in
any party programme prior to 1952 and was only discussed in the most
general of terms, usually with reference to a vague 'incorporation' of
the *campesinado* into a pre-existing society and nation. Immediately
after April there was little change in this attitude since the peasantry
had played a very marginal part in the insurrection and appeared to
be broadly disposed to accept a malleable clientelist relationship with
the new regime. Thus, government leaders expressed a certain confidence in developing limited proposals for change in the countryside.
This was partly determined by pressure from the right wing, which
perceived in an agrarian reform implications for property relations in
general that were far more dangerous than those evident in the nationalisation of the mining companies. The MNR right was only prepared to
countenance a measure that conferred the right progressively to purchase freehold of *colonos'* existing rented plots; it would not accept
the idea of expropriation of other latifundia lands. The COB and the
MNR left, on the other hand, were until October almost entirely bound

up in the question of the mines and possessed no detailed proposals for the rural sphere except to call for an 'agrarian revolution', although some militants were sent into the *campo* to help establish *sindicatos* and the COB occasionally urged direct expropriation (*tomas*) of haciendas by peasants.

The new Minister of Peasant Affairs, Ñuflo Chávez Ortiz, the son of a wealthy *hacendado* from Santa Cruz and a more cautious member of the party's left, attempted to reconcile these two positions. Two months after the revolution he stated: 'We are going to orientate the Agrarian Reform on the basis of strengthening collective communal property and the implementation of the capitalist stage in private property, liquidating feudalism'.[45] This raised fears on the right that collectivisation was to be introduced on a wide scale, but Chávez was in fact separating rural organisation into its two already existing spheres: the latifundia and the *comunidades*. When pressed as to the nature of the proposals, which were in fact only very general ideas of some of his team, the minister made it clear that, 'the Agrarian Reform will in no sense ignore the Right of Property . . . the new system of agrarian labour will be developed on the basis of the existing indigenous communities in order to bring about cooperativisation. . . . It is not possible to proceed to the redistribution of land because this would mean establishing minifundia and be prejudicial to production . . .'.[46] Paz was even more cautious in his pronouncements. At a noisy meeting in the township of Jesús de Machaca, long a centre of *campesino* discontent, he talked (through an interpreter) in the manner of a benevolent *patrón* and offered no tangible promises: 'The government, always attentive to the needs of the indigenous class, has given instructions that they be attended immediately by the various ministries and public institutions . . . I want you to lend your most decided cooperation to the government. How? By maintaining perfect order in the *altiplano*, producing more, working harder . . . we, for our part, will do our best to improve your conditions in every sense.'[47] This was in June, and the reference to 'perfect order' was not amiss for the peasantry was already beginning to realise the possibilities of the April revolution and embarking on independent actions that continued to escalate until and even beyond the final reform decree, signed in August 1953.

Given the essentially parochial conditions of rural existence, the form and intensity of this mobilisation was very uneven. However, by the end of 1952 it was usually taking the form of a simple refusal to work for landlords because of their lack of recognition of the Villarroel decree abolishing *pongueaje*, constant legal appeals for the expropriation of haciendas, and actual seizure and division of estates. At the same time rudimentary *sindicatos*, which bore only a formal resemblance to urban unions, were set up along often chaotic lines but sometimes to immediate effect. For some 15 months the key zones of the Bolivian countryside were immersed in disorder that was often localised to one *finca* (farm) or village but remained constant and was directed primarily at the landlord class, generating within it a sentiment of acute apprehension and even panic that Herbert Klein has justifiably likened to the 'Great Fear' in revolutionary France.[48]

Unrest was centred in the departments of Cochabamba, La Paz and Oruro, evident in the north of Potosí and parts of Chuquisaca, but virtually absent from the rest of the country. Around the shores of Lake Titicaca and in the Cochabamba valley hacienda buildings were attacked weekly and although these petty revolts dissolved through lack of direction or sustained support, they often included large numbers of rural labourers. In November 1952 peasants from Colomi, Cochabamba, blocked the road to the hacienda 'Emusa', wrecked a truck and abused its occupants, and then more than three thousand of them, armed with staves and machetes, entered the village, appropriated its store of firearms, cut the telephone lines, burnt several houses and three hacienda buildings and killed one person. So fragile was the situation that the local reform director blamed the incident on the history of maltreatment meted out by the *hacendado* of 'Emusa', and took no action other than to send two representatives to discuss the *campesinos*' problems.[49] In June, *La Patria* of Oruro registered in some detail 'a horrible crime' on the *finca* 'Catavi' which seems to have been representative of many incidents taking place on the large and arid farms of the *altiplano*. According to reports collected by the eleven soldiers sent to investigate the death of the *hacendado*,

'Señor Rómulo Ruíz (the *hacendado*) . . . had noticed that three steers were grazing on their pasture and, as is common on rural properties in order to avoid possible problems, led the animals to the hacienda house. Immediately, the *indígena* Condori, an ex-*colono* of the Catavi hacienda, appeared and started to remonstrate with Señor Ruíz. Soon violent words turned to deeds and they exchanged punches, with the *indígena* coming off the worst. Wanting to take revenge, Condori gathered most of the *colonos* of the hacienda and outlined what had happened, instigating them to attack the *patrón*. After hearing these bellicose arguments their patience became exasperated, and he led them in a group to the hacienda house. There was no discussion when the *indígenas* invaded the homestead of the Ruíz-Flores couple. Some armed with pikes, others with sticks and spades, they immediately attacked and killed Señor Ruíz with a tremendous blow of a pike to the head and gave his wife a deep wound with a spade. The Señora, who was still alive, was taken to the bedroom where most of the *colonos* went and extinguished the last sign of life with their blows. Alicia Ruíz, twenty years old, who went to the hacienda of her brother Rómulo with the intention of making a brief visit, was an eye-witness to these crimes. She miraculously saved her life by begging for mercy on her knees; she was joined in her pleading by another señora and two girls, whose names it has not been possible to ascertain. The *indígenas* were affected by such an attitude and took them to the church and there, together with their companions, made them kiss the cross and swear that they would never speak a word of what had happened to anyone.'[50]

Señorita Ruíz, of course, immediately broke her vow, and Condori was forced to take flight, a further twenty three *colonos* being captured later in Sicasica. It is hardly surprising that her account and the style of a provincial paper should stress the rude violence of the *campesinos* since, whatever the social underpinnings of these actions, Señor Ruíz and his wife were indubitably dead. The columns of *La Patria*, like those of *Los Tiempos* in Cochabamba, were swamped with landlords' calls for government guarantees and more troops. At the same time many *altiplano* estates were abandoned by their owners and entered the de facto ownership of their peons. On the richer farms of the valley *hacendados* mounted greater resistance and peasants often engaged in more organised activity. In December *campesinos* from Chaparé, Cochabamba, blocked the Aguirre road and collected tolls off travellers for a number of days.[51] In mid-1953 the towns of Tarata, Cliza, Punata and Arani were invaded and searched for weapons. Four people died in fighting, all roads were blocked, and the Cochabamba train halted and forced to return to the city, and the police station at Villa Viscarra put under siege. The townsfolk of Tarata seem to have incurred particular hostility since the peasants returned there the night after the initial occupation, seized the contents of the town's stores and, reportedly to the shouts of 'We will exterminate Tarata', sacked a large number of houses.[52] This region was again to be the scene of prolonged and violent disturbances during the late 1950s and early 1960s as a result of market conflicts between Cliza and Ucureña and a struggle between local leaders of the peasant *sindicatos*.

Very often there was nothing that could be done in such situations; the army was in no shape to undertake operations and anyway strictly prohibited from taking repressive measures; the urban militias and *carabineros* were reluctant to engage with *campesinos* who made formal protestations of loyalty to the MNR, placed the blame for disturbances on the *patrones* and the Rosca, and often possessed appreciable firepower and greater numbers than the urban forces. On occasions, however, the hard-pressed authorities were able to avert explosive situations with diligent mediation. In November 1952 the prefect of Cochabamba and a senior official from the ministry of peasant affairs, Vicente Alvarez Plata, sped to Cliza to intervene in a dispute that seemed set to plunge the whole upper valley into violence. *El Diario*'s local correspondent was clearly impressed by their reception:

> 'As soon as they recognised the Prefect's automobile, the *campesinos* discharged their firearms, and the throaty roar of thousands of *pututus* (horns) wounded the air with baneful portents. This was the greeting for the department's most senior authority. A sea of hands formed waves of the characteristic 'V-sign'. The Prefect gathered together the principal chiefs and requested them in a speech in Quechua that they drop their belligerent attitude since their demands would be considered immediately. The *campesinos* voiced their anger at the fact that their plots (*piojales*) had been snatched from them and that they had already paid their annual dues (*ramas*) to compañero Emilio Pinto, *colono* of Ramón Ledezma.'[53]

The question of payments to 'guarantee' ownership of lands and as contributions to the *sindicato* was frequently identified as a cause of unrest since many less than scrupulous figures would relieve peasants of sometimes substantial sums in return for imaginary services on their behalf with the authorities. Accusations of such practice were often levelled against leaders who fell from favour or were in some form of personal or collective dispute, complicating any wider political allegiances that might be in play. The first, most renowned, but apparently justified victim of this was Antonio Alvarez Mamani, a travelling herbalist (*kallawaya*) from Calacacha who possessed long-standing links with the MNR and had been agitating in the northern altiplano for over a decade. After the revolution Mamani vied with his rival Gabino Apaza to collect *ramas* from the peasants of La Paz and Oruro. Arrested for 'fraud' and 'subversion' four times in a year, Mamani was released according to the needs of the ministry for local alliances and the settlement of quarrels between *dirigentes*.[54] In March 1953, during a spell in jail, Mamani claimed to head 50 *sindicatos* on account of his 'exemplary conduct and service to the nation'. Soon after his release he accused Apaza of being under communist influence and deliberately inciting peasants to subversion; Apaza immediately replied in kind.[55] Such charges were to be a consistent feature in the labyrinthine struggles between rival *dirigentes* over the following 30 years. At this stage, however, it was the landlords, organised in the *Sociedad Rural*, who most often made the accusation. In June 1952 a delegation from the *Sociedad* secured an appointment with the minister of government, to whom it presented 'numerous demands and grievances with reference to the state of agitation which exists in many regions of the *altiplano*, created by professional agitators of communist affiliation'.[56] While tin had been controlled by a tiny elite of three companies, rural landlords comprised the overwhelming majority of Bolivia's backward capitalist class. They now saw not just the threat of loss of lands but also the spectre of mass peasant rebellion which promised the total collapse of social control in the countryside: behind it all, as ever, lay the bolsheviks.

In fact, leftist agitation in the *campo* was very limited. In the 1940s the PIR had some influence in Cochabamba and the MNR had possessed a number of rather unreliable contacts in the *altiplano* but in the year preceding the reform all of these were effectively dissolved in the melting pot of government patronage—still highly unstable on both sides—and outstripped by independent action motivated by the lack of local systems of control, sheer impatience, regional disputes, continued landlord provocation or the activities of the peripatetic charlatan brokers. The only substantial incident of 'communist' influence involved the POR, which under the direction of its erstwhile leader Warqui had established something of a presence amongst the peasants of Ucureña. This was soon to prove ephemeral and had only been made possible by supporting a faction in conflict with the leader of the regional confederation over financial questions. Nevertheless, these facts were of little consequence to the inhabitants of Cochabamba late in January 1953, as *El Diario* reported at some length:

'More than a thousand armed *indígenas* caused panic in Cochabamba last Saturday when, equipped with cudgels, axes, staves and some with rifles, they entered the city after walking through the night from Ucureña to demand the release of Paulino Morales, José Rojas, Napoleón Chacón (and others), all of them of *porista* affiliation. These leaders had been arrested on Thursday for being agitators . . . The distressed townsfolk dispersed rapidly, fearing that the subversives would start an attack. The owners of shops and other stalls quickly closed their doors and carried off their produce as a precaution against possible looting. Happily, the *indígenas* did not touch anything nor did they do harm to anybody.

'Outside the Prefecture the crowd came to a halt and demanded the release of their leaders. The subvertors of order sounded their *pututus* with open belligerence. Señora Rosa Morales Guillén, a well-known MNR leader, addressed the crowd from the balcony of the Prefecture. Speaking in Quechua, she asked for calm and the naming of representatives to resolve the conflict. The *indígenas* would accept none of the propositions put to them, demanding respect for union rights and accusing Agapito Vallejo, current general secretary of the *Federación de Trabajadores Campesinos*, of being a traitor and of having opened an account in one of the banks of La Paz with Bs.60,000, money collected from *ramas* (union contributions).

'When Emilio Chacón, the leader of the demonstrators, tried to speak from the bandstand at the corner of the plaza the official automobiles sounded their horns, drowning out his words. The *indígenas* took their revenge against Agapito Vallejo, who tried to address them, by sounding their *puputus*. When the *indígenas* began to display an even more bellicose attitude the militants of the MNR took up their weapons and surrounded the plaza. At the same time civilian agents doused the plaza with teargas. One of these agents had to flee and had to hide himself in a private house . . . a *campesino* threw a rustic muzzle-loader to his shoulder and attempted to fire at the citizen but luckily the gunpowder exploded without propelling the bullet, otherwise some injury would certainly have been caused.'[57]

I have noted a number of examples of peasant mobilisation to give an idea of its scope and the threat felt by the urban populace of a country overwhelmingly dominated by its rural masses and, when lacking adequate forces of repression, distinctly vulnerable to them. Under these conditions it was no surprise that Ñuflo Chávez and his various 'mobile brigades' constantly toured the countryside, felt obliged to issue statements almost daily that 'there is no agitation' or that 'the harvest/sowing continues as normal', and soon found themselves compelled to adopt a more radical view of reform than that which they had previously entertained. The mines and their workers were indisputably at the nub of the country's economy and political development, but the *campesinado* had to be controlled at any cost to sustain the revolution.

Thus, when Paz finally appointed a commission to draw up a reform decree, at the same time as the indigenous 'subversives' were molesting the teargas-lobbing 'citizens' of Cochabamba, the MNR took the unusual step of including in it leaders of the PIR — Arturo Urquidi, the agricultural expert who was dean of San Simón university in Cochabamba — and the POR — the young and gifted ideologue Ernesto Ayala Mercado. In the event, Urquidi came to dominate the commission's work and the final draft of the decree bore the stamp of the PIR's objective of developing capitalism in Bolivian agriculture on the basis of medium-sized owner-worked or cooperative holdings as an essential stage before widespread collectivisation could be introduced. The 177 clauses of Decree Law 3464, signed by Paz and Chávez on 2 August 1953 in front of 100,000 *campesinos* at Ucureña had six central aims:

1. To provide adequate parcels of land to peasants with little or none, so long as they worked them, expropriating for the purpose latifundia ('excessively large properties').
2. To restore to the *comunidades* usurped lands and cooperate in their modernisation with full respect for collectivist traditions.
3. To secure the complete abolition of *pongueaje*.

4. To increase productivity, investment and technical aid.
5. To protect natural resources.
6. To promote emigration from the *altiplano* to the *oriente*.[58]

The law protected the hacienda house and a proportion of its cultivated land, 'small and medium properties' (the size of which depended
on the region and the extent of cultivation) and 'agricultural enterprises', modern farms largely situated in the department of Santa
Cruz. Since there was no clearly defined overall limit to its scope the
reform was from the start vulnerable to a myriad of loopholes, the
predictable pressure from landlords on local reform officials, and
bargains struck higher up the structure. Moreover, the fact that the
law established three separate agencies, each badly financed, with its
own set of rules, and highly cumbersome in operation, ensured that
the process of establishing a claim, investigation of deeds and complementary evidence, topographical surveying, assessment, appeal and
counter-appeal became so extended that many peasants simply took
direct action without waiting for any official imprimatur. There are
today farms, particularly in the *altiplano*, which still formally belong
to absentee *hacendados* but which have been farmed since 1952 or
1953 by *campesinos* who consider them their property, pay no rent,
and who — provided they are registered in the census as living on or
near the property — could be dispossessed in law only with great difficulty. Direct expropriation continued to take place on an appreciable
scale but with less violence than before and often in simple 'anticipa-
tion' of legal ratification.

However, the effect of the reform on the general pattern of land
tenure fell far short of popular expectations: between 1954 and 1968
only around eight million of some 36 million hectares of cultivated
land changed hands.[59] After two years 51 per cent of the latifundia in
La Paz, 49 per cent in Chuquisaca and 76 per cent in Oruro had been
affected, but in Tarija the figure was 33 per cent, in Santa Cruz 36 per
cent and in Cochabamba only 16 per cent, the national total being 28.5
per cent.[60] This very slow progress was to continue until the end of the
decade; by 1960 23 per cent of cultivated land had been distributed to
28 per cent of rural families. Later the process was to be accelerated out
of both political necessity and an improvement in administration (for
example, the acquisition of an IBM computer), but a constant feature
of the reform was and continues to be the frequent misuse of very

limited credit and an extremely low level of mechanisation. Redistribution was generally seen as an end in itself by the politicians if not by the planners, and this led to further retrenchment of the minifundio, keeping production at its pre-revolutionary level until the end of the decade. In 1959 agricultural property in the department of La Paz was divided into 64,280 separate units, of which 45,281 were less than one hectare in size. The proportion in other departments, with the exceptions of Santa Cruz, Cochabamba and underpopulated Beni, was broadly similar.[61] The MNR had publicly set itself against strengthening the subsistence minifundio but by the end of the decade it was admitted that this had become a major problem while cooperativisation had failed to take off.

Yet, on the day after the reform was signed, Sinforoso Rivas, now head of the Cochabamba federation, told his members, 'the consolidation of the Agrarian Reform . . . requires many years. . . . We have to wait patiently and trust that the process will be realised'.[62] Coming from a former 'communist agitator', such a statement had some resonance; it reflected the fact that, whatever the shortcomings of the measure, there now existed amongst important layers of the peasantry a disposition to accept it as a great achievement. This soon became a generalised sentiment, out of which the MNR was to make enormous political capital. The axis of *campesino* agitation turned increasingly inward, directed towards internal disputes over land, competition over political favours, and control over markets, fairs and price levels. *Pongueaje* was eradicated and many thousands of peasants now possessed their own plots on which they could work full-time; agriculture remained as backward as before but the old social structure had indeed been crippled, dissipating many of the factors that had caused discontent. It soon became apparent that the *sindicato* would replace the hacienda as the central mechanism of social control and become the principal interface between government and the rural masses. The MNR, and Paz in particular, recognised the great political potential of this and would turn to the peasantry over the following years as a dependable ally in the struggle against the militant miners. Although its insufficiencies and failings were legion, the reform succeeded in neutralising independent peasant power for 25 years. The *campo* was by no means a quiet place but neither did it become the site of left-wing mobilisation and, as events were to show, this was of critical importance.

Consolidating the Party

Nationalisation of the big mining companies, agrarian reform and universal suffrage were the three central accomplishments of the MNR and constituted the basis of the national revolution. Yet, the party was to rule for over twelve years on the strength of measures passed in the first 18 months; clearly its success depended on other factors, however popular the core reforms proved to be. In retrospect the most decisive element appears to be its success in coopting or neutralising the leadership of the COB at important junctures. But both this factor and the achievement of broad support from the *campesinado* depended on the MNR's capacity to maintain a following in the urban centres, all of which required not only diligent redistribution of wealth under conditions of increasing crisis — even bankruptcy — but also a sustained populist image and a coherent apparatus that would fulfil the function of ensuring political supremacy and channelling favours.

The first congress of the COB, held in October 1954, reflected the extent to which Paz and the MNR had succeeded in achieving an advantageous rapprochement with the labour movement. The very fact that the congress had been delayed so long was itself an indication of the COB leadership's anxiety to obtain acceptable delegations and a favourable reception for a programme and statutes that marked a clear departure from Pulacayo on apparently subsidiary but still critical issues. In the event, there was remarkably little dissent from the 310 delegates, 60 of whom represented the FSTMB and were therefore largely pledged to Lechín. The industrial unions dominated the congress with 177 delegates, while the 'middle class' had 56, with 13 'special delegates' and only 50 for the peasantry — one for every 50,000 people in the countryside, a purely arbitrary figure designed to preserve a 'proletarian leadership', which in later years was to cause great discontent. Paz was obliged to open the congress by telling delegates, 'You will be our constant guide in all actions of the government', but he quickly made it clear that since they had representatives in the regime they must also take responsibility for the revolution: 'With the present administration, with worker ministers, with all the changes in our economy the unions cannot act with the same orientation and in identical form as they did under the regimes of the oligarchy . . .'[63] This was, of course, the logic behind the MNR's use of worker ministers. Whatever the misgivings of the left as to some of the effects of this, the COB leadership noted 'the perfect identity of interests and feelings that currently exists between the Government and the People'.[64] The programme approved by congress declared that 'today it has been said with good reason that the workers' and peasants' congresses are truly popular parliaments', but this did not mean that they were potential soviets or had brought about a situation of dual power: 'the taking of power' by the unions would be absurd given that they were economic not political bodies. Moreover, this was ruled out by the COB on the grounds that it was in harmony with the nature of the revolution and confident of its ability to influence the course it took:

> 'The growing participation of the masses gives a popular orientation to the Revolution, tending to subordinate the purely bourgeois democratic schema. The ever greater number of worker ministers (now increased to five), the application of workers' control, the COB's participation in legislation and the executive etc., show that our Revolution is a Popular Revolution rather than bourgeois-democratic or proletarian. It cannot be characterised as bourgeois-democratic because the uneven development of Latin American countries impedes such a course here.'[65]

One interesting feature of this position adopted by the MNR left was its orientation towards the Chinese example of national liberation 'through an alliance of several social classes', which at this stage was seen as directly comparable to the Bolivian case.[66] Paz himself had earlier pointed to a perceived similarity, noting that, '[in seeking foreign capital] we are not being reactionary at all since Mao Tse Tung now supports the development of private industry'.[67] At the same time the COB laid down a formal repudiation of the traditional or orthodox parties of the left which it was often to suppress but never entirely discarded:

> It is easy to understand the disgust felt for Stalinism in the light of the 'political barbarism' imposed by a Soviet bureaucracy that has risen like a monstrous cyst out of the stagnation of the October Revolution, brought about by the defeat of the proletarian revolution in various important countries and the consequent 'capitalist siege' of the USSR. On the other hand, the position of the COB should not be confused with that of the epigones of Trotsky, who have capitulated to Stalinism or refuse to recognise the

progress of movements for liberation from the foreign yoke and which take the form of 'political liberation' in countries subordinated by the Kremlin (Yugoslavia) or 'national liberation' in those dependent on finance capital (Bolivia). We defend the traditional strategic line of revolutionary Marxism in demonstrating the fundamental task of the international proletariat to be the conquest of an iron international unity to impose socialist victory and peace . . . [68]

The MNR itself never adopted 'socialism' as a motif, still less an objective, but the COB was always to adhere to it as a formal aim. Furthermore, there were in the programme a number of demands which the government was both unwilling and unable to concede: a minimum wage and a sliding scale of rises in line with inflation; nationalisation of all transport; wholesale cooperativisation in agriculture; popular revolutionary courts; a complete overhaul of the educational system; and workers' control with the power of veto in all economic activities, not just the nationalised mines. Thus, however great the degree of collaboration, there were still important issues of potential conflict between the unions and the party.

All the same, the fact that the COB programme attacked the PCB and POR in their own language and bore many signs of a familiarity with Marxist theory reflected the MNR's success in winning to its ranks key members of the orthodox left, particularly the POR, which consequently entered a profound crisis.

From early 1953 *porista* militants had been the targets of government attacks and periodically arrested for 'communist subversion', César and Guillermo Lora both spending a year in jail. The party was also feeling the effects of its organisational weaknesses which led many *simpatizantes* to join the MNR rather than staying close to a small and doctrinal group which possessed diminishing influence and could offer little in the way of concrete resources compared to a ruling party which appeared to be in the vanguard of the revolutionary movement however hybrid its ideology. In addition, the POR was particularly badly hit by the complex schisms breaking out within the Fourth International: it was certainly important to the Bolivian section that the debates raging in Paris and New York centred not just on the characteristics of Stalinism and the post-war workers' states but also the tactics to be adopted towards reformist parties with a mass base or strong influence in the working class. It was in this charged atmosphere that in 1954 a faction developed in opposition to the 'defeatist' line pursued by Guillermo Lora, who argued that in the short term there was a depression in working-class militancy abetted by the bureaucratisation of the union leadership and that the MNR would retain a more than transient popularity; revolutionary strategy, as a consequence, should be directed primarily towards organisational and educational tasks to prepare a vanguard. The opposition *Facción Proletaria Internacionalista*, allied with Michel Pablo at an international level, believed that there was much greater potential for rupture, especially within the COB, and that the correct line was to move immediately to the offensive for a full social revolution. After a series of heated and complex encounters, which led to the publication of two separate newspapers over two years, the party finally split completely in mid-1956, the dissidents led by Hugo González Moscoso and Víctor Villegas taking the majority and the newspaper *Lucha Obrera* while Lora regrouped his Leninist Workers' Faction around the periodical *Masas*, which survives today with its crisp and pungent style as a testimony to the resilience of the POR's most prolific militant.

However, matters did not end there since many who had backed Lora argued that the logic of their position was that they should actually enter the MNR to influence it from within and win its members to revolutionary socialism along the lines laid down by Trotsky for the work of the French section in the 1930s and in a form being adopted by British Trotskyists in the Labour Party. This group was led by Edwin Moller, a senior figure in the COB who possessed much influence with the POR's trade-union militants. At the crucial meeting to decide the issue Lora was absent (having just returned from a meeting of the International in Paris) under circumstances that still remain contentious. He was quick to condemn the decision to adopt the entryist tactic as capitulationist, but the damage was already done. Moller and Ayala Mercado took a large section of the rump of the POR into the MNR and for a while presented themselves as revolutionaries but soon began to adopt a position very close to that of Lechín and to defend the party against their old comrades. This undoubtedly fortified the MNR left, giving it a militant nucleus and theoretical strength with which to combat the right. (The COB's 1954 programme was actually penned by Agustín Barcelli, an itinerant Peruvian radical

who had previously broken with the Chilean CP over its entry into the
Popular Front but never fully embraced Trotskyism.)

The 1954–56 split signalled the eclipse of the second generation of
Bolivian Trotskyism. Lora, intermittently jailed for his invectives, was
obliged to turn his attention to the small nucleus of party members
working in Siglo XX, where the POR was building a following but still
remained dominated by the PCB. Warqui retired to a smallholding in
Santa Cruz and Alandia retreated to his paintings, while figures such
as Fernando Bravo joined up with González to pursue a high-profile
campaign against the MNR, with little success: in 1960 Bravo and
González stood against Paz and Lechín in the presidential poll and
scored 1,420 votes against 735,713. The miner-turned-schoolteacher
Bravo was to die young after an extended illness aggravated by persecution, but González continued to receive international backing for
his POR (*Combate*) long after it had lost the strength inherited in 1956
and had become simply one of several factions of a now severely debilitated movement. Trotskyism was to return as an important force but
with a new generation of militants and an acute sense of the lessons of
the 1950s.[69]

The success in neutralising Trotskyism was also evident — although
in a much less open and emphatic manner — with respect to the rest of
the left. As befits a populist vehicle incorporating a number of dispar-
ate positions, the MNR sopped up many independents as well as ex-
piristas, stunting the growth of the young PCB as *entrismo* became the
norm in these early years. Yet it achieved surprisingly poor results in
the universities, largely because the party's *Avanzada Universitaria*
adopted belligerent and often violent interventionist tactics which
were quickly perceived as threatening the jealously-guarded autonomy of the institutions of higher education. In fact, the *Avanzada* did
make a direct assault on autonomy in 1955, when, fully backed by
Lechín and the COB, party and miners' militias attempted to possess
the universities. The response was immediate and deeply shocking to
the MNR left, which believed that it was engaged in an unproblematic
weeding-out of falangists. The centres of greatest conflict were Sucre
and Cochabamba, where parties of all persuasions from the POR to
the FSB defended autonomy in a series of strikes, demonstrations and
street battles. The MNR student contingent found itself badly outnumbered and forced to make a hasty retreat. The party lost much
support amongst students who turned in increasing numbers to the

right-wing opposition. This gave the FSB an unexpected boost and led it to expand its conspiratorial activity and to seek greater links with groups that were developing a nascent form of christian democracy.

In other areas statism and the resources available to a governing party proved far more useful to the MNR. Its rigid formal hierarchy, from the *Jefe* down to the lowliest militant of a *comando zonal*, became a conduit for jobs and favours on an unprecedented scale. It is estimated that within four years the civil service doubled in size as a result of the need to accommodate party members. In Cochabamba so many militants were appointed to government positions that new party elections had to be held six weeks after a local poll in order to reduce the number of claimants for formal appointments and clear out supernumerary *paracaidistas* (literally, parachutists, the term used for those who joined the MNR simply to improve their own position).[70] Often the pressure of that traditional Bolivian ailment *empleomanía* led to open conflict; for a number of months after the revolution the MNR's *Comando Regional* in Potosí was in a state of anarchy as various factions battled it out to secure a monopoly on local state resources and power, frequently resorting to the use of militias and strikes by miners. In the end only the daylight assassination of the leader of one faction brought about a modicum of order. Sometimes these conflicts bore some relation to ideological contests, but more often they were simply personalist battles.

The importance of party membership extended well beyond the 'popular classes'. All army officers had to swear loyalty to the MNR, and many of the more prescient took their party obligations seriously, setting up cells in their units as a shield for parallel organisation and political debate. Even urban entrepreneurs joined the ranks; in 1954 an 'Importers' Cell' was established in La Paz, reaping enormous benefit from party affiliation. Over two years this 'cell' bought $6.6 million at an exchange rate of Bs.190 when the market rate rose from Bs.1,415 to Bs.7,768.[71] Small wonder that the reconstructed PIR should concentrate so much of its invective against 'the bourgeoisie of the *compañeros* . . . a commercial plutocracy financed by the state and protected by contraband and speculation'.[72]

The increasingly widespread sympathy for such sentiments, especially amongst those inside the MNR who were suffering acutely from inflation, made it imperative for Paz to secure authority over the repressive apparatus. Once the resistance of the COB had been overcome this proved a relatively easy task. On May Day 1953 Lechín declared to the crowd in La Paz, 'we need to create a Popular and Revolutionary army', finally conceding that a formal military apparatus was necessary; in June he helped open the military college. In November, following an abortive rising by the FSB, Paz moved to tighten his hold over the militias by creating a new force, the *Control Político*, which incorporated all the party militias under the command of General Claudio San Román. Distinct from the workplace militias, which remained intact but largely dormant outside the mines, the *Control Político* was professionalised and highly active. For a decade it was the country's principal repressive organ, acquiring a progressively unpopular reputation as its members imposed a partisan order, availed themselves of petty privileges on the streets, and oversaw a network of prison camps (Coati; Alto Madidi; Pekín) that sprang up as opposition to the party grew in the late 1950s. The *Control Político* was in many respects the antecedent of the paramilitary groups which emerged in the late 1970s and some of its members figured in them, but San Román himself proved so unpopular that even the rightist military regimes which followed the MNR refused to let him return from exile in Asunción.

These sundry elements of resistance to independent worker mobilisation were underpinned by an economic crisis that was eventually to bring all but the verbiage of social change to a halt. Although it was not faced with an overtly hostile US economic blockade as were Guatemala, Cuba and Nicaragua, the economy of revolutionary Bolivia was, as we have seen, peculiarly vulnerable to external market forces that were running very unfavourably for it. This structural problem was made considerably worse by politically-generated reflationary pressures. Within a year of the revolution the cost of living had risen over 100 per cent; over the next year it increased by an even greater proportion. The balance of payments moved from a surplus of $9.7 million in 1951 to a deficit of $10.3 million in 1954.

It was to Washington that Paz turned in order to confront this situation. In October 1953 he wrote an open letter to Eisenhower pleading for immediate aid. Since he had already attempted to devalue the peso in May, and had proved true to his word on nationalisation and the military question, and given the unquestionable severity of a situation which could still favour the radical forces, the US government reacted positively. Eisenhower offered $9 million immediately for famine relief and essential commodities, and promised to double technical aid. Thus began a process that would lead to Bolivia receiving the highest rate of food aid per capita in the world and becoming dependent on US funds for a third of her total budget by 1958. The political cost of such assistance was naturally very high indeed.

3.
REVOLUTION IN RETREAT, 1956-64

In outward form the process begun on 9 April 1952 ended on 4 November 1964 when, in a series of enthusiastic strafing runs, aircraft under the command of General René Barrientos extinguished the resistance put up by MNR *milicianos* from their last redoubt of Laikacota hill in the centre of La Paz. The party's 'National Revolution' was over. Never again would the MNR hold office except as a coalition ally under the strict observation of the armed forces over whose defeat it had once presided. Yet the revolution ended both earlier and later than November 1964. The economy of Bolivia, its social structure, popular memory and political habits would continue to register the changes it had effected well after Barrientos's coup, as we shall see. What is, in some respects, less easy to determine is the manner in which the second and third administrations of Víctor Paz Estenssoro (1960 to July 1964 and August to November 1964) and that of Hernán Siles Zuazo (1956−60) were able to present themselves as the natural continuation of the April revolution when in practice that 'continuation' involved a concerted reversal of the revolution's initial radical impetus, extensive redefinition of its social content and a string of serious − at times violent − ruptures inside the political alliance that staged it.

From left to right Hernán Siles Zuazo, Juan Lechín Oquendo and Víctor Paz Estenssoro with their wives

The talented polemicist Sergio Almaraz, who was deeply involved in political activity during this period, later wrote, 'History would be easy if advances and retreats responded exclusively to alternation between revolutionary and counter-revolutionary governments.'[1] The extended *thermidor* of the Bolivian revolution presents us with a more 'difficult' history than any other period in the country's recent political life; its contours cannot be fully grasped in terms of simple class antagonisms since these were reproduced in the political sphere in an exceptionally distorted manner. The complexities of this interregnum between periods of authoritarian rule and open social polarisation make it more than usually conducive to interpretation along the lines developed by Nicos Poulantzas, with an emphasis on the state less as an instrument for class domination than as a site of class conflict and a recognition of the importance of a dominant bloc rather than a single ruling class as the real instrument if not the ultimate determinant of political power.[2] This is not the place to develop such an interpretation, but we may see some of its relevance in the fact that by the mid-1950s the Bolivian state exercised substantial economic power compared with the private sector, being controlled as well as administered by people drawn overwhelmingly from the petty bourgeoisie whose ideology was more bourgeois than proletarian but who depended directly on the support of a militant working class for their power and legitimation. In observing the opening years of the revolution from relatively close quarters we have seen some of the contradictions and conflicts generated by such a state of affairs; the last decade of MNR rule saw these develop into a general crisis.

The precise characteristics of this process are too varied to be exhaustively surveyed here but they would appear to bear out a number of general comments. First, that the economic crisis which reached its apogee in 1956–57 offered an unparalleled opportunity for Washington to gain influence over key sectors of the MNR and deepen its control of the economy through the management of aid. This intervention was of a progressively general and openly political character, but it took most concentrated form in the Stabilisation Plan of 1956 and the Triangular Plan of 1961. As a result, the MNR administrations registered all the tensions of being obliged to implement US policy whilst endeavouring to maintain their independence, redistributionist popularity and 'anti-imperialist' trimmings. This proved an insuperable dilemma. Yet, it took the form of a general decomposition rather than an abrupt disintegration of the ruling alliance. This was principally because the party's left, centred on the COB, had lost the initiative of the early years as well as the ideological resources and political force to overthrow the centre—right but it still retained sufficient independence and strength to regain ground in a piecemeal fashion. Thus, the leadership of the COB attempted to negotiate with the right and continued to maintain a toehold within the apparatus of government although it was frequently obliged to enter into direct confrontation with the regime by a rank and file it could not fully control.

This variable response was mirrored by that of the dominant conservative sector of the MNR which drew its lifeblood from the gains of 1952 but proved incapable of maintaining a disciplined mass movement with which to challenge the unions on their own ground. The Bolivian revolution therefore differed from those in Mexico, Cuba and Nicaragua in that the ruling party was unable to coopt and control the labour movement largely because of the strength of its syndicalist traditions, which were established before 1952 and gave significant purchase to the Marxist left. As a consequence, the MNR made increasing recourse to the assistance of the peasantry and began to reconstruct the military, forces that it could not control without the help of precisely that working class against which it was engaged in an ever-deepening offensive. As this dependence became more acute the political war of manoeuvre contained within the MNR became one of position and broke beyond the confines of the party. The 1964 coup signalled the return of the army as the principal arbiter inside a dominant bloc which lacked a national bourgeoisie of any consequence and could no longer manage the legacy of 1952 outside of direct coercion of the labour movement.

Stabilisation and Resistance

Between 1956 and 1964 US financial commitments to Bolivia amounted to $327.7 million compared with a sum of $76.4 million over the previous decade; the $25 million disbursed by Washington in 1957 represented 32 per cent of the Bolivian government's revenue.[3] Even for the right of the MNR the size of such aid posed distinct problems for the regime's independence, but Paz and his successor Siles argued that it was the only means by which the country could avoid complete economic collapse and thus preserve the victories of 1952.

The scale of the crisis was impressive, and 1956 proved to be the most critical year of all. The index of food prices in La Paz rose from 100 in 1931 to 7,036 in 1952, 52,627 in 1955, 97,010 in March 1956, and then shot up to 390,492 over the following nine months.[4] The cost of living index as a whole had risen from 100 in 1952 to 2,270 at the end of 1956, the money supply to 2,229, and the free market dollar quotation to 3,104. Foreign reserves in the Banco Central stood at an almost irrelevant $1.2 million. This state of affairs was undoubtedly exacerbated by extensive speculation caused by multiple exchange rates and the unwieldy system of rationing basic goods on a coupon basis. A flourishing black market was directed by '*cuperos*' who usually owed their control of supplies to party affiliation. Goods disappeared from the markets and the spectre of bread riots haunted the government, which had been taken aback by the level of support given to the Falange in the 1956 elections. The MNR's emphatic and ignominious overthrow by the *paceño* middle class in 1946 was sufficiently recent to instil grave fears within the party of renewed popular mobilisation against it.

As a result, one of Paz's last acts as president was to establish a Stabilization Commission in August 1956. This move was widely accepted although it was plain that whatever the nominal composition of the body, it had been set up at the behest of the IMF and was to be supervised by a group of its advisers led by an ardent advocate of monetarism, George Jackson Eder. Eder himself provides an eloquent account of how he, a US citizen, contracted and paid by Washington and responsible to the US government, acquired direct administrative control of the economy of a foreign country. He may not have enjoyed the experience a great deal since he refers to the people with whom he had to work as 'perhaps the most corrupt, incompetent and opportunistic group of politicians that had ever ruled the destinies of the nation'.[5] Furthermore, he was of the opinion that, 'there is not now, and never has been, a successful government enterprise in Bolivia . . . [it] would have been better off if all productive activities had been left entirely to private enterprise.'[6]

These do not strike one as entirely convincing indications of the 'objectivity' of the commission's executive director, whose function was formally that of a technical adviser. Such doubts are borne out by Eder's reference to the fact that every nominee to the commission had to be '*persona grata* to the US embassy as well as to the president and the other council members and at least not too personally obnoxious to Juan Lechín or Ñuflo Chávez'.[7] In fact, two nominations forwarded by Siles were rejected because, 'on referring with the American embassy, I was informed emphatically that neither person would be suitable because of their ideological backgrounds'.[8] Eder recounts that when the stabilisation decree was enacted, it was not the sovereign government of Bolivia which dictated the exchange rate of the peso: 'It is certain that if the President (of Bolivia) had insisted on maintaining a fixed Bs.7,000 rate despite changing circumstances, the Treasury (of the United States) would have refused to go ahead on its stand-by arrangements'.[9] When Siles later attempted to reverse his capitulation on this point Eder describes how he 'marched' into the Banco Central and proclaimed that, 'if the rate were not permitted to fluctuate, I would cable the ICA, and that would probably be the end of the stabilisation fund'.[10]

Such an approach was entirely consonant with the final decree, issued on 15 December 1956. The economic measures that would enable Bolivia to receive $25 million in aid adhered closely to the tenets of monetarism, which are today much more widely appreciated than they were in 1956. In brief, the plan stipulated:[11]

1. Government expenditure to be reduced by 40 per cent.
2. Deficits of all state enterprises to be eliminated, principally through removal of price controls and subsidies in the *pulperías*.
3. Reduction and removal of tariffs; increases in domestic taxes.
4. The exchange rate to be unified; strict reserve limits for banks.
5. Limited compensatory wage increases followed by a wage freeze after one year; increases in domestic rents limited to 200 per cent.

The decree was a direct attack on the popular economy established after April 1952 for although it succeeded in reducing inflation, it quickly contracted production, increased unemployment, reduced credit and cut real incomes in all sectors except the countryside, where the *campesinos* benefited from increases in the price of their produce. The abolition of the black market was achieved, but Eder had mistakenly assumed that the entire urban population purchased its goods there and thus greatly misjudged the effects of an immediate 100 per cent increase in legal prices.[12] He confidently predicted that within three months further wage rises would be unnecessary as prices began to fall, but inflation still reached 115 per cent in 1957 and was only to fall the following year. Local manufacturers were opened up to full competition from abroad but unable to raise credit in order to buy in raw materials; manufacturing output fell by 30 per cent in 1957 and sales of cotton dropped by over 90 per cent. However, the decree had greatest impact in that sector where it was most vulnerable to resistance – the mines.

The ramifications of removing subsidies in the *pulperías* can be judged from the fact that in 1956 they purchased 22 per cent of all imported rice, 13 per cent of powdered milk and 12 per cent of flour, to be resold at prices very much lower than those on the black market:[13]

[Kilo]	Pulpería	Black Market
Meat	Bs.23.9	Bs.800
Flour	8.7	760
Rice	16.9	650
Sugar	11.2	260

The stabilisation plan was so severely deflationary in its effects and so directly aimed at the real income of the miners that it was certain to engender strong opposition, notwithstanding the heights scaled by inflation and the only dimly perceived wider effects on currency management and state planning. Washington had achieved its aim of opening the economy to the discipline of the free market, but Siles was charged with maintaining the contraction of the state sector and limiting wage increases; he was only partially successful.

The MNR left had supported Siles's candidature for the presidency largely to neutralise the ambitions of the right, which, under the leadership of Walter Guevara Arze, had launched a fierce campaign against the COB leadership, effectively ruling out any chance of Lechín obtaining party backing for the nomination. Although in this case, as in 1960, there were claims that Lechín had been previously offered the presidency only to be disappointed at the last moment, the left was satisfied with what it considered a clear majority in the new congress and the vice-presidency going to Ñuflo Chávez. Moreover, initially neither Lechín nor the bulk of the COB leadership saw anything amiss in the stabilisation plan. At first Lechín gave assurances that earning power would not be affected, supplies would be resumed and the economy stimulated by US aid; in June 1956 he reportedly went so far as to say, 'what a pity Dr Eder was not here three years ago'.[14] On the day after the decree was published, Lechín tried to negotiate higher wage increases from Siles but apparently accepted only minimal concessions. The *ampliado* (extraordinary meeting) of the COB called to discuss the plan was postponed for ten days in an effort to stall criticism, but when it finally took place on 27 December it was the worker ministers who were criticised for not obtaining better compensation while the general idea of stabilisation was accepted. Only the Siglo XX deputation attacked the decree as a whole. Lechín claimed that he had not been fully consulted about the plan but this was not accepted as a valid excuse, especially since he had been a member of the commission. At the next meeting of the COB on 4 January 1957 there were calls for the resignation of all worker ministers. The executive secretary responded with a stinging attack on the 'ultra-left' and defended the fundamentals of stabilisation, but he was now caught between two forces and obliged to demand of Siles a number of major revisions.

On 23 January Lechín wrote to Siles on behalf of the COB, reiterating its loyalty to the government, 'of which we consider ourselves a part', and proposing large scale wage increases as well as price controls and a tax on capital assets. All the suggestions were rejected. Siles had already made a Gandhiesque gesture by embarking on a hunger strike against the precipitate stoppage called in Siglo XX, formally renounced the use of violence to impose stabilisation, and perceived that he could split the COB insofar as those sectors that did not possess the privileges of the *pulpería* were much less badly hit than the miners from whom the left drew much of its strength. Thus, when it was obvious that the issue was not going to subside, Siles began to build a campaign against the left both inside and outside the union movement. The stakes at play in this contest were substantially increased when Lechín and Torres proved able to amend only marginally a POR resolution at the FSTMB's eighth congress at Pulacayo in March with the result that the miners' union proposed that the COB should terminate *cogobierno* and announced that they would call an indefinite general strike unless the miners' basic pay was raised by 66 per cent by 30 June.

The issue went forward to the second congress of the COB held at the beginning of June amidst great tensions. There matters took a peculiar turn when the PCB joined the opposition to the left slate, adopting the position that any strike would only drive Siles into total dependence on the US. Lechín equivocated, since he recognised the vulnerability of the radical group to the government's increasingly popular campaign against a 'wreckers' strike' but he also saw that the PCB had aligned itself with sectors (principally the rail, petrol and construction workers) which Siles was attempting to wean into full opposition to the existing COB leadership. The president addressed congress with a strong speech in which he announced that he would never resort to inflationary policies, and castigated the left in a highly provocative manner. The supporters of a strike eventually won the vote but only with 260 votes out of 439; it was clear that they would start the action with the union movement badly split. [15]

Siles's defence and virtual threat of resignation if the strike went ahead shook the leadership of the COB. His accusations of petty sectoral demands at the expense of the commonweal, the mobilisation of party *comandos* and militias, and the isolation of the miners and teachers from nearly all the other unions encouraged the union hierarchy to avert a strike in which the entire concordat established after 1952 might be destroyed. Ñuflo Chávez, one of the most determined opponents of Eder, tried to force the issue by resigning the vice-presidency in the expectation that congress would reject his move and thereby provide parliamentary backing to the opposition. But Siles had gained ground and in a close vote Chávez was forced to leave office. By 25 June, the eve of the strike, the regime's massive publicity drive had obtained the backing of all the main factories in La Paz and the tacit acceptance of most mines, with the resolute exception of Siglo XX. The COB called off the strike at the last moment; the left was disorientated and badly divided, Lechín discredited, and the regime in an excellent position to turn important sections of the labour movement against his leadership.

Within a week of the strike's collapse Siles signalled his intentions by declaring that the COB, 'which had been set up with the full backing of the MNR', should not deviate from the government line and was in urgent need of 'restructuring'. He added that, 'the resolution passed at the last workers' congress calling for a general strike was put through by Trotskyist leaders and backed by falangists. Last week's national pronouncement against the strike shows that the executive committee of the COB should include representatives of other large groups of workers.' [16] That same day the executive committee called a meeting for self-criticism but four days later a communique signed by delegates from all the major unions except the factory workers and miners called on the leadership to resign or accept 'restructuring'. A *Bloque Reestructurador* was set up, driving Lechín into the arms of the militants centred on Siglo, which, according to the young POR leader Filemón Escóbar, had last given *vivas* to the MNR in 1955 and never more would do so. The *Bloque* came under the direct supervision of the Minister of the Interior, José Cuadros Quiroga, a hard rightist who, according to one of its members, financed the new organisation to the tune of Bs.10 million a month until he resigned in mid-1958, only to be succeeded by the equally *anti-lechinista* Walter Guevara.[17] The ministry also oversaw the coordination of the *Bloque*'s activities with those of the special armed *comandos* of the MNR, which now entered into direct conflict with the union militias in a number of camps. As a result of this campaign the COB met in November to issue a 'declaration of unity' and ratify its full support for the Eder plan. Lechín was permitted to stay in office.

The government's position in this confrontation had been greatly strengthened by support for its cause from the unions at the Huanuni and Colquiri camps, which now entered into prolonged conflict with Siglo XX. The Huanuni union had originally been set up by the company, leading to a number of conflicts with the FSTMB in the early years; its first secretary Emilio Carvajal, a bitter enemy of Lechín's, was now president of Comibol. Moreover, the mine had a large number of workers engaged as self-employed *cooporativistas* on a piece-work system known as *pirquín*, explicitly denounced in the Thesis of Pulacayo. These workers were totally opposed to strike action while the large number of potentially dangerous unemployed surface workers at Huanuni were found remunerative employment in the militia of the MNR *comando*, thereby consolidating an effective anti-Siglo alliance. Since Huanuni lay on the road and rail links from Oruro to Siglo, its control by the regime was both politically and logistically critical. Colquiri was less important both in size and location but, as a relatively young mine still expanding its operations, it could legitimately be given large capital sums and better treatment than other camps, although this failed to placate the faceworkers for long.[18]

At the end of 1957 the FSTMB held an *ampliado* at Potosí where the left, headed by Ireneo Pimentel (PCB), César Lora and Filemón Escóbar (POR), all from Siglo XX, achieved a majority of 78 to 8 with 15 abstentions for a resolution calling for major wage increases, the removal of *cogobierno* (already in practice suppressed) and rejection of Eder. Pimentel's support signalled a change in tack by the PCB, which joined with the POR in suppressing criticism of the bureaucracy for a defence of union independence. The victory of the left indicated that although the general strike call might have been tactically mismanaged, the regime's policy of splitting the COB was no less risky, especially since Eder's policies were now beginning to bite. Government forces attempted to break up this meeting with little success. However, at the federation's ninth congress, held at Colquiri in July 1958, the regime moved immediately against the Lechín-left bloc. The local *comando* combined with detachments sent from Huanuni to attack participants before the congress had even got under way. The Colquiri interior workers came to the defence of the federation with a number of dynamite attacks, but the delegates were forced under gunfire to escape to the San José camp, where *cogobierno* was duly pronounced dead and demands made for the dismantling of the MNR's *comandos especiales*, identified as the thugs of yellow trade unionism. The support given by the delegates to the political resolution, which restated that the FSTMB was not apolitical but revolutionary and class-based and denounced the Siles government as anti-popular and pro-imperialist, indicated that, with the exception of those few camps where the *comando* was well-armed and generously financed, the federation had regained its independence and authority if not complete control.

Siles's policy of fomenting rivalry inside the union movement created great difficulties for the MNR, which, from the *Comité Político Nacional* (CPN) to the lowliest *comando zonal*, was still formally subject to internal elections and highly vulnerable to faction-fighting. Even at the peak of his popularity in mid-1957 the president could not be sure of support from all the regional or departmental party organisations. This was not a purely internal matter since, in the towns at least, the *comando* controlled not only a significant part of the local militia but very often the town hall (*alcaldía*) as well, and it could exert much pressure on the prefecture (a central government post) and the army garrison. Thus, administration of the regions depended on obtaining a diligent mix of appointments to the posts of prefect and divisional army commander and the sponsorship of a strong yet friendly slate within the local party. Often this was achieved only for the ensemble to come apart through infighting over the distribution of power in local government rather than because of ideological differences. During this period the army did its utmost to protect its limited resources by marginalising itself from these contests, but there were obvious and recurrent problems in determining the balance of forces between the prefecture, which controlled the *carabineros*, and the *comando*, directly responsible for the militia, and between the *alcaldía*, which administered urban markets and municipal services, and both the prefecture, charged with running the departmental infrastructure, and the *comando*, which even after the suppression of coupons exercised direct pressure on the markets as well as appointments in a range of state institutions. In this way local politics came to assume great importance and even the most provincial townships became highly politicised.

In the mines themselves the *comandos* were at a permanent disadvantage insofar as the *sindicatos* not only covered the entire working population but were also a type of parochial popular front grouping a number of parties (including the MNR) and not simply that of the government. Furthermore, the union generally possessed greater prestige. Once the retention of the *pulperías* had been won, the union also controlled access to cheap supplies and ran its own radio station, which even before the advent of military rule was of inestimable organisational and political value.[19] These factors prompted a further disaggregation of power in a period marked by rifts in the ruling alliance.

Siles tried to reverse this situation by suppressing elections inside the local MNR apparatus and directly appointing interventors to lead the major *comandos*. This reversion to centralisation caused widespread outcry but lasted until early 1959 when, with an election due within the year, it became necessary to allow greater space for pacts to be renegotiated. However, the Siles administration introduced an irreversible bureaucratisation of the MNR, which henceforth divided into various 'sectors' of differing political complexion at all levels while power was increasingly concentrated in the hands of the national leadership.

Paradoxically, the site of greatest tension in terms of the relation between local and central authorities was not in the *altiplano* at all but in the tropical city of Santa Cruz, which throughout this period experienced substantial growth and the sort of political chaos normally associated with isolated 'boom-towns'. Santa Cruz had always been separated in a more than purely geographical sense from the highland–valley system which constituted the heartland of Bolivia in terms of population, industry, politics and culture. Subject to very infrequent but quite potent outbreaks of separatist sentiment, it was suffused with a strong sense of its regional identity, underpinned by the marked distinctiveness of the *camba* character from that of the *kollas** in the highlands, and the city's role as *de facto* capital of the *oriente*, the sparsely populated eastern half of the republic. Except for the regions around the city of Santa Cruz itself, Trinidad and Riberala in the Beni, and some of the rubber lands in Pando, this huge tract of the country was virtually *tierra incognita*, the only forms of communication being by plane to a few airstrips or, more dependably, the complex riverine network which flowed towards the Amazon. Santa Cruz de la Sierra was a long-established colonial outpost dominated by church missions and linked to the Jesuit empire in Paraguay; its sugar industry and cattle-raising had preserved tenuous ties with the *altiplano* but even in 1950 it remained cloistered in near autarky. The MNR had made the city its headquarters in the civil war of 1949 partly because there was no garrison there (none was properly established until 1959), which reflected the relative 'openness' of a society that by no means lacked its share of large landlords but was still governed by very fragile rules of economic competition and social control. The pugnacious populism and relatively disciplined organisation of the party made appreciable headway in such a political circuit, where personal power was applied as much through gangsterism as through petty favours.

The MNR's policy of economic diversification with the oil industry as its vanguard both developed Santa Cruz and brought it closer to the rest of the nation. Throughout the 1950s the state oil corporation YPFB registered a modest but constant expansion in the south of the department while both the government and US aid agencies were attentive to the possibilities of agro-industry in the region. This spurred on the construction of a new highway from Cochabamba, completed two years after the revolution and resurfaced thereafter with large doses of US development assistance. In 1956 monthly truck traffic on this road was 11,755 lorries; by 1960 it had reached nearly 50,000.[20]

* *Camba* is the name for one who comes from the eastern region of Bolivia; a *kolla* is a person from the Sierra.

Between 1955 and 1960 the *oriente* received 57.7 per cent of all credits from the Banco Agrícola against 16.1 per cent for the departments of La Paz, Oruro and Potosí combined. As a result, production of sugar rose from 34,000 tons in 1950 to 1,950,000 in 1964, and that of rice from 10,000 tons to 123,500. Cotton and coffee also expanded but on a more modest scale.[21] Although this growth was to be superseded in later years and had only a partial effect on the national economy as a whole, its impact on the region was great and redynamised a residual *caudillismo*; ever since, Santa Cruz has been the terrain of unusually violent political activity even in times of relative stability.

Under the MNR power struggles in the region were as complex as they were violent since they incorporated all the fluidities evident on the national scene within a local context in which landlords still retained considerable power but had to contend with the agrarian and urban (1956) reforms which had released important tracts of land around the perimeter of the city, providing a valuable resource for the distributionist clientelism of various party leaders. The right— broadly, the landed interests and city elders allied with the FSB-dominated university— operated through the *Comité Pro-Santa Cruz*, established in 1950 to further regional interests and led by the local dignitary Melchor Pinto. Control of the MNR was more unstable but generally decided through forthright engagements with the *Comité* which resulted in the department having 21 prefects between 1952 and 1962. The key figure in the MNR throughout this period was the young lawyer Luis Sandoval Morón, who, along with his brother Edil, displaced first a coalition of moderate old-guard *movimientistas* and then another clan based around the Barbery family in a series of highly-charged *comando* elections in which erratic government patronage mixed with liberal donations of land, disbursement of municipal funds, mobilisation of peasant '*sindicatos*', and depressingly persistent outbreaks of kidnappings, street brawls, castrations and murders.[22] Sandoval first obtained power in January 1954 but lost it again in March when, accused of murder, he was removed and the party 'intervened' by a colonel appointed by La Paz. In September 1955 Sandoval, now 'cleared' without any semblance of judicial enquiry, was returned to power. He held control until the end of 1957, when Siles's policy of intervention allowed the *Comité* to regain influence for a chaotic period of two years during which Sandoval captained an autonomous and semi-legal guerrilla band, making sundry incursions in the style of a nineteenth-century *caudillo*. On one occasion he reportedly entered the city mounted on a white stallion and carrying two pearl-handled revolvers in order to 'treat his men to a drink'.

Comiteismo was too closely attached to the FSB to hold on to power for long; after Siles had effectively lost control of the MNR apparatus in 1959 the maverick Sandoval retrieved his office to direct the city's affairs until mid-1961, by which time the military was taking a leading role in imposing order throughout the country and entered Santa Cruz to curb its factionalism with only short breaks for the next eight years. An idea of Sandoval's political style and independence may be gleaned from a not untypical incident in March 1961, when, during the first rains, the newly-asphalted central plaza of the city disintegrated into lumps of oil and sand. The dismayed and incensed townsfolk, encouraged by the *comando*, took their revenge by holding hostage the CBF engineers working on the job. Paz instructed that they be released immediately but Sandoval complained in reply, 'I don't know, our *pueblo* has no luck; despite all our efforts and concerns fortune defrauds us at every turn. These men are guilty and must be punished. I consider the reaction of the people to be just, although as the local authority we must, of course, maintain public order.'[23] Sandoval's idea of public order in this case was to order the engineers to take off their shoes and march in the mud around the square to the accompaniment of the municipal band and the jeers of the populace. Three months later he was again displaced, his rabble-rousing style and 500 militiamen, complete with their anti-aircraft gun, being insufficient to counter the government backed by those who had been obliged to make forced loans and yield property 'for redevelopment' or lose their jobs in local administration. The Sandoval Morón brothers were certainly somewhat extreme in their methods but their style was essentially in harmony with *cruceño* conditions and not so wayward as to deny them influence at national level, where they engaged in spirited if fleeting alliances, almost always against the incumbent president. Their populist legacy was sufficiently durable to enable them to burst back into national political life, albeit momentarily, in 1979 after years of exile and lightly-worn disgrace.

Although Sandoval Morón was a permanent nuisance for La Paz, he was valued as a bulwark against the Falange, which was particularly deeply incrusted in Santa Cruz but engaged in conspiratorial activity n most urban centres throughout the 1950s. Growth of support for the FSB amongst the urban middle class and students was due less to the attractions of its ungainly and remarkably unrevised ideological paraphernalia than to the simple fact that it resisted the MNR *tout court*, accusing the regime of both selling out to the yankees and being communist, demanding respect for property (principally in the countryside) and yet promising structural transformations even more profound than those introduced after April 1952. By composing itself so completely in opposition the FSB was consigned to the sphere of subversion and became encumbered with all the attendant problems of repression, clandestine activity and the violent squabbles so typically nurtured within sects. Yet, *falangismo* was the only available orbit for the forces displaced from power by the revolution, and it found sufficient recruits amongst those who had scores to settle with the MNR to be able to stage a number of ill-organised armed actions throughout the decade. The most serious of these took place in La Paz on 19 April 1959, when the FSB seized part of the city and held out for six hours. Amongst the fifty people who died in this action was the veteran fascist chief Unzaga de la Vega, found shot in his apartment. Unzaga's cerebral state was certainly not so secure as to make the MNR's claims of suicide appear preposterous but neither was the *Control Político*'s reputation so unblemished that the FSB's denunciation of assassination could be dismissed with ease.

The death of its *jefe* of 22 years unhinged the Falange from its rigid attachment to the doctrines of the 1930s, and under its new leader Mario Gutiérrez it reduced military activity somewhat and began to explore common ground with christian democracy. This lent the party a veneer of respectability and probably accounts for the fact that although it came third in the 1960 elections, the FSB polled 79,000 votes, nearly eight times the support given to the PCB, which had significantly greater support in the working class. The extreme right was, therefore, far from dead and could legitimately be presented as the 'new Rosca' and the most acute threat to the revolution. It certainly plagued the Siles government, but by the time of Unzaga's death Siles was already losing ground to a renewed syndicalist challenge.

The FSTMB's strike of February-March 1959 lasted over two weeks and lost Comibol $2.8 million but finally secured a 20 per cent pay rise and, more critically, the retention of price subsidies in the *pulperías*. Compared with events over the previous two years this was a major setback for the regime, which was able to keep Huanuni and Colquiri working but eventually had to concede defeat over a key component of the stabilisation programme. However, the strike also marked a new shift in alliances inside the miners' federation since Lechín, Mario Torres and other national leaders, concerned at the vulnerability of the Siles regime and the possibility that prolonged action might duplicate the errors of 1957, did their utmost to limit the stoppage and reach a compromise. They thereby lost the support of the left which controlled the independent strike committee, chaired by César Lora. The tension between these two bodies reflected not only longstanding differences between the rank and file and a bureaucracy which had remained virtually unchanged since 1944 but also a division between those who were in conflict with the government but still belonged to the MNR and were prepared to reach an entente to preserve equilibrium and those who, while they did not seek the immediate overthrow of the regime, fought for a rank and file victory in order to reverse the policies of 1956 and rekindle the radicalism of 1952. As we have seen, the PCB oscillated between these two positions, but in 1959 it joined with the POR. The effect was to cripple the *Bloque Reestructurador*, which had been losing affiliates since mid-1958. The *Bloque* finally collapsed in January 1959, when the leadership of the factory workers' union was voted out *en masse* by a rank and file which had been sceptical of the pro-government stance from the start and forced an abstention in the 1957 vote. The *fabriles*'s eventual support for Siles had been rewarded with Abel Ayoroa, their leader, receiving the labour ministry. After the 1959 miners' strike he was removed from union office and denounced as a traitor to the working class, the new leadership of the union being largely composed of militant *lechinistas* led by Daniel Saravia.

This reconstitution of syndicalist unity was sealed early in 1960, when the Siglo XX union finally overcame resistance from the Huanuni *comando*. The original cause of this conflict lay outside union affairs in the independent campaign for the presidency by a central figure in the MNR right, Walter Guevara. Guevara's attempt to win the party nomination was supported by the *comandos* of Huanuni and Colquiri which had received arms and finance from him when he was minister of the interior. However, both the left and centre of the party backed the return of Víctor Paz, who had been able to distance himself from the stabilisation plan whilst ambassador in London and had offered Lechín the vice-presidency in an effort to regenerate the spirit of the pre-1956 alliance. Siles at first supported Guevara but drew back when his protegé made ever stronger attacks against both the COB and Paz, requiring his removal as minister. As a result, the *guevaristas* found themselves isolated inside the MNR and obliged to take strong independent measures. This shift in the balance of forces registered in the Huanuni *sindicato* elections of December 1959, when the old *comandista* leadership gained only half the number of votes given to the left and was then charged with a number of crimes, including that of murder. On 22 January 1960 the displaced *comando* struck back; 120 armed men seized the union building and proclaimed the old leadership restored. When some 400 workers approached the building they were fired upon and had to withdraw. On hearing of this, Ireneo Pimentel and César Lora mobilised 600 workers from Siglo and drove to Huanuni. Fighting lasted for several hours and ten people were killed, including the *comando* leader, Celestino Gutiérrez, whom the attackers left dangling on a rope for a number of hours until Siles arrived to negotiate a 'truce'. Yellow unions would reappear in Bolivia's mines and factories but never again would they attract popular support.

The 1960 election campaign also accelerated mobilisation in the countryside, where Guevara's challenge offered alternative clientelist attachments and exacerbated the deep-seated competition between the regional leaders (*caciques*) over official patronage, control of markets and land, and military power. This last issue was of great importance for although the peasant *sindicatos* were generally ill-organised local or regional agglomerations, they made up for their lack of discipline in the potential for a massive response to leaders who acted in impetuous and authoritarian manner and controlled considerable supplies of arms. In 1953 one source estimated that the 16 'regiments' organised in the countryside comprised some 110,000 *campesinos* under arms; even if this figure were halved it would still represent a formidable force.[24] In some instances intra-peasant conflict remained largely marginalised from the shifts of national politics. This was the case in the generations-old feud over land between the Laimis and Jukumanis in the north of Potosí, where the authorities had always been perplexed by the intricacies of the contending claims and sometimes acquiesced in requests from both sides to stay out of the issue, which could only be resolved on exclusively local and resolutely non-hispanic terms.[25] Yet, this should not be construed as being indicative of a pettyfogging quarrel; late in 1959 260 people died in clashes. Elsewhere the contest for resources was frequently assimilated into the formal politics of the nation, even if many of the participants possessed only a dim perception of the wider factors in play.

Guevara's rupture with Paz and then Siles drew initial support from two leading *campesino* figures, Miguel Veizaga, who headed the small-scale, self-employed farmers from Cliza in the Cochabamba valley, and Zenón Barrientos Mamani, an Aymara chieftain from the department of Oruro. The outward reason for their allegiance was agreement with Guevara's attacks on the bureaucratisation of the MNR and the inertia of the agrarian reform. However, they were also motivated by long-standing feuds with the dominant but still insecure leaders in their respective regions: José Rojas, chief of the Ucureña *sindicato* of ex-*colonos*, and Toribio Salas, the highland *cacique* based in Achacachi. These contests had on occasion broken out of the ritual circuit of intrigues within the ministry, blockades of roads, and competition over 'affiliations' in intermediate zones into direct armed conflict. But it was only from 1959 that the MNR was shown to be incapable of imposing its will and order in the countryside without accepting alliances which gave the *caciques* considerable autonomy. Thus, Rojas, a Chaco veteran and long-standing Cochabamba peasant *caudillo*, was made minister of peasant affairs for six months in that year in order to sustain Veizaga's support for Guevara. When he was finally removed from office because of the manifest excesses of his partisan behaviour (and, one might hazard, the disdain felt by the MNR leadership for a man who insisted on speaking in Quechua but happily toured the countryside in a chauffeur-driven limousine), Rojas blocked the roads to the weekly fair in Cliza for two months and launched a number of attacks, necessitating the intervention of the army. He had been preceded as minister by a non-*campesino*, the MNR apparatchik Vincente Alvarez Plata, who had attempted to curb Salas's power in the *altiplano* but failed to generate sufficient support. In November 1959 Alvarez Plata was killed in Achacachi in circumstances which directly implicated Salas. But such was his authority that the *cacique* was able to survive his expulsion from the MNR, hold nocturnal meetings of his followers, and persist in harassing the settlement of Warisata.

The various peasant chieftains became increasingly involved in constructing regional alliances and defence pacts, some of the most important of which were with the mining camps. In March 1959, 3,000 of Rojas's men were dispatched in a special train to break the FSTMB strike at San José; a month later the Ucureña militia was again mobilised to suppress the FSB rising in La Paz and only kept out of the city with great difficulty after the rebellion had been quashed. Rojas also signed an alliance with the *comando* of Colquiri but this was nullified once the interior workers regained control of the union. Veizaga, on the other hand, had his forces occupy the townships of Tarata and Tolata in January 1960 after the conflict in Huanuni since he held Rojas responsible for the death of the *comando* leader Gutiérrez. In fact, it was this incident (in which Rojas played no direct part) that sparked off a major conflict between the factions of the Cochabamba valley. By the end of January 1960 attacks, kidnappings and occupations had become so commonplace that Paz and Guevara, both now formally candidates in the elections, flew to the area to negotiate a truce. By early March two provinces had been declared military zones, and the army's seventh division was prohibiting the carrying of arms as well as the entry into the region of politicians from either the MNR or Guevara's new MNR-*Auténtico*. But even this was not enough. Large areas of the valley lacked any semblance of order. Rojas was threatening to occupy Cochabamba itself, Veizaga to cut off its water supply. The Rio Retama had been converted from a regional boundary into a fortified line complete with barbed-wire fences, trenches, machine-gun nests and even mortar emplacements. Scores of people were killed in skirmishes and several government commissions were sent to mediate.

Only the election brought a temporary down-turn in conflict. In the several *pueblos* controlled by Rojas every vote went to Paz, yet in Oruro the MNR-A did well, coming within 2,000 votes of the total amassed by the MNR. Veizaga and Barrientos Mamani immediately renounced Guevara, applied to rejoin the MNR, and held discussions with Paz. But it was not until the end of 1960, after the declaration of a state of siege, the deployment of a number of army regiments and the airforce, and the intervention of Lechín, that Rojas agreed to halt his persecution of Veizaga and both *caciques* pledged themselves to hold free *sindicato* elections.

This state of affairs in the countryside reflected a more general atmosphere of tension and conflict which attended the 1960 election. Guevara's split was the first critical fissure in the MNR and placed an enormous burden on the fragile unity of its apparatus. Yet, because Guevara was fighting not simply against the arbitrary and undemocratic nature of both government and party but also for a clearly conservative set of policies, he was unable to sunder the unions from Paz and thereby delayed by three years a definitive schism. Moreover, the leadership of the COB, having obtained Lechín's nomination as vice-president, believed itself to have regained a strategic advantage over the party's right. Even the PCB, which was soon publicly to regret its error, misjudged the strength of Guevara's challenge and mobilised in support of Paz despite the fact that it was standing its own candidates for congress.[26] On a wider plane such a response was not so surprising since Paz was still identified with the core revolutionary reforms; Siles, on the other hand, had lost credibility, and although at the MNR's eighth convention he identified only the extreme left as his detractors, the list of charges he attributed to them had drawn a much wider constituency: 'According to the accusations of the parties of the extreme left, my government has sold the *patria* to the petrol consortiums and made government decisions dependent upon approval from the State Department; it has been responsible for massive unemployment and massacres, the deaths of workers; it has halted the agrarian reform and favoured the ex-*latifundistas*, attempted to denationalise the mines and weaken YPFB prior to its liquidation; finally, it has been the author of the division of the workers' movement.'[27] Siles, unrepentant to the end, went on to accuse the POR and PCB of running a 'feudal fief' and 'dictatorship' in Siglo XX. He called the 1959 strike subversive, defended the Huanuni *comando* and the actions of Rojas's militia, attacked Lora for attempting to stage a re-run of the Paris Commune, and declared that if the stabilisation plan had not been imposed Bolivia would have been driven into communism. When set against this tirade, the measured and conciliatory tone adopted by Paz appeared to herald a new era. In the final poll the MNR returned a high vote, but the combined support for the MNR-A — soon to be renamed the *Partido Revolucionario Auténtico* (PRA) — and the FSB was a third of the ruling party's total, which, under the unchanged voting conditions of bullying, bribery, threats and residual dependence on *oficialismo* for jobs, was a significant achievement. The predictable charges of fraud were treated with disdain by the MNR left, but it was this sector that was to bear the consequences and suffer most under Paz.

Repression and Development under Paz

Lechín and the MNR syndicalists were marginalised so quickly and emphatically under Paz that it might in retrospect be said that they made a serious mistake in supporting him. In a simple sense, of course, they did. But it should be remembered that, notwithstanding all his fighting rhetoric, Lechín remained a *movimientista* and unless he could take a majority of the most militant proletarian sectors out of the MNR he stood to lose his position in the COB by making such a move himself. Since he was utterly opposed to the 'Stalinism' of the PCB and the 'maximalism' of the POR, both of which parties would have placed severe constraints on his now famous manoeuvrability, he could not join them. He adjudged the situation in 1960 not to be conducive to a left break from the MNR to form a new labour party. As a result, neither he nor the rest of the *cobistas* in the MNR had much choice but to negotiate the best terms they could obtain within the party on the basis of the union movement's revival. Their expectations of success in this were raised by the fact that after the election the unofficial 'sectors' that had existed inside the MNR since 1955 took on a much more coherent shape, with the *Sector Izquierdista* seemingly possessing the greatest following. The *Sector Socialista* was restricted to a small group around the new labour minister Anibal Aguilar Peñarrieta and the ubiquitous Edil Sandoval Morón. It espoused a very flaccid socialism indeed, and was seen as a predominantly technocratic faction supported by many *silistas*. Paz's personal following was obliged to follow suit for although the president and the CPN had persistently to denounce factionalism, Paz had used it to his best advantage in order to regain power and, once it was clear that a great deal more was at stake than Siles's personal policies, it became necessary to enter the lists.

From the start Víctor Paz directed both government and party in a closed, bureaucratic fashion with the assistance of a small group known as the '*maquinita*' (little machine). Inside the MNR he returned to the interventionist policy adopted by Siles and used the party's executive secretary Federico Fortún Sanjinés to bypass the unwieldy and divided CPN, consolidate a vertical chain of command, and suppress dissident tendencies in the *comandos*. This approach was mirrored in the cabinet, now largely staffed by young technocrats of the post-revolutionary generation; Lechín was the only leftist in the higher echelons of government and soon found himself deprived of all executive powers.

Paz surrounded himself with men who subscribed to his developmentalist ideas and shared his belief that the modernisation of Bolivia was an absolute priority. He had a clear view of the form such a change had to take: 'All the men and women of the party ought to take stock of this idea: we need to go to foreign capital to develop our economy . . . It has been said that if I came back to government the *cupos* and queues would return. This is false and insidious, as is the accusation that I would destroy stabilisation. The stabilisation plan was necessary. It had to be carried out and we must continue it.'[28] This theme predominated and was pressed home with insistence. Occasionally, however, the veteran economist sacrificed much in the cause of clarity; 'One of the causes of underdevelopment is lack of capital. So, it has to be obtained from abroad. The best thing to do is to raise loans because these, and their interest, are paid off and the country is freed of any obligation.'[29] Paz warned that this 'new stage' of the revolution would not be as spectacular as the first, but its transformative effect would be just as great. He criticised prejudices against private capital, to which he offered extensive guarantees, while Federico Fortún laid emphasis on the more general political and organisational aspects of the new turn: 'The revolution has not always taken a clear attitude with respect to the middle sectors, nor, in practice, have they been considered the natural allies of the revolution . . . immediate and decided assistance must be given to private mining . . . a revolutionary party without vertical organisation is not able to implement a political programme.'[30] Such an approach dove-tailed very smoothly with Kennedy's Alliance for Progress, which sought to counter the effects of the Cuban revolution through expanded US investment in infrastructural schemes that would generate industrial growth, diversify the ownership of land and agricultural production, and give impetus to structural reforms, thereby reducing social polarisation and political radicalisation in a 'modern . . . evolutionary' manner. For Washington, the Paz administration represented an excellent 'partner' to spearhead the Alliance; it had already implemented important reforms, it was civilian and democratic in form, it was clearly under pressure from the left but it had also made significant concessions to the US in 1956 and now seemed even more amenable to direct economic and political collaboration. In Kennedy Paz saw a man after his own heart, a politician capable of substituting for the progressive national bourgeoisie that Bolivia so manifestly lacked for its necessary transformation into a modern state. In 1963 Paz visited the US president, greeting him in language that was typically extravagant but also disarmingly genuine: 'In my *patria* there exists an admiration for this great country, for its technical progress, for the youth and vitality of its culture, for its democratic dynamism and for its contribution to the common task of preserving the values inherited from our forebears which we must pass on to our children.'[31]

Within six months of Paz's inauguration the strengthened alignment with the US had taken tangible form in the drafting of what became known as the Triangular Plan. This project was jointly funded by the US government, the Inter-American Development Bank and the government of West Germany, and aimed at the complete overhaul and refinancing of Comibol, which by 1961 had outstanding debts of $20 million. The plan granted a credit of $37.75 million to the corporation on what are generally known as 'soft' terms, in this case a three-year grace period, 4½ per cent interest and repayment scheduled over ten years. However, the terms of Comibol's 'rehabilitation' were markedly less soft. They required an overall dismissal of more than a fifth of its workforce and the closure of a number of (unspecified) mines. Those enterprises which had not been 'technically rationalised' would receive no new investment or subsidies. At the eleventh FSTMB congress, held at Huanuni in May 1961, Lechín endorsed the principle of the operation, avoiding the issue of redundancies, and arguing for acceptance as the only sure means of renovating the mining sector: 'Some time ago the workers were realistic enough to argue that capital must be found for Comibol, no matter where the credit came from. Thus, if Comibol obtains credits somewhere, it is adopting a progressive attitude which cannot be regarded as counter-revolutionary. For this reason we must support the plan. Some hotheads are trying to push the workers into an isolationist position.'[32] The left resolutely opposed this line, but Lechín was able to harness official support to the weight of his authority, swinging the majority of the delegates into backing the proposal. However, this decision was by no means preordained, and debate was particularly heated because the MNR had already out-flanked the COB in rejecting a much more favourable package offered by the Soviet Union. In October 1960 Krushchev approached the Bolivian representative at the UN with an offer to give credits to Bolivia so that she might build her own badly-needed smelter. In December Brezhnev wrote to Paz confirming this offer, the Czech government also offering generous terms for the construction of an antimony smelter. To consolidate the favourable popular response to these offers, and to place further pressure on a regime that was showing every sign of needing a good excuse to turn them down, Moscow sent a parliamentary mission to Bolivia in December 1960. This delegation ratified the smelter offer and released further plans for $150 million in credits for road-building, YPFB and the railways. The Bolivian congress and the COB welcomed the initiative but Paz was well aware that Washington was totally opposed and therefore reverted to his trusted policy of delaying a decision for 'technical studies'. At the same time the MNR leadership revived an old campaign against the Soviet Union's 'dumping' of tin on the international market which had depressed prices, and necessitated strong action by the International Tin Council. This policy of Moscow appears to have been misguided in every sense since the Soviet Union had by 1959 become a net importer of tin. However, the issue was manipulated with great insistence and to some effect, particularly by the bellicose president of Comibol, Guillermo Bedregal.[33]

The PCB naturally mobilised all its resources to support the Soviet offer. Some worthy citizens were so aghast at the prospect of having Russians set foot in the country that they left La Paz for the duration of the mission's visit, and the Bishop of Oruro led his congregation in beseeching the Lord to impede acceptance of the Soviet offer. In the mines the PCB's oscillations and eventual regroupment behind Paz in 1960 had given a new lease of life to the POR, which was attacking the Stalinists with a venom not seen since the 1940s. This, as the *porista* Filemón Escóbar recounts, led to the Soviet delegates receiving a welcome at Siglo XX of a type that they could hardly have anticipated:

> Their reception was tremendous. The miners, on seeing the Russians, commented that they were gringos just like the North Americans. At this time our party was holding a national training session. It was decided that we would take part in the reception of

the Russians, defending our own point of view. All that night we prepared little red flags with a hammer, a sickle, and the number 4. At eight in the morning, as the miners came off the night shift, they all put our flags on their helmets in the slot that normally contains an electric light. Four thousand of them wore the flag of the international. We also distributed red flags and posters supporting the Russia of Lenin and Trotsky, to distinguish ourselves from the Muscovite bureaucracy. Years later a journalist from *Life* magazine innocently wrote that the miners of Bolivia were so backward that they carried these banners not knowing who ruled the Soviet Union. It was the man from *Life* whose backwardness was thereby exposed for the Bolivian miners had a better understanding of Russian affairs than that journalist.

The communists reacted vehemently to the discovery that the main square of Siglo XX was dominated by the posters and red flags of the Trotskyists but they stopped short of violence because the Russian deputies were addressing their greetings to the workers. Listening to their speeches, César commented that they were not politicians but mere administrators. What the miners wanted to know was how the workers of Russia brought about the 1917 revolution, which was the true basis of that country's progress. Someone spoke up, expressing the view of our party: that if the government refused their offer of a tin smelter we, the miners of Siglo XX, would accept their offer with revolutionary enthusiasm. The Russians were quick to reply — they could only undertake negotiations on a government to government basis, and could not enter into any commitment with labour unions. At the end of the proceedings there were cheers for Russia, on the one hand there was the powerful voice of our party cheering Lenin and Trotsky, on the other, the communists cheered the Russian ruler of the day . . . The Soviet deputies saluted with three fingers, we replied with four.[34]

There is every sign that Paz used the Soviet offer to push Washington into presenting a concrete alternative, but this did not include a smelter. The private mining companies continued to oppose such a measure, arguing that Bolivia possessed insufficient reserves to justify it, although they themselves increased their investment in the excavation of tin. Inside the MNR the issue took on renewed importance as embodying a vital step towards autonomous national development, but although it was enthusiastically supported by René Zavaleta, the young minister of mines, all tangible proposals were effectively torpedoed by the party leadership.[35]

The confidence with which Paz was now acting was most evident in his rapid and efficient removal of Lechín. Lechín had, in point of fact, scarcely challenged the president at all; he had implicitly accepted the limits of the traditionally powerless post of the vice-presidency, supported the Triangular Plan, been disparaging about the Cuban revolution, and even gone to the lengths of visiting Chiang Kai-shek in Taiwan in order to brush up his image and curry favour with Washington. Yet, in mid-1961 the COB leader was deliberately 'set up' when interior minister José Antonio Arze Murillo implicated him in a cocaine scandal through an acquaintance in Cochabamba. In hindsight, it is hard to avoid the conclusion that although innocent, Lechín had been somewhat careless in some of his associations. He resigned and withdrew his resignation several times, but was on such unsteady ground that Paz was easily able to exile him as ambassador to Rome. It may be that Paz recalled that Siles's father had rid himself of a burdensome vice-president by sending him abroad and then impeded his return because of a drug scandal; alternatively, as Paz himself later claimed, it is possible that even by this stage the CIA chief in Bolivia, Lt. Col. Edward Fox, had secured such control over the interior ministry that he could act without reference to the Palacio Quemado.[36]

One critical factor in the increasing belligerence of the Paz government was the expansion of US aid which, as one writer put it, rose 'stratospherically', by over 600 per cent between 1960 and 1964. This further assisted a short-term improvement in the economy, with inflation limited to single figures (and even a negative percentage in 1963) and annual average growth between 1961 and 1964 reaching 5.7 per cent (compared with 1.5 per cent for 1956–61). In the mining sector aid from the plan succeeded only in slowing down the rise in Comibol's costs, but the situation would have been considerably worse had the Vietnam War not suddenly hiked tin prices from $1.17 to $1.70 a pound.

Despite the fact that other important indicators, such as those for oil production and unemployment, were far from reassuring, by mid-1961 the Paz cabinet felt able to press ahead with the Triangular

Plan. There were now few resonances of 1952 in the language of those administering Comibol's 'rehabilitation'. Aguilar stated baldly, 'I am not a worker minister', and in 1960 collaborated with Bedregal, the head of Comibol, to produce a 'Thesis of Telamayu' to counteract the COB's syndicalist programmes. This bosses' charter for the workers contained a smattering of *Marxisant* flourishes but remained firmly founded on its opening postulates: 'with the National Revolution the traditional worker−employer relation disappeared . . . The thesis considers that daily demands ought to be subordinated to the development of the National Revolution.' As a consequence, it was a short step to itemising the travesties of 'anarchosyndicalism', ranging from its 'abuse of co-administration' to the 'subversive use of the general strike', the rejection of links with 'the party that leads the Revolution', 'false internationalism', the suppression of representative democracy in *cogobierno* and the dictatorship of the *controles obreros*.[37] Bedregal went on to castigate the FSTMB for losing $12 million in 'illegal strikes' and insisted upon a reduction of Comibol's work force by a further 5,000 in addition to the 7,700 jobs lost between 1956 and 1960.[38]

In order to pre-empt the predictable response from the left Paz jailed 18 of its national leaders — including PCB general secretary Jorge Kolle Cueto, Guillermo Lora, Ireneo Pimentel, Federico Escóbar and Filemón Escóbar — while the plan was introduced. As a result, the PCB and POR momentarily sank their differences and combined to fight yet another defensive strike centred on Siglo XX headed by the curiously-unjailed César Lora. The 18-day strike won the release of the jailed leftists and lost Comibol a further $1.5 million, but it failed to halt the plan. The support given to the stoppage reflected the popularity of the two men who came to personify the radical traditions of Bolivia's largest mining camp: Federico Escóbar and César Lora. These leaders, the first holding the official post of *control obrero* and the second simply a rank and file delegate, were very different in character and politics but shared a reputation for honesty and principled behaviour that enabled them to draw many apolitical workers into prolonged confrontations with Comibol and the government over political as well as strictly syndicalist matters.

Escóbar was the older of the two, liked for his easy and friendly manner with his fellow workers as well as his complete hostility to the Comibol administration. Escóbar had been a victim of the 1947 'white massacre' and was sacked from a variety of jobs during the *sexenio*, an experience which led him to join the PCB. Although Federico was no intellectual and prone to all manner of political 'deviation' in the course of his union work, he was always to be seen carrying some classic Marxist tract, he exuded all the enthusiasm of an autodidact, and was fervent in his attachment to a fundamentalist revolutionary cause, giving his children names such as Krupskaya and Fidel. However, it is less for this than for his implacable syndicalism that Escóbar became something of a legend in the mines. A student who went to work in Siglo XX in 1971 records,

> What [the workers] remember is all his bullying behaviour towards the bosses, regardless of rank. They say that he once arrived at a meeting with the management, and all the gringos were there. He said to them, 'Here you all are at ease, smoking imported cigarettes while the worker has only his coca and distilled alcohol; you smoke what we earn. Get out of here you bastards.' Everyone left except the manager, who stayed to discuss labour problems with Escóbar and the workers. Escóbar told them to sit down where the gringos had been, and he offered them cigarettes from the packets they had left. Any worker who was not properly served at the company store would go and complain to Escóbar and he would bawl out the employee responsible. Everyone was afraid of him. When he approached a place the [white-collar] employees would begin to tremble, literally tremble.[39]

Escóbar's prestige combined with Ireneo Pimentel's organisational abilities as the union general secretary maintained the PCB's hold over Siglo for many years. Although in 1964 Pimentel renounced his radical past and Escóbar joined the Maoist *PC-Marxista Leninista* (PCML), this hold was maintained under a new generation of leaders, such as Simón Reyes and Oscar Salas (Huanuni), less exuberant in style but more disciplined in their politics. Thus, when Escóbar died in 1966, supposedly of a liver complaint, it was the workforce rather than the party that mourned him.[40]

César Lora was more introverted and intellectually more sophisticated than Escóbar, never acquiring the same level of popularity or even a formal union post. Lora's avoidance of overtly dogmatic behaviour while maintaining a firm party line enhanced a reputation built on almost constant persecution, identifying many workers with a man whose politics were often alien to them but whom they trusted as honest and entirely class conscious. He also possessed a remarkably sure sense of timing in forming tactical alliances with the PCB and then moving sharply against it, heading a particularly venomous campaign at the end of 1962 over Pimentel's alleged mishandling of union funds. Under Lora's leadership the POR regained much ground lost in the 1950s when its maximalist policies appeared to be totally utopian. It was no coincidence that under the conditions imposed by the Triangular Plan the Trotskyists retrieved some of the authority they had held in the late 1940s.

Conflict over the plan peaked in mid-1963 when Bedregal, having managed to remove only 2,000 workers over the previous two years, imposed a lock-out at Siglo XX in order to push through his planned 'rehabilitation'. On 13 June the camp came out on strike and this soon spread to the rest of the pits. Lechín, called back from Rome by Paz, tried to defuse the situation. But this was an impasse which could not be negotiated away: on 3 August Paz issued a decree abolishing *control obrero* and on 23 August implemented an agreement with Washington whereby Bolivia would receive aid in exchange for purchasing almost all its manufactured imports from the US. As a result, a range of goods became very scarce or were only available at high prices. The FSTMB formally declared a national miners' strike, foreign technicians and US embassy personnel were taken hostage in Siglo, and the central mines declared military zones. A full military occupation of Siglo and Huanuni was only avoided by last minute talks between union leaders and the remarkably flexible commander of the Oruro garrison, Colonel Juan José Torres, but skirmishing between militias occurred throughout September. When the strike finally ended, on 1 October, Pimentel and Escóbar were again in jail (where they would remain for over a year) and Lora fired from his job along with many other radicals.

The 1963 strike, one of the longest in the miners' history, sundered the FSTMB and the COB from the MNR for good and hastened the schism of the MNR itself. The political resolution of the twelfth miners' congress in December likened the Paz government to those of the Rosca and declared the president 'a traitor to the aims of the Revolution'. Two weeks later the left was denied any voice in the MNR convention to decide upon the party's candidates for the 1964 elections. Lechín withdrew his delegates and announced the formation of a new party, the *Partido Revolucionario de la Izquierda Nacional* (PRIN), which issued no programme but drew in almost all the *movimientistas* in the COB and began to discuss a tactical pact not only with the PCB but also with all the other anti-Paz forces, including Siles and the FSB. The MNR had lost its links with the organised working class and with them the last of its radical credentials. The *Sector Socialista* began to waver; Paz's dependence on the US and the army deepened.

The Triangular Plan was the most important but certainly not the sole US activity in Bolivia at this time. Even before the stabilisation programme Washington had made its mark on the country's oil industry by advising on and heavily influencing the 1955 petroleum code which justifiably became known as the *Código Davenport*. Paz later defended the code's generous terms for private enterprises on the grounds that the losses suffered by them in exploration could not have been borne by YPFB, the expansion of which was tightly limited after 1956. The debate over policy in the oil industry was heated but rather abstract until 1961, when YPFB began to reach the limits of its existing wells and capacity for exploration while Gulf Oil made a major discovery in its sector and was pumping petrol within a year. This reduced YPFB's ability to stage a nationalist defence—which Paz had consistently opposed—and strengthened Gulf's position substantially, preparing the ground for far greater expansion after the fall of the MNR.

In other sectors, US interests were pursued more directly. A prolonged attempt to reform the Banco Minero by urging a colossal increase in its interest rates and the removal of its monopoly on tin transactions was so manifestly aimed at achieving the best conditions for private banks at the expense of the state that the Banco's executives were able to stage an effective defence of their institution.[41] Late in 1963 and early in 1964 the US embassy moved directly into the arena of labour relations; an embassy officer, Emmanuel Biggs, encouraged and allegedly funded to the tune of $57,000 a still-born 'alternative COB'. This organisation, known as COBUR, was repudiated even by labour minister Aguilar although Paz gave it his blessing. The operation was undertaken under the auspices of the American Institute for Free Labor Development (AIFLD) and the *Organización Regional Interamericana de Trabajadores* (ORIT), widely viewed as a yellow union apparatus with close CIA links.

Another of the most prominent embassy officials involved in this case was labour attaché Tom Martin, who was given a free rein under ambassador Ben Stephansky. Martin concentrated much effort on cultivating close relations with the new minister of peasant affairs, the scholarly Carlos Ponce Sanjinés. His style, however, left something to be desired in sophistication: at one official dinner in Potosí Martin addressed the local notables with the words, 'I have the money of the United States and Ponce has the ideas . . . if you help Ponce you will get the money.' This might have caused a bigger scandal than it did had it not been overshadowed by charges that Martin's assistant offered $50 to one of Ponce's officials for a bout of post-prandial fellatio.[42]

In general, political operations went more smoothly. The admittedly rather incautious Cuban ambassador was declared *persona non grata* after transparent manipulation of his contacts with Achacachi *cacique* Toribio Salas, who was thereby tainted with 'Castroite subversion'. It did, however, prove difficult to persuade Paz to take an unambiguously anti-Cuba line since the MNR originally welcomed the revolution, identified it as similar to their own, and even deigned to offer its leaders their advice. Even after Castro had made his first 'Marxist' speech Paz was reluctant to cut all ties, fearing the obvious consequences for his image. Thus, it was not until mid-1964, after Lyndon Johnson had suspended an economic agreement over the issue, that diplomatic relations were fully severed.

It was the arrival of Johnson at the White House that brought about a discernible change in relations, less in terms of open policy than by virtue of the fact that the Pentagon came to exercise greater influence on foreign affairs. Paz had been on very good terms with Stephansky and he continued to be close to his successor Douglas Henderson, appointed in December 1963. But Henderson himself was soon complaining of pressure from Colonel Fox, particularly on the question of Cuba.[43] Having visited Kennedy only a few weeks before he was assassinated, Paz had decided to run again for president in 1964 because, despite the obvious dangers, he could see no viable alternative. The State Department appears to have supported him in this; certainly Henderson made every effort to encourage him. However, Fox and his minions evidently had other ideas since by early 1964 they were directly aiding the ultra-conservative *El Diario*, which launched a strong anti-Paz campaign.

The central man in this particular operation was Colonel Julio Sanjinés Goitia, a graduate of West Point who sat on the newspaper's board but continued to serve as an army engineer as well as an employee of the US embassy, working on Alliance for Progress programmes. Sanjinés's position as the army's most senior engineer placed him in a particularly influential position inside the US-funded 'Civic Action' programme of road and school building and the establishment of water towers, a programme that had done much to improve the public image of the army, enabling officers to establish links with various civil leaders independently of the MNR. Yet Sanjinés, whose reputation was as an intellectual and a 'backroom boy' (he later became president of the Andean Development Corporation), was essentially a broker in the Pentagon's support for the military. Inside the country he kept a low profile, and his influence within the armed forces was subordinate to that of General Alfredo Ovando Candia, the army commander, and General René Barrientos Ortuño, head of the air force.

These two men were of entirely different temperaments. Ovando, already a senior captain in 1952, was a tight-lipped martinet dogged by a stomach ulcer. Before all else an institutionalist, he had become highly practised at maintaining unity inside the officer corps and was respected by his peers for the manner in which he had kept up good relations with the MNR but also held it at bay and tended the gradual reconstitution of the force. His appointment as chief of staff in 1957 coincided with an upturn in the military's fortunes as a result of pressure applied by Eder. One of the conditions of stabilisation had been that the MNR adopt a distinctly more favourable policy towards the armed forces and allow the US to 'professionalise' them. Siles had adopted this policy only with reluctance and initially did little, but before long the institution was receiving greater funds, more men and new equipment. Its share of the budget rose from 6.8 per cent in 1958 to 16.8 per cent in 1964. Over the same period the army's manpower rose from 5,000 to 15,000; by 1964 it was receiving over $1.5 million in US aid, and some 1,200 officers and men had trained at the School of the Americans in the Panama Canal Zone.[44] The military still had no tanks, its aircraft were extremely old (a squadron of second-hand Mustangs was only bought in 1965), and most of its units spent more than half their time farming. Yet it had reacquired both corporate spirit and organisational stability, possessing sufficient resources to contain the militias. Ovando recognised that Paz in particular had done much to assist this process and he, like many of his subalterns trained in the post-1952 Colegio, was in broad sympathy with the MNR's nationalist ideas. He therefore treated the army's growing involvement in maintaining public order and temporarily filling posts in public administration as an essentially institutional matter, taking care to avoid unnecessary political attachments while always seeking piecemeal advantages. The Pentagon needed Ovando to keep the military in order but could not expect to promote him, however subtly, as a political alternative to Paz.

Barrientos, on the other hand, was both politically ambitious and a popular officer with a high public profile. Born in the Cochabamba valley in 1919, he was of humble background, loquacious, fluent in Quechua, and a charismatic figure. He had been linked to the MNR during the *sexenio*, fought with the party in the 1949 civil war, and was in the leadership of its military cell after 1952. He had also visited the US on a number of occasions and knew Fox from a course for senior airforce officers in Oklahoma. However, if the process of nurturing good military friends had developed into preparation for a coup before mid-1964 both the CIA and the Pentagon might have felt somewhat insecure about a candidate whose machismo often bordered on sheer foolhardiness. As a pilot Barrientos had clocked up an inordinately large number of 'near misses' and accidents even by Bolivia's aeronautical standards; the fact that a goodly proportion of these were attributed to 'lack of fuel' might have raised further doubts. (Bolivian pilots are, in fact, considered to be amongst the best in the Americas and the national airline, Lloyd Aereo Boliviano, is the oldest in Latin America, but the physical conditions under which they operate and the country's airport facilities are amongst the world's poorest.) There was something decidedly double-edged about the attributes of a man who, on learning that three conscripts had died when their parachutes failed to open, went up and made the drop himself with the same equipment. Equally, Barrientos's renowned sexual appetite did little damage to his reputation at large, but when it led him to the spouses of his colleagues and alleged bigamy it began to cause disquiet beyond the disconsolate but mute church and even amongst the ranks of an officer corps rarely accused of either fidelity or sobriety. It has been said of Barrientos that, rather like Marshal Ky in Vietnam, he saw the country as one large aerodrome, but this ignores the general's powerful populist appeal which was significantly more important than his administrative or military capabilities.

It was in the countryside that the military and Barrientos in particular made the most headway in accumulating popular support. Paz had recognised from the beginning of his second term that he required solid peasant backing to counteract the threat of the miners. He therefore revived the agrarian reform, signing 200,413 titles between 1960 and 1964, compared with 47,746 issued between 1955 and 1960; there was a sixfold increase in the area distributed. But by continuing to rely upon the system of playing regional leaders off each other — Rojas against Veizaga in Cochabamba, the rising Felipe Flores against Toribio Salas in the *altiplano*, and Rubén Julio against Sandoval Morón in Santa Cruz — Paz was unable to reduce conflict in the countryside and still lacked a majority following. The Cochabamba valley continued to be blighted by violence to the extent that it remained a military zone through most of 1963. This enabled Barrientos, who was a *cochabambino* and proud of it, to take a central part in negotiating truces and distributing largesse. By September 1963 the airforce general had established himself so firmly in this role that he was able to fly the contending *caciques* to his house in La Paz, where they agreed to sink their differences, drank a champagne toast, and promised to support him as vice-presidential candidate with Paz in the 1964 elections.[45] Later the Cochabamba *campesino* federation nominated him as presidential candidate for 1968—72 without any reference to the MNR whatever.

Barrientos's efforts to gain the vice-presidential nomination appear to have been largely personal in motivation since the armed forces played only a minimal part in pushing his claim and a number of senior officers were clearly unhappy about its ramifications for the institution as a whole. On the other hand, there was little direct opposition within the officer corps since the general's ascendancy did hold out the promise of greater influence and an increased budget. Much greater opposition existed within the MNR itself; at the January 1964 party convention the issue generated such heat that the police had to be called in to stop brawls between the supporters of various candidates angling for a post that had acquired unusual importance because the presidency itself was already decided. In the event, Paz backed his faithful apparatchik Federico Fortún, who was able to muster the necessary votes through adept bureaucratic manoeuvre and strong-arm tactics. Barrientos declared to the press that the nomination 'was a mistake' and retired to the Bar España, where he got heartily drunk, burst into tears, and crushed a champagne glass between his fingers.

However, by early 1964 the rules governing politics had become so unstable that there was no guarantee that the Paz-Fortún ticket would stay intact for the six months up to the poll. As it happened, Barrientos's setback was reversed in an incident that typified the style of the man. Early on the morning of 25 February, in the midst of the conflict caused by the convention and under threat of losing his command, Barrientos was hit in the chest by a bullet as he was leaving the house of his sister in the Miraflores quarter of La Paz. It was quickly spread about that he would have been killed had the projectile not struck the 'silver wings' of the USAF badge that Barrientos wore on his uniform out of vanity and against regulations. The full truth of the matter will probably never be known since no Bolivian doctor ever examined any wound, the general being conveyed with remarkable speed in a USAF plane to a North American military hospital in the Panama Canal Zone where he underwent a 'lengthy operation'. He immediately became a hero, the 'silver bullet' affair generating such sympathy that within ten days Paz, who for all his sophistication could still read the political ground-rules astutely enough, unceremoniously dumped Fortún and cabled Barrientos that he had been designated as the new running-mate. Three weeks later he was standing on the balcony of the Palacio Quemado, declaring that, 'I will not allow the army to be an instrument of political machinations . . . my mission is to accompany and help Víctor Paz Estenssoro so that errors are not committed.'[46] The ambiguity of such words reflected the very uneasy relations that existed from the start between the two men, not least because General San Román, who headed the *Control Político* and disliked Barrientos intensely, was widely suspected of staging the several attacks that took place against Barrientos and Lechín over this period.

This unveiled reversion to gangsterism was underpinned by the consolidation of a strong anti-Paz coalition with which Barrientos maintained close and not very private relations despite the fact that he was running in an election that the *Bloque de Defensa del MNR* declared to be illegal and proceeded to boycott. The alliance extended well beyond the dissident factions of the MNR although its principal figureheads were Lechín, whose PRIN was not yet considered unalterably sundered from the old party, and Siles, who declared in

May that Paz should be replaced immediately and that an extraordinary congress should appoint an interim military administration to preside over fresh elections. Forces as different as the Falange and the POR (González) joined in building opposition to the re-election, with the FSB staging a rather tame but unmolested guerrilla in Santa Cruz and representatives of seven parties joining the re-energised Siles in his favourite ploy of a hunger strike. Once this tactic had failed and the official slate had won the poll, the tenor and scale of attacks changed. By August, Siles, recognising that the unity of the MNR was no longer a valid objective, was openly dedicated to cajoling Barrientos into rebellion, declaring that the Paz government was counter-revolutionary and had to be removed. For his pains he was exiled along with forty other oppositionists.

Paz's gamble on re-election failed; it united not the MNR but the right and left in their opposition to the ramshackle remnants of a party that no longer possessed any popularity beyond that generated through state patronage. The fact that Lechín as well as Siles appeared to perceive the only resolution to the problem in Barrientos was not as extraordinary as it might at first appear since of all the parties only the POR had argued consistently against the reconstruction of the army and any belief that it might resolve the crisis without recourse to dictatorship; the rest seemed to have their minds set on some reincarnation of Busch or Villarroel, an image Barrientos did much to encourage but which barely stood up to any cool examination.[47] Even the PCB, which certainly did not support a military solution of any type, appears to have misread the political situation in its one-sided and overly optimistic expectations of a new popular front during the last weeks of the Paz regime.[48] By this stage the military was patently waiting in the wings and would have had to have been directly attacked and marginalised if it were not to overthrow Paz in the same form as the Brazilian military had removed Joao Goulart for a conservative dictatorship in March 1964, an example which must have weighed heavily in the deliberations of the Bolivian officers.

By September Paz was obliged to rely on constant police action to keep control. Nearly a hundred opponents were exiled, political arrests were commonplace, and, with press attacks growing, censorship was imposed. This hardened a long-standing conflict with the teachers over pay that quickly escalated into a damaging strike and provoked the students into direct confrontation with the government.

In a series of demonstrations and street fights late in October, first in Cochabamba and then in Oruro and La Paz, some thirty people were killed. The majority were shot by the police although in Oruro the carabineros placed blame for casualties on 'the dynamite distributed by elements from San José which, given the inexperience of the students in the handling of this dangerous explosive, is causing grave injuries'.[49] Much of the preparation for these demonstrations was undertaken by the FSB's youth leader Guido Strauss but the left was also to the fore and provided many of the militants who engaged the police and *Control Político* in the streets. This contingent and unsought alliance was also evident on a wider plane: while the Falange's guerrilla made long and grandiose pronouncements from the countryside around Santa Cruz, lorryloads of miners from Siglo XX led by the POR engaged the army in a fierce battle at Sorasora, outside Oruro, to prevent a military occupation of the main camps. It may well have been this clash that determined the final timing of the coup.

Such a state of complete disorder allowed Barrientos — publicly at loggerheads with his president within weeks of the election — to stage a rebellion that he could direct specifically at Paz and generally in favour of order and liberty. Yet the final coup, which began on 2 November, took some time to spread: many commanders were still unsure of the strength of the militias and looked to the inscrutable and procrastinating Ovando for a lead. After a day and a night of 'negotiations', during which Ovando telephoned Paz to say that he was being held hostage in the high command, the army chief eventually arrived at the palace early on 4 November to escort the president to El Alto. Paz flew to Lima still believing that Ovando had remained loyal throughout, whereas he had in reality assessed the balance of forces and then thrown his administrative skills behind Barrientos's rather ill-organised insurrection.

Paz was not alone in his misunderstanding of the nature of the revolt; shortly after the president left the city, Lechín was carried at shoulder-height at the head of a large crowd of workers towards the Plaza Murillo, but they were prevented from approaching the palace by a volley from its new military occupants. In the ensuing melée the head of the COB lost a shoe. A few minutes later, according to the pro-MNR evening paper *Jornada*, an accommodating officer lent him a pair of military boots, the significance of which was not lost on the paper or, before too long, a much wider segment of the population.[50]

4.
THE LONG NIGHT

Aside from Barrientos's most ardent supporters — and in established political circles the majority were far from ardent — few Bolivians would contest the assertion that his regime (November 1964 to April 1969) was a dictatorship. Yet, like all dictatorships, this one had its own distinctive character. Although it was directed by the military, it was not a tight institutional movement of the type being erected at the time in Brazil and which would soon emerge in Argentina (under General Onganía in 1966). There was plenty of anti-communism but only the most rudimentary vestiges of a 'national security state' doctrine. The Bolivian army had been expanded rapidly but it still lacked the professional strengths of military institutions in the neighbouring states. Corporate ideology was backward-looking and served to temper but by no means to eradicate the personal ambitions of senior officers; it had not developed to the point where the armed forces could generate and realise a political project on their own. Repression was meted out in an ad hoc fashion and without sophistication. Hence, Barrientos was able to make the regime his own rather than that of the military as a whole. But his control was not so strong that he could marginalise the institutionalist sectors of the

From right to left General Juan José Torres, General Alfredo Ovando, General René Barrientos and Luis Adolfo Siles Salinas

army grouped around Ovando. This led to an erratic form of collaboration by which Ovando and Barrientos took power together on 4 November; Barrientos held it alone from the 5th, when the army commander was booed off the balcony on their first public appearance; Ovando regained joint control in May 1965 to strengthen the offensive against the COB; Barrientos withdrew from the presidency from January to August 1966 in order to fight an election, the post being held in the interim by Ovando, who finally stood down when Barrientos won a sweeping victory at the polls which gave him 'constitutional' status until his death in April 1969.

This uncertain mix of old-style *caudillismo* and institutional control was characteristic of a regime that in its form and dynamic stood between two political epochs. It was ramshackle and venal, endeavoured to be popular, and exercised much effort to retain a democratic veil in the style of the regimes of the 1940s. But under pressure from the Pentagon, and in the face of the continued threat posed by the labour movement, it constantly edged towards the forms of totalitarian authoritarianism that were to take root in the sub-continent in the 1970s. As a result, political activity was restricted but not entirely closed off, and everyday life was in general not subject to the torments that were to become commonplace a decade later throughout the southern cone; arbitrary arrests, torture and murder were much in evidence but usually directed at the leadership of the left and the unions rather than the population as a whole. At the same time the military became progressively insecure of the form its mission should take; the need for anti-communism was uncontested, but it remained open to doubt whether this should be undertaken in open collaboration with Washington or with a more independent, nationalist orientation. On the one hand, the Pentagon funded and trained the armed forces and the US represented the pinnacle of the 'free world', but its omnipotence was so manifest the collaboration increasingly appeared to be pure parasitism. On the other, many field officers had been educated under the MNR and imbued with a fundamentalist nationalism which was easily incorporated into institutional ideology and proffered a viable line of independent political development, but this threatened a rupture with Washington and required a collective self-confidence and organic cohesion which was still lacking in 1964. Barrientos was therefore able to adopt a resolutely pro-US strategy, and it was only after his death that the tensions this caused came into the open. For more than four years the armed forces adhered to and expanded Paz's policy of 'opening up' the economy, replacing the exhausted system of co-optation and negotiation with direct coercion. At root, the difference with the late MNR regimes rested on an exchange of the State Department for the Pentagon as the country's supervisor.

'Order Restored'

A direct offensive against the COB was not undertaken immediately. Between November 1964 and mid-May 1965 a form of armed truce prevailed; the military prepared to make a move, but was unsure of the outcome. It should be remembered that the conquests on which the COB's authority rested had existed for twelve years and had formed an integral part of the political consensus for much of that time. The *Control Político* was abolished immediately but the workers' militias remained intact and Barrientos was adamant from the start that the armed forces had effected a 'revolution in liberty' that would guarantee and dynamise the legacy of 1952. In the first few months the balance of forces was finer than may perhaps appear in retrospect, and it was not out of sheer deceit that Siles was fêted as an author of the rebellion, the parties of the left largely untroubled or even that Barrientos promised to study the restitution of *control obrero*. Indeed, immediately after the coup the PCB and PRIN joined the COB and parties of the right to form a *Comité Revolucionario del Pueblo*, which in the first instance provided unequivocal backing for the rising. Lidia Gueiler described it in the name of the *Comité* as 'essentially . . . popular, democratic and revolutionary . . . to fight against hunger, against the denial of liberty and justice, and for a social, political, and economic democracy . . .'.[1]

However, it was not long before the adoption of such a position by the parties that had the greatest influence inside the working class was revealed to be an error of historic proportions. The *Comité*'s manifesto outlining a return to the early days of the revolution was willingly approved by the junta, but within days of taking power Barrientos was demanding a 'spiritual and material disarming' of the miners. He received a blunt response from the FSTMB: 'Let them come to the mines and ask the workers for their arms. We will see if they hand them over. When a miner takes up a weapon he doesn't give it away for anything in the world.'² Barrientos's reaction was to tour the camps, dispensing with the services of his bodyguards in a typical act of bravado. He gladly accepted the petitions thrust upon him and expressed a desire to 'get rid of all misunderstandings. You ought to come to the palace to discuss all your problems. We are not going to jail anybody.'³ Some leaders, such as the recently-released Pimentel, praised the new president but the rank and file were deeply suspicious, the overwhelming majority of the union leadership drawing back from any commitment and demanding a show of good faith.

It never came. On the contrary, over the first months of 1965 official invectives against 'extremists' and 'anarchosyndicalist irresponsibility' signalled the regime's direction. By April Lechín had become a clear target, the ministry of the interior declaring that Lechín was in reality a Chilean, which was considered a particularly efficacious slur by a government that like so many military regimes limited its 'nationalism' to invectives against the neighbouring state and strident demands for an exit to the sea. The COB did not respond; indeed, the left was totally outmanoeuvred during this interim period.

By mid-May the threat of a descent into dictatorship was so manifest that, in the face of the COB's inactivity, the miners, factory and construction workers and teachers joined with the *gastronómicos* — whose influence should not be underestimated in a country where eating is highly socialised — to form a pact in defence of basic union rights.⁴ The students continued to support the junta but their backing was not to last for long. On 15 May, three days after the establishment of the pact, Lechín was seized in a midnight raid on his house and put on a plane to Paraguay. A general strike was called but in the cities the lack of preparation was telling and the stoppage failed to take root. It was in the mines that resistance was strongest and where the army concentrated its forces. All camps were declared military zones on 16 May, and with good reason since it was not until the 23rd that the militias had been completely overrun and the troops had control. Even in camps like Viloco and Colquiri, not normally highly militant, fighting was fierce: it was plain that all the gains of nationalisation were now under assault; losses on both sides were high.

The high command issued a statement that was to be the blueprint for future military declarations as to its policy in the mines: 'The workers of the mines are one thing; the leaders are quite another. To the men of the mining rank and file and to honourable leaders we will give every assistance. The extremist leaders will be expelled without mercy because they destroy the political and social stability of the country. . . . In this action alone the armed forces did more than the MNR in its 12 years and therefore deserve the recognition of Bolivians.'[5] The 'liquidation' of the FSTMB, COB and the majority of its affiliates was declared on 17 May, many union and political leaders being exiled or jailed over the following week. On 23 May the new president of Comibol, Colonel Lechín Suárez (Juan Lechín Oquendo's half-brother), sacked all union leaders and announced the end of 'an extremist dictatorship' in the mines.[6] These moves were ratified by the decree of 23 September which prohibited the existence of all but government-controlled worker organisations and expressly forbade anyone who had occupied any political position to hold union office. The FSTMB was badly defeated but not completely smashed, although it would be five years before it fully recovered its rights and authority over the rank and file. The leadership was either exiled or went underground, and many militants were forced to scrape a clandestine living by *jukeo*, the theft of ore by night-time mining which was almost a traditional occupation for unemployed workers.[7] With the aid of the students, who as a result of the 'real coup' of 16 May were turning to the left in large numbers for the first time since 1946, the FSTMB organised a conference of clandestine unions in September, but this was a very partial achievement in the face of a full retreat by the workers' movement. An entire generation of miners was experiencing military occupation and control for the first time, making underground reorganisation a slow and painful process dependent on secondary cadres without great experience or reputation. In September a correspondent from the moderate Catholic daily *Presencia* went to Siglo XX, where instead of the militant proletariat which regularly elected communists and Trotskyists to its leadership he found 'massive demoralisation. . . . I asked the workers why they were not organising their unions. The replies were more or less the same: Because all those who were elected have been sacked. We choose the most responsible, the most serious, those who speak best, even against their own will so that they can represent us, and in a few days they're out. Why should we do more harm to our comrades?'[8] This sense of fear had been sown by the execution in July of César Lora, who had stayed on in the mining zone to piece together a clandestine union in Siglo but soon fell victim to a well-organised man-hunt, being captured and shot near the village of

San Pedro. On 18 September, two months after Lora's assassination, the rank and file of Siglo XX tried to break the military occupation of the camp. A detachment of workers took control of the police station at Llallagua and seized sufficient weapons to drive back the troops sent from Catavi. In the exchange of fire eighty people died and two hundred were wounded; that night the army was forced to pull back and await air support. The miners took possession of the Catavi barracks and further stocks of arms and ammunition. It was, however, a vain effort. The next day reinforcements brought in from Santa Cruz recaptured Llallagua and Siglo, followed not long after by Catavi. The repression was fierce; in all two hundred people died in the three days of fighting. Small wonder that the *Presencia* journalist found demoralisation; the delayed reaction to the May intervention had been a valiant but resounding failure. The security services stepped up their activity, restricting rank-and-file organisation and running the clandestine leadership to ground. In 1966 Federico Escóbar died in mysterious circumstances, and in July 1967 Lora's *porista* comrade Isaac Camacho was killed by the secret police.[9]

The sense of defeat in the mines was not only bred by repression, the destruction of the unions and the assassination of their leaders, but also by the huge cut in wages that lay behind them and was implemented to push through the last stages of the Triangular Plan, held over from 1963. The decree of May 1965 ordained that from 1 June 1965 all wage scales and contracts would be revised to the levels in force in the mine of Quechisla in August 1964 — that is, to the level of the worst-paid mine at the worst time of the year. For workers in the major pits — Siglo XX, Huanuni, Colquiri, San José — this meant a wage cut of between 40 and 50 per cent. The measure was rigorously enforced and, as the figures in Table 3 show, had a telling effect. The regime produced much documentation to prove the 'corruption', wastefulness and drain on resources caused by the FSTMB, but even after the removal of the union and a cut of 15 per cent in all pithead costs, Comibol's losses and debt continued to rise.[10]

Barrientos assured the miners the cut would be limited to six months; it remained in force for a period ten times as long. He also offered a bonus equal to roughly half the daily basic wage, but in order to qualify for this workers had to work seven full days a week all months, a requirement that was not technically impossible since the government eventually found a miner who had completed the task and was duly

Table 3

Comibol Average Wages 1965

	Jan-April		July-Dec	
	No. Employees	Wage (Bs.)	No. Employees	Wage (Bs.)
Face Workers	8,529	867	8,076	527
Face Employees	623	1,221	554	1,086
Mill Workers	2,586	589	2,551	486
Mill Employees	575	970	498	662
Surface Workers	4,531	514	4,711	452
Surface Employees	4,587	862	4,074	690
Total	21,431		20,464	
Average		770		407

Source: Estudio Sociológico de los Centros Mineros de Comibol; Salarios y Costos de Vida (La Paz, June 1970) p. 13.

regaled as an Andean Stakhanov. Since the bulk of what meagre social security arrangements existed inside Comibol were revoked there was a notable lack of desire to work continuous 56-hour weeks and rapidly exhaust an already extremely short working life in order to gain a wage similar to the basic before May. The regime's much-vaunted 'profit-sharing' scheme did little to ameliorate the situation, amounting to a rise of four pesos for interior workers and two for surface workers in December 1965, increased to five in December 1966.[11] In view of this, it is not surprising that the government's efforts to establish a yellow trade-union apparatus came to nought or that even among those miners who supported parties close to the regime little heed was paid to the declaration of the ruling generals: 'Without any demagogic intent, we can assure you, in complete frankness, that the present sacrifices will rebound to your benefit later since when production increases . . . pay will be bettered. . . . Now that the red leaders have been eliminated, fleeing in terror of having to answer for their crimes after many years of tricking and exploiting you, we ask you not to listen to the few extremists that still remain and will continue with their old tactics of lies, intrigues and incitement to violence.'[12] One effect of this offensive was a displacement of the priests working in the major mines from a position of basic anti-communism, which had shaded into anti-unionism, to a more sympathetic attitude towards the rank and file as a whole rather than just their converts. This was marked by a lessening in anti-left propaganda broadcast by the religious radio stations, particularly Pio XII in Siglo. In time this would lead to the open defence of militants and direct conflict with the military.

The regime's labour policy was matched by an emphatic opening up of the economy to foreign capital. In the mining sector the two most notorious cases were concessions to US firms, the International Mining and Processing Corporation (IMPC) and Philips Brothers, a subsidiary of US Steel. In 1966 Barrientos ceded to IMPC full rights to process and export the Catavi *colas y desmontes*, the huge slagheaps of ore which could only be reclaimed through the use of sophisticated smelting techniques and which were at the time valued at $3,500 million. The price for access to a resource of such strategic value to Bolivia was the payment of a royalty of 12 per cent to the state and 8 per cent to Comibol. The concession of the Mina Matilde to Philips caused an even greater outcry since it was to last for a full twenty years and give the firm access to rich deposits of zinc, lead, silver and cadmium valued at a minimum of $200 million, for a rent of only $120,000 a year and $2.2 per ton shipped. The firm was limited to processing certain quantities of ore, which at current market rates had a value of $15 million a year, payments to the state being 1.6 per cent of export value. Moreover, Philips benefited immediately from several years of preparatory work and maintenance undertaken by Comibol at a cost of $5 million, a sum that would only just be recouped by the state over the entire period of the concession.[13] These deals were so clearly prejudicial to Bolivia's interests that they caused much consternation even inside the armed forces and the FSB; they were politically inept as well as economically disastrous.

By 1967 private mining companies accounted for 24 per cent of the country's mineral production. The influx of foreign banks — First City National, Banco Boliviano Americano and Bank of America were the most powerful — had an even more pronounced effect: by 1969 they controlled 58 per cent of national deposits. Yet, while the government and its allies painted a picture of ever-increasing investment, the country had become a net exporter of capital; between 1965 and 1968 private foreign capital investment amounted to $27.7 million while repatriated profits exceeded $320 million. Additionally, the public external debt had increased by around 70 per cent: by 1968 annual repayments of principal and interest had reached $50 million, one third the value of Bolivia's exports.

Discontent was also directed at Barrientos's policy for the oil industry although this was more the result of a long-term weakness with respect to foreign capital, having its origins in the 1955 *Código Davenport*. By 1954 YPFB was producing sufficient oil to meet all the country's needs except for aviation fuel, and production maintained its level throughout the 1950s. However, by the early 1960s the state corporation's lack of exploration placed it in an increasingly vulnerable position with regard to Gulf Oil, which was the only company to strike oil of the 14 which had bought 1.2 million hectares of concessions after 1955. In December 1966 Gulf began to pump oil to Arica and from there to California. Gulf's agreement with the Bolivian state gave it extremely light tax liabilities and the right to repatriate 79.3 per cent of all profits, an extraordinarily generous deal which greatly weakened YPFB. Thus, by 1968 YPFB's reserves were 33 million barrels against Gulf's 187 million. The state company had invested $38 million in its entire operation while the foreign firm was spending $120 million on exploration alone. Under Barrientos the failure to protect nationalised enterprises even to the degree managed by Paz saw the share of oil production in 1964 of 3 per cent to Gulf and over 95 per cent to YPFB change in three years to 82 per cent to Gulf and less than 20 per cent to YPFB.[14] As with the mining contracts this was the cause of much disquiet inside certain military circles while the left, which until mid-1967 was still able to make its voice heard, campaigned effectively against the 'sell outs' of a regime that was entirely in the pocket of Wall Street and the Pentagon.

It was not difficult to give substance to such accusations not simply with reference to private enterprise but also to bilateral state relations. For example, the Barrientos government's acceptance of US imports of wheat and other foodstuffs damaged the plans for self-sufficiency in staple crops drawn up under the agrarian reform. In 1967 only 22 per cent of all rice consumed was produced in the country; in 1968 20 per cent of US imports worth $158.6 million were food-stuffs. As with oil, it should be recognised that the basis for such a state of affairs was laid by the MNR, which had presided over a process that saw national flour production fall from 57,000 tons in 1956 to 7,000 in 1962 while imports rose from 14,800 tons to 111,000 over the same period. The debt to the US for flour reached $23.6 million in 1964, imports from the US being nine times greater than those from Argentina despite the fact that they were 50 per cent more expensive.[15] In line with Paz's decree of August 1963, trading relations with the US were given top priority; in 1968 over 40 per cent of all imports came from the US and 42 per cent of exports went there.

The amount of direct US financial aid to the Barrientos regime did not increase greatly because the rise in tin prices caused by the Vietnam war gave the state a somewhat wider margin of manoeuvre with respect to revenue. However, collaboration on the ground took an ever more visible form. The North American military presence was increased, with the US army acquiring a radio communications station at El Alto which became popularly known as 'Guantanamito' after the US base of Guantánamo in Cuba. The Peace Corps was given free rein and under the auspices of US AID, which throughout the 1960s persisted in the belief that Latin America's problem stemmed from high birth rates, began to introduce contraception and sterilisation into the countryside. This enforcement of an arrogant and unthinking malthusianism in a country of less than five million people and over four times the size of the British Isles quite naturally caused a severe backlash, the subject of Jorge Sanjinés's film *Blood of the Condor*. The regime also received encouragement to develop its apparatus of control. Between 1964 and 1966 the cost of maintaining the state bureaucracy more than doubled with the monthly pay of an army lieutenant being more than twice the average annual per capita income ($120) and four times the salary of the highest grade of teacher.[16] Under Barrientos the economy grew at roughly the same pace as the rest of Latin America and inflation remained low, but the debt continued to climb, income distribution became increasingly inequitable and social spending fell. The policy of hiving off the most profitable sectors of the nationalised industries to foreign enterprise failed to provide an answer to structural underdevelopment and accelerated the depreciation of valuable resources with the most minimal gains accruing to the state. Economic planning in this sector subsided into little more than streamlining plunder; the country's economy took on an aura of stagnation, corruption and decline.

A similar atmosphere prevailed at the political level although after August 1966 the government was nominally constitutional and parliament functioned, giving the few opposition deputies the chance to voice criticism even if this was often punished with spells in jail. Barrientos was never able to stitch together a coherent coalition of civilian forces and was obliged to construct a number of his own political parties, the existence of which was transient in the extreme. The most important of these was the *Movimiento Popular Cristiano* (MPC) which formed the centre-piece of the *Frente Revolucionario Barrientista* (FRB), under which name the general's various cabinets conducted their business. Of the parties of the right only the FSB failed to enter the regime, apparently because its relative strength gave it too much bargaining power and independence. However, the FSB maintained close links with Ovando, both sides exploiting the connection in their manoeuvres to gain advantage over Barrientos. Besides the military, a number of technocrats, and camp-followers in the MPC, the regime received most of its support from the 'Taxi-parties' (so called because their membership was not considered to exceed the capacity of a city cab) of the reconstructed PIR and the *Partido Social Demócrata* (PSD) as well as from Walter Guevara's PRA and the conservative *Partido Demócrata Cristiano* (PDC). The PIR, now headed by Ricardo Anaya, adhered to a 'pure Marxism' which evidently stipulated support for a military dictatorship — which, in this case, returned the compliment by giving its blessing only to 'pure Marxism' — and bore little resemblance even to the policies adopted by the party at its reformation in 1956; its entry into government was the death knell of a political current that had decomposed into complete opportunism and lacked followers beyond a few aged and pious survivors from the 1940s. The PSD was even smaller. Having been founded during the late 1940s in a belated attempt to give the Rosca a more flexible vehicle with which to challenge the MNR, it had made no impact in popular circles. But it numbered amongst its leaders men such as Luis Adolfo Siles Salinas, half-brother of Hernán Siles, René Ballivián Calderón, a senior employee of Aramayo and leading financial adviser to Barrientos, Rolando Kempf Mercado, an influential oil executive, and Roberto Arce, a founding-member and senior UN official. The party therefore possessed an influence out of all proportion to its size and acted as a vital conduit between the regime and US commercial interests. To this link were added Guevara's more political contacts, although once the PRA joined Barrientos it lost much of the popular support inherited from the MNR days. The PDC, on the other hand, had accumulated an appreciable following over the last years of the

Movimiento. Having been founded as the *Partido Social Cristiano* in 1954, the party expanded from the early 1960s under the leadership of men such as Remo di Natale, Luis Ossio and Benjamín Miguel as a moderate alternative to the Falange and with particular strength in student circles. More cautious than its sister parties in the rest of the hemisphere — and significantly less adventurous than the Chilean party in power at the time under the presidency of Eduardo Frei (1964–70) — the PDC soon found itself badly shaken by the experience of participating in a military government as opposed to calling for individual freedoms and democracy from a far less autocratic MNR. As with the rest of the right, the PDC paid the price for an enthusiastic and remunerative embracing of military patronage in an almost Pavlovian response to the fall of the MNR. Under Barrientos Christian Democracy began to lose the support of its youth wing, which was progressively drawn to the radical alternatives developing in the region more on the basis of doctrinal egalitarianism and the rise of liberation theology than through contact with the orthodox left.

This coalition was neither forceful nor steady; each party took its turn to dissociate itself from one action or another of Barrientos, but none had the political resources or will to make a definitive break. Even the general's own MPC finally collapsed in 1967 through squabbles over jobs, being replaced by an even more ephemeral *Partido Agrario Laborista de Izquierda Cristiana* (PALIC), the precise ideological position of which was apparently too sophisticated to merit a programme. In practice these parties provided a pluralist veneer and a caucus of bureaucrats for a government that drew its domestic strength from the military and peasantry.

When Barrientos held elections in July 1966, the peasants hoisted him to constitutional office with 63 per cent of the poll, well ahead of the Falange's candidate, the aged Chaco war hero General Bernardino Bilbao Rioja. Although there was the traditional use of fraud, coercion, petty bribery and manipulation of the media, it should be noted that the left contested the poll. It was, however, disastrously divided, the PCB putting up its own candidates under the banner of the *Frente de Liberación Nacional* (FLIN) and refusing to join the united front erected by the PRIN, the POR, the Maoists, the MNR left and the independent socialists of the *Grupo Espártaco*, which banded together to form the *Comité Democrático del Pueblo* (CODEP). Neither front gained any congressional seats, the MNR itself only managing to take a handful — principally from Paz's base in Tarija — and the parliamentary opposition came to depend quite heavily on the voice of a few independents, the most vocal of whom was the aristocratic young writer Marcelo Quiroga Santa Cruz, and the dissident falangists. Repression played a large part in this lack of electoral success but it does not fully explain the victory of the *oficialista* ticket which derived from the general's popularity not just with the leadership of the peasant *sindicatos* but with many of the rank and file as well.

We have already noted the origins of this alliance in the early 1960s. Under the Barrientos regime it was consolidated by diligent patronage and formalised in what became known as the *Pacto Militar-Campesino*, by which, 'the Armed Forces will ensure that the conquests achieved by the majority classes, such as the Agrarian Reform, basic education, union rights and others, are respected . . . [the peasants] will support and defend, firmly and loyally, the military institution under all circumstances. They will put themselves under military orders against the subversive manoeuvres of the left.'[17] Barrientos spent much of his time in the *campo*, hopping from village to village in a helicopter donated by Gulf Oil which he named Holofernes, less out of any classical allusion than because this had been the title bestowed upon the white charger of the nineteenth-century populist tyrant Mariano Melgarejo (1864–71), who shared the airforce general's birthplace of Tarata and was similarly dependent upon a power-base in the Cochabamba valley. Although Barrientos's peripatetic campaigning, 'down-to-earth' speeches, and liberal distribution of footballs, tv sets and bicycles certainly played their part, it is clear that these would have been of strictly marginal value were it not for the clientelist network inherited from the MNR. Yet, as Table 4 shows, Barrientos did not accelerate the agrarian reform, preferring to award larger plots to fewer people in a more discrete exploitation of the statute for political ends. General Banzer would later adopt the same policy.

The support given to the strategic *campesino* leaders required the imposition of a hierarchical structure of patronage, close screening and control of local dignitaries, and persecution of dissidents and independent forces. It was during this period that the personalist and regionally-orientated divisions in the peasant movement were made more complex by the emergence of a 'nationalist' strata of *campesino* leaders who were pledged to the *Pacto* and owed their influence to the army. This tradition was to prove surprisingly durable and was a

Table 4

Land Distribution by Regime, 1955–74

		% titles	% area	Average title size (hectares)
1955–59	MNR	9.8	4.9	19.1
1960–64	MNR	39.8	27.6	26.4
1965–69	Barrientos/Siles	14.8	21.1	54.3
1970–71	Ovando/Torres	17.7	14.9	32.2
1972–74	Banzer	17.8	31.5	67.6

Source: Servicio Nacional de Reforma Agraria, 1975, quoted in Javier Albó, *Bodas de Plata o Requiem por una Reforma Agraria?* (La Paz 1979) p. 42.

constant impediment to the development both of radical currents and of independent union organisation in the countryside. Nevertheless, the very fact that such a system had to be imposed and did very little indeed to improve the lot of the rural masses signalled a structural weakness that would in time become critical.

With his electoral triumph, the efficient dismantling of the COB and suppression of the left, a secure alliance with the peasant leaders and Washington, and continued guidance from a generally tame cluster of conservative politicians, the Barrientos regime seemed set at the end of 1966 for four years of relatively untroubled rule. There were a number of discontented and ambitious army officers cloistered about the enigmatic Ovando, and the students were demonstrably moving to the left, but these were not exceptional problems given the achievement of having reversed the 'subversive legacy' of 1952. The peasantry was quiescent and the proletariat still in retreat although in the mines a number of concessions, such as the returning of the radio stations, had been wrested from the government and some militants were beginning to resurface. An assessment of the balance of forces that forecast the continued stability and obscurity of an unremark-able South American military regime and predicted the definitive demise of the traditions born of 1952 would at the time have seemed entirely plausible. It was not to be. Precisely at that stage when the country's radical and popular forces were at their lowest ebb and it was ruled by a singularly undistinguished regime, Bolivia came to the centre of attention of a world which may have identified it as Latin

American but was scarcely familiar with its exact location, let alone its politics.

Ñancahuazú

Shortly before 2 p.m. on 8 October 1967 a radio message was relayed through to the headquarters of the army's eighth division tactical group at the colonial town of Vallegrande in western Santa Cruz. The message was for the divisional commander, Colonel Joaquín Zenteno Anaya, and had been picked up by a nearby field station in the hamlet of Abra del Picacho. It was brief but distinct: 'This is *flaco*. Attention, this is *flaco*. I have *Papa*. Over.' The voice was that of Captain Gary Prado Salmón, a US-trained officer of the elite Ranger regiment. Prado was speaking from an isolated spot some forty kilometres to the south of Vallegrande, a ravine known as Quebrada del Yuro; his message informed Zenteno that the Bolivian army had finally captured the world's most celebrated guerrilla, the Argentine Ernesto 'Ché' Guevara. Guevara was wounded in the leg and suffering from an acute attack of asthma, but he was alive. With him was a young miner from Huanuni, Simón Cuba, whose *nomme de guerre* was Willy. Willy had acted as Ché's bodyguard, carrying him on his back during their last desperate effort to evade the circle of troops closing in around the remnants of the guerrilla force in the broken country south of Vallegrande. Together with a third fighter, *El Chino* (the Peruvian Juan Pablo Chang), these men were executed some 24 hours later in the schoolroom of the village of La Higuera. That day — 9 October — and 24 June — the feast of St John the Baptist and midwinter's day, but also the night of a well-planned massacre in Siglo XX — remain two of the most prominent dates in the calendar of Bolivia's political memory; both are drawn from 1967.

Yet Guevara's death was essentially an international event, reported by many journalists who were visiting this obscure country for the first time because of him, and mourned by millions who, in the spirit of his internationalism, paid no immediate heed to the precise locality of his demise. This fact registered in Bolivia, but no more so than the concrete impact of Ché's last campaign at Ñancahuazú. Guevara's unique reputation and remarkable influence had the effect of turning what was in most respects a desultory and quixotic military episode bordering on a complete shambles into a dangerously public and embarrassing threat. In the event, not even the legendary guerrilla fighter could overcome the difficulties he himself played a large part in creating, but he succeeded in shaking the Barrientos regime and bequeathing a legacy which would be taken up inside the country as well as abroad.

Guevara and Ñancahuazú drew the spotlight onto Bolivia for a brief period and much has been written about the event, but of foreign authors only Régis Debray, a leading protagonist in the affair, has drawn out its domestic content and ramifications.[18] It is somewhat ironical that Debray, who was pilloried by the right and hectored by the left for the abstract and essentially idealist character of his defence of the *foco* strategy employed by Ché, should have written two years before the campaign that the unique conditions in Bolivia following 1952 meant that the rural guerrilla would play a subordinate part to revolutionary movements in the traditional proletarian centres.[19] In the event, neither he nor Ché paid sufficient attention to this observation; indeed, many of the problems that dogged the guerrilla resulted from factors that had their origins outside the country even if they were only to take concrete form in the rugged backlands of Santa Cruz.

The *foco* theory itself was grounded in the experience of the Cuban revolution. As theorised by Debray, who transformed the actions of Castro and Guevara into a complete politico-military system, the *foco* inverted the traditional Leninist schema on which the Latin American communist parties had constructed their strategies; it elevated the rural over the urban, the peasantry over the proletariat, and revolutionary violence over organisational manoeuvre. Crystallised in the French philosopher's *Revolution in the Revolution* (1966), the pragmatic tactics of the Cuban rebels in the Sierra Maestra took the shape of an alternative strategy for the left whereby small groups of dedicated fighters would be implanted in the countryside, proletarianise themselves and revolutionise the peasantry in the course of a mobile war that would whittle down the unity and effectiveness of the armed forces and dynamise the contradictions in the system of control through a series of escalating crises. This thesis, it should be noted, drew a number of motifs from the Chinese and Vietnamese revolutions, but it was most directly derived from the Cuban example, which was at the time considered valid for the rest of the sub-continent.

Even before the opening of the Bolivian campaign the left was engaged in a violent polemic over the *foco*, already being essayed in Guatemala, Colombia, Peru and Venezuela.[20] In every case tensions had increased inside the local CPs, the leaderships of which remained tied to Cuba but often at variance with the 'export' of its revolutionary methods and determinedly jealous of their national authority. In the case of Venezuela this had led to particularly deep divisions and open conflict with the Havana leadership.

This is not the place to trace in detail the trajectory of these debates and their effect on the ground. However, we should note that by 1966, when Guevara had returned from a short trip to Africa to advise on the war in the Congo, his position on revolutionary strategy was moving away even from that of the Cuban leadership, which had come under considerable pressure during the Sino-Soviet split to mirror its economic dependence on Moscow with a more balanced policy towards the sister parties in the rest of Latin America. Originally Havana was inclined towards the Chinese position since this appeared to parallel its own criticism of the Latin American parties, which continued to reject the *foco* as adventurist and anti-Leninist. At the time of the split Cuba's neutrality was obtained by a subtle form of words which placed it in the Moscow camp but enabled it to continue pursuing a relatively independent line in its own sphere. Thus, Guevara and Castro were still formally at one, but in practice and personal disposition Castro was backing away from Ché's inflexible insistence on making the revolution through the *foco* with a determined internationalist orientation and little if any regard for the position of the regional CPs, an approach that in many respects put him closer to Peking than to Moscow. Guevara's poor record in state management as minister of industry and his subsequent travels abroad further underpinned this orientation towards permanent engagement and the risks of direct action. Although there was never an open rupture, Castro allowed Ché to go his own way, financed and publicly backed him but desisted from whole-hearted support.

These discernible differences of emphasis at the Cuban end were not themselves the direct cause of Guevara's lack of local support and political isolation in Bolivia, but they served to exacerbate the substantial difficulties caused by the divisions in the communist movement. Guevara was certainly hampered by the fact that at the OLAS Havana conference in January 1966 Castro ensured that a delegation from CODEP, amongst whose members were Lidia Gueiler and Guillermo Lora and which had been directly assisted by the Chilean socialist leader Salvador Allende, was prohibited from taking its place, subjected to a number of attacks and then flown out to Canada. Later Debray himself identified this as a crucial mistake, depriving the guerrilla of support from a non-aligned left that was still very influential.[21] Castro fully backed the FLIN delegation composed exclusively of the pro-Moscow PCB; but, as it soon became clear, this party required more than expulsions from international conferences to aid it in resisting the attacks of Bolivia's Maoist party, the PCML.

In Bolivia the ideological content of the Sino-Soviet split played only a minor part in splitting the PCB. Since late 1963 a dissident tendency had been taking shape under the leadership of Raúl Ruíz González, Luis Arratia, and the *tarijeño* student leader Oscar Zamora Medinacelli, who, as an official of the International Students' Union, had developed close ties with Peking. This group's attacks on the PCB's vacillating stance with regard to the MNR and its 'revisionist deviations from Leninism' soon attracted key union militants like Federico Escóbar and many of the party's student militants, making it a force to be reckoned with. In August 1964 four members of the PCB's central committee were expelled, and by 1965 the new party had taken concrete form, being led by Zamora into adopting a pro-Chinese line to supplement its attacks on the PCB's reformism at home. Zamora had formed part of the expelled CODEP delegation to Havana as a representative of the PCML, but even by mid-1967, nearly 18 months later, he still hoped for improved relations with Cuba and offered aid to Guevara despite the lack of contact with Castro, who dealt solely with the PCB's leadership, Mario Monje, Jorge Kolle Cueto and Simón Reyes.

Although the PCB had a monopoly on political and material support from Havana, it failed to provide more than token backing for Guevara, who had by mid-1966 already established a preliminary presence in La Paz. This may be explained in part by the fact that Ché's scouting party of the Cubans Ricardo and Pombo, in charge of making party links and recruiting, and Debray, charged with surveying likely areas of activity and making an overall socio-political assessment, manifested an independent outlook and maintained contacts with the PCML. However, a more deep-seated reason was that the PCB itself was extremely wary of the guerrilla tactic and very anxious to keep control of operations in its own national territory. Relations were made even more tense by the fact that these initially suppressed sentiments were, until January 1967, channelled almost exclusively through the person of Mario Monje, the party secretary who handled finances from Cuba and promised Castro that he would help the operation but who remained ignorant of its intended scope and the presence of Guevara until the campaign was effectively under way.

It was, as a result, hardly surprising that the PCB, now perceiving a danger of losing ground and prestige to Cubans as well as Maoists and Trotskyists, played a waiting game and hedged its bets. Monje offered to join the guerrilla himself and, at Castro's request, initially lent the services of four of the best cadres in the party, amongst them Roberto (Coco) and Guido (Inti) Peredo Leigue. But as early as 24 September 1966 matters had become so fraught that the Cuban contact in La Paz, Pombo (Captain Harry Villegas), noted in his diary that he had told Monje, '1. They (the PCB) have shown no confidence in guerrilla warfare; 2. They have made no effort to organise themselves, rather, they view it all as not solving anything. They added that they had been concentrating all their efforts towards a general uprising and considered guerrilla warfare as secondary. We asked them what they had done to date; they replied: "Nothing". We told them that we could not sit around for twenty years waiting for them.'[22]

Thus, the campaign began with the guerrillas strengthened by a small number of trusted PCB militants who had studied in Cuba and been drafted in before their party had grasped the significance of the operation, but they were not subsequently added to and relations deteriorated further still once fighting began. Some recruits were gathered from other political circles but Zamora eventually failed to deliver a PCML contingent, the 'Maoists' often referred to as fighting with Ché being a group that was headed by an ex-miner, Moisés Guevara, already expelled from the PCML. Moisés Guevara was unable to recruit any of his ex-comrades and so drafted in friends and contacts, whose aptitude he did not question closely; as a consequence this group turned out to be the least reliable of the fighters, numbered only nine out of a promised forty, and provided several key deserters. At its peak the guerrilla numbered 29 Bolivians and 18 Cubans.

There is little doubt that in spite of the later lengthy and formally correct rationalisations of its conduct, the PCB failed to support Guevara out of sectarian interest as well as programmatic differences.

Yet, Ché and his aides proved remarkably insensitive to the predictable difficulties, some of which were certainly due to their singularly unbending attachment to the *foco* and ingrained distrust of what was, after all, one of the weakest and most cautious of the Latin American parties. However, Guevara's attitude may also be explained by the relative lack of importance he gave to Bolivia itself compared with the continental movement which would radiate from it. As Debray later wrote, Ché's principal objective was not to seize power in Bolivia but to develop there a nucleus of campaigns in several of the five surrounding countries. Bolivia's geopolitical situation made it ideal in this sense, and Guevara clearly intended to regenerate the collapsed guerrillas in Argentina and Peru as well as initiate activity in Brazil. This Bolivarian schema was excessively ambitious since only in Peru had any previous guerrilla activity shown even temporary signs of success in the early 1960s.[23]

In itself this project must have reduced Ché's sensitivity both to specifically Bolivian conditions and to the claims of its local communist party. But Guevara's choice of the *foco*'s original site must also be understood to be a result of his experience of visiting La Paz in 1953, when the revolution was at its height and much of the country in the hands of the popular militias. Compared with that memory and the relatively greater stability of the regimes in the neighbouring states, Barrientos's corrupt and unpopular regime appeared a particularly inviting target despite the low level of working-class mobilisation.

Guevara entered Bolivia from Brazil late in October 1966 on a Uruguayan passport made out in the name of Adolfo Mena González, a 'special envoy of the Organisation of American States'. Disguised as a balding, bespectacled technocrat, Ché was able to move about freely and even to obtain credentials from the president's own office. His arrival accelerated preparations for the establishment of a base in the countryside, which he and the Cubans, who were now congregating in La Paz after a variety of well-disguised routes from Havana, were eager to set up.

Debray had surveyed three potential sites during a brief visit in September. The first was in the Alto Beni region in the north of the department of La Paz, quite densely populated, close to urban centres and with countryside suitable for a guerrilla campaign. Debray himself seems to have preferred this site, and Coco Peredo had even acquired some property there, but it was eventually ruled out, partly because there was a strong military presence but also because the PCB leadership, still in close contact with the Peredo brothers, had learnt of the plan and this was considered dangerous.[24] The second zone was in the Chaparé region of eastern Cochabamba and in key respects similar to the Alto Beni. Ché eventually chose the third site, Ñancahuazú, on the borders of the departments of Chuquisaca and Santa Cruz. Peredo had also bought a sizeable farm there, and the site offered the possibility of moving across the vital Santa Cruz–Cochabamba highway into Chaparé as well as east to Brazil or south through the oil region based on Camiri to the Paraguayan and Argentine borders. From an expansionist viewpoint Ñancahuazú was the most appealing centre.

However, it would have been harder to find in all Bolivia an area less well suited to the fighting of a guerrilla war, especially by the *foco* method. Its selection was almost inconceivable from this angle as both Debray (in retrospect) and many of his critics have pointed out at some length. The area was one of broken hill chains, complex river systems and deep ravines; it offered good cover but was extraordinarily difficult to traverse and had no defensible perimeter. It possessed very little game and, unlike the Sierra Maestra, had few wild fruits. From a socio-political point of view it was distinct insofar as it was very sparsely populated and in that those peasants living there held land in adequate quantities, were highly parochial in outlook, distanced from national political developments, and had never demonstrated any deep-seated discontent or proclivity for radical politics.[25] At no stage during the campaign (November 1966 to October 1967) did any local peasant join as a combatant, although many were happy to sell the guerrillas food (at highly inflated prices) and several betrayed them. As a result, the force never grew, and with the cumulative effects of desertion and illness it soon became too small to undertake effective military activity in the zone itself, let alone to expand operations. Throughout 1967 these factors became increasingly important and relieved the ill-organised Bolivian army of much of its task of wearing down and isolating the rebels; in the last phase of fighting (July to October 1967) some military units were making use of the terrain and peasant contacts in a manner closer to the Cuban experience than were the rebels.

Some of the basic problems of the zone must have been evident by the end of 1966, when the bulk of the force transferred from La Paz to Ñancahuazú. But initial preparations in the setting up of secondary camps and stores, bomb-making, scouting, cutting paths, training the recruits and dividing up tasks proceeded well and consumed much energy and time. At this stage the group also had radio contact with Havana, a network in La Paz (headed by Loyola Guzmán of the PCB youth wing), and contact with the oil town of Camiri through 'Tania' (Laura Gutiérrez Bauer, an East German who had been in the country for two years and had very good cover both in La Paz as a student and in Camiri as a disc-jockey on a late night lonely-hearts programme on which she transmitted coded messages).

It was in the midst of these busy preparations that Mario Monje arrived at the camp escorted by Tania and Ché's principal Cuban lieutenant, Ricardo. Monje had just returned from visiting Castro to whom he had presented his complaints about the Cubans' activities and from whom he had sought assurances about future cooperation, especially critical since he was now under pressure from Kolle Cueto to leave the party if he continued with his plan to join the guerrilla. Castro finally revealed to Monje that Guevara was in charge of operations and this apparently impressed him, although in a message to Ché on 14 December Fidel noted, 'I cannot say what Stanislao's [Monje's] final attitude might be but he might bring in some good people . . .'.[26] Monje and Guevara met in Bolivia for the first and last time on 31 December. As Ché recorded in his diary,

'The conversation with Monje began with generalities but he quickly came down to his fundamental premiss, stated in three basic conditions: 1. He would resign as party leader but would obtain its neutrality, and cadres would be brought for the struggle. 2. He would be the political and military leader of the struggle as long as the revolution was taking place in Bolivia. 3. He would handle relations with other South American parties, trying to persuade them to support liberation movements. . . . I answered that the first point was a matter for his own judgement as party secretary, although I considered his position to be a great mistake. It was vacillating, accommodating and would protect the good name in history of those who should be condemned for their crookedness. Time would prove me right.

On the third point, I told him I had no objection to his trying, but that he would fail. . . . As for the second point, I could not accept it under any conditions. I was to be the military chief and

I would not accept any ambiguities on this matter. Here the discussion ended and we talked in a vicious circle.'[27]

Monje left the camp the following morning and with him went any real chance of active collaboration with the PCB. The party secretary had failed to obtain the only terms upon which both he and a markedly less enthusiastic central committee would cooperate. Monje's position inside the party was weakened and the PCB's attitude shifted from suspicion to extreme coolness. Kolle and other leaders publicly maintained their support for the guerrilla but disclaimed responsibility for it, stressed the importance of organising the masses by traditional means, and implicitly rejected the type of united front proffered by the guerrilla campaign.[28] In practice the party's line was more emphatically antagonistic: in February 1967 Loyola Guzmán, Ché's La Paz contact and the guerrilla's treasurer, was expelled, and in August twenty militants from Cochabamba were threatened with expulsion when it was learnt that they intended to join Guevara. According to Debray, Ché was heard to say, 'The Bolivian Communist Party is our Enemy Number One.'[29] In January 1968 Monje presented to the PCB a detailed critique of the guerrilla, defending his own role and the party line but desisting from any direct criticism of Havana.[30] Oscar Zamora and the PCML, on the other hand, although they also maintained public support for Guevara, later vehemently attacked Monje for sabotaging the campaign and Castro for covering up for him.[31] Of the rest of the left, all of which offered public support, only the POR also made clear at the time its criticisms of the *foco* method.

The guerrillas found themselves obliged to go onto an active footing very much earlier than they had anticipated when, on 19 January, a detachment of police arrived at the *Casa Calamina* in Ñancahuazú guided by a neighbouring farmer named Algarañaz. Algarañaz's suspicions had been roused as early as November by the unusual activity around the recently purchased farm which he first ascribed to a cocaine smuggling operation. Since his curiosity and several visits had been brusquely rebuffed, he called in the local *carabineros*. In the event they found little that was suspicious (the main force was camping away from the house), talked amiably with a couple of Bolivian guerrillas, and confiscated a revolver which they said could be reclaimed in Camiri. The incident was of little importance in itself, but it did indicate that the force was vulnerable to being located at a very early stage. Far greater problems ensued when, at the beginning of February, Ché took the main body on a training march. This was supposed to last 25 days but the heavy summer rains and swollen rivers stretched it into a 48-day excursion, during which two men drowned, a number (including Guevara) became ill, supplies of food ran out, and bickering between the Bolivians and Cubans was frequent and heated. The exhausted force returned to Ñancahuazú on 19 March only to find that two members of the rearguard recruited by Moisés Guevara had deserted and that two days beforehand an army patrol had searched the area around the house, finding a diary belonging to one of the Cubans (Braulio), a number of sketches of combatants (including one of Guevara) and other documents. The guerrilla had been discovered and would soon come under attack.

Four days later, the 23rd, Epifanio Vargas, a local employee of YPFB who had already met the rebels and seen through their story that they were Mexican geologists, guided an advance patrol led by Lieutenant Rubén Amezaga up the Ñancahuazú river and inadvertently into a hurriedly-lain guerrilla ambush. Vargas, the lieutenant and six of his men were killed, and most of the patrol, which included a major and a captain, were captured. According to Guevara, these men 'talked like parrots' but imparted little useful information and were quickly released. The ambush had been a success in its own right but the guerrilla was now embarked upon full-scale military operations well before it was prepared for them.

Forces from the army's fourth division, based at Camiri, occupied the main guerrilla camp in the first week of April, obliging the rebels to go onto the move and retaliate. At first they registered some success: on 10 April a large patrol led by Major Rubén Sánchez scouting around Iripití, some twelve miles from Ñancahuazú, was ambushed by a force led by Coco Peredo with the loss of 19 men. Major Sánchez defended himself a good deal more resolutely than had his confrères and refused to collaborate in interrogation, but his captors rejected the invitation to execute him and released their captives the next day, thereby revealing further important information. By this stage Barrientos had declared four provinces to be in a state of emergency and issued a call to the nation 'to join the fight against the local and foreign anarchists with arms and money from the Castro-communists', but he refused to believe that Guevara was their leader or even alive. For good measure the PCB, PCML and the POR were formally out-lawed although they had long been operating in a semi-clandestine manner.

The ambush of 10 April marked the end of the opening stage of the guerrilla and placed its operations on a new plane. Henceforth it would be in permanent retreat. The rebels' problems were made more acute by the fact that they had been joined a couple of weeks before by Régis Debray and Ciro Bustos, an artist from Buenos Aires who had been contacted by Tania as a potential organiser in Argentina. On the 16th, when it had already been decided that in view of the scale of operations and the pressure on the force these two should be smuggled out of the zone, an Anglo-Chilean journalist by the name of George Andrew Roth made contact, having mysteriously wandered through the army's forward positions. Guevara decided to split the force, send-ing the visitors and those who were ill south with a detachment led by the Cuban Joaquín (Comandante Julio Vitale Acuna Nuñez). This group left on the 17th and two days later left the visitors near the settle-ment of Muyupampa. They had expected to escape from there with-out great difficulty but were almost immediately picked up by officers of the DIC (Criminal Investigation Department) and handed over to the fourth division.

The capture of Debray in particular caused a sensation outside of Bolivia and greatly increased the profile of the campaign. All three foreigners were charged with being guerrillas although the enigmatic Roth was released in July. Since they were indicted under military law their alleged offence was punishable by a maximum of thirty years in jail for Bolivia had abolished the death penalty. However, few Boli-vians believed that anybody could survive a thirty-year sentence in a military prison and noted that, with the exception of those who had actively collaborated with the army, no guerrillas had been captured alive, reviving interest in the army's traditional respect for the *ley de fuga*, under which prisoners were shot 'whilst attempting to escape'. The prisoners' lives were, therefore, understood to be in great danger. As a result of this and the growing awareness that Ché was in the country, Bolivia began to attract visitors the like of whom it had never seen before. Debray's publishers Feltrinelli and Maspero arrived in La Paz to protect the interests of their author, the latter being promptly expelled for his pains. A certain 'Señor Khan' managed to insinuate himself into Camiri, where with somewhat misguided enterprise he endeavoured to take snaps of local officers. He turned out to be the Pakistani Trotskyist Tariq Ali, who lacked even rudimentary Spanish. This somewhat delayed comprehension of his claims that he was not a guerrilla but did not impede his departure from the country — which was even more speedy than that of Maspero. These events, and one of the first detailed reports both of Debray's situation and the growing US presence in Camiri, were noted by Perry Anderson and Robin Blackburn, Marxist intellectuals who momentarily dropped their duties as editors of the London-based *New Left Review* to report for the *Observer*. Debray's capture also brought a letter from de Gaulle, who had impressed senior officers during his visit to Cochabamba in 1964, but this did little to diminish the francophobia that had infected the local press.

On the military front, the effort to smuggle the visitors out had resulted in a critical division of the guerrillas' forces, which were never able to link up again. The rebels now numbered some forty men, divided into two groups, and Tania. Neither group knew where the other was, and they faced 1,500 troops. Joaquín lost more men in skirmishes while extricating himself from the Muyupampa region, and Guevara offered a depressing assessment for the month of April: 'We are still totally isolated; sickness has undermined the health of some comrades, obliging us to divide our forces, which has now taken away much of our effectiveness. We still have not been able to make contact with Joaquín. The peasant base continues to make no progress although it may be that through planned terror we will succeed in getting the neutrality of some; support will come later . . . '.[32]

If things were bleak on the guerrilla side, the armed forces were certainly not making major gains, either militarily or in public relations. Official versions of what was occurring 'at the front' were at first cautious and then entered a phase of voluble contradiction, hyperbole and untruth. Barrientos took to holding press conferences in which he adjudged the rebels' strength at one stage to be 500 men, called for the invasion of Cuba, and alternated wildly between claims that the existence of Bolivia was in the balance and confirmation that large numbers of guerrillas had been 'eliminated'. The seasoned foreign press corps was summoned to the Palacio to hear that 'the ideology of Fidel Castro is that of a madman who uses millions by the day, or by the month, to pay agents who in the last resort do nothing more than satisfy the hunger of communist China', or that Bolivia's economic ills were due to the expansion of its population, which, in accordance with a hitherto unknown economic law, had reduced production.[33] Journalists were also exposed to the delights of one of the military's favourite exercises: a 'spontaneous demonstration' by the people of La Paz on a day when all government offices were closed at 3 p.m. Official employees who neglected to participate lost five days' pay. The affair started well with contingents from the newly-created *Comité de Damas Cristianas* and the *Frente Anticomunista de Bolivia* selling flags and raising shouts of 'Debray killed, Debray must die' and 'With the armed forces against the red *bandoleros*' to the strains of 'Bridge over the River Kwai' provided by a military band fortuitously passing at the time. But as the day wore on numbers dwindled with chants against the regime and in support of 'Fidel' beginning to emerge from the crowd. Even at the peak of the campaign Ovando ruefully admitted, 'Bolivians are repelled by communists but as yet they haven't demonstrated this repulsion'; it proved impossible to mobilise broad anti-guerrilla sentiment, and the government soon turned its attention to directly military matters, from time to time calling on the services of Archbishop Clemente Maurer to confirm that the Church was unalterably opposed to those 'who are drenching the country in blood, carrying foreign flags and misusing the word "*guerrillero*" '.[34]

At the ill-defined front between Camiri and Santa Cruz the two divisions charged with 'eliminating' the rebels — the eighth advancing from the north and the fourth from the south — were slow in adapting to conditions of a guerrilla war and the troublesome presence of journalists. At first the airforce happily admitted to its use of napalm and even dropped it from a plane carrying a reporter. In Camiri there was a closely-observed state of near chaos; in August the commander of the fourth division was hard pressed to explain the death of his chief intelligence officer, a Captain Padilla, shot with his own revolver in the Hotel Chapaco. The claim that he had been executed by the urban cell of the *Ejército de Liberación Nacional* (ELN) whilst interrogating a female suspect was discreetly abandoned when it was discovered that the lady concerned had been more than a little inebriated and her husband known to be unsympathetic to the attentions she was receiving. A manifest issued by the ELN (formally declared by Guevara at the end of March) suggested that if the official version was to be believed they could only assume that interrogation techniques currently being disseminated in the Panama Canal Zone stipulated that boots and belts be removed during questioning. One reason why officers were engaged in such diversions was that very few of them were prepared to court the undoubted risks of entering the countryside, a task which was largely left to subalterns and NCOs.

This situation caused alarm in the US military, which had been keeping a close eye on matters. As early as 9 March General Robert Porter, head of US Southern Command in Panama, flew to La Paz to talk with Ovando and the general staff; three days later a five-man counter-insurgency training team arrived in the country. In mid-March four members of the permanent US military mission flew over the guerrilla zone in the company of CIA agent Aurelio Hernández. This activity inevitably drew attention, and before too long La Paz was awash with rumours that Bolivia was to be sent 25,000 marines like the Dominican Republic the year before. Much publicity was given to a train sent from Argentina which was supposed to be carrying flour but widely thought to be transporting munitions and troops. Both General Stroessner and General Onganía deployed large numbers of men on the Paraguayan and Argentine borders and cooperated closely with the Bolivian high command. This provoked something of a nationalist backlash and rather punctured Barrientos's denunciations of 'foreign intervention'. Colonel Zenteno, backed by the powerful chief of staff General Marcos Vázquez Sempértegui, argued that external military aid should be kept to a minimum and that the conflict should not be internationalised. Ovando coincided with this position and by mid-year had bullied Barrientos into changing the key local commanders, sending Zenteno to Santa Cruz and Luis Reque Terán to Camiri, where they began 'Operation Cynthia', a pincer movement designed to force the rebels to more open ground in the north-east. The results of this operation were slow in coming but eventually rewarding. It was, in fact, not until September, when the guerrillas were clearly cornered, that the full contingent of 600 Rangers trained at La Esperanza outside Santa Cruz by Colonel Joseph P. Rice, Major Robert 'Pappy' Shelton and some twenty US Special Forces men ('Green Berets') were thrown into the zone. The US presence at Ñancahuazú was largely confined to representatives of the CIA who took a leading role in the interrogation of captives.

The fundamental weakness of the guerrillas—that, in the words of Debray, 'their political base did not coincide with their theatre of operations'[35] — was brought home with brutal force at the end of June, when the regime momentarily turned its attention away from the combat zone to Siglo XX, only 160 miles distant. That the guerrilla had unsettled the government and fortified opposition was made clear as early as 19 April, when a general assembly at Catavi called for restoration of wages and reinstatement of all those sacked since May 1965 and pledged itself to provide the rebels with food and medicines, to hold a march in Oruro on 8 June and a FSTMB conference together with student delegates and those of other unions on 24 June. The declaration of a state of siege cancelled out the demonstration, but it proved difficult to halt preparations for the conference, which showed every sign of becoming the broadest and most powerful political meeting to be held since the 1964 coup. In Siglo the parties of the left were united on the basic demands and had entered into an agreement by which they would take turns to stand guard over the approaches to the camp and the *sindicato* building. On the eve of the conference, the night of San Juan, the township of Llallagua was transformed by the infusion of visiting delegates, the sight of many bonfires and the sounds of merriment as the miners and their families celebrated the traditional midwinter feast. It is said that on this occasion Comibol was unusually generous in the distribution of beer, and organised dances in league with the church radio station Pio XII, something that had never occurred before; by midnight many of the camp's inhabitants were in high spirits. One who was not overly inebriated was Rosendo García Maismann, a PCB militant whose turn it was to guard the *sindicato* and who, along with Simón Reyes, had passed a relatively sober evening. At around 4.30 a.m. García got up and went to the *sindicato* where he joined the 18-year-old Juan Carlos, a disc-jockey on La Voz del Minero broadcsting music to awaken the first shift interspersed with advice to maintain vigilance in case the army attempted to break up the conference.

When García entered the building troops were already filtering quietly into the outskirts of the camp having been disembarked from a train that had free-wheeled to a halt a mile down the track. Their first objective was the radio station, but as they broke in García was able to reach the siren and sound the alarm. He was shot down but killed the officer leading the attack as he fell. Organised resistance was impossible, and the army's score of casualties was later ascribed to the fact that the police, which had also been prepared for the operation, mistakenly fired on their colleagues. It was, however, the miners and their families who suffered most under fire from bazookas and machine-guns for nearly two hours. The army initially listed 16 dead and 71 wounded but it soon emerged that at least 87 people, including many women and children, had been killed and many more wounded. (The true figure was obtained partly because the new 'sink and float' plant had replaced the calcination ovens which the army had used in the past to dispose of bodies.)

The massacre of San Juan was not the bloodiest but certainly the most carefully and callously planned in the tragic history of the Bolivian mines. In reply to the accusations of murder in cold blood that inevitably attracted the attention of journalists covering the guerrilla Barrientos stated,

> 'I'm not making up a story; the fact is that subversion developed in the following way. First there were militant meetings at which the participants declared their support for the guerrillas and collected money for them. Then they threatened the constitutional government. Later the radio stations of Huanuni, Catavi and Siglo XX made broadcasts inciting the people to overthrow the government, start the class struggle and set up a proletarian government. Finally the reds and corrupt old union leaders declared the three most important mines in the country to be *territorio libre*, where nobody could enter without their permission. Because of this the government instructed the armed forces to occupy the mines and restore order and authority. This would have happened in any country.'[36]

Some 30,000 people attended the funeral of those killed in a formidable display of solidarity and protest, but a meeting held the same day inside the mine on level 411 produced a more tangible response in the call for a strike; this was heeded with remarkable discipline. The stoppage eventually lasted two weeks despite the complete military occupation of the camp and was only ended when the local commander forced the company clerks who had replaced the elected union leaders to call the strike off or face further 'measures'. By this stage the university in La Paz had also been declared *territorio libre* and Barrientos and Ovando 'enemies of the people', requiring much use of tear gas and the occupation of the campus to regain a semblance of order. Rumours of a coup grew but both Vázques Sempértegui and

Ovando resisted making a move because of the continued threat in the east, and Barrientos weathered the storm.

The events in the *altiplano* coincided with a series of skirmishes between the army and Ché's group well away from the main zone of operations and dangerously close to the Santa Cruz—Yacuiba railway, the road to Cochabamba, and to the city itself. The clashes at La Florida, Piray and El Filo were not major encounters but they worried Zenteno who failed to realise that Reque Terán's incursions from the south were in fact forcing Guevara to the north-east and that Ché was not attempting to gain control of the Cochabamba highway. However, illness—from mid-June Ché could only move on horseback because of his asthma—and hunger required that the main rebel force obtain provisions and medicines: the most logical place for this was the village of Samaipata, on the main road. On 6 July, in what was to be the most celebrated of their actions, the guerrillas hijacked a lorry and bus full of students from Oruro returning from an anti-government demonstration in Santa Cruz. All traffic was halted outside the hamlet of Las Cuevas while the rebels instructed a local German woodmill-owner to telephone Samaipata and tell the municipal authorities that they would occupy the village that night. This does not appear to have generated much excitement since when, shortly before midnight, the vehicles approached the Samaipata *tranca* (the traffic control post outside almost every settlement of any size in Bolivia) the transport police came forward to inspect their papers with customary nonchalance and were easily overpowered. Once in the town, goods were purchased at generous prices (and not with counterfeit money, as the regime claimed) and the small garrison, asleep in the school, was disarmed with only one soldier offering resistance and being shot. Within 30 minutes the guerrillas were off, dropping their military hostages at Las Cuevas and disappearing south of the main road. The country was electrified at the daring of this raid but it proved to be the peak of the guerrillas' campaign, a propaganda coup that masked the desperate situation of the rebels.

This was confirmed by further desertions early in August and the collapse of the now isolated urban network with the arrest of Loyola Guzmán (who was only released in exchange for German hostages taken in mid-1970). But the most damaging blow came on 31 August, when Joaquín's group, which had sought in vain to link up with Ché for a number of months, accepted the offer of a peasant named

Above The mine at Colquiri. *Below* Making the *Pacto Militar-Campesino* work: René Barrientos and *campesino* leaders in the Palacio Quemado

The Rangers regiment, Vallegrande, and, below, their quarry,
Ernesto 'Ché' Guevara, near Nancahuazú, 1967

Honorato Rojas, whom they knew from earlier encounters, to guide them across the Rio Grande at a place called Vado del Yeso. Rojas's farm had been billetted with soldiers dressed as peasants and he had arranged with Captain Mario Vargas Salinas the point at which he would cross the river. Late in the afternoon of the 31st Rojas led Joaquín's group, which numbered ten including the now very depressed Tania, into an inescapable ambush. All were killed, either immediately or once they had been interrogated. Three days later Ché's group passed the same spot; the two groups had come within several hours' march of each other.

The remaining group of 17 men headed west in a further attempt to break the tightening circle. On 22 September they entered the village of Alto Seco, where they participated in a party and gave political lectures. One peasant wanted to join but a Bolivian fighter put him off with the words, 'Don't be silly; we're done for . . . we don't know how to get out of here.'[37] They were never able to hide their position for long and four days later the fourth division had them pinpointed moving towards the settlement of La Higuera. At midday on the 26th the vanguard under Coco Peredo was intercepted and wiped out, but it required the deployment of the Rangers over the next fortnight to nail Guevara down.

The action not far from La Higuera in which Captain Prado captured the guerrilla leader was not the final event in this isolated and unkempt war. A group headed by Inti Peredo, which had been dispatched on what seemed like a suicide mission to hold off the main army attack down the Quebrado del Yuro, managed against all odds to break out. Of these ten men, four died on 14 October 20 miles north of La Higuera and one (the Bolivian Ñato) was captured and executed when nearly away from the zone at El Mataral. Of the full force a total of five men escaped: three Cubans, who crossed the Chilean border in February 1968 and were escorted by Salvador Allende to Tahiti from where they travelled to Prague and Havana, and two Bolivians—Inti Peredo and Dario (David Adriázola Veizaga)—who reached Santa Cruz, caught a plane to Cochabamba, and went into hiding. Their freedom was, however, to be short-lived. Inti was gunned down in La Paz in September 1969 and Dario finally run to earth and executed in January 1970. In delayed retaliation the reconstituted ELN and its friends abroad killed the peasant traitor Rojas late in 1969 while he was living under army protection in Santa Cruz; Zenteno's intelligence officer, Colonel Roberto Quintanilla, was killed in Hamburg in 1971. In May 1976 Zenteno himself was shot down in the streets of Paris, but although the regime of Colonel Banzer blamed the ELN for this, all the available evidence suggests that the government itself supervised the assassination since the general was manifesting increasing independence and opposition to it.

With the death of Guevara Barrientos declared the guerrilla vanquished, but he was still left with the problem of Régis Debray, whose court martial had begun on 26 September and was still underway when Ché was captured. Although external pressure for a proper trial and the insistence upon a full interrogation by the CIA (in the shape of one 'Dr' Eduardo González, a Cuban exile) had saved Debray from summary execution, Barrientos's directive that he be tried by court martial had created more problems than it solved. The junior officers baying for blood were somewhat placated but the court offered little semblance of justice, while allowing Debray to make an impressive speech that had much the same effect as Castro's defence after the assault on the Moncada barracks in October 1953.[38] Besieged by journalists, the officers in charge of the trial found themselves entirely out of their depth; Colonel Efraín Guachalla excused himself from answering all the questions because he was 'not a *homo sapiens*', while the prosecutor, Colonel Remberto Iriarte Paz, promised to look into claims that the trial was in breach of the constitution only to apologise when he returned to the courtroom in the afternoon that he had left the relevant notes in his other jacket.[39] Even more embarrassing for the army was the case of Jorge Vázques Viaña, the guerrilla son of the respected historian Humberto Vázquez Machicado and a PCB militant who had been captured with severe wounds near Monteagudo on 27 April and transferred to a hospital in Camiri. After several days of interrogation by the CIA agent González, Vázquez disappeared, the army claiming that he had fled to Argentina although the man was completely immobile and still in post-operative shock. With a macabre sense of propriety the authorities left an empty chair for Vázquez in the courtroom since he was a 'witness for the prosecution'. A journalist asked Iriarte if Vázquez would be presented and was told of the hospital 'escape', to which he replied that he had information that Vázquez would appear on 2 November. Iriarte smiled and remarked upon how well the press was informed, failing to register the fact that 2 November is the day of the dead.

The reputation of the Bolivian authorities was more permanently tarnished by revelations of the CIA role in the counter-insurgency operation. Journalists had noted the visibly important part played in Camiri and Vallegrande by Eduardo González and Félix Ramos, both of whom were formally incorporated into the Bolivian army as captains. The following year Barrientos's far from liberal minister of the interior, Antonio Arguedas, suddenly left La Paz and appeared in Havana, where he passed to Castro a copy of Ché's diary which had been photographed by Ramos and sent to the US almost before the Bolivians had known of its existence. Arguedas's extraordinary *volte face* and no less damaging revelations as to the extent of CIA operations inside the country deeply wounded the *amour propre* of the Bolivian services, which embarked upon a series of judicial investigations of the matter in July 1968. In these a string of senior officers, including Zenteno and Colonel Andrés Selich Chop, duly proceeded to list the names and recount in detail the activities of the US agents in Bolivia which had been central to the defeat of the guerrilla.[40] Although these revelations only put flesh on the bones of a story that was already widely known, they reflected and deepened antagonisms that had appeared inside the military. Superficially at least, these correspond to differences between the followers of Barrientos and those of Ovando, generally field and junior officers. The members of the military tribunal, supporters of the president, were all promoted to generals after the trial while Zenteno and Reque Terán, the key commanders in the field and broadly in favour of Ovando, remained colonels. Such disparities were also evident lower down the hierarchy: Captain Vargas Salinas, whose military exploits extended to machine-gunning people stranded in the middle of a fast river from an impregnable position on its banks, was immediately promoted major and dubbed the 'Lion of Masicuri', while Captain Prado, who had captured Guevara, and Major Sánchez, who had displayed greater tenacity and personal courage than any other officer, retained their rank. Indeed, the rather upright Prado was selected as the scapegoat for the execution of Guevara which had been ordered by La Paz and preceded by a visit to La Higuera by Ovando, Zenteno and the fierce Croat Selich, who is reported to have discharged his pistol into Ché's arm during interrogation, which was directed by Ramos. The truth both about this affair and the fate of Guevara's cadaver will probably never be known, not least because so many of those involved have since died, some under distinctly suspicious circumstances. Most accounts identify Ché's actual assassin as a sergeant, Mario Terán, and the large number of bullet wounds in his extremities may well be accounted for by the version which holds that once the guerrilla leader had expired a number of lesser ranks were permitted to 'participate' in his execution. No doubt the cult erected around Ché ordained that such questions should attract an excess of asinine comment and fuel the mountains of commercialised detritus rapidly collecting in the sensation-hungry metropolitan states; for Bolivian political life their consequences were to be a good deal more surreptitious but also more significant.

The guerrilla proved to be a catalyst for a number of changes in political life although in the short term the Barrientos regime remained unchallenged. The example of the Ñancahuazú rebels had a particularly strong impact on the students for whom their abnegation and heroism contrasted strongly not only with the doctrinal constraints and apparently slothful organisational orientation of the established left but also with the transparent spiritual blandishments of the parties of the moderate right, particularly the PDC. As elsewhere in Latin America, guerrilla warfare provoked largely generational divisions in the major political groupings and motivated interest in new ideological currents that attempted to merge the social critique of Marxism with a combative Christian humanism. In Bolivia the development of this strain amongst the youth of the middle class took a slightly distinct path. The Church was itself very weak, having fewer priests even than Uruguay, the most secular of all Latin American states, and depending heavily upon the support of the Vatican, which had the effect of restricting the growth of liberation theology amongst young national priests. On the other hand, the relative lack of authority of the hierarchy enabled dissident elements inside the PDC to develop independent ideas without overbearing constraints. Many, such as Néstor and Jaime Paz Zamora, acquired an ideological radicalism abroad, often in Chile or at the University of Louvain in Belgium. Some, like Adalberto Kuajara, later to be a leader of the PCB, moved to an openly syndicalist stance, while many student leaders, such as the *cruceño* firebrand Oscar Eid Franco, began to adopt a directly adventurist and pro-guerrilla attitude.

This process was uneven and confused, being signalled rather than consolidated in the formation of the PDC-*Revolucionario*, which had the effect of jolting the left of the MNR, now completely disorientated and disorganised, into reconsideration of its position. Although the principal rupture occurred inside the PDC, what developed over the two years following Ñancahuazú amounted to a general crisis for the parties of the centre and the political circles of the urban middle class and intelligentsia. Despite its failure, the guerrilla provided a kind of quantum jump from the orbit of 1952 and challenged those sectors that were lodged between the popular masses, the small but politically pugnacious bourgeoisie, and the army to reconsider their position. The impetus for this was further strengthened by the continued absence of the COB and any discernible advance in reconstituting militant syndicalism as the primary axis of the left, in addition to the regime's lack of any perspective other than degeneration into a completely unencumbered dictatorship at the beck and call of Washington.

In fact, the experience of the guerrilla had increased US doubts as to the dependability of Barrientos, who was now showing signs of an erratic independence as well as failing to tighten up an apparatus that was a good deal less stable than it appeared. Recognising that the guerrilla war and the high US profile in his regime had unsettled certain sectors of the military and caused shifts in the centrist parties of the middle class, Barrientos tried to refine his style: 'I ought to reaffirm a definition which my government has made in an absolutely clear form: yes we are anti-imperialists, but we are for the Alliance for Progress, because in this new context we find all the possibilities for being able to put into effect a real plan of government.'[41] Other declarations were even more confused, giving the humourists of La Paz, led by the urbane and acerbic 'Paulovitch', a field day in parodying the military style of political discourse.[42]

Throughout 1968 Barrientos found himself losing political and military support. The cabinet parties no longer possessed any real popular base and the FSB was showing a dangerous interest in backing Ovando and cultivating support amongst officers who held nationalist criticisms of the regime's economic policies. The man emerging as the figurehead of this movement was the ex-*falangista* General Juan José Torres, one of the army's most senior and respected officers who was pushing Ovando to make a break with the president. However, the most tangible challenge to Barrientos did not come from this more institutionalist and technocratically-inclined sector but from an old-style military caudillo, the chief of staff General Marcos Vázquez

Sempértegui, who in August 1968 launched a coup attempt, which collapsed immediately when both the military nationalists and the FSB failed to support it, justifiably fearing that Vázquez aimed simply to replace one dictatorial personalism with another.

In response to this and the growing threat posed by Ovando, Barrientos began to build independent sources of support inside the military. He paid particular attention to the elite parachute brigade centred in his home town of Cochabamba, the CITE (*Centro de Instrucción de Tropas Especiales*), but also set up early in 1969 a paramilitary force independent of the high command and loyal only to himself — FURMOD (*Fuerzas Unidas para la Represión y el Mantenimiento del Orden y el Desarrollo*). The appearance of FURMOD, which soon began to act in a manner reminiscent of the *Control Político*, increased fears that the president was preparing to launch an open dictatorship. If this was the case it is doubtful if it could have lasted for long since Barrientos now lacked firm backing from any sector except the peasantry, despite the fact that there was no obvious popular figure who might challenge him: Ovando signally lacked the populist touch. The immediate question of the future of the regime was resolved suddenly and violently but without obvious political consequences when, in April 1969, Barrientos's helicopter crashed after leaving a weekend peasant meeting near Arque, Cochabamba. It has never been proved that the crash was an accident or the result of sabotage although no bullets were found in the bodies recovered from the wreck. Accusations and suspicions continued for many years and for a while a well-known and impetuous officer, Major Faustino Rico Toro, was held on charges connected with the president's death, but whatever the case, the incident in which Barrientos died was far from foreign to the way in which he had lived his life.

Barrientos's death left the country in a vacuum which was not to be definitively sealed for over two years. He was succeeded by his elected vice-president, the mild-mannered Social Democrat Luis Adolfo Siles Salinas. This step was sanctioned by the high command which was itself badly disorientated since Ovando was in the US recovering from treatment for his stomach ulcer on a medical leave which had also been inspired by political motives. In the event, it suited Ovando to acquiesce in Siles's assumption of power since the new regime patently lacked popularity or a political base despite its civilian character. Siles's lack of independence from the military restricted his actions almost completely as he attempted to loosen political restrictions somewhat while still operating within the framework established by Barrientos. Ovando quickly returned home and began to make claims on the legacy of his late colleague through the *Pacto* although his personal style was unsuited to such activity. At the same time he engaged in the now critical task of deliberating between the various factions of the divided officer corps, attempting to piece together a viable project for a new phase of military rule. This process was very directly influenced by the nationalist military regime established in Peru in October 1968 by General Velasco, who was already presiding over a string of nationalisations, preparing a new agrarian reform and putting substantial distance between his government and Washington to some effect and not without popular acclaim. By the end of September 1969 Ovando, who had been quietly studying the Peruvian experiment, had secured sufficient agreement between his commanders to make a move. On the 26th the hapless Siles, who in recognition of his plight had once said, 'I came into government alone and I shall leave it alone', was detained while on a visit to Santa Cruz and bundled out of the country. The five-month echo of the Barrientos regime, which had been the product of a constitutional nicety and lack of preparation on all sides, collapsed without great consternation. Its fall opened a period of highly-charged political manoeuvre and experimentation wherein the residues of 1952 and Ñancahuazú would play a central part.

5.
CRISIS OF HEGEMONY, 1969-71

The end of the 1960s and opening years of the 1970s saw the demise of the 'post-war boom' in the metropolitan nations and witnessed even sharper political crises in the neo-colonial states. The view that the years 1968 to 1975 represent a determinate 'revolution-ary moment' not only in the backward countries but also in Europe does not withstand sober analysis (even when North America is exclu-ded), but it is certainly the case that the economic and political system established after 1945 was profoundly fractured. While popular memory may not recall the 1967 devaluation of sterling, a currency long since dispossessed of its global authority, or that of the dollar four years later — with infinitely greater consequence since it marked the collapse of the post-1945 financial system set up at Bretton Woods — it has certainly registered the rise in oil prices as well as a series of bitter conflicts that in some senses have not yet become part of history. Amongst these we might mention the barricades of Prague and Paris in 1968, followed by the 'hot summer' in Italy; the Tet offensive; riots in the urban ghettos of the US; the Portuguese revolution, followed by the collapse of Lisbon's moribund empire in Africa and — it should be noted, if only in recognition of the plight of the forgotten people of

East Timor — Asia; and, most acute of all, final, humiliating defeat for Washington after the long, barbaric and extraordinarily expensive war in Vietnam, Cambodia and Laos.

This social and political turmoil was fully evident in Latin America even though many of its countries were still under the military rule which had contained the initial impact of the Cuban revolution. The massacre of some 300 students in the Tlatelolco quarter of Mexico City in October 1968, an event covered by the international press arriving to cover the Olympic games, confirmed that rebellion was by no means the monopoly of European youth: their American peers engaged in such activity under very different conditions. In Guatemala, Venezuela and Colombia young people from the urban middle class continued to dominate guerrilla groups, which, despite persistent reverses, represented more than a peripheral nuisance to the regimes undertaking extensive counter-insurgency campaigns against them. Elsewhere this generational radicalism was overshadowed by broader mass mobilisation and industrial discontent in weakening the apparatus of control erected in the wake of the Alliance for Progress and General Maxwell Taylor's all-embracing security doctrines. In May 1969 the car workers of Córdoba, Argentina, took to the streets in a semi-insurrectionist movement which prompted the fall of the Onganía regime, radically reduced the scope of succeeding military governments (Levingston and Lanusse) and paved the way for the return of Perón. In Chile the weight of the parties of the left, the unions, and expectations aroused by the reforms of the Frei administration enabled Salvador Allende to take power in 1970. His *Unidad Popular* government was critically debilitated by the lack of an overall parliamentary majority, but it was still the first freely elected regime of avowedly Marxist character in the post-war era. When this triumph was added to the radical tenor of General Velasco's Peruvian regime it appeared that Washington's fear of an anti-US bloc in the southern cone was not entirely without foundation. Apart from the almost Ruritanian Stroessner regime in backward Paraguay, the sole dependable US allies were Uruguay, where the lingering threat of the Tupamaros and the strong showing of the *Frente Amplio* in the 1971 elections were only finally nullified in the coup of 1973, and Brazil, where the mobilisations of April and July 1968 failed to unhinge the system based on the 1964 coup and provoked a severe 'institutional' clampdown. Further north the attention of the State Department was directed less towards the simmering but still firmly suppressed social discontent in Nicaragua, Guatemala and El Salvador than to the pistol-packing populist caudillo General Omar Torrijos, whose 1968 coup was construed as a major threat in strategically vital and hitherto pleasantly containable Panama. Although the 1977 canal treaty was finally to lay the fears of many to rest, it should not be forgotten that for many years Torrijos's sharp tongue and unpredictable nature kept the North American right in a state of near apoplexy.

When viewed in such a context, the two years of political confusion in Bolivia following the Ovando coup can be seen as at least reflective of a wider disruption of US hegemony in the hemisphere, with local dominant blocs being forced into frantic manoeuvre and alteration of the means by which mass mobilisation was contained. It would, however, be incorrect to understand this instability as being solely, or even predominantly, determined by Bolivia's manifest vulnerability to the influence of her powerful neighbours, whether this be the implicit support for the forces of radicalism that was offered by Santiago, the continued nurturing of military cooperation and pressure for advantageous economic deals from Buenos Aires, or the increasingly open and adventurous advances of Brazilian 'sub-imperialism' concentrated on Santa Cruz. These factors played an important part, but the crisis of 1969–71 was more directly a product of the legacies of 1952 and Ñancahuazú, which combined in an uneasy and often contradictory manner to place proletarian independence, armed struggle, and popular power back on the political agenda. The response to this — a 'left' or 'revolutionary' nationalism directed by the military — was rapidly exhausted, reflecting the scale of popular mobilisation, the advances made by the left, and the extremely limited scope for restricting reform within the parameters laid down in 1952. The alternatives, as soon became clear, were either a complete rupture with such a system forced from below or violent imposition of the direct control introduced by Paz and refined by Barrientos.

The regimes of Generals Alfredo Ovando (September 1969 to October 1970) and Juan José Torres (October 1970 to August 1971) differed from each other in style and form but shared the fundamental aim of attempting to bisect the extremes which were identified with April 1952 and November 1964/May 1965. The fact that these officers, and the institution over which they possessed very unsteady control, had lived through and were closely associated with the essential contradictions in this political calendar obliged them to engage in particularly tortuous pirouettes. Moreover, it rapidly exposed the weaknesses both of recycling a MNR-style nationalism and of the armed forces as the vehicle for such a project. The military could draw on potent precedents in Busch and Villarroel and even its role in the heyday of the MNR, but it could not exorcise the more powerful memory of 1952. The COB and the left, on the other hand, were confronted with all the problems of constructing a strategy that would overcome two historic failures: that of 1952, when the working class held armed power but possessed no independent political leadership, and that of 1967, when such leadership was proclaimed on the basis of armed actions that were of almost negligible consequence because they were completely distanced, both geographically and politically, from the mass of workers and peasants.

Ovando Changes Course

Aside from Barrientos himself, nobody was more closely associated with the regime of 1964 to 1969 than Ovando. He had guaranteed the success of the original coup, acted as interim president, controlled the army, and been to the fore in the defeat of the guerrilla, the execution of Guevara and the massacre of San Juan. That he had exhibited scarcely-veiled personal disdain for Barrientos, sought to check moves towards a full dictatorship, and in 1966 displayed a degree of independence in negotiating a contract with the German firm of Klockner to build Bolivia's first tin smelter at Vinto hardly served to temper the image of a die-hard *gorila*. However, the coup of 26 September met with no popular opposition and was even cautiously welcomed. The most obvious reason for this was that the COB and the left were in no state to undertake a major political offensive, but they were not in any case disposed to engage with the new regime, which in its rather extended gestation and initial pronouncements appeared to be seeking a reversal of the direction taken by Barrientos.

The main evidence for this lay in a document that was published on the day of the coup and presented as the ideological basis of the new government: the *Mandato Revolucionario de las Fuerzas Armadas de la Nación*. This manifesto had been drawn up by General Torres, the new commander-in-chief widely identified as the leader of a nationalist faction inside the army, but it was also signed by a number of senior officers — Generals Rogelio Miranda and David Lafuente and Admiral Alberto Albarracín — who had been dedicated *barrientistas*. At the time it was thought that these officers had put their signatures to a document they believed to be nothing more than a variant of traditional military verbiage, allowing them to cash in on the Peruvian experiment as a justification for removing Siles's meddlesome civilian regime. In fact, Miranda and the others had opposed the *Mandato* as 'too communist', but once Ovando had overruled them, their formal endorsement did initially commit them to acquiesce in a policy by which the armed forces,

> 'place themselves at the service of the revolution and commit themselves to the struggle for social justice, for the greatness of the Patria and for authentic national independence, today in risk of foreign subjugation.
>
> The Armed Forces recognise the immediate necessity of confronting the chaos with a truly revolutionary government which counterposes an integrated revolution to the simple use of violence that becomes an end in itself, and which realises a rapid and profound transformation of economic, social, political, and cultural structures to confront the dependency, poverty, disorientation and the Vietnamisation of Bolivia in new and sterile fratricidal destruction.'[1]

This primary objective of eradicating the threat of further guerrilla foci is evident throughout the *Mandato*, but is set down in terms that deviate somewhat from those employed in the counter-insurgency manuals issued by the US army: 'Revolutionary power is instituted in order to put an end to a pseudo-democratic order, which is antinational, falsely stable and characterised by ... the existence of a government infiltrated by the Rosca, ideologically and politically dependent upon reaction and the right, and disqualified from waging the national battle against terrorist adventurism and against dependency and backwardness.'[2] Having made this assessment, the document goes on to outline the military's prescription: 'The development of a country like Bolivia which belongs to an area of misery and dependency cannot be based on an exclusively capitalist system nor upon a completely socialist system but only on the national revolutionary model where there is a coexistence between state property, social, cooperative and communal means of production, and private property.'³ Amongst the eighteen points by which such a balance would be achieved were promises to defend and develop national capital whilst retaining guarantees for foreign investment, to undertake 'responsible and efficient' wage rises, to implement an extensive programme of public works, and to exercise complete independence in foreign policy, including the establishment of relations with the Soviet bloc.

In the wake of the Barrientos regime and a period of humiliating and economically disastrous 'cooperation' with the US, such a programme appeared much more adventurous than it was. Ovando himself declared that one of the central issues was the absence of an authentic national bourgeoisie and the need to take up the tasks historically bestowed upon such a class.⁴ Given that such a substitutionism had been a core objective of the MNR, it was not surprising that he also pronounced the new government to be a continuation of April 1952, but at no stage did he repudiate Barrientos, frequently presenting himself to the peasantry as the late caudillo's natural successor and strongly upholding the *Pacto*. Moreover, Ovando did not hesitate to declare that, 'we do not want socialism'⁵ or make comparisons with Velasco's regime, in which popular participation was extremely limited: 'Obviously no two countries are precisely alike, their problems differ and their approaches to these problems differ. But fundamentally our revolution is the same as Peru's.'⁶

One of the key elements of the analogy lay in the thesis — propounded most consistently by Torres — that the real frontier in underdeveloped countries lay not on their formal boundaries but internally, in the main centres of production where the imperialist presence was most powerful. This meant that the principal task of the military — the defence of the frontier — should not be restricted to border garrisons but, as in Peru, also be undertaken through the political and administrative defence of national enterprise and direct involvement in government.⁷

Such ideas contained a great appeal for many of the middle class intelligentsia who had opposed Barrientos but baulked at the guerrilla option or membership of the parties of the traditional left. Just as Velasco had surrounded himself with some of the brightest of Peru's radicalised professionals in order to advise officers whose technical training rarely rose above quartermastership, Ovando sought out able and independent figures from the middle class elite to give his cabinet some glamour as well as bureaucratic ability, which was considerably lower in the Bolivian officer corps than in that of Peru.[8] The role of the civilians in Ovando's first cabinet was distinct from that of those who had served Barrientos in so far as they had the opportunity to introduce novel measures and take advantage of the lack of confidence and direction evident in most military circles. Although their time in office was short and distinctly uncomfortable, these were no run-of-the-mill 'Donatos' (the term applied to the omnipresent and generally servile civilian collaborators of military rulers after the example of Donato Muñoz, minister of government for the infamous General Melgarejo). Most renowned of Ovando's young team was Marcelo Quiroga Santa Cruz, the aristocratic writer from Cochabamba who, over the previous decade had shifted his sympathies from the Falange to a left nationalist position, being jailed by Barrientos for the only attempt in Bolivian history to impeach a serving president. Quiroga was made minister of hydrocarbons, a critical post because Gulf Oil was identified as the single most important beneficiary of the Barrientos era within striking range of the regime. He was joined by his political co-thinker Alberto Bailey, minister of information, and by his defence attorney, José Luis Roca, a progressive Christian Democrat from the Beni, as minister of agriculture. Mariano Baptista Gumucio, an independently-minded *movimientista*, prolific writer and influential journalist, took over educational affairs and began to popularise the ideas of Freire and Illich whilst the capable and diplomatic technocrat José Ortiz Mercado took charge of planning. These appointments added substance to the intellectual influence on the regime during its first phase of the Brazilian writer Helio Jaguaribe, one of the foremost defenders of 'state capitalism' as a 'third way' between imperialism and socialism. To balance this potentially headstrong contingent Ovando recruited three figures from the private mining sector (*minería mediana*): Oscar Bonifaz (ministry of mines), Antonio Sánchez de Lozada (finance), and Eduardo Quiroga (secretary to the presidency). He could also, of course, rely on the decidedly less than radical credentials of the military members of the cabinet led by the ambitious martinet Colonel Juan Ayoroa Ayoroa, who controlled the powerful ministry of interior and showed no sign of relaxing the grip this office had held under Barrientos.

Almost all of the political capital amassed by the Ovando regime in its brief span of a year and a week derived from the nationalisation of Gulf Oil, undertaken on 7 October 1969, *Día de Dignidad Nacional*. This was less than a fortnight after the government had come to power, giving the impression that Ovando had the measure well prepared and agreed upon beforehand. In fact this was not the case: a number of military leaders held out against Quiroga and his allies until the last moment. On 27 September Ovando discounted the possibility of nationalisation and only promised a rescheduling of the company's taxes.[9] In cabinet discussions the general maintained his usual inscrutable silence while the civilians, anxious to take early and decisive measures and win popular support, cajoled their reluctant colleagues into agreement, not the least of their methods being the employment of economic arguments beyond the grasp of the officers. The position was so insecure that on the night of the 6th some members of the cabinet slept away from home for fear of arrest, but Ovando put the operation in the hands of Torres, who supported Quiroga and had Gulf's offices and installations occupied by troops by dawn, well before the decree was formally signed.[10] In his speech announcing the nationalisation the president drew attention to the fact that Gulf controlled 90 per cent of Bolivia's gas and was 'an enterprise that has acquired an economic and political dominance similar to that of the tin barons'. But he also stressed that it represented a unique case, that the government offered full guarantees to private enterprise, and that although it would not accept 'either dependence or blackmail', international laws would be respected (that is, compensation would be paid). He also went out of his way to mollify Santa Cruz, which would lose important royalties from oil and gas production before YPFB could restore levels.[11] This was a necessary step since the expropriation of Gulf had provoked a powerful protest from the *Comité Pro-Santa Cruz* as well as *El Diario* and *Los Tiempos*, but the right had no popular support for its campaign. The COB, the students and even the oil workers applauded the measure as a vital move and interpreted it, with varying degrees of confidence, as an indication of the potentially progressive character of the regime.[12]

The response of the US government was to criticise but acquiesce in the nationalisation and embark upon a campaign to extract the greatest possible compensation. Ambassador Ernest Siracusa may have counselled this 'soft approach', which did not entail invoking the Hickenlooper Amendment and imposing an official economic boycott, because it was clear from the start that the international oil companies would stage their own boycott of Bolivian petroleum. As a result, the Ovando regime lost $14.4 million in export revenues and was soon confronted with soaring interest rates and a badly weakened peso. Unemployment rose too, but it was private industry, organised in the *Confederación de Empresarios Privados de Bolivia* (CEPB), that proved to be the most consistent critic of the government's economic policies, demanding greater support for private investment and 'an end to uncertainty'.[13] Such an attitude must have been partly determined by the fact that the US radically cut back bilateral aid to the regime, from $21.5 million in 1969 to $8.0 million in 1970, a clear sign of political disapproval. This might appear somewhat heavy-handed given that the Ovando regime was avowedly anti-communist and unmistakably military in character. However, Ovando himself had delivered an early speech criticising Nixon's Latin American policy, pronouncing the Alliance for Progress a failure, and declaring that the US did better out of dispensing aid than did its recipients.[14] Perhaps even more worrying than this was a speech given by Torres to the Inter-American Defence Council, a conclave of the region's most senior officers, when it met in La Paz in November. The commander-in-chief denounced formal democracy as a sham, made a fervent nationalist attack on dependency, and criticised existing thinking on counter-insurgency as ill-conceived and insufficient.[15] Both the Pentagon and the army commanders of neighbouring states began to fear that the Bolivian armed forces were running out of control. The more prescient may have perceived a coherent and far from radical strategy in Torres's ideas and the more powerful may well have been informed by their intelligence services that the general represented only a small majority inside the military, but one should not underestimate the importance such groups place on unquestioning fraternity as well as their ingrained aversion to experimentation.

Aside from the nationalisation of Gulf the Ovando regime undertook very few positive measures. To complement the nationalisation the 1955 petrol code was abrogated, and the Banco Minero retrieved its monopoly on the sale of minerals. Relations with the Soviet Union, Romania, Hungary and Czechoslovakia were established and commercial treaties with these states were negotiated, but the issue of Cuba proved too sensitive with the officer corps and was quietly left to one side. Bolivia also joined the Andean Pact, established at Cartagena,

Colombia, which, with its restrictions on the repatriation of profits and initial promise of regional integration and economic planning, appeared to offer a substantial antidote to US preponderance in a manner close to the regime's industrialist orientation. Yet, in almost every other respect the government limited itself to providing the basic conditions for an *apertura* (literally, 'opening') by rescinding Barrientos's security law, legalising the parties of the left and the COB, and lifting censorship. Alberto Bailey managed to make some advances in reducing the extraordinary power of the traditionally reactionary press by allowing journalists a column in which to express opinion independently of their editors, and by fostering a paper run by the journalists' union, *La Prensa*. For this he suffered the increasing attention of Colonel Ayoroa, and Jorge Carrasco banned any mention of his name in *El Diario*.

The response of the left to the government fell into three broad groups. First, there were those, largely without party affiliation, who followed the line of the Argentine writer Jorge Abelardo Ramos, renegade Trotskyist and principal ideologue of 'left nationalism', who argued that the major contradiction was between Ovando and Siracusa. Impressed by the assault on Gulf and convinced of the possibilities of the military moving further still to the left and directing an authentic national liberation movement, the supporters of this line urged a policy of non-provocation on the part of the left.[16] They were, however, a small minority, composed primarily of middle-class intellectuals.

The second identifiable tendency comprised the established parties of the left and evidenced marked differences of tactical approach within it. The common denominator was a recognition that the military was not monolithic and could at times display independence from the Pentagon's ordinances. However, it was necessary to defend working-class independence, regain basic democratic rights and place pressure on the regime to undertake further radical measures. Taking the softest approach inside this framework were the PRIN and PCB, both of which had been badly bruised over the previous five years and showed an almost instinctive desire to regain security and credibility by limiting their actions to the traditional syndicalist sphere. Jorge Kolle (PCB) described the regime as, 'reformist with some anti-imperialist elements, of vacillating patriotism and of undoubted but veiled reserve with respect to the "popular danger" ... a percentage democracy'. Ovando's government was the result of the failure of the Alliance for Progress but neither he nor his collaborators would fully confront imperialism and reaction.[17] Typically, the POR, which enjoyed more internal confidence and an external prestige perhaps unparalleled in its history, gave an essentially similar assessment a much more ringing tone, placing greater emphasis on the government's limitations and urging forthright mass action.[18] It is worth adding that, despite the use of a markedly different language, the assessment of Ovando produced by the *francesito* Debray from his Camiri cell was at root in agreement with this thesis. Although Debray made some surprisingly optimistic remarks about the 'middle-class character' of the military — no doubt indicating the first steps in a revision of the excesses of *foquismo* — he captured an essential element of the regime in describing it as '*for* not *with* the people'.[19]

The third tendency on the left formally concurred with much of the analysis produced by the PCB and POR but argued that the key characteristic of the regime was its link with Barrientos. The most forceful exponent of this view was Oscar '*Motete*' Zamora of the Maoist PCML. At a week-long political forum organised by the students' union (FUL) of San Simón university, Cochabamba, in January 1970 Zamora clearly distinguished himself from the rest of the left in effectively disregarding the reformist elements of the regime, marginalising the tasks of mass organisation, and maintaining that the counter-revolutionary character of the government (a quality it shared with that of Allende in Chile) required the initiation of a 'People's Revolutionary War'. This, he strongly implied, was ready to begin.[20] Tracing a similar trajectory, although with a good deal less bombast and rectilinear analysis, was the PDCR, whose sympathisers and members appreciated the possibilities of mass work but, being largely middle class, still tended to the view that armed struggle was one of the tasks of the moment.[21]

Unsurprisingly, it was the traditional parties which held greatest influence in the debates during the COB's critical fourth congress in May 1970. There is no doubt that this meeting was the most politically contentious in the organisation's history, principally because it involved self-criticism of the policies pursued during the rule of the MNR and in November 1964. Lechín, who had kept a very low profile over the preceding months, was the natural target of the left. At the FSTMB congress held in April he had been obliged to suffer the indignity of not being re-elected to his post by popular acclaim and was required to defend his candidature in what was only the second card vote in the federation's history. His opponent was Víctor López, the politically independent general secretary from the Siete Suyos mine who was backed by the POR and even some of the rank and file of Lechín's own PRIN.[22] However, the PCB rallied to Lechín and he won narrowly, only to face a COB congress where there was yet another close vote during which his opponents raised chants of 'No to the traitor of the working class' and 'Against political opportunism'.[23] The COB was clearly divided and its leadership under severe attack but in the ensuing debates it contrived to produce a political thesis that was to play a major part in determining the course of events over the next year.

The *Tesis Política* produced by the COB in May 1970 was built around a resolution presented earlier to the FSTMB by the POR. The essential features of this document were its restatement of the necessity of working-class independence and the connection made between the anti-imperialist struggle and that for socialism. These aims were not contested; indeed, in the light of the COB's experience under the MNR they were almost taken as read. However, the PCB could not accept a number of paragraphs that clearly upheld the trotskyist critique of the 'revolution by stages', tore the thesis of *cogobierno* to bits, and discussed the working-class seizure of power and the dictatorship of the proletariat as less than distant objectives. The PCB gained support for a number of its objections because a good part of the opposition to Lechín and the more generalised discontent over the COB's recent record was not so much political as syndicalist in character, directed precisely against subordinating the interests of union to those of party. Thus, following a sophisticated and highly-charged political debate, a number of communist amendments were carried while other critical *porista* positions — particularly that on *cogobierno* — were ratified. The final result was a most extraordinary confection wherein various sections manifested Trotskyist positions only to be followed by paragraphs clearly drafted by Stalinists. For example, section two, 'Socialism and State Capitalism', paragraph four, opens, 'The experience of 1952–64 shows us that in order to be victorious the revolution must not be halted but continued through to the end, and that the decisive problem is knowing which class holds power . . .'.[24] This is scarcely compatible with the PCB line that appears in section five, 'Anti-Imperialist Worker Unity', paragraph four: 'In order to

arrive at socialism it is necessary to unify, beforehand, all revolutionary and anti-imperialist forces . . .'[25]

Despite these contradictions the POR considered that its position
had been made sufficiently clear within the document to allow the
party to vote for a hybrid thesis, especially since if it failed to do so it
would lose further ground.[26] This situation mirrored the results of the
elections for the FSTMB's senior posts which, apart from Lechín, were
now occupied by the independent López, Simón Reyes of the PCB, and
Filemón Escóbar of the POR, popularly known as the 'troika'. One further and highly important result both of the debates and the effective
balance of forces between the PCB and the POR was the agreement to
establish a *Comando Político* of all the leading parties of the left, the
COB, and the major unions in their own right. This body would act as
the political leadership of the popular movement in accordance with
the COB thesis, which was certainly open to widely differing interpre-
tations on a range of issues but also unequivocal on key tactical questions.[27] Initially this united front had a rather shadowy existence but
before too long it was to be thrust to the forefront of affairs, in which
Lechín was obliged to participate as a member of a collective and
under close political supervision, rather than in his accustomed style
of independent caudillo.

By the time of the COB congress, the Ovando regime was embarked
upon a concerted lurch to the right. It had failed to build upon its
early measures and showed every sign of responding to pressure from
the officer corps to reassert its authority against a popular movement
that was recuperating rapidly and evidently under the leadership of
the extreme left. In February 1970 Ovando, who was officially presiding over an institutional movement, was forced by the La Paz garrison
to let eighty of its officers interrogate the civilian ministers over their
conduct and plans. By all accounts it was a stormy meeting in which
the ministers' facility for long words and complex ideas exhausted the
patience of a cluster of vocal but none-too-intellectual colonels. The
ministers survived the day but the writing was on the wall.

The most consistent indication of military disdain for the democratic aspects of the regime lay in the actions of Colonel Ayoroa, who felt
at liberty to close down *La Prensa* and investigate with remarkable
sloth a number of political assassinations, which — as opposed to
wholesale massacres — were extremely rare in Bolivia. The deaths of
Alfredo Alexander, the owner of *Ultima Hora* and *Hoy*, Jaime Otero

Calderón, another journalist who was investigating the circumstances of the killing of Alexander and his wife, and the peasant leader Jorge Soliz caused particular consternation because they were linked to the cover-up of a very lucrative and illegal arms deal with Israel set up by Barrientos. Moreover, the circumstantial evidence indicated that the assassins were closely connected with Ayoroa himself, Colonel Rafael Loayza, the chief of military intelligence (G-2 or *segunda seccion*), and Captain Luis Arce Gómez, chief of security at the Palacio Quemado. The culprits were never found but the regime's image took on a decidedly murky aspect.[28]

This slippage into discrete acts of terrorism was matched at the political level in July, when Ayoroa, encouraged from the wings by General Rogelio Miranda, succeeded in ousting Quiroga and his group from the cabinet. They were replaced by other civilians of a much more compliant nature and firmly under military tutelage. A few days later the hardliners achieved a further success in persuading Ovando to abolish the office of commander-in-chief of the armed forces, thereby sacking his friend Torres, who represented the greatest institutional impediment to those trying to claw back the powers they held under Barrientos. Torres was packed off to develop his interesting ideas at the Non-Aligned conference in Lusaka while Miranda took command of the armed forces in his capacity as army chief, to be followed in rotation by the heads of the airforce and what had started as a river and lake patrol force but now rejoiced — for perfectly sound political reasons if nothing else — in the title of navy, the cause of some merriment in the chancelleries and barracks of neighbouring states.[29]

The replacement of Torres by Miranda weakened Ovando's independence even further and gave Ayoroa the confidence to allow more open attacks by the extreme right. The most important of these was the assault on San Andrés university in August by gunmen of the FSB and a well-known gang of thugs known as 'the Marqueses'. The forty assailants were paid and armed by Alfredo Candia, the local chieftain of the World Anti-Communist League, and assisted by Captain Arce Gómez, eager to even the score with the left-dominated FUL which was attacking the regime. This was no hit-and-run raid but a complete armed occupation involving heavy shooting, a score of casualties and the cessation of all academic activity. The occupants remained untroubled for a week until Ovando was obliged by popular demonstrations to order Ayoroa to remove the falangists and their gangland friends as discreetly as possible. A similar invasion of the Gabriel René Moreno university in Santa Cruz was, however, permitted to endure until the fall of the regime. Although the FSB had an appreciable capacity for acts of vandalism and mindless violence, the university occupation also stemmed from the aim of neutralising what was correctly considered to be the principal source of support for the ELN, which in July 1970 broke out of a prolonged period of clandestine preparation and launched a rural guerrilla campaign around the mining settlement of Teoponte in northern La Paz.

The Teoponte guerrilla was in every respect a tragic affair, a pale shadow even of the Ñancahuazú debacle. Politically misconceived and militarily inept, it resulted in the death of all but 8 of the 75 insurgents within eight weeks whilst the hardliners in the military were presented with an excellent opportunity to extend their power well beyond the guerrilla zone and prepare for a full reactionary coup. The leader and principal instigator of the Teoponte campaign was another member of the Peredo family, Osvaldo or 'Chato', who returned from exile in Chile to take up the cause for which his elder brothers had died. However, Peredo was not a lone idealist and neither was the ELN a lost cause amongst the students and young professionals. Over the previous two years it had amassed significant support for an organisation of its type and its first manifesto after 'embarking upon operations' carried the signatures of ten well-known student leaders who had left the PCB or PDCR to take up the armed struggle. Also amongst those who entered Teoponte on 19 July in the guise of literacy volunteers were a number of young doctors, the theological teacher and poet Néstor Paz Zamora, and the folksinger Benjamín Cordeiro (Benjo Cruz). In the short span of their activities these amateur fighters recruited some *campesinos* and miners, but Teoponte was at root a middle-class endeavour and its failure registered most strongly in that sector.

The literature produced by the ELN in this period showed little sign of any revision of the *foco* thesis that served Guevara so ill. The fact that Siracusa had accepted the nationalisation of Gulf was taken—in what could only be a wilfully one-sided interpretation of the conjuncture—as evidence of the absolute identification of Ovando with imperialism, requiring an outright offensive. More important than this, though, was the belief that such resistance against imperialism should first take the form of a military struggle, the necessary precursor to any political work: 'It is necessary to defeat imperialism in an open confrontation which begins an unlimited war. Only then do communiques, conscientisation and manoeuvre take the form of deeds rather than words.'[30] Peredo reiterated the need to conduct a campaign in the countryside on exclusively military grounds: 'Experience has proved that the city is the worst enemy because all the strength of the repressive apparatus is concentrated there. . . . Ché's idea, which we continue to hold, was that of organising an army on the basis of the *campesinado*, but with a proletarian ideology, which might defeat another army, the upholder of the system. This new army cannot be formed in the city but in that terrain where we can move more freely and with greater possibility of development.'[31] The degree to which Guevara's ideas remained intact inside the ELN is evident in the correspondence Peredo had with Debray, the Frenchman emphasising the political origins of military activity and suggesting in comradely but forceful terms that the existing balance of forces was not propitious for the launching of a new guerrilla. Peredo's reply was unequivocal: 'The phrase of Lenin and Clausewitz, that "war is no more than the continuation of politics by other means", must be put the other way round for most of our countries: the continuation of politics by other means is nothing more than war.'[32] Such clumsy defences of militarism reached a sad apogee in the ELN's contention that 'revolutionary violence is to invest lives and sacrifices for the people'.[33]

The Teoponte campaign, if indeed it merits such a term, proved Peredo wrong on every count. The guerrilla's only tangible achievement was to exchange two German mining engineer hostages for Loyola Guzmán; the sum of $300,000 handed over by the West German embassy remained firmly in military pockets. This was on the second day of the campaign; thereafter the rebels were driven into a headlong flight in terrain and climatic conditions of which they had no knowledge and against which their urban constitutions possessed minimal resistance. Several fighters, including Nestor Paz, died of exhaustion; two more, caught stealing cans of sardines, were executed by their comrades. The majority either deserted or were quickly captured. In every case, and in direct contravention of Ovando's declaration that all who surrendered would be given full guarantees, these people were executed on the spot. The Rangers soon had the zone cordoned off and, as a result of the lessons learnt at Ñancahuazú, suffered minimal casualties. By early September the few remaining survivors had split up and were totally reliant upon the support of sympathetic miners and peasants to get them out. In the end this was only made possible by the fall of the Ovando regime and the ability of the local populace to oblige the troops to obey Torres's orders that the remnants of the guerrilla be spared. In what must have been a highly impressive demonstration of the errors of his strategy, Peredo was saved from summary execution by the population of Tipuani, which lined up along ten kilometres of road to ensure that he and his comrades were not captured by the army. One of Peredo's lieutenants, Gustavo Ruíz Paz ('Omar'), wrote in his diary that he and his companions were reduced to tears by the fact that people who showed them so much affection and risked their lives for them could also make such stringent criticisms of the *foco* in which the survivors had held such a devout belief.[34] What was left of the revolutionary vanguard was delivered to safety thanks to the masses they had come to lead. Despite this experience and the fact that its principal leaders were exiled to Chile, the ELN continued to function, but henceforth its actions would be limited to the city where it found popular mobilisation much better cover than the jungle.

There is little doubt that the survival of Chato Peredo and his companions was facilitated by the fall of Ovando and the consequent inability of the reactionaries in the high command to finish off their task of exterminating the guerrilla for the purposes of boosting military morale and dealing a terminal blow to the 'infantile left'. However, the initial coup against Ovando on 4 October was staged precisely by this right-wing group and inspired by its successes at Teoponte and the president's inability to restrain the repression meted out by local commanders. The sentiments that prevailed in these circles, and no doubt in the US embassy as well, were that the political relaxation begun in September 1969 had gone too far, that Ovando should be removed, and that political conditions were ripe for a decisive institutional coup. However, their assessment of the balance of forces both within the military and, more critically, outside it proved to be badly flawed, creating a situation in which it was the left rather than the right that gained the advantage.

In Bolivia the coup d'etat generally takes the form of a declaration of rebellion by a senior officer of a powerful unit, backed by expressions of solidarity from fellow-conspirators. There then normally follows a period of frantic negotiation during which garrison commanders consult their officers before pledging support to one side or the other or, as frequently occurs, remaining 'neutral' until matters have advanced somewhat. The *golpe* involves a concerted war of nerves and depends not solely on the perceived validity of the rebels' demands but also on the type of unit (armoured/infantry/airforce) that is supporting them, the background and personal ties of their figureheads, the geographical spread of support, and the decision with which they are acting. The outcome of a coup is normally decided over the telephone well before fighting between units might take place although it frequently involves threatening deployment of troops and dummy attacks by aircraft. Rebel commanders must not only be assured of a substantial caucus of support beforehand but also be capable of 'reading the silences' from those garrisons where they have limited backing or lack an alliance with senior officers. The staging of a coup is, therefore, a veritable art, the iconology of which is familiar to the people of Bolivia in much the same way as the population of Europe is conversant with the devices of parliamentary elections.

The garrison of La Paz and its environs is the strongest in the country, and rebels must win a majority of it to their cause if they are to have a chance of success. The key units in the capital are the Tarapacá tank regiment (the most powerful unit of all) stationed at El Alto, the Bolívar artillery regiment and the Max Toledo motorized unit stationed at Viacha, 15 miles from the city, the Colegio Militar, the Ingavi infantry regiment that guards the Estado Mayor at Miraflores, and the Colorado infantry regiment, the principal batallion of which provides the presidential guard, billeted at the Sucre Barracks. Finally, but by no means of lesser importance, there is the airforce base at El Alto which is the headquarters of the *Grupo Aéreo de Caza* (GAC) fighter command and *Transportes Aéreos Militares* (TAM), which has limited firepower but provides the only means for rapid troop transport. The garrisons of Cochabamba (seventh division) and Santa Cruz (eighth division) are less powerful but each possesses key units capable of shifting the balance of forces: the NCO training school and CITE paratroop regiment in Cochabamba, the Manchego regiment of Rangers and the airforce college in Santa Cruz. Aside from these centres, only Oruro, with the nearby Andino motorised regiment at Challapata, possesses more than a local garrison of infantry conscripts, capable of holding a town and its environs but not of launching major offensives outside the locality.

It is clear that at the beginning of October 1970 General Rogelio Miranda, the army commander and acting commander-in-chief, had good reason to feel that the institutional tide of opinion was running heavily against Ovando. Not only had the Association of Retired Generals and Colonels, a body of no little influence in military circles, published a communiqué calling for him to stand down, but there was also a strong movement of junior officers led by Majors Humberto Cayoja and Norberto Salomón that wanted elections. Accordingly, Miranda struck early on the 4th by announcing that Ovando, who was on a visit to Santa Cruz, had been removed from his position and that he (Miranda) had taken presidential powers pending further institutional decisions, a move that received the political support of the MNR and PDC. Troops directly dependent on the EMG and from the Colegio invested the city under the command of Colonel Hugo Banzer Suárez.

However, Ovando was able to turn both the clear identification of the coup with the forces of the right and his absence from La Paz to his advantage by securing in person pledges of loyalty from the garrisons of Santa Cruz and Cochabamba, support which enabled him to fly to the capital protected by CITE and force Miranda to negotiate. The rebels were further debilitated by lack of backing from the Tarapacá and the GAC, which had either proclaimed themselves neutral or made no pronouncement, and the powerful second batallion of the Colorados, which, under the command of Major Rubén Sánchez, was firmly opposed to the coup. Moreover, Miranda, in a remarkable lapse of military efficiency, had failed to silence Radio Illimani, reportedly asking his aides if any of them had friends in the electricity company who could arrange to cut its supply.

The critical division in the officer corps became even more pronounced during negotiations between Ovando and Miranda at the Papal Nunciature, with both generals being accompanied by large groups of bodyguards who came close to a shoot-out. After a day of tense and interrupted talks, incessant troop movements and confusion, both men agreed to step down. On the 6th power was formally handed over to a triumvirate composed of the commanders of the three services: Generals Efraín Guachalla (army) and Fernando Sattori (airforce) and Admiral Alberto Albarracín. The junta declared that it would rule until 1972, when elections would be held.

Although the officers of the La Paz garrison had voted 317 to 4 for Ovando's removal and telegrams from provincial units showed a similar balance of opinion, there was no such consensus about the junta. This confusion strengthened a third challenge for power launched without warning on the evening of the 6th by the recently returned General Torres, who made his way to the El Alto air base and secured the support of the officers and men of the CITE, GAC and the surrounding units against the formation of the triumvirate. Torres's counter-coup was given added weight by the backing of those who had previously supported Ovando, particularly Rubén Sánchez, whose unit was already moving on the Palacio Quemado as the fighters of the GAC began to strafe the zone around Miraflores. However, as Torres himself later admitted, there can be no doubt that his final victory was due primarily to the decision of the *Comando Político* to call a general strike for the 7th. The strike was formally against the junta but broadly interpreted as being in favour of Torres, a fact that rapidly persuaded the triumvirate to hand over to him the power it had held for a mere nine hours on a day when Bolivia was ruled by no less than six presidents. Torres's only firm military backers were the airforce and the Colorados, commanded by an officer who was known to be a maverick, but the support of the COB, which had sown panic throughout the officer corps, enabled him to take power on the 7th to a popular acclaim which far exceeded that which had greeted Ovando a year before. The general strike call had proved crucial, but it remained to be seen whether the *Comando Político* would offer full political support to a general, however popular he was or leftist his credentials. On the other hand, it was clear that Torres had very limited positive support inside the armed forces, the majority making a tactical retreat into neutrality while a sizeable minority remained in sullen opposition.[35]

Torres and the Popular Assembly

The worst fears of Miranda's supporters were realised on 7 October when Torres, in recognition of the part played by the general strike call in his victory, invited the COB to participate in the new administration. For eight hours on the 8th the *Comando Político* debated the issue of *cogobierno* with the arguments for a positive response being upheld by the PCB and a group of union leaders who had left the PRIN to form the *Frente de Acción Revolucionaria Obrera* (FARO).[36]

However, given that Torres initially offered only one third of the cabinet seats and that the COB's *Tesis Política* contained a number of unequivocal denunciations of *cogobierno*, the opponents of the proposal were able to force a rejection. Torres's leading advisers — Jorge Gallardo and Hugo Torres Goitia — counteracted by increasing the offer to half the cabinet and making the proposal public. This increased the pressure on the *Comando* and after further heated discussion the proposal was finally accepted, but the names put forward as potential 'worker ministers' were all of minor union figures who would clearly act as delegates under the control of the *Comando*.[37] In the face of evidence that both the offer and the debate surrounding it were generating a further coup attempt — this time by Ayoroa's brother, Miguel, commander of the Ingavi — Torres, who was anyway disappointed with the names presented to him, withdrew the offer. The COB did not insist and was evidently somewhat relieved to leave the president 'at liberty to form his own government'.[38] The COB offered its 'militant support' to Torres and recognised 'our common struggle to smash fascism, wherever it is found', but warned that, 'at the first sign of any deviation or retreat we the workers will be the first to denounce the fact to the people and occupy our own barricades'.[39] The same day the *Comando* published a twenty-point programme that called upon the regime not only to grant it official recognition but also to fulfil all the demands made in the COB *Tesis*; although it could not possibly do so, the government quickly signalled its acceptance.[40]

As a result of this initial testing encounter with the left, Torres's first cabinet was more military and arguably more right wing in character than Ovando's first ministerial team. The COB was quick to denounce the presence of Generals Via Soliz and Lafuente as well as the appointments of Siles's trusted strike-breaker Abel Ayoroa (minister of labour) and General Luis Reque Terán, a leading architect of the Ñancahuazú defeat and self-styled 'expert in defence against nuclear attack', as army commander. Yet, while it was the case that Torres was at great pains to protect the armed forces, made minimal changes in its commands, and limited himself to exiling Miranda alone, his government was palpably much more vulnerable to the labour movement than Ovando's had been. The offer of *cogobierno* was an astute tactical move but it was also made from a position of weakness.

In the first months of his rule this weakness was not fully apparent to the masses, in no small measure due to the enormous personal popularity that Torres enjoyed. Although his reputation has been greatly enhanced after his assassination in 1976, 'Jota Jota' ('JJ') endeared himself from the start to the populace more than any other soldier and possibly more than any other president in the modern era. In the first place, he had, of course, defeated a rightist coup, something that went a long way to occlude the fact that he subsequently protected its leaders out of feelings of loyalty to an institution which he had served for thirty years and which he held in almost mystical esteem. Torres's strength lay in his ability to capture personal affection in a simple style of speech, honest smile, and the knowledge that he came from humble origins, rising through the ranks after a childhood spent peddling sweets outside the cinemas of Cochabamba. To his transparent conviction that what he was doing was correct and proper should be added the identification of his appearance and persona with a typical middle-aged husband and father attempting against all odds to make ends meet. This air of domesticity was strengthened by Emma Obleas, a woman who came from a more elevated background but whose liberalism and *simpatía* was a critical complement to the attributes of her spouse. Torres possessed neither the mock-Kennedy features of the *blancoide* Barrientos nor the hispanic hauteur of Ovando; his thick moustache, shock of dark hair, and squat stature marked him out as a *cholo*, like the majority of Bolivia's townsfolk. (Sometimes, it seems, his staff remained oblivious to the advantages of this: on one occasion an unevenly tutored aide flew into a rage when a leftist leader referred to the president as 'bonapartist', thinking that the reference was to his lack of height.)

Although his regime was quickly revealed to be weak and vacillating, almost afraid to govern or upset the social forces that were bearing in on it, Torres did not lack ambition or the style with which to project it, as his first speech in the Plaza Murillo made clear: 'I am a child of this people and the doors of my office will be open 24 hours a day to receive my brothers, the workers. With you, workers, *campesinos*, revolutionary intellectuals and soldiers, we will construct a new social order where justice reigns and there is no more poverty and misery in Bolivian homes. ... We will impose an order of social justice which wipes out the distinctions between rich and poor, for everybody born in the territory of our Patria has the same rights, they are equal and deserve a common destiny...'[41] The objectives of the

Torres regime were similar to those of Ovando but necessarily pursued with greater urgency. The government saw its aim as that of obtaining genuine sovereign control over productive enterprise with greater state participation in a mixed economy where the interests of foreign capital were strictly limited.[42] This proved a great deal more problematic than was at first assumed, but there were several areas where the regime could not afford to dawdle if it was to retain its popular impetus.

The most important of these was undoubtedly the question of miners' pay, which the military had prohibited Ovando from returning to its pre-May 1965 levels. Comibol's real labour costs were $6 million lower in July 1970 than they had been in April 1965, and the rank and file was fully mobilised around an issue with which the military was unambiguously identified; Torres had no option but to authorise increases.[43] The agreement signed at the end of November provided for the regime the kind of dynamic that the Gulf nationalisation had given the Ovando government, but it did not fully meet the demands of the FSTMB, which was under pressure from a revived but still suspicious mass movement. When the delegation led by Filemón Escóbar ('Filippo') arrived in Siglo XX to explain the terms of the decree which granted *reposición* it scarcely received militant acclaim:

> 'When Filippo and the other union leaders came, the miners began to protest at their late arrival. There was booing and hissing for about twenty minutes, during which shouts of "petty bourgeois", "sell out", "bought off" and other insults in a similar tone were bandied about. . . . Seated on the ground, they listened to Filippo speaking on the restoration of wages and prices of contract. Filippo explained this patiently, clearly and repeatedly. He made comparisons between soft, medium, and hard rock, the scale of prices in 1965, the fall they had suffered up to 1970 and those that would now prevail, which in some cases was superior to those of 1965. The miners questioned him aggressively; they knew how to defend their wages resolutely and demanded that facts were explained until they understood things with absolute clarity. When they had finally taken stock of the position they did not fully believe that the things explained to them would take place. They said that in order to assure themselves that the restoration of the wage had been put into effect they were going to wait until payday.'[44]

Partly to help pay for the measure and partly to bolster an egalitarian image Torres also accepted the FSTMB's demands for cuts in the pay of the Comibol bureaucracy, fixing a ceiling of $1,000 (Bs.12,000) a month on all state salaries. In Comibol this meant a pay cut for nearly 250 people, in YPFB for another 145, some of whom earned up to sixty times the basic rate for a manual worker — Bs.600.[45] Military pay was not affected. On the other hand, the government only promised to consider sympathetically the other principal demand made by the union, that of *cogestión* (worker participation in management) with the power of veto. The very uneven record of the *controles obreros* under the MNR and the cautious attitude of the rank and file when faced with the possibility of formal participation in management gave the regime some space on this issue. But in March 1971, when the demand was picking up support quickly, Torres, aware of the more conservative and bureaucratic character of the petrol workers' union, declared *cogestión* in YPFB with himself as its chairman. This took the form of union participation rather than control since the workers' representatives and those of the management and the government were equal in number, the workers had no power of veto, and the government chairman had a vote; it was far from the model being championed by the FSTMB's 'troika'.

From the start the regime was less able to control events outside the state sector. On the day of the coup a number of workplace occupations were staged. The most important of these were in the press, including *El Diario, Los Tiempos* and Radio Indoamericana, in Potosí. The removal of proprietor Carrasco and de facto institution of a workers' cooperative in *El Diario* was the most important and enduring of these, turning the traditional organ of conservatism into a mouthpiece for the left. This fuelled debate over the issues of freedom of expression and ownership of property, pitting the rights of the individual against those of the collectivity in a particularly sharp manner, similar to the cases of Radio Renascença during the Portuguese revolution and *La Prensa* in the first stages of the Nicaraguan revolution. To this day each issue of *El Diario* carries on its second page the words, 'Usurped on 7 October 1970 for defending liberty and justice, restarted publication 1 September 1971' — a reminder from Jorge Carrasco of this short interregnum in his family's control of the paper and the means that were necessary to regain it. After much prevarication the regime eventually decided to ratify the cooperativisation of the newspaper even though it was taking a line that was far from *oficialista*, and the US embassy had made it clear that it saw the resolution of the occupation as a litmus test for the attitude of the government towards private enterprise.

Siracusa would surely have taken this line in any event, but he gave it particular prominence because the US government's own property at the Centro Boliviano Americano (CBA) in La Paz and Sucre and the US Information Offices in Oruro and Cochabamba were broken into, ransacked and occupied by students; in La Paz several US marines were beaten up, allegedly threatened with death, and ejected from the CBA. The ambassador angrily demanded $45,000 in compensation, full guarantees and an immediate return of the property. The government promised to comply and made some headway in negotiations, but the La Paz CBA, like the similarly occupied Jesuit resource centre IBEAS, remained under the control of the *Comité Revolucionario* of San Andrés, which mounted guard over offices it declared had been repossessed from imperialism for the use of the people. Since a score of people had been killed by the army in Oruro during Miranda's coup and huge crowds were attending the funerals of the Teoponte guerrillas in La Paz, Torres refused to bring troops out of their barracks to retake the occupied properties for fear of rekindling anti-militarist mobilisation.

The high command and many officers were further angered by Torres's statements about arming the people. During his triumphal tour of the major mines following the restoration of wages the president was continually besieged with demands for the distribution of weapons. In Siglo he responded by saying, 'the workers will be armed only if the armed forces should no longer be, as they are now, with the people'.[46] A fortnight later he promised the people of Potosí that if they were 'defrauded by the military, I will give weapons to the workers'.[47] Declarations like this raised expectations on one side and fears on the other, neither of which were fulfilled.

The right-wing backlash was further spurred on by a struggle between Torres and the high command over the release of Debray and the other Ñancahuazú prisoners. Late in November Reque Terán denied that there was any possibility of an amnesty for the Frenchman although the government had said that it was considering the matter positively.[48] Just before Christmas Torres furtively approved his release and sent a special detachment to Camiri which to all intents and purposes smuggled the prisoners out to Chile against the will of most officers. The following week Reque Terán demonstrated his anger by telling the press that there had been differences of opinion over the matter.[49]

Military opposition to the regime was soon identified as being centred on two leading supporters of Miranda: Colonels Hugo Banzer Suárez and Edmundo Valencia. Within weeks of the coup these two officers were sufficiently sure of themselves to break military protocol and challenge Lechín to a public debate over his accusation that they were fascists and supported imperialism. The students offered a venue and full guarantees but the colonels wanted a television studio instead of a 'live' audience and said that the FUL was incapable of providing minimal conditions for free debate. In mid-December Banzer, who still retained his post as commander of the Colegio Militar, was thwarted in a coup attempt when Torres failed at the last moment to appear at the institution's graduation ceremony, at which he was to be held hostage. Banzer read out a barely-veiled *pronunciamiento* anyway and held on to his post.[50] Such a state of affairs could not persist for long. A month later the two officers, better prepared, armed with $60,000 donated by the outspoken Brazilian ambassador General Hugo Bethlem, and supported by the bulk of the young officers who had backed Miranda, took over the Estado Mayor and declared themselves in revolt.[51]

The Banzer–Valencia coup of 10 January 1971 was defeated in much the same manner as had been Miranda's October *golpe* — by a general strike and critical divisions inside the officer corps. The speed with which the strike was called and miners shipped into La Paz to brandish their Mausers and take over the city centre clearly warded off support for the rebellion. The strength of popular mobilisation was significantly greater than that in October and offered the prospect of major clashes if the coup was to be sustained. On the military front the rebels had been driven to take Reque Terán and the chief of staff, Colonel Samuel Gallardo, hostage, indicating lack of support at the top and impeding intra-institutional negotiations. Moreover, the airforce and the Colorados remained loyal, isolating and attacking the *golpistas* in Miraflores while crowds of workers filled the city centre. Reading the balance of forces, the commanders of many units who sympathised with the rebels' denunciations of anarchy and disorder and the release of Debray simply sat tight and watched the coup fizzle out in a matter of hours.

Torres, who had seconded the *Comando Político*'s call for full mobilisation, and had finally been obliged to expel Banzer, fifteen accomplices and Bethlem, went to the Plaza Murillo to address the large crowd collecting there. The suppression of Banzer's predictable and precipitate rising was widely identified as the work of the masses themselves and demonstrably increased confidence and a general sentiment in favour of speeding up the process begun in October. This watershed was evident in the Plaza, where Torres, the victim of his own speechifying, engaged in a remarkable exchange with the crowd below. He denounced the 'small group of fascists' who had staged the revolt, committed himself to distributing arms 'when there is money to buy them', and promised to 'deepen the Nationalist Revolution' against a volley of slogans—'Arms for the People', 'Mina Matilde to the State' and 'Enemies of the People to the firing squad'. Eventually this barracking reached such a pitch that the president was obliged to break from his speech and respond to chants of 'Revolución Socialista' in an impromptu and uneven dialogue. Unable to persuade the crowd of the merits of his 'Nationalist Revolution', Torres finally declared, 'We are here to proclaim that the Nationalist Revolution will go wherever the people want to take it.'[52] Such a rhetorical flourish was, of course, made in the heat of the moment and represented neither the regime's completely open character nor its abdication of all responsibility for policy, as some have claimed. It did, however, illustrate an essential lack of authority and direction, which was to become increasingly evident over the months that followed.

The events of January obliged the Torres regime to take further radical measures or risk being overtaken by the left, which in its strike call had described the government as weak, vacillating and incapable of resisting reaction. On the day after the abortive coup further US government offices were attacked in Santa Cruz, and the CEPB's own radio station, Radio Progreso, was declared to be under workers' control. Torres won back a measure of credibility by renationalising the *colas y desmontes* at Catavi that Barrientos had ceded to IMPC, and three months later, on the eve of May Day, he yielded once more to popular pressure by finally expropriating the Mina Matilde group, probably the richest site handed over to a US corporation. Thus, Barrientos's principal measures in favour of foreign capital were reversed but the cost was high. In March Nixon announced that the General Services Administration would sell off more of Washington's stockpile of tin, the advance news of which alone began to affect the world price. More immediately Bolivia found that her exports of zinc were being boycotted both in North America and in Europe, forcing a frantic search for alternative markets. Loans from the Inter-American Development Bank and the World Bank were held up in what the *Washington Post* later called the most open action ever by a treasury secretary to manipulate international credit for political ends. The loan from the World Bank was for the construction of a gas pipeline from Santa Cruz to Yacuiba, a project that hardly depended on the political colour of the regime in La Paz but was vital to Bolivia's export effort. However, Treasury Secretary John Connally was both a close friend of the president of IMPC, Frank Tye, and convinced that 'the US can afford to be tough with Latin Americans because we have no friends left there anymore'.[53]

Recourse to nationalisation as a means of strengthening the state sector and drawing off radical pressure soon proved to be insufficient if only because direct US investment in Bolivia was not great. Nor was it always very profitable; the regime was highly reluctant to take over the South American Placers operation at Tipuani, despite the fact that it was being sabotaged and under virtual siege from the local population, because it was known to be a failing enterprise.[54] Yet, anti-US sentiment continued to rise. In the wake of the Banzer coup Lechín, who was now taking a more prominent political role, delivered a forceful anti-US speech, in which he declared that, 'while the Pentagon and the CIA remain General Torres won't be able to sleep peacefully either at home or in the palace, and the workers will be even less secure. If we want to embark on a period of political tranquillity we will have to throw the North American military mission out of this country . . . if fascist elements are still to be found in the army, why not liquidate them at once? When I say liquidate I mean kick them out and take the power of their weapons. Instead of kicking out eighteen, kick out tens and hundreds; remove all the fascists from the army.'[55]

Two months later, addressing the miners of San José after Nixon's announcement of the buffer stock sales, the COB leader gave full backing to the *Comando*'s proposal for an *Asamblea Popular* as an independent organ of popular power, demanded that 'the gringos . . . who have sucked the blood of the people for five hundred years' be chucked out, and insisted that armed struggle was the only way of doing this: 'the enemy has taught us the use of violence and we will now employ Bolivian violence.'[56] If, in making such statements, Lechín was regressing to the spirit of 1952 this was because he was responding to a situation which was in many respects similar to that which had prevailed nearly twenty years before. The tide of anti-imperialist sentiment was not restricted to the students, although they certainly undertook most of the practical initiatives, including the organisation of a vociferous 'Anti-Imperialist Week' at the end of May. As a result of continuous demands, demonstrations and temporary occupations, Torres was forced to make further concessions in this quarter. In February he closed down the *Centro Boliviano de Educación Sindical* (CEBES), an ORIT- and AIFLD-backed union organisation. In May he announced the expulsion of the Peace Corps, and when the US embassy hesitated, exerted pressure to ensure that its volunteers left the country by the end of the month. Shortly afterwards the regime rescinded the US government's contract to use the 'Guantanamito' base as a satellite-tracking station, Torres making rare recourse to irony in his explanation that the foreign base constituted a grave danger to the security of the state because it was so close to Bolivian military installations. At the same time Julio Garrett, the ambassador in Moscow, signed an agreement with the Soviet Union for the installation of an astronomy station in La Paz. Such moves incensed Siracusa and deeply concerned the high command, but the president refused to expel the US military mission, knowing that this was bound to provoke more than tight-lipped discontent.

In almost every case these actions were undertaken to pre-empt the left, which — usually in the shape of the students or the revitalised ELN — threatened to take matters into its own hands. Very frequently it did so, revealing the government's lack of authority. In February miners from San José and students took over the offices of the DIC (*Dirección de Investigación Criminal*) in Oruro to protest the appointment of *barrientistas* to senior police posts; similar occupations in Potosí and Sucre during March forced the resignation of several officers.[57] Threats of raids on the US embassy in search of CIA agents prompted the exodus of a number of diplomatic personnel. In Oruro the FUL occupied a mansion owned by the Patiño Foundation and turned it into a popular cultural centre, having already expelled the civic *Sociedad 10 de Febrero* from the university because its members were 'representatives of the bourgeoisie'.[58] The students of Potosí followed suit by expropriating the Freemasons' social club while those of Cochabamba and Santa Cruz 'repossessed for the people' several properties belonging to Barrientos. In a slightly different manifestation of this youthful adventurism a group of female students from UMSA's faculty of social welfare equipped themselves with shotguns and made a midnight raid on the only motel in La Paz. Allegedly to the cry of 'Hands up, Socialism has arrived!', the commando extracted eight underdressed couples and demanded that the building be turned into a nursery because it had become a centre for prostitution and drug-taking. In all likelihood these demands would have been met had the motel staff not protested that their livelihood was threatened and called in the police. Minister of Interior Gallardo—who wrote in his political memoirs that there was not one week during the Torres government when he was not required to solve some crisis caused by direct action—was roused from his bed to patch up a reluctant truce whereby the building would remain a motel but be cooperativised.[59]

The regime's unwillingness to employ the police or troops encouraged direct action as a means of wringing concessions from the state even by sectors which were not normally prone to such an attitude. In Potosí the minister of housing was held hostage for several days to obtain departmental finances and ensure the building of a new telephone exchange. In Coroico the prefect of La Paz and a number of engineers suffered a similar fate, and the local 'Revolutionary Committee' blocked all roads to support its demand for guarantees that the road to Santa Barbara would be completed. The mayor and council of the isolated town of Rurrenabaque successfully impounded a DC-3 owned by Lloyd Aereo to extract a promise of more frequent flights and a better airstrip.[60] Perhaps the most concerted and politically-charged instance of this localised mass mobilisation was the campaign to remove the headquarters of the army's second division from the centre of Oruro. This demand stemmed directly from the killings that had taken place during Miranda's coup; it proved so popular that, after numerous exchanges between the *Central Obrera Departamental* (COD) and Reque Terán, it led to a call for a departmental general strike. At the last minute Defence Minister Lafuente relented and handed the barracks over to the ministry of education, as demanded by the *cabildo abierto* (mass meeting of all citizens). This humiliating climb-down caused more ire inside the officer corps than any other incident, even the Debray release, since it appeared to encapsulate the weakness of the *'institución tutelar'* and the scorn with which it was held in popular circles. Retired and serving officers bombarded the press with letters protesting the 'appalling insult' and 'disgrace'.[61]

Manifestations of popular discontent and the breakdown of public order which usually accompanied them occurred at frequent intervals throughout the first half of 1971. Before May they seemed only to constitute a generalised chaos, but after the largest celebration of labour day ever seen in the country they took place in a new political context. This was determined by the May Day declaration that the Popular Assembly planned by the *Comando Político* would meet for the first time on 22 June in the legislative palace. The formal establishment of 'an organ of workers' and popular power' that was completely independent of the government led to a marked alteration in the political climate; a confused phase of making myriad demands on the regime and embarking on independent actions had grown over into one in which the regime's power and legitimacy were put under challenge by an alternative source of authority. For nearly two months this remained little more than an expectation, but it was an expectation that influenced events and groomed political behaviour. Even the regime, which certainly did nothing to assist the formation of the assembly, endeavoured to win the new body to its side and gave the impression of being almost relieved at the appearance of a new initiative. The fact that the assembly, which from the moment of its declaration showed signs of developing into a soviet-type body rather than a mere debating chamber, could be founded without official hindrance a full seven weeks before it opened its sessions signalled the degree to which the *Comando* had acquired a broad legitimacy and the left held the upper hand.

Such conditions led to the establishment of two new political parties that were to accumulate considerable popularity over the coming decade and pose a major challenge to the orthodox organisations of the left, which continued to place a premium upon programmatic clarity and internal discipline rather than mass appeal. The first of these, the *Partido Socialista* (PS), was set up on May Day in a fusion of FARO, Marcelo Quiroga's UNIR (*Unión Nacional de Izquierda Revolucionaria*), and the remnants of the *Frente de Liberación Nacional* (FLIN), which had become dominated by ex-members of the MNR left led by Mario Miranda Pacheco. The PS's orientation was towards an independent radicalism built upon a united front and anti-imperialism, couched in Marxist language but devoid of strict strategic limitations. It was in many ways similar to Allende's party in Chile and certainly did not lack a presence in union circles, but in this first phase of its existence the absence of a tight programme enabled it to span a number of contradictory positions which would before long engender internal crisis. The PS declared itself independent of Torres, but both the background of its leaders and the loose character of its platform indicated a fundamentally centrist approach designed to maximise tactical opportunities. Before too long the left of the PS would find that its greatest strength lay in those lowest common denominators of Bolivian popular sentiment: anti-militarism and anti-imperialism. But the party was always hampered by the lack of a disciplined organisation that is so essential to sustain a permanent presence in the working class. The PS was also debilitated by the competition it faced in the circles of the radicalised urban middle class by the other political grouping to emerge in this period.

This was the *Movimiento de la Izquierda Revolucionaria* (MIR), which began to operate from the end of May but was not formally founded until September 1971. In its early stages the MIR was a party that proclaimed an unambiguous Marxist line, adopted extremely radical postures, and appeared to be set to displace the authority of the PCB and POR with a bold and youthful politics that skirted the traditional stumbling-block of syndicalism. Before all else a generational party, the MIR was the product of a fusion of the PDCR, led by Jorge Rios Dalenz, Antonio Aranibar and Adalberto Kuajara, the *Movimiento Revolucionario Espártaco*, a group of young intellectuals led by the *tarijeño* economist Pablo Ramos, and a number of prominent figures, such as Jaime Paz Zamora and René Zavaleta Mercado, previously attached to the PDCR or the left of the MNR. Like the socialists, the MIR adopted a number of contradictory positions; even in June Aranibar was stressing the vanguard role of the proletariat while Kuajara held up the *campesinado* as the principal force in the battle for socialism.[62] Within a year this was to result in the formation of two marked tendencies within the party; later it was to contribute to the jettisoning of many of the original Marxist objectives, a sharp shift to the right and a high turnover of militants. However, in 1971 the MIR displayed few of these traits; it established close links with the ELN, criticised the orthodox parties for being lethargic, and invoked Lenin in attacks on military populism and nationalism:

> 'It is not a case of the people supporting and trusting in a few progressive officers, but of these soldiers supporting, trusting and following the people. It is our revolutionary duty not to suppress this Marxist-Leninist truth out of fear of 'upsetting' the progressive officers or because we are frightened to push them in "an infantilist manner" to join with their reactionary comrades in arms at the moment of crisis . . . the MIR considers that in the present conjuncture the principal contradiction is not "between the oppressed nation and imperialism" but between the exploited classes of the dependent nation and imperialism.'[63]

With such a line the new party quickly captured the support of many of the students and radicalised urban youth, taking over the leadership through Oscar Eid of the national students' union (CUB) as well as the La Paz FUL, which had previously been subordinated to the informal *Comité Revolucionario* led by Jorge Lazarte and Víctor Sossa of the POR.

The emergence of the MIR undoubtedly increased pressure on the PCB and POR, both of which redoubled their resistance to 'ultra-leftism' and insisted upon the importance of building a revolutionary movement within the working class and out of its existing aspirations and organisations rather than imposing it from without through 'adventurism'. While the younger members of the POR in particular concurred with the necessity of the armed struggle, the party directed its attention to the Assembly, arguing that the *Comando Político* itself possessed the characteristics of a soviet and that the *Asamblea* would consolidate these, bring about a state of dual power, and provide the basis for an assault on state power.[64] Attacking the MIR's line from a position more sympathetic to Torres, the PCB stressed at its third congress in June that it was 'not anti-militarist', and preferred to itemise the positive elements rather than the insufficiencies of a regime that, 'is moving towards a popular, progressive character with anti-imperialist features'.[65] On the other hand, for some months before the consolidation of the MIR the PCML had been adopting positions and engaged in activity that stood to its left. In pursuit of their objective of initiating the *guerra popular*, the Maoists had responded to the Torres coup by organising the *Unión de Campesinos Pobres* (UCAPO) in the north of Santa Cruz and leading it in a disorganised occupation of the Chané hacienda owned by the powerful landlord Raúl Bedoya, a leading spokesman of the private sector. In the first instance Torres attempted to negotiate a compromise because the peasants possessed a number of irrefutable claims and Bedoya had failed to repay a large state loan used to expand his cattle ranch. However, in January the central government lost control of the situation when, in the face of lack of official action, UCAPO reoccupied the estate and provoked further *tomas* in the region, including those of a large rice mill and even a leprosarium. The Rangers quickly moved in on their own initiative and shortly afterwards announced the capture of four 'guerrillas', including a certain 'Comandante Rolando', who transpired to be none other than Oscar Zamora himself and whose arsenal comprised a pair of revolvers and a stack of pamphlets by Mao. Zamora was summarily exiled but soon returned to the country while his party continued to fuel mobilisation in the countryside and city of Santa Cruz, where popular discontent with the political preponderance of the far right and the large agro-industrial interests had reached an unprecedented level.

The policy of armed struggle was pursued with greater efficiency by the ELN, which concentrated its actions in the towns. Varying its tactics, the ELN took to rapid occupations of radio stations as well as kidnapping important entrepreneurs. In smooth and widely-publicised operations it abducted the Swiss mine-owner Alfredo Kuser and the German owner of Bolivia's largest paper and printing concern, Johnny Von Bergen, from whose family the guerrillas extracted $50,000. Although an attack on the airforce base in Santa Cruz mounted in support of UCAPO went badly wrong, the ELN succeeded in bombing the houses of several leading landlords and rightists in a campaign of *ajusticiamiento* that stretched from minor police spies to Colonel Quintanilla, shot down in Hamburg. Some actions, such as a raid on the premises of the chamber of commerce in Cochabamba which yielded a hoard of documents implicating local businessmen in plans for a coup, proved popular and justified direct action, but others, like the planting of booby-trap bombs which killed humble policemen, induced popular repugnance as well as needlessly antagonising the military. Throughout this period the ELN remained in clandestinity and concentrated on provoking the right; it was the only force on the left not to have representation in the *Asamblea*, but it had many friends there who sympathised with the guerrillas' methods and saw them as an indispensable factor in constructing the socialist movement.

The Popular Assembly has been the subject of considerable controversy in Bolivian political debate. A few have dismissed it as a transient and thoroughly ineffectual body, a talking shop for self-seeking ideologues who met for only ten days, spent five of them immersed in bureaucratic minutiae and the rest in provoking a coup against which they could provide no leadership.[66] The left has, in general, defended the experience although it differs considerably as to whether the Assembly represented a 'school' (PCB), possessed 'the characteristics of a soviet . . . and the germs of dual power' (MIR), or was a body with much more pronounced soviet characteristics born out a state of dual power (POR).[67] Some of the heated and detailed debate over the Assembly has certainly been rendered either irrelevant or highly abstract by the fact that circumstances determined that it never developed beyond a cursory experiment. However, it was an experiment that possessed a very distinctive character, represented a conscious and practical attempt by the left to build on the experience of 1952, and terrified the right.

The Assembly's initial orientation was given by the COB's May 1970 political resolution, but in the weeks up to 22 June these were refined in the drafting by the *Comando Político* of the new body's 'constitutional bases', which were discussed and approved in the opening debates. This document stated that the Assembly 'cannot be a form of bourgeois parliament', but was 'an organ of popular power', which would 'execute its decisions using the means of struggle that belong to the working class'. In order to ensure a consistently proletarian line, 60 per cent of all delegates and members of commissions were drawn from industrial unions, which had a total of 132 delegates. The 'organisations of the middle class' were given 53 delegates, the *campesinos* (in effect, the PCML-dominated *Bloque Independiente*) 23 delegates, and the parties of the left — initially, the PCB, PCML, PRIN, POR (Lora), PDCR and *Espártaco* — 13.[68] Such a composition generated two major criticisms: first, from the far left, that the peasantry was ludicrously underrepresented, and secondly, from the government, that although the MNR had been formally excluded, it in fact possessed a majority through its militants in the unions. Throughout the Assembly's sessions the first point was rejected both by the COB and by the majority of the political parties not only on the grounds that the working class must have a majority because of its vanguard role but also because the *campesino* movement was still badly split and, apart from the *Bloque*, largely pledged to its pacts with the military; to give the peasantry representation on a numerical rather than political basis would be to consign the Assembly to the control of the right. The criticism about MNR representation was in a sense more taxing since the left was well aware that despite its proscription by the *Comando* the MNR did enjoy a powerful presence. Yet, in practice the party's union militants, while they might object to the revolutionary parties' occasional domination of proceedings, stood well to the left of their party leadership, now split between Paz and Siles.[69] In the event, these delegates adhered to the line taken by the FSTMB and COB. Although Paz had initially supported the idea of the Assembly, he had been quickly rebuffed, and even Torres had refused to negotiate a political deal with him, forcing the old caudillo into a *golpista* position completely contrary to the wishes of the MNR's worker militants.[70]

The *Asamblea* began its sessions in the legislative palace on Tuesday 22 June with the tacit approval and under the concerned observation of the Torres regime. For the next ten days it was in almost continuous session, many of its debates lacking direction or discipline and being greatly at variance with the formal protocols of the legislature that occasionally occupied the same chamber. This was the least of the concerns of delegates who had explicitly rejected a parliamentary role; it was also to be expected that the new body establish firm rules for procedure and constitute specialist commissions before it moved on to substantive debate. Although the threat of a coup was always in the air, it is only with the privilege of hindsight that the preliminary organisational concerns of the Assembly can be seen as so critical in their consumption of time. The first days were taken up with the establishment of a 'commission of powers' to consider applications for delegations, and the institution of further commissions to study *cogestión*, a united workers' university, and the establishment of a workers' militia and popular courts. All of these commissions were staffed in strict ratio to the Assembly's general composition, and all produced reports and draft resolutions within a week.[71] However, some delay was caused by the election of a president in which Lechín was again opposed by Víctor López. This resulted in the division of the FSTMB delegation, but even with the backing of the factory workers, the PCB and the POR López could win only 58 votes against the 103 logged by the leader of the COB, who carried the entire peasant delegation as well as the petrol and railway workers and the students.[72] Lechín's frequent absences from the chamber, a seven-hour debate over the election of the second vice president, and a day and a half of arid discussion over the PCML's insistence upon a vote of support for Zamora and the Chané–Bedoya occupation combined to stall progress. Zamora, who was not a delegate, gave a 'clandestine' press conference in which he attacked the POR and PCB for sabotaging the revolution, but his party's action only succeeded in alienating many union delegates, some of whom called for the exclusion of all political parties. Further problems on this score were averted by an eventual agreement to condemn 'repression of any type against any person or organisation engaged in the struggle for national liberation and socialism'.[73] These perhaps predictable difficulties arose both from the Maoists' manifest depreciation of the value of the Assembly and the equally marked reluctance of many union delegates to deviate from a series of concrete questions, most notably that of *cogestión*, to which they perceived the far left attached little importance. None the less, the first three days of discussion produced approval of a set of statutes whereby 'the Popular Assembly is constituted as the leadership and unifying centre of the anti-imperialist movement, and its fundamental objective lies in the achievement of national liberation and the installing of socialism in Bolivia. It is an anti-imperialist front directed by the proletariat. It is constituted by the COB, the national union confederations and federations, popular organisations, and by political parties with a revolutionary orientation.'[74]

The first substantive resolution was proposed by Lora and received unanimous support, effectively ruling out the government's hopes of coopting the Assembly. It noted that the right was planning a coup, affirmed that the workers would make recourse to revolutionary violence, called for a general strike and workplace occupations in the event of any reactionary offensive, and asserted that in such circumstances the Assembly would exercise military as well as political leadership of the popular forces. Although the adoption of such a position was essential to challenge both the right and Torres, the practical problems it posed were soon encountered when the commission on militias and popular courts made a preliminary report. In the subsequent discussion it was agreed that so long as the Assembly lacked the

From top, clockwise Juan José and Emma Torres, Filemón Escóbar, Guillermo Lora and Juan Lechín

Above Tolata, Cochabamba, January 1974. *Below* General Juan
Pereda and the electoral commission, 1978

coercive resources to impose its decisions popular courts would lack credibility. The difficulties of providing arms for the militia were also overwhelming whilst Torres refused to distribute weapons and the bulk of the troops remained loyal. As a result, the PCB had the commission's report referred back for further study.

The principal debate was over *cogestión*, lasting three days and pitting the major unions, the PCB and POR against the students, the PCML and the constituent parts of the MIR. The far left did not formally oppose the FSTMB motion put up by Noel Vázquez and Filemón Escóbar, but maintained that workers' control was highly vulnerable to bureaucratisation and at root a distraction from the seizure of state power, which could only be resolved by the armed struggle. While López responded by emphasising that control of Comibol was a political and economic issue central to the exercise of power in Bolivia, Lora found himself in the exceptional position of being applauded by the FSTMB leadership and PCB when he called for an end to 'verbal terrorism' and, instead of the repetition of formal truths, recognition that 'You cannot go to the workers when they are about to go on strike for more pay and tell them, "tomorrow you go to the civil war". The masses make the revolution. It has to develop from their daily necessities, otherwise you isolate yourself and commit suicide.'[75] There were, of course, powerful and recent examples that could be employed to support such a line, but there were equally salient problems with the organisation of workers' control, even with the power of veto, and although the Maoists and the MIR finally voted for the motion, their warnings about the necessity of confronting the fascist threat proved to be better founded than was supposed by the other parties. They were not, however, greatly assisted by the ELN, which on the final day of discussion distributed a strident manifesto announcing that it had taken on responsibility for the defence of the Assembly and would continue to protect it provided the delegates ordered the immediate arrest of all *golpistas*, the nationalisation of enterprises that supported them, and the deployment of armed workers' and students' patrols throughout the city.[76]

With most delegates running short of funds, the basic statutes approved, and further reports and resolutions on a workers' university, the militias and popular courts in preparation, the Assembly's first session was closed late on 2 July. Delegates were instructed to reconvene on 2 September, having reported back to their unions and received new mandates. In the meantime, the *Comando* reassumed political leadership and departmental popular assemblies were convened on the same basis as the national body. These began to meet in a number of provincial capitals from early July and, although more limited in geographical scope, proved to be just as popular and no less radical than their model in La Paz. Freed from wider political constraints and faced with concrete local problems, the departmental assemblies seemed set to become popular versions of the traditional *cabildo abierto* and generated considerable apprehension amongst local entrepreneurs and army officers. Though the Assembly's deliberations had been short and in many respects inconclusive, it now became clear that it set off a national movement that possessed great momentum and represented a direct threat not just to a notoriously weak regime but to the country's entire social system.[77] The large number of foreign correspondents who had descended on La Paz to cover the Assembly transmitted a similar message abroad, where figures such as General Bethlem were not slow to opine that, 'with the help of an illegitimate government there has been installed in Bolivia the continent's first soviet under the direction of Russia'.[78]

Evidence of planned destabilisation and preparations for a coup by the right *en bloc* — a phenomenon not fully seen since 1946 — was not hard to find. As was later to occur in Chile, the self-employed transport workers were to the fore, first reducing services and charging arbitrary fares and then declaring a full strike in June. Supplies in the markets became increasingly scarce as the large agricultural enterprises held back production and wholesalers began to speculate; the cost of bread, milk, rice, sugar and coffee suffered the most notable increases, in some cases up to 20 per cent a month. As Torres later admitted, the government faced a campaign of economic sabotage centred in Santa Cruz not only as a result of the expropriation of Gulf but also because of the establishment of national sugar and coffee marketing boards as a first step towards nationalisation. This move threatened foreign companies like Grace and local enterprises such as Gasser, the firm run by German immigrants who held a virtual monopoly over the refining of sugar in the east of the country. Another Santa Cruz group which had been badly hit — this time by squatter occupation of valuable but undeveloped urban property — was the Foianini family, which had close ties with Banzer, known to be in constant contact with regional business interests during his several secret incursions into Bolivia over the first half of 1971. Banzer's campaign in his home town was greatly aided by the cooperation of the Brazilian military, which in all probability decided to move from assisting destabilisation to providing direct aid for a coup when, in mid-August, Torres rejected a Brazilian tender to mine and process iron ore from the border deposits at Mutún and instead awarded the contract to the Soviet Union.[79] Bethlem had already given vent to his idea for the dissolution of Bolivia into a protectorate of the larger neighbouring states; now he publicly urged direct intervention, receiving only a formal rebuke from the foreign ministry in Brasilia which had come to appreciate the need for a strong military protegé to replace Torres and counter Argentine interests.[80] In Buenos Aires the replacement of the relatively flexible Levingston by the much more ambitious Lanusse provided further impetus for *golpistas* under the cover of the Argentine president's proclaimed 'neutrality' in Bolivian political affairs. The Argentines' prime candidate was General Remberto Iriarte Paz, but they also gave succour to Miranda and Juan Ayoroa.

The closure of the first session of the *Asamblea* and the prospect of a second within two months gave the conspirators both a basis upon which to build support within the country and a time limit within which to stage their coup. On the political front Banzer, who was recognised by most opponents as the leading challenger if not as a natural president, benefited greatly from a close alliance with leaders of both the MNR (Guillermo Bedregal, Ciro Humboldt, Raul Lema Pelaez) and the FSB (Arturo Violand, Hector Ormachea, Carlos González). His military contacts were handled by Major Humberto Cayoja, who some considered was being cultivated separately by *cruceño* business interests as a kind of right-wing reincarnation of Villarroel. On a wider political plane this activity found ample resonance in those groups predictably left aghast at the 'communist danger' and continuous social mobilisation: the *Confederación Nacional de Instituciones Femeninas* (CONIF), Opus Dei, the freemasons, local chambers of commerce, and not a few members of the diplomatic corps. Perhaps this circuit found nothing more disturbing than the publication of a pastoral letter by the Archbishop of Sucre, Cardinal Clemente Maurer, which called for 'justice not violence' and urged a popular orientation for the church. The day after its appearance a number of prominent Catholics from the country's placid capital threatened to crucify their cardinal if he continued in this vein.[81] Inside the military a trauma of similar proportion was provoked by the publication in July of a lengthy and radical manifesto by the clandestine *Vanguardia Militar del Pueblo* (VMP), indicating a measure of success for the left in its attempts to gain support from the non-commissioned officers, who play a vital role in Bolivia's largely conscript and often bilingual army.[82] When the demands of the VMP, which were essentially institutional in nature, were added to the expulsion of the second division, the release of Debray, and the continued activities of UCAPO and the ELN, they amounted to an almost irresistible invitation for the officer corps to support, if not to initiate, the coming coup.

In the last resort, the rebellion was not quite the rapid success its authors expected. It began on 18 August, when military intelligence was alerted to the presence of Banzer in Santa Cruz. Officers from the local police arrested him at the Foianini household. One version has it that as he was taken away in his pyjamas, Banzer, fearing with good reason that he was about to be put up against a wall and shot, divulged details of the conspiracy.[83] A number of other leading plotters were indeed taken prisoner soon after, but the core activists — Major Cayoja and Captains Tito Vargas, Mario Oxa and Ernesto Campos — remained at liberty to urge the commander of the Rangers, Colonel Andrés Selich, to rebel and take over Santa Cruz. Notwithstanding his strong anti-communist views and high ambitions, Selich vacillated even at this late stage. As a member of the Gasser family freely admitted six months later on a German television programme that revealed the extent of support for the coup from the expatriate business community, it took a generous infusion of cash to persuade the colonel to move his troops from Montero and effect the seizure of the eastern capital for the rebels on the 19th.[84] Banzer had already been flown out to La Paz but the coup now had a firm base from which to build support.

Even before Selich had gained control over the city centre Brazilian planes were landing at El Trompillo airport with large consignments of distinctive INA machine-pistols, distributed to FSB paramilitary forces that had adopted the title of 'The Christian Nationalist Army'. The following day flights were resumed, although this time the aircraft sported freshly-painted Bolivian markings. Brazil's intervention was scarcely discreet; on 15 August she had declared the full mobilisation of troops on the border, little or no attempt was made to conceal the identity of the planes making regular flights into Santa Cruz from the 18th to the 20th, and the country's consul in the city, Mario

Amorín, was wounded whilst participating in the fighting.[85] After a brief fight outside the prefecture Selich went on the radio, now broadcasting in the name of the *Frente Popular Nacionalista* (FPN), to announce that attacks had been made on a number of militants of the MNR and FSB, 'the authors of which were severely punished, eight of them being put to death'.[86] This declaration effectively gave notice that opponents would be executed and that Selich had reverted to his accustomed mode of operation, but resistance was maintained for several hours at the university. Upon its fall a further two dozen people were put before a firing squad.[87] According to the Red Cross, 98 people were killed and 506 wounded in Selich's thirty-hour operation.

It took two days for the rebellion to take root in La Paz, in part because the airforce held back from supporting it until the very last moment. Military resistance was very limited. Reque Terán attempted to persuade Torres to resign, misled the cabinet over the extent of support for the coup, and then entered into talks with the local *golpistas* with the result that he was shot and wounded in one of the many confused incidents that are typical of the early stages of a coup. Units of the Andino regiment sent by Torres to support the miners attempting to surround the rebels in Oruro simply halted outside the city and entered into an agreement with their colleagues who were in opposition to the regime to wait until matters were more clearly defined.[88] Only the Colorados under Rubén Sánchez opposed the coup until the end, and because of this, as Torres later remarked, were no longer deemed to be members of the armed forces by the rest of the institution.[89]

Although he was supported by one solitary unit of the military, Torres still refused to distribute arms to the people. Gallardo writes that even the ministry of the interior was refused access to weapons for its defence and was forced into the extreme measure of buying them off the FSB, the very party now in revolt.[90] On the night of the 20th, when the general strike and popular mobilisation declared by the *Comando* were already in effect, a delegation (Lechín, Mercado, Lora, López, Reyes and Eid) went to Torres and demanded the immediate distribution of weapons; he refused and added that anyway there were none left in his power.[91] Although it made little difference at such a late stage, this was virtually the case. When the crowds assembled by the *Comando* outside the stadium were finally sent by their amateur commanders to take the army's central stores they found only 1,200 aged Mausers and a very depleted stock of ammunition. Bolstered by small contingents of the ELN and the Colorados, the students and workers used these weapons throughout the 21st in a desperate attempt to recapture the estado Mayor and hold on to the strategic Laikacota hill. The manifest lack of military preparation led to the loss of many lives, but this was also caused by the fact that the popular forces believed that both the airforce and the Tarapacá remained loyal; they were, therefore, completely unprepared when these units moved in to liquidate the last vestiges of resistance to the rebellion. One reason for the delay in the decision to change sides was a breakdown in the rebels' communication network, which was only remedied when they were given radio facilities by the US military attaché, Major Robert Lundin. Lundin's role was given wide coverage in the US press only two days after the coup, but the contention that he knew nothing about plans for the rising and had only acted in support of Banzer at the last moment was shown to be false when it was revealed that the US embassy — from which a number of people were shot and killed on the 21st — had on the 18th advised all US citizens to stay at home until the 22nd. [92]

By late on the 21st the Torres regime had collapsed and Banzer was freed, declaring himself president before other contestants could lodge their claims. The students of San Andrés held out for another 48 hours until they were bombed and machine-gunned into submission with further casualties. Colonel Banzer declared with all the confidence of a complete victor, 'there will be no more teargas but bullets'. His political ally Víctor Paz, speaking in Lima, offered a characteristic interpretation of events by announcing that the coup enabled the conditions for 'realising the outstanding tasks of the national revolution and preparing the transition to the socialist stage, which ought to be reached tomorrow'. [93] The killings in Santa Cruz and La Paz precluded further active resistance by the left. Its members went underground to embark on extended self-criticism and establish some form of organisation. The defeat it had suffered was the most severe in the history of the working class, outstripping even that of 1946.

6.
THE *BANZERATO,*
1971-78

Hugo Banzer Suárez ruled Bolivia for almost exactly seven years. His regime was the country's longest in over a century, spanning the bulk of a decade in which open political activity was the exclusive prerogative of the military and its closest collaborators. The August coup and the dictatorship built upon it radically altered public life, which for the majority was subordinated to the risky negotiation of daily and civic affairs. Banzer certainly encountered opposition, but inside the military he was able to contain it with adroit manoeuvre; popular discontent and resistance, on the other hand, was repressed without quarter. This drove many sectors of the population into an anguished resignation that was abetted by the parlous state of the left, for much of this period entirely preoccupied with the arduous and painfully slow tasks of reorganisation. Banzer's ability to uphold this system of rigid control was due principally to the unequivocal support he enjoyed for several years from Washington, from an economically expanding and politically ambitious Brazil, and from the dominant agro-industrial interests of Santa Cruz, now the dynamo of the economy as a result of a massive increase in the price of oil and the boom in export agriculture. The matrices of Bolivia's economy were transformed

General Hugo Banzer

almost to the same degree as the country's politics, these alterations being trumpeted so loudly that it seemed to many that a new era had indeed arrived.

This illusion was greatly bolstered by the advent of similar regimes throughout the southern cone of Latin America. The coups of June and September 1973 in Uruguay and Chile established governments that were even more extreme than Banzer's and acted from their inception with a radicalism and confidence that lent substance to ambitions to hold sway for at least a decade and possibly to the end of the century. The shift to the right in Peru with the 1975 overthrow of the ailing Velasco by General Morales Bermudez was less emphatic but marked a general trend which was fully confirmed by the establishment of General Videla's institutional regime in Buenos Aires in March 1976. A 'Southern Cone Model' emerged, characterised by the prohibition of independent and union activity, an authoritarian garrison state, the pugnacious celebration of 'western christendom' and 'nationalism', and corporativist systems of social organisation. Repression was generalised and extraordinarily harsh; the left was defeated on a regional scale with the death and 'disappearance' of tens of thousands. Economic management was handed over to the enthusiastic acolytes of Milton Friedman and the 'Chicago School' of free-marketeers who dismantled the apparatus of protectionism, pared down state enterprise, scythed through welfare expenditure, and made a frontal assault on wages. Although in the medium term the results were in every case disastrous, it should not be forgotten that some spectacular immediate returns were registered by local financial groups as well as foreign capital.

If Bolivia did not exhibit the extremes evident in the large neighbouring states, it was largely because the ecological limits to her economy were simply too tight. Following his *autogolpe* of November 1974 Banzer dispensed with the services of his civilian allies, founded an exclusively military administration, and introduced a string of corporativist decrees similar to those promulgated by Pinochet. The model of an 'organic regime' was fully embraced with a formal but not inconsequential realignment of the ideology of August 1971. This system was to remain firmly intact for a further three years. Its eventual collapse, which only became visible at the end of 1977, was most obviously underpinned by economic factors and pressure from the Carter administration, but it was also accelerated by the resurgence of political forces that reformed and took advantage of unexpected opportunities with great rapidity. Thus, despite its remarkable longevity, the Banzer regime was by a long margin the first of the southern cone dictatorships to crumble, its 'New Bolivia' proving to be too threadbare a construction to endure once economic expansion was exhausted and external patronage removed.

'Paz, Orden, Trabajo'

Banzer was a talented career officer to whom political extravagance was alien. His political skills, which were not for some time fully appreciated by his peers, centred on an ability to control the armed forces through a diligent management that frequently required decisive pre-emptive action but was generally based on negotiation. He was not overly encumbered with novel ideas, never very popular with his colleagues, neither physically nor personally imposing, and only over time did he develop into a capable public speaker. The new president was the grandson of German immigrants, the son of a senior but undistinguished commander in the Chaco War, and well connected with the influential expatriate business community in his home town of Santa Cruz. Aged only 44 when he came to power, Banzer had graduated as a sub-lieutenant in the immediate aftermath of the 1946 counter-revolution when anti-militarist sentiment was rife. As a lieutenant he survived the purges of 1952 and was promoted rapidly under the MNR, becoming a colonel at the age of 35 after attending a number of advanced courses in the US. An expert in logistics, he served as Barrientos's minister of education and then as attaché in Washington. Trenchantly conservative in outlook but without party affiliation, respected by his colleagues, trusted by the North Americans and feted by the *cruceño* bourgeoisie, the diminutive Machiavellian was in almost every sense the perfect leader for the new Bolivian counter-revolution.

The trinity of 'peace, order, work' became the *leitmotif* of Banzer's rule and was seen by many as confirming its fascist character. However, in August 1971 neither Banzer nor the military as a whole felt able to advance without the support of the country's most powerful parties of tradition and historic antagonists: the Falange and the MNR. Both parties were given four seats in the new cabinet, in which seven out of fifteen members came from Santa Cruz. The FSB's leader Mario Gutiérrez was made foreign minister in recognition of his party's role in the August rebellion, but Víctor Paz, who before the end of the month was declaring with entirely misplaced confidence that 'I am the caudillo of Bolivia and people believe in me', preferred to manage his party's affairs without taking up a government position.[1] In a move that was soon to provoke some institutional discontent, Banzer signed a pact with the two parties to form the *Frente Popular Nacionalista* (FPN), by which the military formally became part of a political movement. The CEPB was also included in this new front, which was financed by 'donations' of 1 per cent of all state salaries, deducted at source.

Within days of the new regime coming to power the *New York Times* declared with marked relief that it 'confirmed that the United States still has friends in Latin America and that political change does not necessarily have to be to the left'.[2] The *Washington Star* concurred: 'Bolivia returns to its senses'.[3] Both journals looked to a rapid improvement in relations with the US; they were not disappointed. Banzer was quick to decree a new investment law which gave foreign capital excellent terms and effectively did away with the Andean Pact's restrictions on the repatriation of profits. This was followed by the 1972 hydrocarbons law that dissolved YPFB's monopoly and obliged it to issue contracts to foreign firms, fifteen of which eventually took up concessions. The new regime also made amends with the enterprises that had been nationalised over the previous two years; a foreign loan was raised to pay Gulf increased compensation of $100 million, Philips was paid $13.5 million for Mina Matilde, and IMPC received $1.5 million for the loss of the *colas y desmontes*.[4]

The response from Washington was predictable. John Connally brought Nixon's 'warmest wishes' to La Paz and praised Banzer's 'great courage'. In Washington itself newly-appointed ambassador Colonel Valencia went to the White House to hear the US president promise close cooperation 'throughout the 1970s', indicating that both sides had expectations of a prolonged rule. Indeed, for a number of years the rising price of tin proved to be virtually the only fly in the ointment; in 1973, following a period of steady increases, Nixon finally decided that it had reached a point that merited the reduction of the US stockpile from 232,000 tons to 40,500 tons, starting with a sale of 18,500 tons at the end of the year.[5] The threat to the Bolivian economy was very great and had been anticipated for some time, but Banzer was in no position to challenge the sales, particularly since his regime was benefiting from unprecedented amounts of US aid. Between 1942 and 1970 Bolivia received a total of $6.7 million from the US for 'administration and government'; over the 16 months between August 1971 and December 1972 Banzer collected a total of $32 million under this head. In his first year of office, military assistance from Washington was double that for the period 1968 to 1970, with total US AID loans exceeding $60 million; the grants of military aid for 1973 and 1974 were three times as great as any previously made by the US to a Latin American country.[6] The scale of this support from Washington prompted a congressional debate in which Defence Secretary Melvin Laird was unable to determine any reason for such largesse other than 'domestic insurgency', since it was now publicly accepted by the Pentagon that Cuba no longer threatened a country like Bolivia.[7] Banzer was, of course, especially privileged because until mid-1973 Bolivia was the most critical strategic redoubt for US interests in the southern cone.

Similar geographical interests lay behind Brazil's policy towards the regime. Brasilia was traditionally concerned to counter Argentina's interests in the *altiplano*, and this it could now do without great difficulty by favouring Santa Cruz, which lay firmly within its economic and political orbit. Less than a month after the coup Brazil granted Bolivia $10 million in credits for machinery to build a railway between the eastern capital and the border town of Corumbá. Over the following years annual grants averaged $46 million, underpinning a series of economic agreements by which Bolivia was to provide her giant neighbour oil, gas, rubber, manganese and iron ore at preferential rates.[8] The terms of some of these agreements were so generous that opposition to them extended well beyond the now embattled friends of Buenos Aires, obliging Banzer to qualify somewhat the enthusiasm with which he had initially embraced the new alliance.[9] Although Bolivian oil and gas were for a time of more than minor interest to Brazilian economic planners, the country offered only a limited export market, and one should not underestimate the more strategic motivations of the Brazilian military. These encompassed not only control over a zone of manifest political importance but also the forging of inroads through to the Pacific seaboard. This latter objective was naturally hampered by Chilean possession of Bolivia's coastal territory, but with a compliant regime in La Paz Brasilia's influence in that sector was markedly increased; once Pinochet came to power the possibility of an accord between governments of similar ideological disposition was further enhanced. The Brazilian generals made few efforts to conceal such aims; in 1972 the 'Superior School of War' published a document which stated that, 'The armed forces ought to intervene in instances of border disputes between other countries of the continent with concern for national interests, the ramifications of armed conflict, and the activity of international communism, whether it be in the country itself or in other countries.'[10] If Banzer and his colleagues were alarmed by this untempered interventionist ethic they made little show of resisting it in practice. In April 1974 Bolivia passed to Brazil 12,000 square kilometres, including the villages of San Ignacio and Palmarito (population: 3,000) in a revision of the border. In 1976 a further 27,000 square kilometres were lost in similar style; a year later the island of Suárez in the Beni changed hands, this time through direct Brazilian occupation. In several zones of the north east progressive colonisation by Brazilian nationals reached such a point that by 1974 the Bolivian chancellery was obliged to request its Brazilian counterpart to restrict the flow since national sovereignty was at risk. There was no reply.[11]

The compliant nature of the Banzer government in its relations with the US and Brazil was complemented by its severe treatment of dissidents inside the country. Both legal and de facto repression exceeded that imposed by Barrientos, being particularly fierce in the opening phase of the regime. Banzer appointed Selich as his first minister of interior, closed the universities for six months, reinstated the death penalty, and did nothing to curb those in his camp who proclaimed that 'for every nationalist who is killed ten extremists must die'.[12] After the fall of San Andrés on 23 August armed resistance was minimal and posed no threat whatsoever, but 'communist subversion' was almost always cited as the reason for arrests, deportations and the closure of newspapers or radio stations; those people who died at the hands of the military were invariably described as 'subversives' or 'Castro-communists'.

By supreme decree 09875 (7 September 1971) the regime formally declared the 1967 constitution to be in force, 'in every respect which does not contradict the spirit and nature of the Nationalist Government and its actions'. Having conferred upon itself the right to act unconstitutionally, the government only bothered to legalise the death penalty and the right to hold suspects for an indefinite period (supreme decree 10295, 3 June 1972). In the immediate aftermath of the coup Selich was given free rein to liquidate opponents, two of the most important of whom were Alcides and Félix Sandoval Morón, shot in police stations in Santa Cruz, where the populist clan was still feared by the vested interests that had suffered at its hands in the 1950s.[13] On some occasions, such as when he accused Torres of leading the ELN and Ovando of masterminding its operations from Madrid, Selich's imagination proved to be a little too fertile, even for the purposes of constructing a rationale for repression.[14] Mostly, however, he acted with absolute disregard either for life or the external impact of gratuitous killing. When, in November 1971, a pro-Torres army captain and ten other prisoners persuaded five of their guards at the Alto Madidi concentration camp to help them capture a plane and flee to Peru, Selich bombed and strafed the camp before closing it down.[15]

By January 1972 Selich was acting so zealously and had concentrated so much power in his ministry that Banzer, fearing a coup attempt, sent him to Asunción as ambassador. Four months later he was removed from that post. This did not, however, signal any relaxation on the part of the regime, as was vividly illustrated in May 1973, when Selich himself was arrested in La Paz by officers who had previously worked for him, interviewed by the new minister, and then beaten to death. The official version that he had thrown himself down a flight of stairs 'during a nervous attack' convinced nobody and caused outrage in the military, which forced a public inquiry. Perhaps the greatest irony of Selich's fate was that his death provided one of the best documented revelations of how the system he had instituted undertook its operations.[16]

The work begun by the defunct colonel was continued by Colonels Mario Adett Zamora and Juan Pereda Asbún who, as ministers of interior, controlled the much feared *Departamento de Orden Político* (DOP), the main instrument of political control. For most of the *banzerato* the DOP was headed by Colonel Rafael Loayza, whose principal henchman, Abraham Baptista, had been a vigorous chief of police under Barrientos. Captain Carlos Mena was another prominent officer who showed great appetite for the department's work, but many of its most infamous operatives — Guido Benavides, Fernando 'Mosca'

Monroy, 'Danger' Salamanca and Daniel Torrico, who at the weekends transformed himself into the popular wrestler 'Mr Atlas' — were civilians recruited from the lower ranks of the FSB or the criminal fraternity. A large part of the DOP's activity was organised around the jails, interrogation centres and concentration camps at Madidi, Achocalla, Chonchoroco, Viacha and the Titicaca island of Coati, which, like Madidi, had to be closed down for a while when 67 prisoners escaped to Peru after overpowering their guards during a football match in November 1972. Although most people who fell into the hands of the repressive state apparatus in Bolivia were eventually accounted for — unlike in Chile and Argentina, where the verb 'to disappear' acquired a sadly transitive form — it is hard to enumerate the effects of repression with any precision. However, the copious documentation collected by various human rights organisations yields a figure of 200 as the minimum for those killed between October 1971 (after the initial offensive) and December 1977. Some 14,750 people were jailed for 'offences against the state', almost every one of them without semblance of judicial process and generally suffering the kind of interrogation techniques described so vividly by Domitila de Chungara in her book *Let Me Speak*. A further 19,140 were forced into political exile, the number of virtually permanent economic refugees already totalling some 780,000.[17] Throughout this period, additionally, there was no independent union activity, no freedom to participate in politics except for members of the FPN (although by August 1972 Víctor Paz was complaining that members of the MNR were being jailed and tortured), and a strictly censored press; in all, 68 journalists were exiled, 32 jailed and 20 radio stations 'intervened' or closed down.[18]

These figures may appear very moderate when compared to the horrific statistics of persecution for the other states of the southern cone, but it should be borne in mind that Bolivia had a population of less than six million people, most of whom still lived in the countryside. In the urban and industrial centres where political and public life was concentrated the impact was considerable. Yet, since these circles were in relative terms very limited there was no exodus comparable to that from countries with big urban conurbations or large middle classes, such as Uruguay, Chile and Argentina, whence refugees streamed into Europe on a scale not seen since the 1930s. In these countries one of the predominant characteristics of repression was the use of sophisticated techniques of detection and control whereas one cannot avoid the conclusion that in Bolivia brutality and gut enthusiasm generally outweighed professionalism in the maintenance of public order and the suppression of opposition. In March 1973 Colonel Adett managed to expel 119 Soviet diplomats, only to apologise for a 'clerical error' when he was informed by the ambassador that there were no more than 40 in the country and that one of those listed as 'endangering the security of the state' was a four-year-old girl. Earlier the minister had declared the guerrillas were operating in Oruro and imposed a state of emergency. This information was promptly and vehemently denied by the local commander, Colonel Cayoja, who was within a matter of hours packed off as attaché to Washington. Cayoja's much publicised return of Banzer's 'expenses' cheque of $5,000 served as a sharp reminder that dissidence was not wholly confined to the civilian spheres.[19] Normally such discontent was contained by corruption or limited institutional sanctions but in the case of his most senior competitors Banzer did not hold back from more forceful measures. Generals Iriarte, Zenteno Anaya and César Ruíz Velarde, and Colonel Miguel Ayoroa, for example, were successively deported to more or less comfortable exile, where they joined the voluble Reque Terán to challenge or denounce the regime. The outcast Torres remained a case apart since he had joined the *Frente Revolucionario Anti-imperialista* (FRA) alongside the PCB, MIR, POR and PRIN. Although he did not remain in the alliance long and the FRA itself collapsed within a year, the ex-president's lone propaganda campaign had sufficient socialist motifs and popular impact for Torres to become the target of the regime's more imaginative claims; Pereda's accusation that the general was forming a guerrilla by the name of 'Black Condor' in league with Régis Debray was but one of a number of colourful inventions produced by the ministry of interior for public consumption.[20]

Whatever its flaws, the imposition of a blanket control enabled Banzer to enforce the highly unpopular economic measures required of his government by the IMF. The first of these was implemented on 27 October 1972, when the regime devalued the peso by 67 per cent in order to obtain a $24 million loan from the Fund. The devaluation increased the cost of living by 39 per cent over the following year while wage rises were limited to between 10 and 20 per cent, resulting in a minimum loss of earning power of 19 per cent.[21] Following traditional practice, Banzer announced the measure on a Friday evening to delay popular mobilisation and allow time for troops to occupy the centre of La Paz over the weekend, when a full state of siege was declared. Nevertheless, on the Monday afternoon, after a series of meetings which led to the declaration of an eight-hour protest strike, several hundred workers took to the streets of the capital. This first open demonstration against the 'fascist, anti-worker dictatorship' was suppressed quickly and with maximum force. According to the government, clashes with the troops left 14 people wounded, but up to 20 deaths were reported in the foreign press.[22]

The popular economy suffered an even more severe blow when, in decrees first announced in October 1973 but eventually delayed until 20 January 1974, Banzer removed or substantially reduced state subsidies on a range of basic goods and services. The subsidy on flour alone amounted to $20 million a year, the withdrawal of which would represent a considerable saving for the state. In the event, this commodity was one of the least badly hit, the price rise introduced in January in order 'to bring it into line with the world market . . . and reduce contraband' being limited to 150 per cent. The cost to the consumer of cooking oil, eggs, sugar, coffee, meat, rice and pasta rose by an average of 219 per cent.[23] Fully aware that inflation to such a degree required wage compensation if public order was to be maintained, the regime decreed a complicated system of bonuses for the industrial labour force, but this covered only half the rise in prices.[24] In the towns the response to this measure was stronger than that of October 1972. The day after it was declared more than a hundred factories in La Paz came out on a 36-hour strike. Two days later a national factory workers' strike received the support of the miners and bank workers. Housewives protested outside the presidential palace brandishing pots and pans, and there were a number of clashes between students and the police. Seventy people were arrested, the church issued an extraordinarily strong condemnation of the decrees, and the CEPB stated flatly that it could not afford to pay the stipulated wage bonus. Yet it was in the countryside that the removal of price subsidies produced the gravest crisis.

The spontaneous mobilisation that took place in the upper Cochabamba valley after the introduction of the price rises stemmed from the fact that the *campesinos* received no compensatory bonus at all and were prohibited from increasing the market price of their produce. Moreover, many did not produce the goods affected and, like the urban workers, were obliged to purchase them at the new prices, which was nigh-on impossible in January when stocks from the last harvest were exhausted and the next still far from ripe. Trouble began early on the morning of the 22nd when, adhering to the strike call, workers at the large Manaco shoe factory at Quillacollo, 15 kilometres from Cochabamba, held a protest march. This soon drew the support of other factories and became so large that the local detachment of police had to withdraw. The next day demonstrators attempted to blow up three bridges, and then held a public meeting at which demands were raised for the withdrawal of the decrees, freedom for all political prisoners, the devolution of 'intervened' radio stations, and the dispatch of a government commission to discuss terms. As a result of the symbiosis between town and country in Cochabamba news of the Quillacollo events was soon known in most of the valley. On the 24th the road to Santa Cruz was blocked. The next day blockades extended from kilometre 20 as far as the turning to Sucre at kilometre 126. Despite extremely heavy rain some 20,000 peasants congregated at the major points at which the highway was barricaded. Their demands for the removal of the decrees and that Banzer come immediately to negotiate with them were presented first to the minister of agriculture, Colonel Alberto Natusch Busch, on the 25th and then to the newly-designated military 'interventor', General Pérez Tapia, on the 28th. Refusing either to make a deal with subordinates or to go to La Paz, the *campesinos* insisted upon Banzer's presence as the only condition for lifting the barricades. The president's response was curtly to reject 'any dialogue under pressure', declare a state of siege, and send the Tarapacá to reinforce local troops.

Early on the 29th the *campesino* leaders held a further meeting with General Pérez, the talks lasting until mid-afternoon. On returning to Cochabamba, Pérez was surprised to encounter a column of six tanks and eight armoured cars moving towards the first roadblock. Having made some progress in his discussions, he ordered the column to halt but was informed that Banzer had commanded a complete 'mopping up of the subversives'. The regime later announced that Pérez had been taken hostage and was only released on the 30th after action by the armoured column.

What was soon dubbed 'The Massacre of the Valley' began at the village of Tolata at 5 p.m. on the 29th. When the column approached, the *campesinos* gathered round thinking that Banzer had finally arrived. The commanding officer ordered them to disperse. First there was silence and then a woman threw a stone at the leading tank. The attack that followed combined the use of fighter aircraft with the automatic weapons of the armoured vehicles but was described by the high command as 'a simple dissuasive action'. One conscript later told a priest, 'we have seen mounds of corpses, *campesinos* stacked up like wood'. Another counted some thirty covered trucks travelling to the airport from Tolata, and said that after the attacks some soldiers refused to go on while others had deliberately fired into the air.[25] Later that night some 700 peasants were attacked at a bridge near Epizana; 15 corpses were found and twenty people 'disappeared'. The next day military operations produced more casualties, but the remaining roadblocks were cleared without further loss of life.

The total death toll was estimated at between 80 and 200, one factor in the uncertainty being ignorance of the fate of 65 people who had 'disappeared'. There were no military casualties. Tolata was Banzer's San Juan and described by the church as 'another My Lai'. It effectively terminated the alliance between the military and the *campesinado* for although the *Pacto* continued to be signed every year by official leaders, it now patently lacked any credibility among the rural masses. The president's response was to claim that the protest had been planned by the Cubans in league with the exiled Chilean socialist leader Carlos Altamirano. Two days after the Tolata killings Banzer gave a speech to tame peasant leaders from the *altiplano* in which he persisted in his theory, stating, 'To you, *campesino* brothers, I am going to give direction as your leader: I authorise you to kill the first agitator that goes into the *campo*, I take full responsibility. If you don't kill them, bring them here so that they can deal with me personally. I will give you a reward.'[26] In practice Banzer had already dispensed with many of Barrientos's methods in upholding the alliance with the peasantry since it no longer played the crucial role of ten years before. With the working class in full retreat and the armed forces greatly strengthened the regime could exist with neutrality rather than popularity in the countryside. The appointment of hardliner Natusch, who had declared 'we will be totally radical' with the Cochabamba protestors, was one indication of this new approach. Neither Natusch, a *beniano*, nor Banzer, a *cruceño*, spoke an indigenous language or cared to cavort in populist style. The president rarely made rural tours, and when he gave speeches seldom deviated from bland celebrations of 'nationalism' and warnings about its opponents: 'I have heard that you don't like politicians. I don't like them either because they come to cheat you. The Communists want to take away your land, to give it to the state; the politicians just want to cheat you. They only want peasant votes in order to get into office, where they forget about their false promises.'[27]

The official confederation led by Oscar Céspedes progressively lost support, undermined by the events of January 1974, more general repression and the regime's economic policies. It was also challenged by independent currents, which expanded with predictable unevenness but gradually acquired an appreciable following outside the parameters of state patronage or the clientelist circuits of powerful local *caciques*. One such group was drawn from the remnants of the Maoist-controlled *Bloque Independiente* but this was soon overtaken in size and influence by the signatories of the 1973 Tiwanaku Manifesto, the most visible of whom was Genaro Flores from the province of Aroma in La Paz. Flores had been the peasant leader most favoured by Torres but shifted to support radical, independent organisation during his exile following the 1971 coup. The group around him possessed tenuous but vital links with the urban working class and sought to transcend the localism that had hampered the rural labour movement so greatly in the past. At the same time there occurred a tangible consolidation of those groups which subordinated economic demands to the more directly political claims of Bolivia's indigenous peoples. Although these groups varied considerably in the degree to which they were prepared to accept the existence of the creole republic or negotiate with *blancoides*, all maintained a resolute defence of the *indio* as a distinct race and the *Qheswaymaras* as a people defrauded of their nation (Kollasuyo). The oldest of these organisations, Fausto Reinaga's *Partido Indio*, was founded in 1962 and had never expanded beyond a propaganda group, but it was typical in its evocation of the Incas and Tupac Katari in defence of a heritage that had to be revived and realised:

'Do you swear by the God Inti, the Goddess Pachamama, our martyrs Tupac Amaru, Tupac Katari, Thomas Katari, to be a responsible militant of the *Partido Indio de Bolivia*, to obey its authority, to respect its regulations, and to struggle with your own life for the triumph of the Indian Revolution?

Yes, I swear.

If you do so, the Gods of the race and the Central Committee of the Party will reward you, if you betray us Inti and Pacha-mama, the martyrs and the justice of the PIB will punish you by taking your life. Amen.'[28]

A more secular group to emerge in the 1970s was known as MINK'A after a traditional form of collective work in the countryside. Led by Julio Tumiri Apaza, this body began as an articulate group of activists dedicated primarily to publicising the oppression of the indian and drawing up programmes that would both raise consciousness and dynamise the nascent indigenous movement. For the supporters of MINK'A La Paz remained Chuquiapu, the colonisation of which was incarnated in the fact that at the end of the 1960s the city was adorned by 39 statues in public places, 36 of them being of *gringos* (including Kennedy, Baden Powell, Humboldt and Mervin Jones), only three of Bolivian *mestizos* (Murillo, Abaroa and Busch) and none of any native of Kollasuyo.

'When we talk about the American people, we mean the Indians; when we talk of the Andean region, we recall the Tawantinsuyo of the past. To ignore this reality is, we feel, an outrage, a *lèse majesté* . . . For Bolivians, using the word "peasant" is just another way of calling the Indians "*indios*", but it also means killing them culturally and physically by confining them to being no more than a "social class". . . . For the Indians independence will come on the day when they take the leadership and administration of their people into their own hands. This they are entitled to do by right.'[29]

By 1975 MINK'A had developed into a fully-fledged political party — MITKA (*Movimiento Indio Tupac Katari*). After Banzer's fall, MITKA split, with one sector led by Constantino Lima adhering to a more extreme line which bordered on outright racism, rejected religious precepts and the validity of political divisions into 'left' or 'right', and maintained that 99 per cent of change would be achieved through the use of violence.[30]

These parties never displayed the kind of organisational system that characterised the urban political movements, and they were frequently dominated by caudillos like Lima who paid scant attention to democratic procedures. The experience of the Banzer regime did, though, enhance their popularity and swell numbers of 'members' so that by the end of the decade the militants of Flores's MRTK (*Movimiento Revolucionario Tupac Katari*) were virtually interchangeable with the members of the *Confederación Sindical Unica de Trabajadores Campesinos de Bolivia* (CSUTCB), which after the fall of the dictatorship became by far the largest peasant organisation and a member of the COB, marking a watershed in relations between urban and rural workers.

In much the same manner it served to regenerate this autochthonous politics, the Banzer regime provoked increasingly open opposition amongst the clergy. While there were not a few in the hierarchy who upheld the traditions of an 'apolitical' church—most notably the rector of the Catholic University and director of *Presencia*, Monseñor Genaro Prata—many national priests as well as the predominantly Catalan and Canadian members of the orders not only adhered to but actively mobilised behind the courteous but firm protestations against repression and economic policy regularly published by the Justice and Peace Commission, established in 1973.[31] The Commission was not simply a vehicle for liberation theologians although it did incorporate those sectors of the clergy which formed the local branch of *Iglesia y Sociedad en América Latina* (ISAL), which as early as September 1971 had declared, '[The regime] attempts to be Christian simply and solely solely by calling itself anti-communist. Not all the affirmations of Marxism are anti-Christian. On the other hand, many of the dogmas of capitalism are. By calling itself Christian a revolution has to prove that it is in favour of man. To date it appears to us that the new government has shown itself to be otherwise inclined. It entitles itself "nationalist". However, it is already taking the first steps towards handing over the riches of the country to voracious international concerns.'[32]

Such sentiments clearly bore the imprint of those at the foot of the hierarchy, but they gained the sympathy of some senior clerics like Archbishop Jorge Manrique of La Paz and Bishop Jesús López de Lama of Corocoro, both of whom had their houses and offices raided by the DOP. After the Commission published the pamphlet *La Masacre del Valle* in February 1975 a number of its members were exiled and it became the victim of the very repression it was denouncing. This long-delayed move, it later transpired, was part of what was called the 'Banzer Plan', by which 'the Church as a whole should not be attacked, still less the bishops as a body, but only a part of the Church vanguard, such as Archbishop Manrique . . . to separate him from the hierarchy and create problems with the national (Bolivian-born) clergy.'[33] The operation, which was described with enthusiastic attention to detail by Bolivian delegates to the third congress of the Latin American Anti-Communist Confederation held at Asunción in March 1977, included the cooperation of the CIA and soon became standard practice for dictatorships of the southern cone and Central America. It succeeded in keeping *Presencia* in line, tempering the content of Radio Fides, and forcing the church to maintain a low profile within the *Asamblea Permanente de los Derechos Humanos* (APDH) but did little to deter the Canadian Oblates administering the periodically-silenced Pio XII radio station in Siglo XX or the Jesuits working in the *Centro de Investigación y Promoción Campesina* (CIPCA). Given the absence of an organised left for much of this period, these and other religious groups cautiously shouldered much of the responsibility for defending democratic rights.

The discontent and divisions in the Church reflected similar trends inside the middle class, which by no means reaped uniform benefit from Banzer's heavy-handed policies. At times such pressures showed up inside the MNR, FSB and sectors of the military, but these generally amounted to little more than domestic quarrels and seldom troubled the stability of the regime. As long as the parties continued to lend him political capital Banzer was not prepared to create trouble over matters such as the malversion of $22,500 by the falangist who was director of the national lottery, Paz's half-hearted criticisms of the devaluation, or even the division of the FSB in February 1973 caused by the intemperate Carlos Valverde, who resigned as minister of health and rushed back to Santa Cruz 'to set up a guerrilla'. However, by the end of 1973 internal wrangling had reached a state that placed the future of the FPN in doubt. The principal cause was Paz's belated recognition that his party's popular credentials had been extremely badly tarnished by its support for Banzer. The severity of the economic decrees first publicised in October 1973 allied with continuous friction with the Falange and the vague promise of controlled elections in 1974 finally led the old caudillo to make a break while the MNR still had the opportunity to salvage something of its popularity. However, many of Paz's senior colleagues had no intention of vacating the well-paid posts they occupied, and he was unable to pull all the members of the party out of the cabinet after he withdrew support for Banzer late in November 1973. When, six weeks later, the *jefe* was unceremoniously sent into exile, the leader of this sizeable rump, Ciro Humboldt, expelled him from the party with the explanation that, 'The cult of the personality is a result of the myth of the infallible man despite the fact that history has taught us that to err is human. . . . I ought to reiterate on this occasion our support for and solidarity with the leader of Bolivian nationalism, General Hugo Banzer Suárez. Our president has entered deeply into the heart of the masses as an example of civic responsibility, a constructive spirit and unlimited abnegation . . .'.[34]

Such is the language of obsequious placemen, but it did Humboldt little good since within five months he too was in exile, implicated in one of the few genuine coup attempts against Banzer. This was a short but potentially dangerous rising staged early in June by a group known as the 'Movement of Young Officers'. Composed principally of junior colonels and majors, this movement had coalesced after the August 1971 coup as a result of what it perceived to be the total betrayal of the nationalist beliefs espoused by a regime many of them had helped establish. Discontent had been sopped up to some degree by the creation at the end of 1972 of COFADENA, a military development corporation which was charged with a number of important economic initiatives in order to retain some elements of the Ovando-Torres policy that remained popular with the junior officer corps. Yet after an early flourish, COFADENA was marginalised and prohibited from pursuing the fully statist line many of its supporters sought. Further alarmed at the regime's economic policies, the group's principal leaders—Colonels Raúl López Leytón, Rolando Saravia, Gary Prado and Arsenio González—decided to make a pre-emptive strike. López Leytón's regiment, the Tarapacá (which may well have still been suffering the effects of its activity in the Cochabamba valley) occupied the centre of La Paz on 4 June and called upon the high command to support its demands for Banzer's resignation, a completely military government followed by early elections, the trial of all those who had enriched themselves through the state, and clarification of the meaning of 'political crimes'. The senior commanders did not deliberate long before these demands were rejected and the 24 ringleaders sent abroad. Nevertheless, Banzer felt constrained to reincorporate most of them within a matter of months since they represented a substantial body of opinion amongst those officers who had graduated after 1952 which the president needed to mollify to some degree if he was to remain at the helm for long. Additionally, they could be better controlled by the intelligence service in provincial garrisons than in exile. At the time this appeared to be a prescient move, swinging military discontent away from Banzer himself, but it helped keep alive a faction which continued to agitate for change from within and would in the future present a major obstacle to the military hardliners.[35]

The abortive Tarapacá revolt combined with the manifest exhaustion of the FPN and the impressive example of corporativist military rule being essayed by Pinochet helped to convince Banzer that he no longer required civilian allies and could proceed with the institution of a completely military administration operating wholly on its own terms. Distinct from the other southern cone regimes in that the new order did not represent a fundamental alteration in the balance of social forces, the '*autogolpe*' of 9 November 1974 was nonetheless a significant political watershed. Its rationale was contained in supreme decree 11947, which opened with the declaration that, 'The wish to constitutionalise the public authorities through elections for political parties only represented an end in itself, for the satisfaction of their own needs and not a means by which to serve the Patria with plans and programmes for the progress of the country.' All political parties were therefore declared to be 'in recess' and public administration placed exclusively in the hands of the armed forces until 1980. Obligatory civil service was introduced for everyone over 21 years of age, enabling the military to 'recruit' all adult citizens and subject them to martial law at any time. All existing officers of trade unions, professional, business and student associations were dismissed and replaced by government-appointed '*coordinadores*'. Any meeting not officially authorised was subject to sanction under martial law; strikes and any other form of work stoppage were strictly prohibited. In order to bolster civic morale further still, the number of public holidays was reduced.[36]

The November 'coup' certainly closed a number of outstanding loopholes in the apparatus of control but its real importance lay in the unqualified acceptance of the Pinochet model and a clear determination on the part of the high command to rule alone for a further six years. Only twice before in the twentieth century had there been purely military administrations, and on both occasions—1930 and

1951 — these had been formed in the midst of a political crisis, placed under great duress, and lasted for a very short time. In 1974 the armed forces faced no major challenge and were confident that the upturn in the economy would maintain this situation.

Managing the Boom

Banzer's economic strategy had two main goals: the attraction of direct foreign investment by removing all but the most minimal constraints on capital, and the fostering of rapid, export-led growth centred on Santa Cruz. The privatisation of chunks of the large infrastructural state sector was recognised to be unattractive to private enterprise except in a very few areas, and it was only in the exploitation of oil and gas that this made appreciable headway. By the end of 1974 the extent of economic expansion appeared to vindicate the strategy. However, the real cause of substantially increased export earnings was not a restructured manufacturing sector dynamised with fresh foreign capital but massive leaps in the price of oil, supported by a subsidiary boom in agro-industry that was fuelled by even shorter-term price fluctuations and an over-abundance of credit. The complete mismanagement of this transient 'loophole' in the terms of trade meant that when price advantages were reduced the Bolivian economy was plunged into a crisis comparable only with that of 1956. The principal features of this crisis were, as elsewhere in Latin America, the accumulation of a massive foreign debt and persistent inflation.

The failure to attract foreign investment did not stem from any lack of effort on the part of the government. The September 1971 investment law freed capital movement to enable substantial repatriation of profits, removed tariffs not only on capital goods (which in this case included vehicles of all description) but also on primary materials, abolished taxes on production and manufactured exports, and laid down exceptionally generous terms for the assessment of capital depreciation.[37] With the removal of key tariffs the tax level on imports fell from 10.2 per cent in 1972 to 5.6 per cent in 1978. The loosening of credit was no less emphatic: over the same period local bank loans rose from Bs1.3 billion to Bs.5.0 billion while foreign lending was considerably more generous. Yet over these six years the liquidity coefficient (the relation of money in circulation to the value of production) increased from 0.2 per cent to 0.8, indicating that the large sums of money being made available were not being matched by increased output.[38] One central reason was that foreign capital simply did not arrive, total direct external investments over the *banzerato* amounting to only $96.8 million, of which more than 65 per cent came from just three firms: Atlas Copco Andina in metallurgy, Sociedad Aceitera de Oriente in agro-industry, and Sheraton Hotels.[39] However generous and politically stable it might have been, the Banzer administration proved unable to persuade foreign capital that Bolivia had ceased to be a high-risk zone. More critically still, it was hindered by the fact that the country had a very small internal market and a low level of internal and regional integration, which despite the availability of cheap labour meant unacceptably high production costs. Thus, the comparatively high export of capital during the 1970s was not primarily accounted for by repatriated profits, as might at first seem natural from the terms of the investment law. These were only $70 million (12 per cent) while the much larger figure of $314.4 million (88 per cent) left the country in the form of interest payments on the government's escalating borrowing.[40] Yet, the policy of opening up the economy did not just fail to 'take off' since the removal of import controls actively prejudiced the interests of a highly vulnerable local industrial sector. Although between 1971 and 1978 imports of consumer goods rose only marginally from 20.1 to 21.5 per cent of the total, those of capital goods fell substantially from 49.1 to 42.8 per cent, while primary materials that were frequently in competition with local products rose from 29.6 to 35.0 per cent.[41]

When set against such a picture, the government's policy of dynamising the economy of Santa Cruz seemed to be an unqualified success. This strategy, as Table 5 demonstrates, was not new but it was pursued much more emphatically by Banzer than by any other regime since 1952.

Up to 1971 official largesse towards Santa Cruz was generally directed at the oil industry. This support continued under Banzer, but one of the major features of his government's policy was the assistance given to the development of export crops, particularly cotton, coffee, sugar and wood. The presentation of a barrage of statistics in tabular form does not make for very easy reading, but a scan of Table 6 should be sufficient to show that the policy produced a number of impressive results.

Table 5

Agricultural Credit (1970–75) and Budget of Regional Development Corporations (1975) (Per cent)

Region	Credit from Banco Agrícola			Regional Development Budget
	1955–64	*1964–70*	*1970–75*	*1975*
ALTIPLANO	16.1	18.53	4.75	14.9
La Paz	11.0	13.53	2.45	3.6
Oruro	2.5	2.04	1.16	3.3
Potosí	2.6	3.14	0.69	8.0
VALLEY	26.4	17.40	6.61	12.1
Cochabamba	13.5	9.92	2.69	0.5
Chuquisaca	5.7	3.86	1.22	8.5
Tarija	6.7	3.60	2.69	3.1
ORIENTE	57.5	64.07	88.63	73.0
Santa Cruz	42.6	43.12	69.64	71.0
Beni/Pando	14.9	20.95	18.99	2.0

Source: Eduardo Arce Cuadros, *La Economía de Bolivia* (La Paz 1979) pp. 269; 281.

Table 6

Agricultural Exports (1972–78) (US$ millions)

	1972	*1973*	*1974*	*1975*	*1976*	*1977*	*1978*	*Total*
Nuts	1.3	1.5	2.1	2.2	2.2	2.6	3.1	15.0
Coffee	4.7	5.9	4.3	7.0	13.1	18.7	16.7	70.4
Hides			0.3	0.6	2.5	1.5	4.6	9.5
Rubber	0.8	1.1	1.9	2.3	2.4	4.0	2.1	14.6
Sugar	0.4	12.4	21.9	17.4	39.7	22.9	14.2	128.9
Cotton	7.6	9.7	22.0	18.1	12.0	17.7	14.8	101.9
Wood	3.7	7.7	12.9	11.1	10.0	12.0	12.6	70.0
Meat	2.3	3.1	0.2					5.6
Beef	1.8	0.7	0.3	0.8	2.1	3.0	2.6	11.3
Others (a)	5.8	3.3	4.2	3.5	4.6	10.7	15.9	48.0
Total	28.4	45.4	70.1	63.0	88.6	93.1	86.6	475.2

Note: a. Includes quinine, wool, tobacco, cotton seed etc.
Source: Banco Central de Bolivia: Pablo Ramos, *Siete Años de Economía Boliviana* (La Paz 1980) p. 144.

There are, of course, statistics and statistics, and the figures in Table 6, which were predictably publicised by the government, conceal as much as they reveal. Sales of coffee, for example, were boosted by 444 per cent in value while the volume of production only rose by 28 per cent. This was a result of the temporary collapse in world supply and price increases caused by frosts in Brazil, floods in Colombia and political problems in Angola in the period 1976–8. In similar fashion, the price of sugar suddenly rose late in 1974 to $65 a quintal when production costs in the Caribbean remained stable at around $10, indicating an essentially speculative rise in the market which could not be expected to endure. Nonetheless, the Banzer regime not only desisted from collecting taxes from sugar producers as a means of retaining the subsidy formally removed in January 1974 — a measure that effectively financed mill-owners to the tune of Bs.98 million in fiscal year 1976 — but also pressed ahead with an enormous expansion of mill capacity.[42] The result was that when the price came down to less than $10 a quintal the government had no option but further to subsidise mills working well beneath capacity for minimal returns. By 1979 this subsidy amounted to an annual disbursement of $15 million, or $7.0 for every quintal of sugar produced.[43]

However, the most outstanding instance of mismanagement occurred in the expansion of cotton. Adopted as a favoured crop in the expectation of substantial price rises, cultivation was encouraged with a full 52 per cent of the Banco Agrícola's loans under Banzer. Between 1972 and 1975 the area sown in cotton rose by over 70 per cent, leading to the replacement of other crops, particularly rice, and even the employment of thousands of troops during the harvest because of the lack of sufficient labour in Santa Cruz. Again the boom was temporary in the extreme. Prices fell from their peak in 1973/74 because of global over-production, compelling a reduction of land in cotton of 37 per cent per year between 1976 and 1980. In this case the government's subsidy consisted in failing to recall the Banco Agrícola's loans, which to all intents and purposes disappeared into thin air. In 1979 69 per cent of the unpaid debts to the bank of $666 million were owed by large *cruceño* family interests.[44] Some observers maintain that, in the face of the collapse of cotton as the foundation for agro-industrial growth, a number of local concerns turned their attention not just back to sugar, rice and ranching but also towards a carefully-planned expansion of another 'non-traditional export':

cocaine.[45] Family firms, such as Gasser-Bowles, Bedoya, Suárez, Said and Elsner, as well as companies with international links — Grace, Hansa — and the influential Banco Santa Cruz de la Sierra not only made huge windfall profits but also soaked up large quantities of government loans, considerably enhancing their economic and political power. Through his acquisition of a vast estate near San Javier in the north of the department Banzer himself became a member of this regional oligarchy, further consolidating its influence in the management of the state. It appeared that the locus of national power had been displaced from La Paz to Santa Cruz in much the same way as Sucre had lost its political hegemony to La Paz at the end of the nineteenth century.

Nothing underlined this fact more than the eastern location of Bolivia's deposits of oil and gas, which, as a result of the enormous price rises of 1973/4 generated revenue that made the advances in agro-industry pale into insignificance. While sales of agricultural goods moved from 4.1 per cent of total exports to 5.6 per cent between 1970 and 1975, those of oil and gas rose from 5.7 to 31.6 per cent.[46] The impact was considerable but, as Table 7 shows, it was not to be prolonged since the boost given to the balance of payments was exclusively due to the rise in price rather than in the volume of production, which in the case of oil was falling rapidly by the end of the decade, while that of gas stayed static.

Between 1970 and 1976 YPFB's gross profits rose from $18.29 million to $96.4 million, and they would have been appreciably greater had the domestic price not been kept low, increasing domestic consumption and restricting export capacity. (In 1976 YPFB exported eight million barrels of crude for $112.6 million and sold 6.6 million barrels to the domestic market for $64.3 million.) A much less defensible drain on the corporation's resources was the payment of large royalties to the department of Santa Cruz, which of all the regions of Bolivia was the one that needed them the least. In 1977 this departmental royalty amounted to $25 million but YPFB's attempts to reduce its size and expand investment were blocked by Banzer without serious discussion. As a result, an increasing proportion of the corporation's investment had to be financed through foreign loans, which by the end of 1978 had reached $355 million. The greater part of this investment was directed towards expanding and modernising refinery capacity in line with the expectations of the regime's 1975—80 development

Table 7

Export of Crude Petroleum and Natural Gas by YPFB, 1972–8

	Petroleum			Gas		
	Volume (000 m³) (a)	Value (000 US$)	Price (US$ per m³)	Volume (000 m³)	Value (000 US$)	Price (US$ per m³)
1972	1,740	31,711 (b)	18.22	1,005,141	9,863	0.28
1973	1,883	48,860	25.95	1,570,154	18,101	0.33
1974	1,716	163,928	95.48	1,546,063	29,188	0.53
1975	1,316	111,428	84.62	1,556,669	42,453	0.77
1976	1,282	112,571	87.79	1,571,241	54,896	0.99
1977	713	67,442	94.50	1,639,143	66,802	1.15
1978	445	42,331	92.99	1,581,390	78,505	1.41

Notes: a. Cubic metres
          b. YPFB calculated its 1972 sales as if the peso had been devalued at midnight on 31 December 1971.

Source: Banco Central de Bolivia: *Boletín Estadístico*, no. 234.

plan that production would grow from 40,000 to 180,000 barrels a day. In fact, production never exceeded the peak of 1973; by the middle of the decade it was evident that Gulf's discoveries of the early 1960s and that of YPFB at Monteagudo in 1969 were becoming depleted. Between 1971 and 1977 YPFB and the private companies spent a total of $120 million on exploration but found reserves of only 20 million barrels of oil and 50 million cubic feet of gas. In October 1978 five exploration teams hired by the state corporation ceased work because YPFB could not afford to pay them. By contrast, YPFB's outlay on refineries was $160 million, in order to achieve capacity of 70,000 barrels a day when domestic consumption did not exceed 25,000.[47]

The failure to discover large deposits was due in no small measure to Bolivia's extremely complex geology. Of the 15 foreign companies which began prospecting in the six million hectares of concessions made under the terms of the 1972 hydrocarbons law only two — Occidental and Tesoro — found commercially viable deposits, and Occidental's Tita site only came onstream late in 1978. These problems were, however, made much more severe by the refinery-orientated strategy and the lack of new production methods, the fall in production being accompanied only by a rise in YPFB's labour force, principally white-collar workers.[48] Beyond this, matters were not helped by factors such as the payment of generous commissions — alleged to be the cause of the excessive capacity of the Tita pipeline — or 'sweetheart deals', like that with the sixth division of the Paraguayan army, which was sold petrol at a price 30 per cent below that charged inside Bolivia itself.[49] Thus, although the country avoided the disastrous impact on the balance of payments that backward nations without oil suffered during the 1970s, expectations of a future oil-based expansion had disappeared before the end of the *banzerato*. By the end of the decade it was widely feared that, having failed to take advantage of the opportunities of the early 1970s, Bolivia would soon have to import oil to meet domestic demand.

The Banzer regime also enjoyed a remarkably favourable situation with regard to the market in tin. After stagnation in the 1950s and a sluggish, uneven rising trend in the 1960s, tin prices registered an increase that was significantly more moderate than that for oil but still critical for an economy which continued to depend on the industry for 70 per cent of its foreign currency earnings. Between 1972 and 1978 the price rose from $1.69 to $5.72 a pound. Yet, as with petrol, increased export value — from $113 million in 1972 to $374.4 million in 1978 — corresponded solely to the price rise and not to greater production, which in fact fell (from 30,277 tons in 1971 to 29,697 in 1978).[50]

The most marked characteristic of the organisation of mining in this period was the officially-sponsored ascendancy of the 25 larger firms of the private sector organised in the *Asociación de Mineros Medianos* (ANMM). Between 1973 and 1976 the value of Comibol's exports rose by 55 per cent while taxes on its operations increased by 99 per cent; over the same period the ANMM's revenue from foreign sales rose by 76 per cent but its taxes by only 26 per cent. Rates of profit as a consequence varied widely, Comibol's falling by 107 per cent and the ANMM's growing by 27 per cent.[51] Boosted not only by favourable government treatment but also by price rises for subsidiary minerals in which it had obtained a sizeable share of control (Tungsten: 70 per cent; antimony: 100 per cent; copper: 65 per cent), the ANMM increased its labour force by 80 per cent and accounted for a fifth of national mineral production. The dominance of an aged state operation mortgaged to foreign banks was placed under acute challenge by private companies which were almost without exception linked to international firms (US Steel; W.R. Grace, IMPC etc.)[52] In this respect, one of the first and most telling of Banzer's appointments was that of Guillermo 'Willy' Gutiérrez Vea Murguía to the executive directorship of the national investment institute. Gutiérrez was head of the Avicaya mining company, linked to the Grace group, but more importantly he had been a senior adviser to Aramayo and was the Rosca's leading candidate in the 1951 elections. His appointment strongly suggested a desire to return to the days before Comibol existed.

However serious their consequences, none of the features of the regime's policy summarised above were to have such a profound and lasting effect on the country's economy as the Banzer government's recourse to loans since, in the absence of any meaningful direct foreign investment, the policy of rapid growth had to be financed by foreign debt. This was, of course, not an abnormal course for a Latin American state in the 1970s, but the scale of Bolivia's borrowing was for a country of its size and productive capacity appreciable even by the unenviable standards of the region. In 1971 the foreign debt stood at $782.1 million, by the end of 1978 it had risen to $3,101.8 million. This increase of $2,319.7 million was not, moreover, matched by a corresponding rise in exports, the debt service rising from 17.3 to 32.0 per cent of export value over the same period.[53] Furthermore, the cost of this credit became progressively higher as international agencies and foreign states drew away from lending to be replaced by private banks, which imposed more stringent terms. In 1971 less than 4 per cent of the debt was with private banks, by 1978 they controlled 43.1 per cent. In 1972 Bolivia's debt service — the return of principal and payment of interests and commissions — was 36.7 per cent of the amount borrowed whereas in 1978 it was returning 66 per cent to the lenders. Between 1971 and 1978 the average annual debt service was over half the sum borrowed.[54] As is now widely appreciated, such a situation leads to yet further borrowing to cover balance of payments deficits and to regenerate production. With the exception of 1974 — the year blessed by the oil price rise — every year of Banzer's rule ended with a balance of payments deficit on the current account; and yet the objective of accelerated growth had scarcely been attained: the average growth rate to 1977 was 5.3 per cent, compared to 5.5 per cent over the 1960s. The 1975 five-year plan had projected a rate of 8 per cent per annum for 1978, 1979 and 1980; the figures registered for these years by the UN's *Comisión Económica para América Latina* (CEPAL) were 2.8, 2.8 and 1.2 per cent respectively.[55]

In terms of both the form in which it was generated and its consequences, such growth was manifestly not co-substantial with genuine development. It did, though, provide a veneer of modernisation. The short-run commodity booms prompted an increase in speculative activity, an expansion in the size and average income of the professional middle class (state spending on services quadrupled), and — in line with the need to accommodate and cater to the new consumerist aspirations of this stratum — a rise in urban construction. While Santa Cruz grew outwards, La Paz expanded both outwards and upwards, with the progessive emergence of ugly but prestigious tower-blocks populated by a young middle class escaping the constraints as well as the support structure of the parental home. Those who directed and funded this activity built themselves opulent suburbs, such as Calacoto and Cota Cota in La Paz, where a conspicuous and competitive consumption was concretised on a scale that would be the envy of many a European executive. With the advent of cocaine these redoubts of the elite were supplemented with even more extravagant examples of spacious, *arriviste* architecture.

The government celebrated such tangible transformation of the landscape as progress incarnate, but it would be more accurate to describe it as just one side of inflation. For the great mass of urban dwellers as well as a peasantry now substantially integrated into the money economy neither housing nor any other item of expenditure became cheaper, better in quality or more plentiful. Banzer's economic team were profligate free-marketeers but, as we have seen, only one side of the market was free. For seven years Bolivia experienced nothing that appertained to 'free collective bargaining' and registered the lowest number of strikes for three decades; there might be discussion over the form and degree of the rise in the cost of living but dreary accusations of 'wage-push' inflation were patently devoid of any validity. The impact of the principal factors in the rise of the cost of living—the 1972 devaluation and the 1974 removal of subsidies—has already been outlined; they contributed to an average inflation rate of a little over 30 per cent per annum. According to the COB, this was accompanied by a drop in the wage-earners' share of national income from 47 to 31 per cent.[56] The miners' real wages, which have been the object of a close study, fell by at least 14 per cent. Figures for the overall loss of earning power vary very widely indeed, the lowest acceptable figure being between 8 and 10 per cent, the highest around twice this.[57]

The computation of economic statistics such as these is rarely free of trouble, but the margins of error are not so generous as to make the obscure mathematics employed by the government believable. In 1976 it assessed per capita GDP at $600 a year, in 1977 at $729.[58] The World Bank, on the other hand, estimated the 1975 figure to be $360, but in 1979 its local director voiced the opinion that the official figures on which its estimates were based were highly inflated; at the time the Bank was making available to Bolivia soft loans reserved exclusively for countries with a per capita GDP of less than $280 a year.[59] Furthermore, the bank—against which charges of radicalism would be extraordinarily hard to sustain—concluded that 'Bolivia has one of the most deformed income distributions in Latin America'. Table 8 bears this out.

Although 25 years after the revolution Bolivia had undoubtedly been transformed in a number of ways, this transformation in no sense amounted to a rupture from abject underdevelopment. Its population had risen from 2.6 million to nearly 6 million but the country still remained unevenly and very sparsely populated: 16 per

Table 8

Income Distribution, 1970–74

Proportion of Total Population (%)	Share of National Income (1970; %)	Average Income (1974; US$)
Lowest 20 per cent	4	59
Next 20 per cent	9	132
Middle 40 per cent	28	206
Highest 20 per cent	59	867
(Top 5 per cent	36	2,115)

Source: World Bank, 'Income Distribution in Under-Developed Countries', mission estimates.

cent lived in the *Oriente*, which covered 60 per cent of the land mass, while overall density rose from three people per square kilometre to five — so much for Mr McNamara's population explosion.[60] More crucially, in 1976 less than 37 per cent of Bolivians could read or write; the region with the lowest rate of literacy was, paradoxically, Santa Cruz, with a figure of 21 per cent.[61] By the same date the number of telephone lines had reached 112,600, the university population 34,500, and over a third of the population possessed a radio, but 66 per cent of homes lacked electricity and 78 per cent had no plumbed water or sanitary facilities. The stock of doctors available to deal with the inevitable consequence of such a state of affairs was only 2,134.[62] Since 86 per cent of the medical staff were located in towns of over 10,000 people the situation in the countryside was a great deal worse than the median figure suggests. Many doctors agree that the official infant mortality rate of 130 per 1,000 live births is a substantial underestimate, it being difficult to obtain dependable statistics in a society where few births are medically attended, many abortions are self-administered, and still-born infants are generally deemed never to have lived rather than to have died. Those infants with chronic illnesses lucky enough to find themselves in La Paz's Hospital del Niño — often abandoned there by desperate mothers — are still subject to a cruel lottery whereby only the most 'saveable' will be put into incubators, which are so scarce that they must be shared even though this greatly increases the chances of cross-infection. The incompetence that has greatly exaggerated such conditions is by no means exclusively military: early in 1983, after the return of a civilian government and the appointment of a supposed 'leftist' as minister of health, the health ministry pointedly refused to back an application to foreign agencies for funds to establish a special ward in the hospital for the control and treatment of infant malnutrition, despite the fact that over 80 per cent of children under 15 do not consume the minimum diet recognised by the UN as adequate for a healthy existence. Those few physicians working in this critical field do so largely in the face of indifference from colleagues content to languish in private practice. There is, quite naturally, no economic motive either for pharmacies, which are not restricted by prescription controls, or the big companies, such as Bayer or Roche, to alter this situation. One of the very few saving graces of the economic crisis over the last five years is that it has made the cost of imported (largely Dutch) powdered milk so prohibitive that the level of breast feeding remains very high by any standard.

'Nueva Bolivia' in Retreat

Although the boom of the 1970s was short-lived, growth rates slumped disastrously, and the level of inflation crept ever upwards, these factors underlay the decline and eventual overthrow of Banzer's regime rather than directly causing it. The full extent of the crisis accumulating over the decade was only to become clear later, and the principal fissures in the edifice of the dictatorship were primarily of a political and superstructural nature. By their very nature dictatorial regimes encourage the primacy of democratic demands in opposition, but in the case of Bolivia the weakness of any parliamentary tradition tended to disaggregate the movement for constitutionality into the defence of the most salient freedoms it guaranteed, rather than any system *tout court*. Thus, for a long time badly-weakened forces sought to gain ground tactically and chip away at the edifice of the dictatorship; there was minimal agreement over a broad strategy of how and with what it should be replaced. This was clear at the very end of its days, when a rank-and-file movement for a complete political amnesty broke the momentum of the *banzerato* but was channelled without great difficulty into electoralism: there seemed to be no ready alternative, even though by taking such a route Banzer gained considerable advantage in making his retreat. The enthusiasm of the major political formations for this strategy and the importance of elementary democratic liberties served to dazzle the working class and peasantry. The form in which Banzer's extended rule was eclipsed soon proved to be of more than passing importance; indeed, it provided the framework for the apparently endless political crisis that followed.

The first consolidated assault on the system was mounted by the FSTMB and resolutely syndicalist in character. In January 1975, only two months after the *autogolpe* Siglo XX–Catavi staged a fortnight-long strike in demand for the return of the local radio stations closed down by the regime. The action not only achieved its aim but also indicated that although national union federations no longer had any formal existence and plant unions were in the hands of the *coordinadores*, rank and file organisation remained intact and the *Comités de Bases* led by the left enjoyed broad support. Over the following 18 months the impetus given by this partial victory encouraged mobilisation on the question of wages, which, as we have seen, were badly affected in the mining sector. Proscribed FSTMB leaders returned quietly to the country and began to organise a national union congress in order to formulate strategy. Although it was illegal, the regime made no move to suppress this meeting, which eventually took place at Corocoro on 1 May 1976. The main demand was for a rise of some 200 per cent on the daily basic pay of $1.75. The government refused to accept the figure of $4 as the minimum necessary to sustain a family of four and offered increases of between 30 and 50 per cent. Although the PCB argued strongly against any precipitate strike and urged piecemeal tactical moves, the congress was swayed by a radical bloc of the PRIN, POR and MIR that succeeded in winning support for issuing an ultimatum to the government that if there was no satisfactory response within thirty days a national miners' strike would be called.[63]

While the Corocoro congress was still underway news arrived in Bolivia of the assassination of General Zenteno in Paris by a previously unknown 'Ché Guevara International Brigade'. There was no discernible grief in the popular sectors, but no great jubilation either, for it was widely believed that the killing was the work of the right, a suspicion confirmed by police leaks to *Le Monde* which implicated the regime and Zenteno's own embassy staff.[64] Two weeks later another Bolivian general was killed in exile, but this time the impact inside the country was considerably greater: the victim was Juan José Torres, gunned down in Buenos Aires early on 1 June. Soon after the Videla coup (24 March) Torres had been threatened by the Bolivian military attaché, and he was clearly at risk in the new 'internal war' being waged by the Argentine security forces, which had kept a continuous watch on his flat. The death of this popular figurehead was immediately linked to Banzer, and dynamised an already tense situation. Black awnings and flags appeared in the popular quarters of the towns, and in Siglo XX 20,000 people attended a demonstration of protest and remembrance on 3 June. In what was perhaps the most completely cynical gesture of his rule, Banzer declared public mourning and sent an aircraft to Buenos Aires with the offer to the ex-president's wife of bringing back the corpse. However, when Emma Obleas insisted that Torres's body be laid in state at San Andrés and the FSTMB offices and then interred in the cemetery at Siglo, Banzer, who had suggested a rapid and discreet burial, felt obliged to withdraw his generous proposal. President Echeverría brought this macabre incident to a close by offering 'asylum' to Torres's remains in Mexico, where they remained until June 1983.[65]

Torres's death and the spontaneous demonstrations of protest that followed it terminated the regime's cautious attitude to the strike call. On 9 June the reoccupied FSTMB offices were raided, their occupants arrested and six of the federation's national leaders deported to Chile, where General Pinochet had them interned in an isolated camp in the south. Siglo XX came out on strike the next day and, as troops invested the camp and began a house-to-house search, the strike leaders took refuge inside the mine, using shafts and exits only the miners knew. The government immediately closed the *pulperías* and threatened to cut the electricity. Within a few days the stoppage had spread to the other camps and received the support of the factory workers, who came out for 24 hours. All the Comibol camps were occupied by the army, two workers being shot dead in Siete Suyos; press censorship was imposed but did not impede the regime from offering Bs.70,000 for the capture 'dead or alive' of Cirilo Jiménez, one of the Siglo leaders, a longstanding delegate for the Beza section, and a supporter with Filemón Escóbar of the recently-created *Vanguardia del POR*, a predominantly miner-based split from Lora. Domitila de Chungara, nine months' pregnant, was also pursued with much energy but eventually smuggled out of the mine to have her child in the camp hospital under the protection of the Red Cross.[66]

The regime's employment first of unusual tact and then unambiguous force proved successful; it drew the opposition out and provoked
the direct confrontation that had been anticipated for a year and a
half. Although Comibol was losing $800,000 a day during the strike,
it had reserve stocks of 70,000 tons, which was sufficient to cover three
months' production. The stopping of food supplies and presence of
the troops wore down resistance in the smaller mines, which, lacking
national leadership or coordination, began to return to work after a
fortnight. Siglo itself held out for 25 days in an unequal trial of
strength. The PCB had expressed pessimism about the strike all along,
but an open assembly of the Siglo workforce had as late as 29 June
voted overwhelmingly for its continuation, underlining the fact that
once the decision to fight for increased wages had been taken at Corocoro there was little alternative but to pursue it through to the end.
The Banzer regime had initially been shaken but, as its tactics showed,
still possessed the strength to overcome any opposition. The failure of
the strike did not vindicate a policy of negotiation but simply emphasised the unequal balance of forces. In mid-1976 it seemed certain that
Banzer's mandate to himself to rule until 1980 would be fulfilled to the
day and hour of his choosing.

It was only with the confidence bred of such supremacy that the president could possibly have embarked upon his celebrated diplomatic
adventure with Pinochet to negotiate an exit to the sea. The recuperation of the coast lost after the War of the Pacific in 1880 had always been
an issue to unite the most extreme political protagonists, being of the
utmost importance to the armed forces, which nurtured the memory
of heroic defeat as a core institutional myth and preparation for
recovery as a rationale for generous budget allocations. The fact that
there existed an enormous imbalance between the military capacities
of the two countries did very little to weaken this ideology of revindi-
cation. (On occasions this was backed up with spectacular military
imagination, such as when it was proclaimed that the carburettors of
Chilean tanks would not function on the *altiplano* — a fact that may
not have unduly concerned Pinochet's airforce, for which La Paz represented a magnificent target. During 1978 and 1979, when Chile had
serious border disputes with Argentina and Peru, and was indeed on
the verge of war, opportunist jingoism enjoyed a marked revival, especially because the latter year was the hundredth anniversary of the
outbreak of the war. Even as late as 1982 a senior airforce officer

privately declared that the acquisition of 53 military aircraft he sought to buy from Belgium would not only give him parity with the Chileans but also enable the FAB to 'bomb the shit' out of the pleasant little coastal town of Arica, which had in fact belonged to Peru before 1880.) Banzer was, therefore, taking the bull by the horns in seeking a diplomatic settlement, which from the very start implied recognition of Chilean sovereignty over much of the disputed territory and would very probably entail further concessions on the part of the dispossessed Bolivians.

Following the famous *abrazo* in February 1975 between one dictator of German origin and another of French descent at the Bolivian border village of Charaña, diplomatic relations with Chile were re-established for the first time in 13 years. (They had been broken off in 1962 over Chile's claims to the Rio Lauca.) Willy Gutiérrez was sent as ambassador to Santiago and negotiations began. Banzer happily admitted that he personally rather than the cabinet or the high command had proposed the *rapprochement* with Pinochet, which may have been something of a deviation from the letter of the November 1974 decrees but could do his image little harm while matters were proceeding smoothly and an exit to the sea remained within his grasp.[67] But by the end of 1975 the Chileans' draft proposals under discussion were so clearly not going to meet the expectations of the Bolivian populace that while he accepted them, Banzer kept the terms secret. The central requirement was the acquisition of a corridor to the sea over which Bolivia would exercise complete sovereignty, but the Chilean offer fell far short of this: 'The territory ceded by Chile will be declared a demilitarised zone and, as agreed in previously held discussions, the government of Bolivia will be obliged to obtain the express guarantee of the Organisation of American States with respect to the inviolability of the ceded zone.'[68] In response to this clear denial of sovereignty Banzer replied that he was in agreement but would have to discuss the matter with the other interested party, Peru. The Bolivian president also failed to reject article 'I' of the draft agreement that gave Chile full use of the waters of the Rio Lauca, which had hitherto always been steadfastly resisted by La Paz. In December Gutiérrez, who was a party to these exchanges, rashly declared, 'I modestly say to my *pueblo*, it now has the sea.' Banzer, meanwhile, had been preparing public opinion for the treaty by stressing, 'It is a question of negotiating, a metre, two metres, ten kilometres, I don't know. We want to be tremendously flexible in this.'[69] Such flexibility involved a straight 'exchange' of lands with Bolivia being unable to keep troops in her corridor while Chile would obtain unqalified control of the new territory obtained in return for a small portion which she had seized nearly a hundred years before. Banzer argued that this was the only way to get an exit to the sea, but he had badly misjudged both the degree of Chilean intransigence and the strength of sentiment over the issue in Bolivia. Press criticism was unusually forthright and the agitation of the *movimiento generacional* inside the army found sufficient resonance to force the regime to draw back from signing any accord. The negotiations stumbled on through 1976 and drew particularly fierce criticism from the MIR, which couched its anti-militarism in left nationalist terms and undertook a very effective propaganda campaign. At the end of the year the press in Santiago published maps of the border area showing three large chunks of Bolivian territory as belonging to Chile. If the move was calculated to sabotage the talks, it succeeded; by early 1977 military discontent had reached such a pitch that Banzer effectively gave up his scheme. In February 1978 relations between the two countries were once again severed. For three years Banzer had juggled over-confidently with an issue that he could not control; his image as a 'nationalist' was badly tarnished, relations with a valuable ally wrecked on the rocks of needless rivalry, and dissent inside the armed forces increased, especially amongst the junior officers.

A not dissimilar effect was caused by the publication early in 1977 of a letter written in November 1976 by Guido Strauss, the busy falangist who had helped stage the 1964 coup and was now sub-secretary of migration, to General Juan Lechín Suárez, now minister of planning. This letter revealed that the Bolivian government had held discussions with and received promises of financial aid from a number of European states as well as South Africa to assist the migration to the country of 30,000 white families (approximately 150,000 people) from Rhodesia (now Zimbabwe) and Namibia to the Beni and Santa Cruz over a period of seven years. The previous year Bolivia had amended its immigration law to facilitate such an influx, and neither Strauss nor a number of other senior officials bothered to deny the existence of such a plan. When questioned about it, government spokesmen stressed the importance of the superior skills, resources and 'impressive work ethic' of the Anglo-Saxon settlers for an underdeveloped country

like Bolivia.[70] For a while the regime continued in this vein, apparently judging that its relations with the Non-Aligned Movement were
less important than the prospect of large sums of money from the metropolitan states and the advent of thousands of enterprising pioneers
accustomed to maintaining social relations of the type the *cruceño*
landed oligarchy so admired. However, its external image was further
damaged when an advance team from Rhodesia publicly expressed
amazement at the appalling conditions of the rural labourers of Santa
Cruz, while other potential immigrants in Namibia made comments
about both creoles and 'indians' in Bolivia that were so steeped in base
racism that even the government could not avoid criticising them.
This only encouraged a domestic campaign against 'importing apartheid' that both further impugned the regime's nationalist credentials
and revitalised interest in local racial problems. In the last resort, the
effort to provide Bolivia with the class of settler which was seen to have
done so much to develop countries like Argentina and Chile foundered because whether the Rhodesian whites were suffering a 'collective psychosis' as Strauss claimed, or not, there was very little to attract
them. The whole affair was not exactly an anachronism since the
epoch of politically-motivated migrations has proved to be unending,
but it was based upon anachronistic assumptions. The country had,
in fact, never been the site of great immigration. After the decline of
Potosí at the beginning of the eighteenth century settlement by Spaniards fell off sharply, and the number of negro slaves imported during
the colony was never very large although several thousand of their des-
cendants remain, speaking Quechua and retaining their identity in
tight communities in the Yungas region of La Paz. In the twentieth
century Bolivia had taken in small groups of European Jews, followed
within a decade by some of their nazi persecutors, and greater quantities of Koreans and Japanese, all of whom had made their mark in
various economic circuits and retained their social identity; but none
of these immigrations had been provided with the grand economic
schema that attended the southern African debacle. It was this that
made a potential tragedy almost comic, the scope of the regime's
ambitions making its failure to realise them far more damaging than
might have been the case. Yet by the time the issue was in the open the
Banzer government was more concerned with the consequences of
Jimmy Carter's election to the US presidency, which affected it as
acutely and as rapidly as any other administration in the hemisphere.

The adoption of human rights as a major feature in aligning US foreign policy towards the Third World marked a critical shift in the relationship between Washington and La Paz. One certainly does not have to believe the rhetoric of this policy or imagine that Carter himself, Linowitz, Vance or Brzezinski had any great affinity with liberalism to accept that their erratic pursuit of the issue contributed to the dislocation of US hegemony in several important zones. Perhaps the most striking instance was Iran, but Latin America was the region most consistently affected. In Central America Somoza was deprived of the total support he needed to resist the *Sandinistas* in the 1978 – 9 civil war, Guatemala was put into quarantine, and the overthrow of the regime of General Romero in El Salvador (October 1979) actively encouraged, having infinitely more disastrous consequences than the State Department could possibly have imagined at the time. Only the signing of the Panama canal treaty in September 1977 produced a result that approximated to the objectives of the policy. In contrast to the cases of South Korea, Indonesia and the Philippines, the dictatorships of South America were put under pressure to limit their excesses, modify their methods and proceed with a modicum of liberalisation. This was met with an outburst of pugnacious nationalism in both Argentina and Chile, the latter selected for special attention for a while at least because of the sheer arrogance of its secret police (DINA) in slaughtering Allende's ambassador to the US, Orlando Letelier, and a North American colleague in Washington, an event which drew public attention to the fact that the Nixon administration had played an important part in the 1973 coup. The Brazilian regime reacted with less virulence since it was already embarked upon an extremely graduated *apertura* after many more years of unchallenged control. Bolivia, on the other hand, was not only a much less significant regional power but also a great deal more vulnerable in economic terms. Exhibiting a palpable loss of internal dynamism and unity — but not to such a degree that any relaxation sponsored by the US seemed likely to exceed the carefully-controlled limits envisaged for 'redemocratisation' — the Banzer regime presented a relatively unproblematic target for the human rights policy. This, though, was no guarantee of success; over the following five years the State Department found itself continually obliged to intervene in Bolivian affairs in order to sustain a policy that was first marginalised by Carter himself and then entirely reversed (except for Poland and Afghanistan) by

Reagan. This was in part because redemocratisation proved so persistently vulnerable and in part a result of the emergence of a new complicating factor: cocaine.

The first step in persuading Banzer to consider a gradual withdrawal
was taken by Assistant Secretary of State Terence Todman, who visited
La Paz in May 1977 and held 'secret discussions' with the president.
Todman was heavily lobbied by human rights organisations, but it
appears that he made little headway since the government's activity
remained unchanged and Banzer reconfirmed that elections would
not be held until 1980. Nevertheless, the pressure applied by the US
embassy over this period must have convinced Banzer that a change in
tactics would not necessarily prejudice his wider strategy. Early in September he flew to Washington to attend the signing of the Panama
canal treaty and talk with Carter. It seems likely that this meeting was
decisive since on 30 September the president declared that elections
might well be brought forward. This was the first time in three years
that such a possibility had been admitted, the reason being advanced
by Banzer revealing his major worry: 'We want the Armed Forces to
withdraw at the opportune moment and not when they might be
exhausted by the exigencies of politics. ... If tomorrow or the
day after we start to have a political carnival there will be no elections.'[71]

However guarded, such a statement changed the tempo of public
life completely. A rapid tour of the garrisons secured support for such
a move, the success of which now depended almost entirely upon containing popular mobilisation. On 9 November Banzer announced that
elections would be held in July of the following year although he made
no move to lift the restrictions that impeded the political campaign he
had to all intents and purposes declared open. This was not surprising;
the military last sponsored elections to succeed an institutional regime
in 1940. There was no experience of the tactical problems this entailed
and no established system as, for example, in El Salvador or Guatemala, whereby the military could guarantee an acceptable result
whilst formally permitting open competition. As a consequence, the
nine months following the announcement of the poll were characterised by ill-organised and frenetic efforts to obtain a victory at all costs
and with little concern as to the wider effects of clumsy manipulation.
As Banzer declared towards the end of the campaign, 'We support
continuismo and we are satisfied because we have just embarked upon

the task of economic development and it is logical that we should continue the work we have just begun.'[72]

Perhaps the only perspicacious move that Banzer made in his efforts to secure this *continuismo* was to hold back from standing as a candidate himself. On 6 December his minister of interior, the airforce general Juan Pereda Asbún, was declared 'the candidate of nationalism' with full support from the government and the armed forces. This was, in fact, not quite the case since the army was less than happy at the prospect of an airforce officer taking charge, and the candidature of Colonel Alberto Natusch Busch had been canvassed in some barracks as an alternative.[73] Banzer's choice of Pereda as his dauphin was surprising in so far as he was an extraordinarily poor speaker — experiencing great difficulty in pronouncing virtually the only word that could not plausibly be omitted from his anodyne speeches: *constitucionalización* — and being about as uncharismatic as it is possible to be outside the British diplomatic service. These qualities were, though, excellent in a man who could be handed formal power and yet not be expected to wield it independently. Pereda, a *cruceño* and long one of Banzer's most faithful acolytes, had patently been chosen not as a genuine institutional successor but as an interim 'front-man' so that the president himself could continue to direct affairs from behind the throne. Both the strategy and the man selected to realise it proved to be calamitous; but this was certainly not predictable at the end of 1977, and once the step had been taken the army threw itself behind Pereda and the *Unión Nacionalista del Pueblo* (UNP) created to run his campaign.

Following the declaration of Pereda's *oficialista* candidature, Banzer made the first move in rolling back the restrictions in force since August 1971 and enshrined in the decrees of November 1974. On 21 December he duly announced an amnesty, but in terms so limited as to cast grave doubt on the possibility of any genuine opponent returning to the country, let alone contesting the election. The measure expressly prohibited the return of 348 'political dissidents', including Juan Lechín, Marcelo Quiroga, Hernán Siles Zuazo and many leftist militants as well as two children aged eight and twelve, one person who had been killed by the police several years before, and a number of people who were paid the dubious honour of having their names listed twice.[74] In real terms the result of the 'amnesty' was that 33 people were released from prison and 19 of these sent for trial; nobody sacked for political or union activity, including 950 miners dismissed after the 1976 strike, was entitled to redress.

The popular response to this artless manoeuvre took an unexpected form but rapidly proved to be uncontainable. In what seemed a misguided move during the Christmas holiday, when they could expect little publicity, the wives of four exiled miners (Aurora de Lora, Nelly de Paniagua, Angélica de Flores, and Luzmila de Pimentel) entered the offices of Archbishop Manrique together with their children on 28 December and declared themselves on indefinite hunger strike until their demands for a general and unrestricted amnesty, work for all those who had been fired, and the withdrawal of the troops from the mines were met in full.[75] Initially the hunger strike appeared to be no different to any other staged by desperate individuals with a particular grievance, but circumstances dictated that within days it was transformed into a mass movement at the centre of national affairs. On 31 December a second group formed from representatives of APDH, the university, and the Unión de Mujeres de Bolivia (UMBO) began to fast in the offices of Presencia, replacing the wives' children who had become ill. The editor of the paper, Huascar Cajías, was less than cordial in his response to this, but given that Manrique had given full support to the action, he could scarcely eject the occupants. From that point on the strike spread rapidly: after six days 61 people had joined; after fourteen some 500 were fasting, and at its end (18 January) over 1,000 were on strike in all of the country's major cities with a great many more lending active support. On 6 January the regime — which had put the armed forces on a 'state of emergency' and steadfastly refused to meet with ex-president Luis Adolfo Siles who had been elected as a mediator by the strikers — organised a counter-demonstration which all public servants were obliged to attend. The torrential rain that persisted throughout that day proved to be a great deal more inconvenient for those who had turned out simply to admire Pereda's oratorial skills than for the thousands of dragooned civil servants who gratefully and none-too-slowly vacated the Plaza Murillo. The demonstration of mass support for the government and its mumbling candidate dissolved before Pereda's eyes and had later to be reconstructed for the press through the employment of creative photography. On the 16th the regime's coordinadores in La Paz declared a 24-hour strike against the fast — a measure that amounted to a general lock-out — and the police forbade the movement of vehicles in the city. This was made a pyrrhic victory when the rank and file union committees announced that their support for this stoppage was to express solidarity with the hunger strike and not repudiation of the action. A number of police posts were attacked and one schoolchild was shot dead by police. On the same day Banzer had reluctantly begun to negotiate with the strikers' representatives, but in the face of their intransigence and the loss of order on the streets he opted to suspend the talks and resort to force. Early on the 17th police raided a number of sites occupied by the strikers. In La Paz some fifty heavily-armed men charged into the offices of *Presencia* in military formation, and with much shouting began to order the strikers out, only to be brought to a halt by a young doctor who informed the irate commander that she would hold him and his superiors entirely responsible for any harm that befell people who had taken nothing but water for twenty days and could not be moved without ambulances. After some delay, during which the officer conferred with the ministry and those on fast gave a barely-audible rendition of 'Viva Mi Patria Bolivia' to an audience of now shame-faced policemen, ambulances were fetched and the 'prisoners' transferred to clinics around the city.

The use of repression succeeded only in increasing the popularity and vindicating the cause of those against whom it was directed. Under the new rules of the game Banzer could scarcely expect to derive any benefit from the sight of half-starved individuals being manhandled by troops in helmets and flak jackets. Moreover, there was a ready stock of volunteers to replace those who were removed. After a stormy cabinet meeting, the president went on television at midnight on the 17th to declare a full amnesty and the 'resolution' of the strike. However, those on fast refused to halt their action until they received written guarantees against persecution, which took a further day to extract from the regime. The final agreement granted all their demands except the removal of the troops from the mines. This was a key issue, but the strike could clearly not continue without loss of life and had already gained all the concessions that could feasibly be expected of such a tactic. It was lifted on the evening of the 18th. Although it was to be some time before it was fully evident, the hunger strike was the single most important factor in bringing the *banzerato* to an end and laying the basis for mass mobilisation over the coming period.

From January the regime was thrown onto the defensive and forced into increasingly frantic manoeuvre to control the election. At a meeting of 160 senior officers early in April Banzer tried to gain support for a suspension of the poll or, failing that, the launching of his own candidature.[76] This move came to nought because a majority of the officer corps now considered that such a manifest reversal of the *apertura* would lead to even greater opposition. Thus, although 35 people were arrested for staging a prohibited May Day demonstration and San Andrés university was closed for a month after student protests against the regime's refusal to respect autonomy, the campaign went ahead.

Once the full amnesty was granted on 20 January and trade-union liberties conceded four days later, Bolivia experienced an abrupt political dislocation whereby not only the groups and parties which had been in existence before 1952 but also those which had come to maturity during Banzer's rule came into the open and began a breakneck campaign to recoup their constituencies, formulate policies for the new democratic era, and settle scores with their enemies. On the left, the MIR was the party expected to pick up much support from the urban middle class disenchanted with Banzer's economic management and the *entreguista* (sell-out) policies of his government. The MIR had shifted steadily to the right over the previous seven years, exchanging the Marxist tenor and emphasis on the armed struggle of its early days for a pugnacious populism and the belief that it represented a second-generation MNR. This evolution into a muscular social democracy restricted its appeal inside the organised working class and, since it possessed virtually no following in the countryside, compelled participation in an electoral front if it was to maximise its opportunities. The focus of such a front was provided by Hernán Siles, whose MNR *de Izquierda* (MNRI) was now several years old and had captured sufficient followers from the old party to stand in opposition to Víctor Paz. The MNRI was a conventional party of Latin American social democracy, drawing in broad left currents of the MNR which had not previously deserted to the PRIN, MIR or PS, basing itself firmly on old clientelist attachments, and defending the record of the MNR up to 1960. In sum, it was hardly 'left' at all but presented a reformist image and a focus for cautious anti-militarism. Once it was clear that Paz could not persuade Siles to rejoin his sector of the party, the MNRI gained the support of the MIR, the pro-Moscow PCB, and Genaro Flores's MRTK to form the *Unión Democrática y Popular* (UDP) as a centre–left electoral front.

The very mild programme of the UDP, Siles's own less than radical record, and the presence of the PCB ensured that much of the left would not support it, seeing it as a reformist popular front incapable of providing a radical solution to the country's problems. The POR was alone in arguing for a positive blank vote whereby it would stand no candidate but urged voters to put a ballot paper (*papaleta*) carrying the main points of the party's programme into the box. The POR was now, though, badly divided, its attacks on 'parliamentary cretinism' carrying little weight in popular circles. The rest of the left fell into two broad groups, both of which contested the election. The first was Marcelo Quiroga's sector of the PS, later denominated PS-1, which had split from the centrist wing that was led by Guillermo Aponte and pledged to support the UDP. Quiroga's party stood alone on a platform that was markedly more anti-militarist and radical on economic questions than that of the UDP, but it depended largely on its leader's rhetorical skill and popularity rather than any organised following. The second, much more powerful, force was the *Frente Revolucionario de Izquierda* (FRI), combining the PRIN, which continued to be Lechín's personal property rather than a full political party but still carried weight in union circles, the much-expanded and revived PCML, Filemón Escóbar's *Vanguardia Comunista del* POR, the POR (Vargas), and the political heir to the ELN in the *Partido Revolucionario de los Trabajadores de Bolivia* (PRTB), which had minimal popular support but had certainly evolved from the pure *foquismo* of the late 1960s and enjoyed a certain sympathy on the left for its attachment to that lineage. The left was, therefore, divided, with the UDP the clear front-runner and likely to pick up the tactical votes of many who supported the FRI or PS-1. Although the FRI took the bold step of making the Maoist *campesino* leader Casiano Amurrio, who had been a vice-president of the Popular Assembly, and the charismatic Domitila de Chungara its presidential and vice-presidential candidates, the effect of this in the *campo* was largely nullified by the fact that the MRTK had blocked with the UDP while those inclined to a protest vote possessed a more authentic sectoral alternative in MITKA, which was standing Luciano Tapia Quisbert.

The peasant vote was clearly going to be decisive to the result of any honest election, but the sympathies of the *campesinado* as a whole were deeply divided since neither the UDP nor the FRI had the time or resources to wage an effective campaign against both Pereda, whose UNP was busy distributing government favours in the countryside, and Paz's MNR. Paz's party, now labelled MNR-*Histórico*, was still perhaps the single most popular party in the country. For many peasants its support for the 1971 coup was either unknown or less important than the memory of the agrarian reform and the legacy of more than a decade of clientelism. Although Pereda's name was plastered on a thousand walls and cluttered the airwaves, in many areas of the countryside Paz was the most recognisable and historically identifiable figure running in the election. Siles, by contrast, had never been very closely identified with the agrarian reform and now had to contend with the oft-repeated accusations that he was a 'communist' as a result of his alliance with the PCB. The MNRH's alliance with Walter Guevara's PRA also improved its standing with those sectors anxious to see a firm alliance with Washington, guarantees for private capital, and a continuation of export-based growth without the restrictions and dangers of dictatorship. Pereda could be expected to pick up much support in Santa Cruz, but his status as a puppet deprived him of a monopoly of sympathy from traditional conservatism. He was, however, less threatened by the only other military candidate, retired General René Bernal Escalante, a rather eccentric reactionary populist of Aymara blood and humble origins who stood for the renovation of *barrientismo* and was backed by the PDC, which could find no suitable candidate from its own ranks and still proved incapable of suppressing the connection with the military established in 1964 and so manifestly vital to the protection of its right flank. Thus, on paper at least, the elections of 9 July 1978 were fought between the forces outlined in Table 9.

The likelihood that the differences of political complexion between these various parties and fronts would prove to be of purely academic interest increased throughout the campaign as the government threw itself enthusiastically into the task of providing Pereda with victory at any cost. The first indication of preparations for a fraud were given in the figures presented by the electoral commission (Comisión Nacional Electoral) for registered voters. Since registration required presentation of either a *libreta* of military service, identity pass (*carnet*), marriage or birth certificate, or a signed declaration of identity from at least two guarantors—documentation that it is estimated less than a

Table 9

The Election of 9 July 1978

Slate	Main Parties	Candidates
1. **Unión Democrática y Popular** (UDP)	MNRI MIR PS-Aponte MRTK MIN PCB	Hernán Siles Zuazo Edil Sandoval Morón
2. **Unión Nacionalista del Pueblo** (UNP)	MNR-Rubén Julio FSB PRA-Gamarra PIR	Juan Pereda Alfredo Guachalla
3. **Alianza Democrática de la Revolución Nacional** (ADRN)	MNRH PRA	Víctor Paz Estenssoro Walter Guevara Arce
4. **Partido Demócrata Cristiano** (PDC)	PDC PRB	René Bernal Escalante Remo Di Natale
5. **Frente Revolucionario de Izquierda** (FRI)	PRIN PCML PRTB VCPOR	Casiano Amurrio Domitila de Chungara
6. **Partido Socialista** (PS)	PS-Quiroga	Marcelo Quiroga Carlos Gómez
7. **MITKA**	MITKA	Luciano Tapia Isidoro Copa

third of the rural population possesses — the CNE's overall figure of 89 per cent registration of an already disputed figure of 2.4 million eligible voters was incredibly high. As it turned out, registered voters in Cochabamba and Santa Cruz, areas of support for Pereda, exceeded 102 per cent of those eligible to poll. In a number of constituencies government control of the lists produced spectacular demographic trends: the village of Yata, with a total population of 32, yielded 300 voters; in Florida 100 people mutated into 300 voters; and Nazareth, a border garrison populated by a dozen officers and a regiment of conscripts, who, because they were less than 21 were ineligible to vote, appeared on the electoral register for the first time with a compliment of 600 voters. In other areas where support for the opposition was strong, registration was greatly hampered; there were, to give just two examples, no inscriptions at all at the Mina Bolivar, and thirty per cent of the voting population at the MNRH stronghold of Guayamerín were mysteriously excluded from the lists after they had completed the bureaucratic requirements for registration. The MNRH appears to have been the principal target of this practice, but having obtained an increase from 1.8 to 2.1 million voters within three weeks of the poll, the CNE/UNP had provided itself with a seemingly cast-iron guarantee against all challengers.[77]

Once the hustings got under way teachers were obliged under threat of violence to turn their pupils out for UNP rallies, of which there were a great many since Pereda was being ferried about the country by the FAB (Fuerza Aerea Boliviana). Opposition meetings, on the other hand, were frequently attacked, sometimes by civilians blessed with ample supplies of teargas, and on a number of occasions by the uniformed police. The UDP was fined $2,500 for putting its propaganda on the sacred white walls of Sucre and told to pay up within 48 hours while the entire country was pasted over with posters extolling Pereda's virtues. Both Paz and Siles were prevented from travelling to hustings in the Beni and Santa Cruz, where landing strips were blockaded, the local authorities regretting that they were unable to guarantee the safety of the candidates rather than exercising themselves to remove the odd tractor or bulldozer from the runways. In Guayamerín the leader of the MNRH youth movement was kidnapped by the navy and later found hanged. More often oppositionists were simply beaten up.

The media were directed with great clumsiness in favour of Pereda. Although the miners' radio stations and a few others kept up generally objective commentaries, many stations were suborned into favouring the 'candidate of nationalism'. The programmes of the state-controlled television channel were particularly partisan and access for the opposition was strictly limited; Quiroga's one election address was cancelled 'for technical reasons' four days before it was due to be transmitted. With the exception of *Presencia*, the newspapers were either disposed to favour *oficialismo* anyway or sufficiently cowed either by direct threat or by the political use of advertising accounts into limiting their coverage. However, it was in the mechanism of the vote itself that the regime exercised most effort to bring Pereda home. Under the existing system voting was by different coloured ballot papers, with each slate responsible for delivering its papers to the polling stations. Since Bolivia's roads are so few and tightly controlled by the

traffic police (*tránsito*) at the *trancas* outside each town the confiscation of opposition papers was a relatively easy matter and took place
on a wide scale over the week before the poll; at many stations no
opposition ballots were available at all. In some places — Apilla Pampa
(Cochabamba), Concepción (Santa Cruz), Mineros (Santa Cruz) — no
vote took place on 9 July; but most of the identifiable fraud took the
traditional form of stuffing boxes, exchanging them, or simply 'losing'
them. One of the most notable cases involved was the dumping of a
number of boxes into Lake Titicaca, which was immediately brought
to the notice of the over-worked international team observing the
count.[78] At those centres where opposition observers were not intimi-
dated, or it proved difficult to 'fix' the count, the UNP was easily overhauled by the UDP. A computation of 60 per cent of the vote from the
provinces of La Paz gave Pereda 15,223 votes against 139,236 for Siles
and 12,847 for Paz. On this basis the UDP would have scored a total of
232,000 (74.9 per cent) in the department against 25,371 for the UNP
(8.2 per cent), but the official result gave Pereda 194,946 votes (52.9
per cent), well ahead of Siles's 124,192 (33.7 per cent).[79] In no
department did the turn-out fall below 84 per cent, a miracle in a
country with such appalling communications and insufficiently
explained by the provision of beer, sandwiches and a free ride in army
lorries for those *campesinos* prepared to vote for *el general*. In Santa
Cruz the turn-out was an impressive 100.9 per cent, but this did not
compare with Chuquisaca's achievement of 104 per cent.[80] At the
other end of the scale, the official result in San Luis (Tarija) gave
Pereda 300 votes but Víctor Paz only 2, denying him the support not
only of his home town but also of a large section of his family, which is
not small and had been conspicuous by its presence at the voting
stations.

In the event, the fraud was so blatant that it defeated its own purpose. The FSTMB threatened to strike if it was not investigated; the
PDC, MNRH and UDP agreed not to recognise the result, and Siles
embarked upon his traditional hunger strike. The international team
was unanimous in its opinion that there had been widespread mal-
practice. Banzer, who even prior to the poll had given up all hopes in
Pereda and considered the staging of the election a lost cause, put as
much distance between himself and the UNP as possible and seemed
set to sacrifice his heir. Pereda, who had naturally pronounced himself the victor long before the count was over, was now induced by his

advisers to steal a march on the opposition and ask the CNE for an annulment because of the irregularities, although the fact that they had been conducted in his favour was not deemed worthy of extensive consideration. Confronted with universal repudiation of an exercise that was designed primarily to impress, such a move was virtually the only one open to the UNP. On 19 July the CNE, itself at the heart of the fraud, duly obliged. That same day Banzer signalled his complete break with Pereda by announcing that if the CNE had no winner to declare he would hand power over to a military junta on 6 August. On the 20th Pereda, fully aware that with no electoral victory to his name he was of minimal value to Banzer, visited the garrisons of Cochabamba and Santa Cruz. The next day he declared himself in rebellion 'against international communism' and immediately received the support of the Rangers and the FAB. Twenty hours of stalemate followed as Banzer held on to the allegiance of the La Paz garrison but made little progress in limiting support for the coup outside the capital. In the end, the FAB's threat to bomb him out of the palace forced Banzer to concede the day on the established rationale of averting bloodshed between brothers. After making a prolonged and lachrymose speech on television, he retired unmolested to his home. For three hours a junta of service commanders held power until Pereda flew in to don the presidential sash, finally obtained by the preferred methods of his fraternity.

7.
IN SEARCH OF DEMOCRACY, 1978-80

Following the overthrow of Banzer, Bolivia plunged into political chaos. Between July 1978 and July 1980 two further general elections were staged, five presidents held office (none of them as a result of victory at the polls), and of the cluster of coups under almost constant preparation four were essayed in practice, one failing and three successful. This chronic instability reflected both the inability of the constitutionalist camp to wrest initiative from those who wished to sustain the *banzerato* and the incapacity of the forces of the right fully to suppress the *apertura*. Even though General García Meza's coup of 17 July 1980 seemed, in the first instance, to have decided the issue firmly in favour of dictatorship, this regime was also to run out of steam within the space of a year. We can, however, divide the last four years of the period under study into two phases — after July 1980 the contest for power became almost exclusively an institutional affair. Until July 1980 the same structural crisis took the form of much more open encounters between badly-divided political forces of all the major social classes.

The very existence of constitutional democracy was at the heart of the conflict, in part simply because it was abhorrent to powerful

Establishment of the CSUTCB, 1979

sectors of the right, but largely because the principal political formations failed to provide anything resembling a coherent alternative to
the Banzer model. The natural competition of party politics quickly
decomposed into stagnant sectarianism, reflecting not just the lack of
an indigenous parliamentary tradition and the ambiguous legacy of
the MNR era but also a lack of confidence and unity in the ruling class.
The dominant bloc fought shy of the modicum of risk involved in a
popular front (UDP), covered its bets by patronising two variants of
reactionary civilianism (Víctor Paz and Banzer), neither of which was
sufficiently distanced from the policies of the last decade to attract
majority backing, and yet was reluctant to pledge itself to outright
dictatorship in view of the growing fissures inside the armed forces
and the defensive strength of the popular movement. The parliamentary left was less divided but very far from strong, the UDP failing
to capture the sympathies of an overwhelming majority as it became
increasingly immersed in partisan manoeuvre and desisted from
mobilisation that might jeopardise the balance of forces on which
constitutionalism depended for its survival. As a consequence, the
popular front encountered a growing apathy amongst the masses
which showed up to some degree in increased support for the PS-1 but
was evident less in terms of numbers of votes than in a broader disen-
chantment with parliamentarianism. The great popular mobilisations of this period were against dictatorship and assaults on the
popular economy but not in support of any specific political front. In
each case the cause of constitutionalism was pursued by rolling back
the initial gains in the streets and workplaces. Exhausted and confused, the populace gave the UDP a clear majority in June 1980 but
was in no state to resist García Meza's coup that followed the victory.

The process of polarisation that spanned the two years between
Pereda and García Meza was neither uniform nor inexorable; it followed shifts in the balance of forces both within and between the
democratic and authoritarian camps. However, the confusion of this
period was constantly underpinned by the economic crisis aggravated
by Banzer, and it served to emphasise that however internally divided
they might be, the principal political forces in Bolivia remained the
military and the COB. The crisis of constitutionalism was, therefore,
not simply conjunctural, not just a case of bad timing, wrong politics
or collective ineptitude, but the result of a social structure that allowed
minimal space for those who wished to uphold the formal division of

powers and reverse the 150-years' dominance of the executive over the legislature. Such objectives are not achieved overnight, by grasping good opportunities, or by courtesy of more or less benevolent foreign sponsors. This is particularly the case in Bolivia, a country that is economically backward but politically advanced; constitutionalism was weak not because it was nascent, a stage about to be achieved, but because it had never represented an adequate means of control for the ruling class or a historic source of liberties for the masses. Here the distinction between finite democratic rights and the complete apparatus of electoralism is critical: while the system owed the strength of its mystique to its incorporation of such rights, these had invariably been obtained in practice by collective action and within the orbit of a direct, popular democracy rather than that of parliamentarianism. In this context it is possible to view the project of formal democracy as a kind of tactical option for both sides, emerging at the end of the 1970s precisely because the military had lost its political dynamism and the organised working class was still too disorientated to provide a coherent alternative. There was a political vacuum.

Negotiating an Exit

The coup d'etat is a political mechanism that frequently lends itself to personalism, and there can be little doubt that Pereda's ousting of his long-time boss was provoked by the thwarting of his ambitions. Yet Pereda was no caudillo, even of the back-room, scheming variety, and his assumption of office owed much to the belief in military circles that Banzer had short-changed an heir who, for all his manifest shortcomings, was the obvious man to preside over the damage-control exercise necessitated by the fraud. No sector of the armed forces sought an immediate withdrawal to the barracks; almost to a man the officer corps believed that a further period of military government was essential, some simply wanting to prolong the *banzerato* with or without its leader, others seeking a measured retreat in good order.

Aside from averting the threat of international communism, Pereda was never fully clear as to the rationale for his coup. In his first speech he asserted that he 'represented the collective will' but stopped short of openly claiming to have won the poll.[1] For the first fortnight of his regime it appeared as if the new president sought simply to refurbish and renew Banzer's dictatorship. He declared that new elections would be a waste of time because the losers would always complain about fraud; he jailed over 100 oppositionists and sent troops to the Yungas township of Coripata, where a score of peasants were killed after demonstrations against the rigging of the poll. The cabinet was firmly in the Banzer mould, including the aged *pirista* and Barrientos aide Ricardo Anaya as foreign minister, Román Vaca, a key figure in the Santa Cruz oligarchy, and the hardline Colonel Faustino Rico Toro as interior minister. Rico Toro came from one of the *tandas* (graduating fraternities) associated with the *movimiento generacional* but was not closely linked with its policies nor disposed to argue the case for further relaxation. However, neither the external nor the domestic conditions were propitious for a bland continuism. The US was quick to react, the coup being an acute embarrassment for the Carter administration, which had held up the elections as the first triumph for its human rights policy in the region. Ambassador Paul Boeker, who had previously complained about the fraud, was now directed to cut all contacts with the Pereda regime. The State Department declared that the military rising was 'a serious setback for the democratic process', and urged Pereda 'to move quickly to re-establish a genuine process of democratic development'. Boeker stopped endorsing aid requests, and Pereda was informed that Bolivia would lose $70 million unless new elections were scheduled.[2] The new president quickly announced that another poll might be held in 1980 but that it would be impossible to have elections in 1979 because it was the centenary of the War of the Pacific during which Bolivia required a strong and stable government. Almost without exception the political parties demanded a new poll before the end of 1979, the FSB joining the UDP in insisting upon elections within six months.

Although the UDP had launched no mobilisation against a fraud of which it had been the prime victim — the only concrete action had been a 48-hour strike by the FSTMB — the rare unity of the civilian parties on this issue had deepened the worries of many officers. Confronted by both inactivity and unanimous opposition, sectors of the military gained the confidence and incentive to press for change. After a tour of the major garrisons in the first week of August, Pereda discovered that although many had backed or acquiesced in his coup as an emergency measure, the position of the US and the claims of the political parties had persuaded a majority that further elections should take place; feelings ran highest in the La Paz garrison, which was dominated by the *movimiento generacional* and threatened that unless guarantees of a new election were given immediately it would publish its document demanding a poll within six months.[3] Accordingly, Pereda formally announced on 6 August that elections would be held in 1980 and that he would not be standing again. He released all those detained after the coup and lifted the state of siege, which enabled the resumption of diplomatic and economic relations with the US. Thus, although he had given himself a two-year reign against the wishes of the majority of the political parties and a powerful minority in the military, Pereda had been forced to acknowledge the interim character of his regime and prevented from consolidating *continuismo*. He began his term in a very weak position.

This was quickly recognised by the opposition forces, which banded together to demand that the government set a date for further elections before 9 September 1978 and that the poll take place before July 1979. Pereda formally rejected this call but was forced to set up a commission to study the issue and hold talks with the major parties. At the same time he withdrew Banzer's security state and obligatory civil service decrees in an effort to establish his democratic *bona fides* and win some badly-needed political space. He was not successful, being obliged within a month of taking office to accept the press unions' demands for a public promise that the military would not intervene in the media; the government was also compelled to 'recognise the justice' of the FSTMB's claim for a seventy per cent wage increase whilst offering only 35 per cent, thereby antagonising all parties concerned. Furthermore, on 2 August, '*Día del Indio*', Pereda made the extraordinary admission that Banzer not he was head of the *Pacto*—a critical sign of weakness. None the less, this concession to the pressure applied by the unreconstructed 'nationalist' peasant confederation failed to secure a truce with his old patron, who declared that the 'nationalism' of 21 August 1971 had ceased to hold sway on 21 July 1978, rejected an offer of the post of ambassador in Buenos Aires, and moved freely about the country to test the possibilities of a comeback.

Faced with a popular movement that was regaining strength and yet could not be repressed without courting the dangers of further rupture with Washington, and simultaneously deprived of support from the undisputed leader of the military right, Pereda's regime was on the run. By early November matters had become critical. Banzer, after finally accepting the post of ambassador to Argentina, returned to Santa Cruz after four days at his desk and seemed set to stage a coup. The junior officers demanded and obtained a new cabinet with increased military representation as a counter-measure. Yet, Pereda further weakened his own position by cutting gas supplies to Argentina and announcing a new deal with Brazil on terms that were widely viewed to be just as prejudicial to the country's interests as those proposed by Banzer several years before. At the same time, in an effort to mollify the popular forces, Pereda promised a reduction in senior state salaries and a campaign against corruption; he then visited Santa Cruz to declare that the customs service would be purged in order to wipe out contraband, which was estimated by the Banco Central to be worth $600 million a year and had become a major feature of the Santa Cruz economy. Instead of complementing each other, these measures had the effect of depriving Pereda of any lingering support or neutrality. Banzer's challenge received vital support from the very regional interests that had accepted his removal only four months before while the UDP, clearly sensing the opportunity to reduce the Pereda regime to a mere holding operation, called for mass mobilisation on 24 November in demand for elections during the first half of 1979.

The UDP's move was a critical ultimatum and served as an excellent pretext for the *movimiento generacional* to curb Banzer's recidivism. In a well-planned coup the young commanders removed Pereda early on the 24th and replaced him with the army commander General David Padilla Arancibia, one of the few senior officers who had been promoted by the book and not by virtue of political favours, a straight-laced but respected *institucionalista* and a man who favoured prompt elections because, like his subordinates, he wanted the military to retreat intact and in good order.[4] The demonstration went ahead as planned, except that it was now to celebrate the new regime's first pronouncement that a poll would be held on 1 July 1979. The praise given by the UDP leadership to Padilla and the colonels who had given him the presidency was sufficiently fulsome to confirm the popular view that the coup had been launched with the prior knowledge of the front. This was not to be the only instance of civilian parties relying on action by the armed forces to secure their objectives for them, but at the time the longer-range implications of such a dependence were not the subject of widespread preoccupation.

Padilla's was the only regime since 1964 to complete a self-determined term of office. As its leader declared in his first public speech, its fundamental aim was to 'return to the people their rights and liberties, including the election of their leaders by universal democratic vote'.[5] The government provided the holding operation that Pereda could not supply and marked the ascendancy of the post-1952 generation inside the armed forces. In some respects this alteration of the balance of forces inside the institution was quite marked, and the most prominent members of the *movimiento generacional* were given important cabinet posts: Gary Prado (planning), Raúl López Leytón (interior), Rolando Saravia (MACA), Simón Sejas (education, after the failure of Colonel José Olvis, a man with *falangista* sympathies, to deal with the militant teachers), and Jorge Echazú (mines). None of these figures was a liberal and all professed a strong anti-communism, but they were committed to retrieving the armed forces' reputation, firmly nationalist in spirit, and convinced that political stability could be achieved through a disciplined hand-over. Given the political situation, this required a great deal more than realising the ideal of 'apolitical professionalism' that was making something of a come-back in the vocabulary of the Pentagon under Carter. Necessarily pledged to interventionism, the leading figures took a series of tough measures against the *banzerista* apparatus. Saravia, who was the most outspoken minister, broke up the official peasant confederation and ordered its offices to be handed over to the independent organisations. López Leytón accused the CEPB of funding a planned counter-coup and in January conducted a wave of raids on the homes of prominent rightists. Although this had the effect of subduing the CEPB, the regime returned to the offensive in April, attacking private enterprise for destabilising democracy in refusing to pay the wage increases it had authorised. At the beginning of its nine-month rule the government did nothing to impede the ex-*movimientista* labour minister Aníbal Aguilar Peñarrieta from initiating a civil case against Banzer, Pereda and Mario Gutiérrez for a series of common and state crimes, thereby opening the way for a full impeachment after the elections. Padilla also fired Banzer as ambassador and retired him from the army, and he raised the possibility that court martial be established to consider the deaths of Selich, Zenteno and Torres as well as the Tolata massacre. In the event, this idea was dropped for fear of provoking anti-militarist sentiment, the regime contenting itself with the much less risky enterprise of prosecuting 1,600 of Banzer's union *coordinadores* for defrauding their organisations of more than $3 million.[6]

These measures enabled the Padilla government to contain the right, which on a number of occasions late in 1978 and early in 1979 came close to rebellion. By April 1979 a form of truce had been established around acceptance of the coming elections, to which the right now devoted its attentions. The price paid by the regime was the removal from office of the vociferous Saravia and, later, the fiercely anti-Brazilian foreign minister Raúl Botelho Gonsálvez. However, the bulk of the *movimiento generacional*, who pointedly did not promote themselves in order to stress their honesty, retained their posts and influence.

Although it certainly moved resolutely to restrain the right and guarantee the *apertura*, Padilla's government exhibited an 'even-handedness' typical of the vacuum-filling bonapartist role it saw itself obliged to play. The regime refused to remove the troops from the mines, ratified the *Pacto Militar-Campesino* and prohibited showings of Jorge Sanjinés's '*Coraje del Pueblo*', which depicts the massacre of San Juan. Moreover, its image became slightly less spotless than it would have liked as a result of some irregular practices concerning the foundation of a large new smelting plant at Karachipampa near Potosí, earning the young officers the sobriquet of *Karachipampas*, which was not entirely damning since it captured their attachment to the idea of autonomous industrial development as much as any flexi-bility in the means of acquiring it. A good deal less ambivalence was involved in the condemnation of the importing of a cargo of rotten rice from Pakistan which was alleged to have been highly profitable to the industry minister, the dapper little naval captain Oscar Pammo, whose radical credentials derived from leading the operation to nationalise Mina Matilde in 1971 but who before long would jettison any *institucionalista* attachments for good.

The essential caution and conservatism of the Padilla regime was most clearly evident in its refusal to take any iniative on the economic front, particularly in terms of devaluing the peso, increasing taxes or removing price subsidies, all of which were demanded by the IMF as conditions for the disbursement of a badly-needed stand-by loan to cover repayments of the debt incurred by Banzer. The rationale for this was that as an interim administration it had no mandate for the initiation of major economic policy, but in reality the military was

highly reluctant to attract the opprobrium of a whole-hearted deflationary policy after the examples of 1972 and 1974. If the debt was to
be rescheduled such steps had to be taken, but outside the context of
dictatorial rule they promised to unleash such popular opposition
that the army was only too happy to leave them to an elected civilian
government. On the same managerial grounds it refused to grant
major wage rises and restricted increases in the state sector to the lowest limit admissible for the retention of an uneasy union neutrality. Its
principal problem in this regard was with the Maoist-influenced
teachers, who through a very vocal campaign managed to get rid of
education minister Olvis but failed to gain their full demand for a Bs.
5,000 minimum wage.

This sum was adopted by the COB as the minimum for all state
sector workers at its fifth national congress in May 1979. The COB's
first congress in nine years was the scene of tearful reunions between
old comrades, many of whom had not seen each other for nearly eight
years. Aside from the remembrance of those who would never return,
the most emotional moment was perhaps the election as honorary secretary for culture of the old Argentine anarchosyndicalist Liber Forti,
who, sporting his customary beret and pipe and unable to hold back
the tears, accepted belated recognition for over thirty years of cultural
agitation on behalf of his adopted people.[7] The congress then went on
to reaffirm the 1970 Corocoro thesis, adding a resolution that restated
the COB's independence from any political current — a setback for
supporters of the UDP, who had agitated for alignment with their
front. The debate over this issue was predictably heated, but the
exchanges between backers of the UDP (PCB; MIR; MNRI) and the *Lechi-
nistas* in league with the revolutionary left were not nearly so contentious as those between all these groups and the PCML, which had argued
from the moment the organisational subcommittee first met that the
congress should be postponed because the old executive had no authority to run it. The leader of the Maoist current inside the COB, René
Higueras del Barco, the secretary of relations, further disputed the
recognition of the MRTK and MITKA as representatives of the *campesino*
movement in addition to the now very small *Confederación Independiente* led by his co-religionist Casiano Amurrio, the 1978 presidential
candidate for the FRI. Branded as divisionists, the Maoists took some
30 of the 600 delegates out of the congress. This split was one of the
worst since the days of Siles's presidency, and it was fully confirmed

when Higueras's speech turned into a slanging match with supporters of the POR (Lora), causing a fight during which a member of the PCML drew his revolver and fired at the Trotskyists, wounding a bystander.[8]

The principal cause of this apparently quite unnecessary conflict was the decison of the PCML leadership to break free from its allies in the FRI and join the ranks of the new front being organised by Víctor Paz: *Alianza*-MNR. For many on the left this was a qualitatively different act from that of the PCB in supporting the other MNR caudillo Siles because, while they were both accepted to have held 'anti-worker' positions in the 1950s and 1960s, Paz had been a party to the *banzerato* whereas Siles had opposed it, defended basic democratic rights, and seemingly moved substantially to the left, virtually imposing the MIR's leader, Jaime Paz Zamora, on the reluctant MNRI and PCB as his running mate in the 1979 elections. The popularly-held view that 'Motete' Zamora's 180-degree turn corresponded to advice from Peking to ally with 'the most advanced sector of the bourgeoisie' was largely borne out by attacks on the new line by orthodox *pekinistas*, who accused both Zamora and Deng Xiao Ping of making a mockery of Mao's thought in base opportunism.[9] The line of the PCML leadership, by contrast, was that the AMNR, 'constitutes a broad front of classes which seek a democratic option, one that is popular and anti-imperialist, within the great process of the Bolivian revolution . . . the Alliance is . . . the most solid obstacle to the ultra-right . . . and opens the road to national liberation.'[10] While Paz now made himself vulnerable to attacks for being 'communist' — attacks that were without delay levelled by Banzer — he succeeded in countering Siles's contract with the *muscovitas* with the support of a political force that had grown appreciably under Banzer, had a strong presence in certain unions and sufficiently radical credentials to freshen up the jaded image of his alliance. Zamora's motives for making a pact were a good deal less obvious: his mutation from 'Comandante Rolando' the exponent of 'peoples' war' to a responsible, besuited statesman could scarcely be dubbed as simply tactical, it greatly antagonised many of the party's leading cadres, and seemed set to deprive the PCML of the gains it had made over the previous eight years. Having said this, it should be noted that the Maoists' differences with the PCB extended only to their choice of the 'multi-class' popular party they attached themselves to, Zamora's choice effectively being made for him once the PCB allied with Siles. With respect to strategy there was little to

distinguish them, the pro-Moscow PCB defending its participation in
the UDP in terms very similar to the PCML's rationale for its alliance
with Paz: as strengthening a popular front capable of restoring
democracy, putting the economy at the service of the masses, fortifying the workers' movement, reincorporating the military into society,
and establishing a democratic, popular and anti-imperialist government.[11] A peaceful, electoral road to socialism was the common denominator, the final objective not being achieved but approximated to
when their respective fronts took office.

The most important new force in the 1979 elections was *Acción
Democrática Nacionalista* (ADN), set up by Banzer in April when
René Bernal refused to ally with him. Resurrecting the old slogan
'Paz, Orden, Trabajo', and drawing the support of a strong dissident
faction of the FSB, the PIR, and the rump of the official peasant confederation led by Pascual Gamón, Banzer rapidly set his new civilian
apparatus into action, gained the backing of many erstwhile employees, and presented Paz with a strong challenge in the competition to
win middle-class sympathy. His pugnacious campaign was based on
the encouragement of fears in the military about left-wing subversion,
attacks on the two main fronts as vehicles for communism, and frequent declarations that the poll would be fraudulent, which did
nothing to endear him to the regime. He got barely veiled support
from *El Diario*, which described the elections as 'an odious obligation
rather than a civic duty', and *Los Tiempos*, which stated baldly that
people did not want to vote. There was a germ of truth in this since the
final registration was only 70 per cent of those eligible to vote (although
registration was not now officially inflated), and even the left-wing
paper *Aquí* noted a perceptible apathy in the popular sectors.[12] There
were widespread fears of fraud or, if the UDP was allowed to win, a
coup.

The campaign was in some respects similar to that of the preceding
years. Siles was prohibited from visiting Santa Cruz when the FSB
occupied the airport, killing one person. Paz received similar treatment in Sucre, and Banzer was stoned and ignominiously chased out
of Huanuni having proclaimed that a vote for the ADN was 'the last
chance to save Bolivia'.[13] However, the poll of 1 July was neither particularly violent nor conducted in a flagrantly dishonest manner; it
did not meet the requirements set in those countries where elections
are a regular feature of political life, but it may be said to have given

Table 10

The Election of 1 July 1979

Slate	Date Founded	Main Parties	Candidates	Votes	Seats
UDP	13/4/78	MNRI MIR PCB MIN (a) ALIN (b) MPLN (c) PRIN PS-Atahuichi MRTK-Ramos PRTB Alfredo Ovando	Hernán Siles Jaime Paz	592,886	46
AMNR	9/4/79	MNR PDC PRA MRTK-Chila PCML	Víctor Paz Luis Ossio	539,744	54
ADN	20/4/79	ADN FSB-Moreira PIR CNCB (d)	Hugo Banzer Franz Ondarza	225,205	21
APIN (e)	11/4/79	MARC (f) FSB-Gutiérrez	René Bernal Mario Gutiérrez	61,362	5
PS-1	13/3/79	PS-1 OST (g)	Marcelo Quiroga Jaime Taborga	72,527	5
MITKA	27/4/78	MITKA	Luciano Tapia Eufronio Veliz	34,456	1
PUB (h)	27/1/78	PUB	Walter González	19,997	1
VO (i)	26/11/78	VO	Ricardo Catoira Filemón Escóbar	17,192	0

Notes:

a. *Movimiento de la Izquierda Nacional*, led by Edil Sandoval Morón.
b. *Alianza de la Izquierda Nacional*, led by Rubén Sánchez.
c. *Movimiento Popular de Liberación Nacional*, led by Ramiro Velasco, a split from the ELN-PRTB.
d. *Confederación Nacional de Campesinos de Bolivia*, led by Pascual Gamón.
e. *Alianza Popular de Integración Nacional*.
f. *Movimiento Agrario Revolucionario Campesino*, led by René Bernal.
g. *Organización Socialista de Trabajadores*, led by Sonia Montaño, a Trotskyist group affiliated to the Argentine PST of Nahuel Moreno.
h. *Partido de la Unión Boliviana*, led by ex-police colonel Walter González.
i. *Vanguardia Obrera*, led by Filemón Escóbar. The POR (Lora) split at its XXIV congress (1975), the dissident group itself splitting in 1977 into the POR *De Pie* (Cirilo Jiménez and Benigno Ojeda) and the *Vanguardia Comunista del* POR (Escóbar and Víctor Sossa). In 1978 Sonia Montaño left the VCPOR to form the OST, while Escóbar formed VO and Sossa continued to head the VCPOR.

Source: *Coyuntura*, 1 June 1979; *Latin America Political Report*, 29 July 1979.

a reasonably accurate reflection of Bolivians' wishes for their next government.

The first point to be noted about the result is the anomaly between the number of votes cast and the number of seats won, particularly between the UDP and AMNR. This derived from the very uneven distribution of constituencies and the reservation of a quota of seats in the lower house for the second-place party in each constituency. This proved particularly prejudicial for the UDP, which enjoyed most support in the heavily populated urban areas that had comparatively few seats. Nonetheless, the UDP's failure to win an overall majority could not be blamed on this alone since the right (AMNR; ADN; APIN; PUB) possessed a clear majority of votes, even when the remarkably good result returned by the PS-1 was added to the UDP total. The UDP was clearly the most popular front but it was equally clearly not going to form the next government because it lacked a parliamentary majority or allies of sufficient strength with whom to form a viable coalition. On the other hand, the ADN steadfastly refused to support its principal competitor Víctor Paz, thereby ruling out the only other obvious alternative.

The resolution of this stalemate, which was in no small measure due to the bifurcations of the MNR and PCB of the 1950s, had, according to the constitution, to be decided by the new congress. Thus, while Hernán Siles and newcomer Jaime Paz staged a hunger strike in defence of their popular mandate in the lobby of the legislature, the deputies and senators engaged in a prolonged debate about how to break the impasse. This took place under a renewed threat of military intervention since even Padilla was now losing patience with a seemingly abortive exercise. Foreign dignitaries, including Mrs Rosalyn Carter, had to postpone their visits for the inauguration until, after a week of complex deals and endless votes, a compromise was eventually reached in the appointment of Walter Guevara Arze, president of the senate, as interim president for a year until yet further elections were held in June 1980. Although it was not reached with any ease, this decision reflected the need of both the major fronts to avoid forming a minority government or an interim administration, particularly since the debt question had become so critical, making the adoption of highly unpopular economic measures unavoidable if the IMF was to be placated. Guevara's appointment was, in fact, in line with the constitutionally-ordained line of precedence — it could have been made almost immediately if the major parties had not insisted upon haggling for advantage — but it also represented something of an historic resolution, bringing the third figure of the MNR of the 1950s between his two erstwhile colleagues. Although Guevara's PRA had sided with Paz in the election and was a concertedly conservative force, its leader had in the past opposed Paz, was viewed as a man of independent temperament, and was expected to resist military overtures against congressional interests. Moreover, he had the personal and statutory authority to act as temporary president even if he lacked the popular votes. Thus, although not highly popular, his appointment possessed a certain credibility. Equally, both main fronts seemed to have protected their flanks, the MNR by having an ally in government whom it could utilise and influence but also jettison without great difficulty if the regime should prove unpopular, the UDP by becoming the effective opposition and yet retaining the 'moral victory' of its vote, a combination that appeared unbeatable for building up a majority in 1980.

Guevara duly proceeded to appoint an 'apolitical' cabinet of conservative technocrats whose disposition was for fiscal sobriety, negotiations with the IMF, and a judicious maintenance of the status quo. Like the Padilla government, Guevara's had no mandate to undertake major economic initiatives, but unlike the previous regime, it lacked an independent coercive capacity. It was answerable to congress but congress would do nothing to aid it in distress; it held nominal authority over the military but the armed forces were, if anything, even less disposed to take its side, enjoying for the first time in a decade the political advantages of 'serving' a civilian administration. The position of each group was not without a certain logic, but the sum of the parts looked far from stable.

This was shown to be the case when, within a fortnight of Guevara's inauguration, congress embarked upon the impeachment of Banzer. The move was led by Marcelo Quiroga Santa Cruz who, on behalf of the PS-1 but with the tacit support of the most diverse groups outside the ADN, charged the ex-dictator and many of his ministers and closest collaborators with some 234 separate instances of civil and common crime. In a 14-hour speech that was richly furnished with supporting documents, laced with an oratorial ardour and skill that congress had not witnessed since the Catavi massacre debate of 1943, and — on the insistence of the speaker — fully covered by state television as well as radio, Quiroga provided a punctilious condemnation of the entire

banzerato.[14] This was both extremely popular and decidedly dangerous for although Quiroga on several occasions accused Banzer of
breaking statutes and abusing the military institution, the tendency of
the impeachment was indisputably towards an indictment of the
entire armed forces. Even those such as Padilla, who nurtured no
great love for Banzer, had occupied positions of authority under him,
accepted the 'institutionalist' character of his regime, and were by no
means disposed to reject its record lock, stock and barrel. Moreover,
the very popularity of Quiroga's invective threatened to unleash a
fresh wave of general anti-militarism, further alienating those officers
who agreed with a greater or lesser number of specific allegations.

The impeachment — Quiroga's second — established the PS-1 as a
radical force prepared to use parliament with the objective of wider
mobilisation, a fact which soon showed up in a marked increase of
support for a party that lacked the organisational strengths of the rest
of the left but seemed to possess a singularity of purpose and an adher-
ence to principled independence. However, the matter did not end
with Quiroga's speech; witnesses were called, testimonies noted, pro-
cedural objections tabled, and then counter-impeachments initiated,
with the ADN rehearsing in detail the crimes of Paz, Siles and Ovando,
who had returned from exile in Madrid to support the UDP. As the
debates went on the political struggles of the previous twenty years
were relived with increasing acrimony and to no clear end.[15] What
had begun as a provocative but considered — and, arguably, necessary
— parliamentary motion had been transformed into a name-calling
free-for-all. The warm reception in popular circles to the vilification
of Banzer was qualified by the absence of any concrete action and the
perceived irrelevance of much of the debate; the armed forces were
antagonised by a legislative assembly that was availing itself of all the
privileges of free speech at the earliest opportunity, and emboldened
because it was doing so with minimal military protection.

At the beginning of October the patience of the officer corps was
taxed further by Lechín's proposal that the economic crisis could be
greatly alleviated if defence expenditure were radically reduced. Inviting senior officers to debate the issue with him on television, Lechín provoked even the moderate Padilla to describe him as the 'ancestral
enemy' of the armed forces. Well-attended celebrations of the anniversary of Ché Guevara's death did little to calm military tempers over the
following days, during which Padilla, now commander-in-chief, was

hard pressed to maintain discipline. Early on 11 October the sixth division, based in Trinidad (Beni), finally broke ranks and declared itself in revolt, calling for Guevara's resignation, the dissolution of congress and the appointment of a military junta to guarantee security at the OAS meeting due to take place in La Paz at the end of the month. Since Trinidad is an isolated town and not a major military centre Padilla had time to hold back other units, deny that the rising was political in nature, and dispatch a mission under Colonel Alberto Natusch Busch to negotiate a settlement. For his part, Guevara restricted himself to stating that the revolt was no more than the manifestation of excessively high spirits following a party attended by the division's general staff on the night of the 10th. The ADN failed to attend the emergency congressional debate on the rising, raising suspicions of direct involvement, but in the event Natusch returned to La Paz remarkably quickly, having patched matters up with his *beniano* colleagues.[16] The UDP, which had adopted a policy of forthright conciliation with the military since Padilla's coup and was registering its request for the removal of troops from the mines in the most courteous of tones, did not push for an aggressive or punitive response to the abortive *golpe*, accepting the government's line that it was an aberration.[17]

The rapid failure of the Trinidad rising did not reduce political tension. On the 24th the COB, making a carefully-judged move to place pressure on the UDP and pre-empt any deflationary package arranged by Guevara at the behest of the IMF, presented its own *paquete económico*. In a comprehensive but essentially tactical document the COB proposed a substantial increase in the minimum wage to Bs.5,000, tight exchange controls and restrictions on foreign travel, a price freeze or a sliding scale of wages in line with inflation, a moratorium on the foreign debt followed by extensive renegotiation of the terms of repayment, tight limits on rent increases, prohibition of the import of luxury goods and cars, and steep price rises for high-grade petrol (used for private transport) as well as the nationalisation of public transport.[18] Although the UDP had no precise economic proposals and only the vaguest of strategies — orientated around 'responsible' renegotiation of the debt rather than a moratorium, and the expectation of new bilateral aid and soft loans from Europe — they clearly fell far short of the COB's recommendations.[19] The Guevara administration was neither willing nor able to accede to the package, but was still obliged to respond rapidly since its publication aggravated an already severe crisis inside the government. From 13 October, two days after the Trinidad rising, Guevara had been negotiating with the two main fronts in an attempt to reverse their effective abstention from government. Guevara's position was that there existed a stark choice between holding elections and solving the economic crisis. First he attempted to gain an extension of his term, which was, he argued, the only means by which the debt crisis could be properly confronted. Having failed in this, the president demanded greater cooperation and participation in government. Since he had achieved a great success in gaining a 25–0 vote in the OAS (Chile abstained) in favour of Bolivia's right to an exit to the sea his reputation was riding sufficiently high for him to make some initial progress. However, Guevara had only been able to maintain a tenuous control with the tactical support of the ADN, and open collaboration with Banzer's party was repugnant to a majority of both the UDP and the MNR. On 29 October, one day after a tentative agreement had been made to acquiesce in the strategy of a rapprochement with the far right in order to avert a coup, the major parties withdrew once again. Guevara declared, 'we are all in the same boat, if it goes down we all go down'. This statement was no idle threat since although the president was receiving intelligence reports not available to the parties, it was plain to all that military insurrection was in the air.

On 27 October Oscar Sanjinés of the COB had openly accused Colonel Natusch of preparing a coup; Natusch had responded by declaring himself totally innocent, demanding proof and threatening to sue for defamation. At the same time the colonel had given both Guevara and Padilla a pledge of loyalty, and since Cyrus Vance—in La Paz for the OAS meeting—had reiterated that Washington would not recognise any regime that came to power through a coup it was felt that there was no immediate danger. However, Natusch's 'resolution' of the Trinidad affair had been no more than a tactical move to impose uniform timing on the preparations for a rising. At 2 a.m. on 1 November, when many OAS delegates were still in the city, the tanks of the Tarapacá, commanded by Colonel Arturo Doria Medina, occupied the centre of La Paz and the Palacio Quemado. By 7 a.m. the entire city was controlled by the rebels, led by none other than Colonel Natusch, who was declared president later in the day. Guevara and Padilla went into hiding, the COB immediately declared an indefinite general strike.

Despite the large number of troops employed in the opening offensive it quickly became apparent that Natusch's coup was not exactly a traditional rightist insurrection in the Banzer mould. In his first pronouncements Natusch promised collaboration with the congress and the COB, stating that he wanted to replace a weak democracy with a strong one. He pledged himself to respect trade-union and democratic liberties, human rights and university autonomy, made no immediate assault on radio stations or newspaper offices, and appeared to be engaged in an enterprise modelled on Busch and Villarroel. The reason for this became clearer when it was known that the rebel regime enjoyed the backing of a number of politicians who had decided that the Guevara government was totally moribund and that they and their interests were better served by collaborating with the most prominent military strongman and steering him clear of the normal pitfalls of *golpismo* into a more considered form of bonapartism. The most important counsellors were José Fellmann Velarde and Guillermo Bedregal of the MNR, Edil Sandoval Morón (the UDP vice-presidential candidate in 1978), Abel Ayoroa and Germán Condori of the MNRI. Bedregal was appointed foreign minister and soon emerged as the regime's leading ideologue despite the fact that in 1971 he had published a book vilifying the military. Yet he insisted all along that he had only backed Natusch because Paz had been in favour of the coup.[20] However true this might have been — it was widely believed on the left and in the working class — Paz quickly denied the charge and offered no support to the new regime.[21] The collaborators were immediately expelled from their parties, and even the ADN, sensing the climate of resistance evident from the start, offered no formal endorsement, simply allowing its members to enter the regime in a personal capacity.[22] Although, in accordance with tradition, Natusch had struck at the end of a week and therefore given himself a weekend's grace, it was soon clear that he would receive no broad support and encounter stiff resistance, at least in the streets and workplaces. No further politicians rallied to his cause and, apart from the several hundred troops billetted in the Quemado, Natusch was left alone with the initial fellow travellers and one foreign collaborator whom the population of La Paz — with that humour born of adversity — identified as Johnny Walker.

An hour after its first strike call the COB announced that the strike would be for 24 hours only, being prolonged according to the situation.

Picking up on this, Natusch invited Lechín to discuss matters with him on the 2nd. After a far from unanimous decision by the executive committee, the COB leader attended at the palace on the 3rd but was not long in rejecting an offer of *cogobierno* and implementation of the COB *paquete* in exchange for an end to parliamentary rule. The strike was continued at 24 hour intervals, it being obeyed in a disciplined fashion throughout the country. At the instruction of the CSUTCB work was halted in many areas of the countryside too; Bolivia came to a standstill in the face of the first general strike since October 1970. On the day of the coup congress convened openly for an emergency debate but lacked a quorum. The acting president of the house of deputies, the *movimientista* Leónidas Sánchez, suggested that it adjourn until the following Monday, but this proposal met with almost universal opposition since young people were now dying in large numbers on the streets by demonstrating in defence of parliament, which would do its cause little good by going on holiday. Having condemned the coup and voted not to cooperate with the *de facto* regime, congress was immediately declared illegal by Natusch and forced to go underground. Guevara and Padilla meanwhile issued messages urging total resistance, Guevara's remaining an inordinately long time in the possession of the president of the house, Lidia Gueiler, while Padilla's was of greater propaganda than organisational value since the leading *Karachipampas* had already been put under arrest.

Faced with such opposition, Natusch revised his tactics. At the start of the new week — 5 and 6 November — he allowed Doria Medina's troops to run amok in La Paz, blew up a large part of the COB building, and imposed a regime very similar to that of August 1971. Despite the widespread deployment of armoured vehicles and the heavy machine-gunning of the city's popular quarters from a helicopter rented from the US construction company Groves Ltd, demonstrators continually returned to the streets, dug up the cobbles and constructed 'moral barricades'. Over 200 died, 125 'disappeared' and 200 were wounded. As many Bolivians perished in 14 days under Natusch as under seven years of Banzer.[23] The impact of this butchery was heightened by the fact that it took place almost exclusively in La Paz and in the space of a very few days (most of the deaths occurred on 5 and 6 November). The Natusch regime became known as the 'Massacre of All Saints' and its principal architect, Colonel Doria Medina, won the title of 'Marshal of Death'.

Both the initial coup and the repression that followed it seemed to have been designed precisely to invite international opprobrium. US ambassador Paul Boeker was immediately directed to realise the threat that had been issued the year before to Pereda; the army's bluff was called, diplomatic relations cut, and $60 million of economic and military aid frozen. The Andean Pact issued a strong condemnation and also cut ties while Chile, still smarting from the vote at the OAS, was quick to disclaim any involvement although this did not protect Natusch from accusations of being pro-Chilean. After two weeks in power the government had been recognised only by Egypt and Malaya; not even the southern cone dictatorships were prepared to rally round once Washington had signalled its opposition. The colonel's civilian advisers had not served him well on the diplomatic front.

On the 7th, recognising that the killings on the streets were no longer serving any political purpose and anxious to find some way out of the impasse, Natusch declared an end to the state of siege and called for further talks with the COB and congress. Parliament did not resist and the executive committee of the COB, perceiving the need for some form of mediation, lifted the general strike. However, the rank and file of the FSTMB refused to return to work and held out for several days more, serving notice on the COB leadership that its actions were under close and critical scrutiny. Padilla and Guevara also rejected negotiations and urged continued resistance, the deposed president pursuing this cause by insinuating himself into the reconvened congress disguised in a wig and sports clothes to make a defiant speech before escaping from the security forces by way of the parliamentary pantry.

The proposal presented by Natusch to his opponents was for a tripartite regime consisting of himself on behalf of the armed forces together with representatives of parliament and the COB. This idea of a triumvirate was received favourably not just by the ADN but also by the PCB, which under the pressure of the moment gave evidence of preferring a bonapartist alliance to weakling civilian government. The sharpest criticism of this line came from the party's UDP partner in the MNR, which had, however, itself accepted negotiations with Natusch. Despite the fact that the PCB repeatedly defended its democratic *bona fides* it was not able seriously to dispute the fact that it had supported a triumvirate with the military, a tactical error of no little consequence and the cause of subsequent self-criticism, most notably by Simón Reyes.[24] Between the 10th and the 15th the COB continued to reject the idea of a triumvirate after making consultations with the rank and file; too many lives had been lost and feelings were too strong to permit any concession on this point. Congress was markedly less reluctant but, whatever their desires, its leaders knew that without the COB no coalition was possible. The comportment of parliament during the crisis was little different to that over the previous weeks, failing to match both the level of popular mobilisation and the example set by Guevara and Padilla: 'Instead of fortifying itself, the legislative power made itself weaker, lost prestige before public opinion, and neutralised itself in debate of little or no national interest.'[25]

The temperamental Natusch had himself wanted to resign once popular resistance failed to crumble under the initial repression, but by that stage he had become a virtual prisoner of his own high command, which had thrown all its resources behind the coup. The eventual decision to negotiate a withdrawal on the part of the hardline *golpistas* now commanding the armed forces may well have been prompted by the realisation that to avoid bankruptcy they would have to declare a devaluation. On 5 November the government had closed the banks in order to stop a run on the peso and pay generous bonuses to officers and troops who, in the face of continued resistance, the passive non-cooperation of the police, and almost universal animosity were proving distinctly unsteady. Apart from the fact that in the space of a fortnight some $18 million had disappeared from the vaults ($3.5 million of it after a visit to the Banco Central by an army jeep in the afternoon of 6 November), this closure had revived the free market in the peso, which immediately shot up from 20 to 35 against the dollar. No doubt in the midst of the melée someone also told the generals of IMF documents which emphasised the inescapability of a devaluation. Having completely mistimed their assault, being confronted by unexpectedly stiff opposition which was allowed to consolidate before it was frontally attacked, decisively ambushed by Washington and jilted by their regional colleagues, the army command had no desire to worsen an already critical situation by provoking full social revolt. It had to retreat; it was only the terms of such a withdrawal that needed to be agreed. The sole option that the rebels refused to accept because it would entail a complete loss of face was a return to the *status quo ante* with Guevara and Padilla retrieving their positions. Once it was clear that Natusch was on his way out, the COB leadership withdrew from discussions in which it was widely accepted it had become too deeply involved for its own good. The congressional negotiators accepted the military veto on Guevara and returned to the schema they had adopted in August, this time proposing the president of the lower house as interim president until the 1980 poll. The army accepted and returned to its barracks. The country was given its second appointed president in three months, and in Lidia Gueiler had the first woman head of state in its history.

Poll versus Putsch

The designation of Lidia Gueiler Tejada as president maintained the monopoly of figures from the old MNR on high office in the post-Banzer era. A woman of comfortable background who had made her mark first as a militant member of the bank workers' union in the late 40s and then, as we have seen, in the MNR's *grupos de honor* during and immediately after the revolution, Gueiler was well-known and broadly respected. However, her political career had been less than smooth. Initially a sympathiser of the MNR's right wing, she was sufficiently involved in the January 1953 coup attempt to merit two years of diplomatic exile in Germany. After her return she loyally supported Paz but under the influence of her second husband, the ex-*porista* Edwin Moller, moved steadily to the left and became a founding member of the PRIN. Almost constantly in exile after 1964, Gueiler separated from Moller, whose political activity had been eclipsed by an enthusiasm for astrology, and returned to the country briefly in 1970/71 to help establish UMBO, and again in 1978 to become vice president in the FRI on behalf of the PRIN. However, her old attachments to Víctor Paz encouraged her to follow the PCML out of the FRI and join the AMNR, for which she became a deputy in 1979. Thus, her appointment marked a clear swing in favour of the MNR at government level. Banzer's alliance was given 11 of the 17 cabinet posts, the ministry of urbanisation going to the Maoist René Higueras who had disrupted the COB congress earlier in the year, and that of the interior being handed to Gueiler's fellow deserter from the PRIN, Jorge Selúm Vaca Diez. The MNRI received only two posts, accepted Paz as the power behind the throne, and sought to turn his control of office to its advantage.

Within days of the removal of Natusch and the celebration of a popular victory this control was shown to be of an almost exclusively formal character and limited to civil appointments. On 22 November General Luis García Meza Tejada, who was not only Natusch's army commander but also Gueiler's cousin, led a movement to reject the new president's military appointments, particularly that of General René Villarroel as commander-in-chief. In a concerted effort to restrict the damage inflicted by Natusch's defeat his principal military appointees staged what can only be described as a 'passive coup' by occupying the Miraflores barracks and refusing to accept orders from the new commanders as well as launching a bitter attack on Víctor Paz for his 'betrayal' of Natusch. This situation continued for three days with both military factions publishing angry advertisements in the press and impeding each other's representatives from entering their offices in open internecine conflict that further demoralised the institution and threatened to wrench it completely apart.[26] The impotence of the new government in the midst of this affair was vividly illustrated by its failure to exercise any control over the ministry of interior, the only civilian office possessing any coercive capacity. When Jorge Selúm attempted to fire Colonel Freddy Quiroga, Natusch's appointee as commander of the *Servicio de Inteligencia del Estado* (SIE), Quiroga simply refused to budge, saying that he took orders only from the general staff (EMG). Since Natusch's commander-in-chief, General Edén Castillo, retained control of the EMG and Quiroga had surrounded his offices with troops there was nothing that Selúm could do. This confrontation, which at the time seemed relatively minor compared to the dispute over the military high command, brought back into the public eye the figure of Colonel Luis Arce Gómez, a plump 49 year-old colonel of no apparent merit who had graduated in 1955, been expelled from the army in 1960 for alleged rape of the daughter of a superior, taken up a career as society photographer for *Presencia*, and been reincorporated into the military after Barrientos's coup to specialise in intelligence and security matters, albeit without great sophistication, as was demonstrated by his activities under Ovando.[27] Upon taking power, Natusch immediately made Arce chief of military intelligence (G-2 or *segunda sección*), and it was in this role that he turned up at SIE headquarters on 22 November with a squad of troops and three trucks to relieve Quiroga and remove from the building all the files inherited from the DOP by the SIE—documentation that provided detailed information on Banzer's opponents from all walks of life and political currents. Selúm raised violent protests but was powerless, Arce returning empty-handed to the ministry tailed by the press, which duly recorded the smiling colonel's 'understanding' with the irate minister. On the advice of his subordinates Selúm henceforth refused to utter a word about the affair, tarried a couple of months before resigning his post, and not long after died a natural but very early death.

The military crisis of 22 to 25 November was resolved to the clear advantage of the *golpistas*. Villarroel was not appointed, his place being taken by General Armando Reyes Villa, not a man given to pugnacious activity or abrasive statements but nevertheless distinctly sympathetic to the García Meza clique. The designation of General Rubén Rocha Patiño as army commander was the only real gain for the *institucionalistas*. The *golpistas* gained control of the navy, replacing Rear Admiral Walter Nuñez with Ramiro Terrazas of the same rank, and retained control of the FAB, with General Jaime Niño de Guzmán and Colonel Waldo Bernal being ratified as commander and chief of staff respectively. García Meza remained at the head of the Colegio Militar and Arce Gómez was ratified as chief of intelligence.[28] Even the field commanders directly responsible for the repression held onto their posts: Doria Medina, Colonel Alberto Grybowski of the Ingavi, Major Víctor Peredo of the Max Toledo, Colonel Moisés Chirique of the Manchego, and the voluble Colonel Mario Oxa, who had distinguished himself by leading the attack on the palace but was more widely known for almost epileptic demonstrations of support for 'The Strongest', a club he chaired and over whose financial affairs he presided to no discernible disadvantage. Although the rebels failed to secure the promotion of Colonel Mario Vargas Salinas — 'the Lion of Masicuri' — and Natusch to general in the December round of promotions and appointments, they succeeded in stopping the *institucionalista* candidates, Miguel Ayoroa and Humberto Cayoja Riart, both erstwhile hardliners who had clashed with Banzer and subsequently moved closer to the *Karachipampas*, from rising to this rank. They also consolidated their hold on the garrisons of Santa Cruz (Chirique at Montero, and General Hugo Echeverría as commander of the army second corps) and Cochabamba (Vargas Salinas as commander of the seventh division).[29]

Having endured the traumas of this immediate repudiation of its

From top left, clockwise Marcelo Quiroga Santa Cruz (1931–1980); Alberto Natusch Busch; police help the wounded during the Natusch coup, November 1979

Lidia Gueiler Tejada

The establishment of CONADE, April 1980. *From left to right* Oscar Eid (MIR), Víctor Paz Estenssoro (MNRH), Juan Lechín (COB), Hernán Siles Zuazo (MNRI), Antonio Aranibar (MIR) and Walter Guevara Arze (PRA)

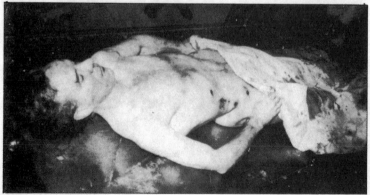

The body of Luis Espinal (1932–1980)

authority, the fledgling Gueiler administration was thrust straight into the arms of the IMF. The political dangers of any devaluation or reduction in state expenditure (from price subsidies to the military budget) could not have been more vividly illustrated than by the events of the preceeding three weeks, but the IMF was adamant. For two years there had been no coherent policy for the management of an external debt that now exceeded $3 billion, production in agriculture, mining and the oil industry had fallen by 5.5 per cent since 1976, currency reserves had slipped from Bs.3,047 million to Bs.1,226 million over the same period while public sector expenditure had continued to rise, from Bs.8,988 million in 1976 to an estimated Bs.17,000 million in 1979. The negative overall growth figure for 1979 was expected to be even greater in 1980, and on its assumption of office the Gueiler government did not have sufficient funds to cover state salaries and running costs for December.[30] The MNR team accepted the need for an immediate devaluation but wisely held back from implementing a readjustment of the currency by the 50 per cent or more that the Fund felt was necessary. Thus, on 30 November the government devalued the peso by 25 per cent and in addition lifted subsidies on petrol, oil and kerosene, the price of which rose by up to 120 per cent. In return it was promised a standby loan of $111 million for the first half of 1980.[31]

The November economic package, or '*pazquete*' as it was dubbed in some circles, engendered widespread popular protest, but nowhere more forcefully than in the *campo*, where the increased price of petrol threatened greatly to inflate transport costs for agricultural produce. The extent and resilience of the *campesino* mobilisation against the Gueiler measures took even the COB unawares and certainly shook the government; it was the largest and most radical independent campaign in the countryside since 1952. One major reason for this was the establishment of the CSUTCB at the end of June 1979, marking the final emergence of a single *campesino* movement allied only to the COB and without official patronage. Although the new confederation lacked the organisational strengths of many of the urban and industrial unions, and its following was unevenly spread throughout the country, it consolidated the movement towards independent organisation evident in the *altiplano* and the Cochabamba valley from the late 1960s, drew in tens of thousands of rural workers, and was led by young and popular figures whose political leanings were towards the left and who were more than prepared to undertake direct action. In this instance much of the preparation had already been undertaken both by the COB's repeated warnings against a devaluation following the June elections and by the partial establishment of road blocks in support of the general strike against Natusch. However, on 30 November it was the peasants and not the COB that took the leadership, moving immediately to seal off the country's main roads and isolate the towns. The action was highly successful, bringing almost all motorised transport on the *altiplano* and in the valleys to a halt for a week while the CSUTCB sought promises from the government to restrict transport price rises to an absolute minimum, make no change in the prices of flour, rice and sugar, reduce taxes on agricultural produce, create new markets and grant *cogestión* in the Banco Agrícola. Food supplies were only allowed to pass through to the mines and certain factories, as agreed with the COB.

The strength of mobilisation in the countryside was not matched in the towns, partly as a result of a downturn in militancy following the defeat of Natusch and partly because the COB leadership deliberately held back from making an all-out offensive for fear of jeopardising the fragile constitutional regime that had just been won back from the military at great cost. As a consequence, the regime's snub of declaring the devaluation only two days after opening economic negotiations with the COB was not answered with the force that might have been expected. On 4 December Lechín told a 50,000-strong crowd demonstrating against the devaluation that the measure should be rescinded and talks continued, but there was no immediate strike call and it was only after the COB's executive committee had reached agreement for limiting transport price rises to thirty per cent that a token one-day strike was called for the 10th, by which time food supplies in the cities were returning to normal. In the major towns feelings were running high against the *transportistas*, who stopped work in protest at the attacks made on them because of fare increases, but the COB urged the CSUTCB to come to terms, thereby consolidating the implicit social contract embodied in Gueiler's appointment.[32] By following this line the COB leadership not only committed itself and its members to the electoralist path but avoided, consciously or otherwise, taking an unparalleled opportunity for making a major assault on the existing economic system, which was more vulnerable even than in early 1971. In the face of a demoralised and divided army and a frightened, unrepresentative administration the decision to follow the *campesinos* would almost certainly have created a profound political crisis and opened up the possibility of realising many of the objectives of the COB's 1970 thesis. Yet the COB possessed no independent political plan as to how to reach such objectives, and as a syndicalist body was perhaps predictably surprised and disorientated by the acuteness and particular form of a crisis that cut right across expectations of a gradual realignment towards constitutionalism. The hegemony of parliamentarianism should not be underestimated here since it was clear that although the working class had by early December expended much of its political energy in combating militarism, it had also registered a substantial victory against the army, tilting the balance of forces sufficiently in its favour to make objectively possible further and more radical advances. This did not happen, the syndicalist left falling in behind the UDP to construct the struggle against Natusch as one in support of the electoral system rather than as one in which democratic rights were defended as part of a wider movement against imperialism and bourgeois rule. In its toying with the idea of a triumvirate the PCB had, paradoxically, glimpsed the essential contradiction at play, but it first inverted its terms and then rapidly retreated to the constitutionalist camp. The overall result was to abet the downturn in working-class militancy, which was aided by an awareness that an electoralist strategy restricted agitation on economic issues and constrained political activity to party campaigning and a fundamentally defensive posture against a further coup. For the *campesinado*, effectively denied the realisation of the much-vaunted worker-peasant alliance at the moment of its greatest need, the retreat was even more marked.

The only full discussion of these issues within the labour movement took place at the FSTMB's eighteenth congress at Telamayu early in April 1980. Following union practice, a number of resolutions were presented by political currents in the name of various mines. Of the 18 forwarded at Telamayu that of the PCB, presented by Oscar Salas for Huanuni, quickly emerged as the majority document since the party had well over a hundred delegates and increased its representation on the executive from 11 to 18 of the 48 members. The strength of the UDP was further bolstered by the MIR, which had 80 delegates and 7 executive members, but the MIR's supporters were far from vocal at the congress since their party was pledged to support a resolution presented by Catavi and drawn up in collaboration with the fiercely anti-electoralist POR *De Pie*, a result of the local balance of forces rather than a wider political empathy. The PS-1 was the third largest political force, having 60 delegates and 5 executive members, but it too was marginalised from early on, lacking the experience to push congress in the direction of a united left front in the poll. This line was also taken by Filemón Escóbar of *Vanguardia Obrera* who, speaking on behalf of Cañadón Antequera, urged a left front organised in a single COB slate, thereby projecting an amplification of the traditional limits to syndicalism and pushing Lechín to declare his candidature against Paz and Siles. Yet Lechín had never received the same degree of support in his political endeavours as for his union activity and while the PRIN was standing in the election, it had little chance of offering the UDP a serious challenge. A resolution that fell even more rapidly was that of Siglo XX-Muruchi which presented the PCML's defence of its alliance with the MNR; the party's line was attacked with considerable rancour and its representation on the executive fell from seven members to one, the dissident Maoists taking one seat. In the event, the minority document chosen by the platform to be debated against the PCB's resolution was that defended by Ascensio Cruz of the POR (Lora) on behalf of Siglo XX. This choice reflected the strength of the PCB on the platform since Cruz's orthodox Trotskyist resolution denigrated 'parliamentary-cretinism', attacked both the major slates as bourgeois, stressed that formal democracy had no historic roots and was too weak to provide any solution to the crisis even in the short term, and called for the building of a revolutionary movement towards the establishment of the dictatorship of the proletariat. Although Cruz gave his traditionally good speech, both he and the organising committee knew that the POR's intervention was designed for propagandist ends, had minimal support, and would easily fall in the face of the PCB document.

Nonetheless, the PCB's organisational strength was no guarantee of success since a good many independent delegates were doubtful of the merits of a resolution that effectively pledged them to support a front led by Hernán Siles Zuazo. Salas attempted to counter this current of dissent by arguing that, 'we are not defenders of Dr Siles because the character of the front is given by the fact that it is made with other classes, not with individuals'.[33] Reyes, taking full advantage of the platform's choice of Cruz to present the minority document, reduced all opposition to the pro-UDP line to 'Trotskyist infantilism': 'the real position here is that we are arguing in all honesty that the task of the movement is the defence of a democratic process that permits us to advance; those who are set against us say that the issue is fascism or the dictatorship of the proletariat, which would mean us going down to an inevitable defeat, as has happened in the past.'[34] Although events would before too long prove the Trotskyist analysis a good deal more correct than it seemed at the time, Reyes's attempt to push home the advantages of 'common sense' was taken too far. As the delegates prepared to vote a large body that sympathised with neither resolution and resented having to choose between them demanded that Lechín take the floor. The old leader, who possessed little love for the PCB and was fully able to dispatch the POR with patronising indulgence, took less than an hour to sabotage the Communists' expected majority in a speech of wit, constant historical reference, and tactical self-criticism. He rehearsed the errors of the MNR period, recognising that he himself had erroneously believed Paz to be on the left, and reminded the delegates that on 9 April there emerged, 'two positions which were concretised in trilogies, the first defended by the miners: nationalisation of the mines, agrarian reform and full liberties for the people. The second was proposed by Siles: to return, to conquer, and to pardon — abstract words while we were proposing concrete measures.'[35] Having dwelt on the reconstruction of the armed forces under Siles's presidency, Lechín described the PCB resolution as 'honest but confused' because although it contained no clear call for a vote for the UDP, this was its underlying and unacceptable message. He rejected calls for his own nomination on behalf of a COB slate but appeared to endorse the idea of an independent workers' candidate; his final proposal was that the new executive elaborate a new document, 'taking the feelings of the mining proletariat into account', and this proved to be an acceptable compromise for the majority of delegates.[36]

The outcome of the Telamayu congress was demonstrative of the wider political condition of the working class over the months before an election that was seen as the last chance to secure parliamentary democracy. The UDP remained the most popular front but it was unable to push its claims for the formal endorsement of the union movement and was severely doubted on a number of issues. Yet the opposition raised by the revolutionary left remained distinct from that of traditional syndicalism, confirming the trend towards a repetition of the state of affairs in 1979: a generalised sentiment of caution that often merged into apathy or pessimism but did not detract from the conviction that the electoral process should be defended; an equally widespread conviction that the UDP represented the only viable progressive force and therefore deserved a tactical vote; and limited but continued gains for the PS-1 as the major left-wing challenge.

The backdrop to this was a growing sense of discontent on the economic front following the inconclusive response of the COB to the devaluation. Over the first months of 1980 the Gueiler government was vexed by a number of industrial disputes bred of sheer exasperation rather than a coordinated campaign. The bank clerks came out in December to obtain payment of a minimum wage of Bs.3,500 agreed the previous August; they were followed by workers in LAB, the national road service, the milk processing plants, the teachers, and the construction and mill workers. By late April the COB was directing most of its attention towards the campaign for a minimum wage assessed on the basis of an agreed set of consumer needs or 'shopping basket'. Naturally enough, estimations of this ranged widely — from the Cochabamba teachers' figure of Bs.12,405 to that of Bs.6,382 presented by the ministry of industry; the COB itself pushed for Bs.9,273.[37] The unanimity of the working class on the wage issue forced an already weak regime to cede much more ground than it desired, finally agreeing to bonuses for inflation ranging from Bs.5,000 for workers in the private sector to Bs.2,000 to pensioners. Although sixty per cent of the wage-earning population received less than Bs.3,000 and thus would still have an income less than that considered 'minimal' by the COB, the increase was sufficiently large to be rejected immediately and unreservedly by the CEPB, some of the affiliates of which were now demonstrating considerable fear of the economic consequences of a UDP victory and looking, albeit less demonstrably, to alternative possibilities.

The campaign by the *golpistas* to retain and extend their influence within the armed forces, keep the Gueiler administration under tight control, and destabilise the electoral process gained momentum and became increasingly explicit from the start of the year. In the second week of January an *ampliado* of the CSUTCB gave rise to rumours that an 'indian invasion' of the capital's middle-class suburbs was imminent. The *campesino* union attacked airforce chief of staff General Waldo Bernal for propagating this rumour and attempting to fan it into a panic.[38] A fortnight later *El Diario* carried an advertisement in the name of a mysterious 'Committee for Public Health' claiming that elections had failed and calling on the military to 're-enter the political scene'.[39] Early in February nocturnal troop movements became uncommonly heavy; and on the 8th the offices of the independent left-wing weekly *Aquí* were bombed and badly damaged. *Aquí* had not been alone in warning against the danger of a new coup in almost every edition, but it was considered particularly repugnant by the right because its Jesuit editor, Luis Espinal, and his small team of journalists (Edgardo Vázquez, Gastón Lobatón, Lupe Cajías and René Bascopé) had over the paper's year-long existence produced a series of detailed investigative reports that were qualitatively more harmful than the vacuous prose that was the customary house style of the local press, right and left wing alike. The bombing seemed to be the handiwork of Colonel Arce, who had been trained in the use of explosives by the Spanish army and was known to have a great interest in curbing Espinal's activity. On the same day airforce commander Niño de Guzmán issued a public statement warning against the threat of an 'anarcho-syndicalist dictatorship', which prompted Ambassador Boeker to reiterate at some length the Carter doctrine and spell out Washington's stance to the increasingly belligerent generals:

> The explosion of interests at the moment is the product of too many years of *de facto* government. . . . The conflicts have their origins in these *de facto* governments. . . . As has occurred elsewhere, when such a government falls, a government that has repressed liberties, there is a social explosion, which represents a greater danger to society. . . . We will cooperate with governments of various types, we've done it in the past and we are going to carry on down that path, but we maintain our position in the sense that the system which has the best perspective for resolving the tensions and problems that can take a society to the verge of destruction is a democratic system.[40]

On 28 February fears of an impending coup prompted Gueiler to go to congress and deny that she would ever resign, promising to lay down her life in defence of democracy; at the same time the decidedly supine Reyes Villa was prevailed upon to declare that, providing there was 'no subversion', the armed forces would support the electoral process. However, the strategy and state of tension continued to prevail;

on 4 March the COB, which had been trying to restrain the flood of coup rumours, revealed that it had received information that there existed plans for a 'St. Bartholomew's Day Massacre' or 'Night of the Long Knives', in which some 300 political and union figures, including Lechín, Siles and Quiroga, would be assassinated. A further strike was called by the *transportistas*, and the Comité Pro-Santa Cruz urged the department's 16 deputies to resign because the regime had authorised the siting of a new sugar mill in the department of La Paz.[41]

The next day the COB and the principal political parties (excluding the ADN but including the MNR) issued a 'Call for the Defence of Democracy', which was to lead to the foundation a month later of a *Comité Nacional de Defensa de la Democracia* (CONADE).[42] The COB's participation in the establishment of CONADE marked its full and formal incorporation into the electoralist project since the organisation's sole purpose was to prevent any coup against the poll by means of a general strike and road blocks as in the resistance against Natusch. The likes of Paz and Guevara now accepted that this was the only way by which they could be assured an untroubled election. The PS-1 was reluctant to sign such an accord since it represented a cross-class and purely defensive agreement to uphold the elections and not an unconstrained worker initiative, but Quiroga eventually took his party into the pact against the criticisms of the revolutionary left and with well-publicised reservations as to its limited scope and potential dangers.[43]

The unity of the COB and the leading political parties appears less to have instilled a sense of sobriety in Miraflores than to have hastened activity in the face of pre-emptive moves by the constitutionalists. On 12 March the badly-tortured body of Luis Espinal was discovered at a municipal abattoir on the outskirts of La Paz. *Aquí* itself, now deprived of its founder, editor and film critic, was not slow to point an accusing finger at Arce Goméz, stressing that the killing bore a marked similarity to the style of the Argentine military, which was reported to have several score advisors working in La Paz. Espinal and his staff were well aware that for several months they had been closely observed and followed by operatives of G-2 and possibly other paramilitary groups that were believed to be organised under Arce's direction and with the advice of the Argentines; in mid-April *Aquí* claimed that such groups controlled 17 'safe houses' in La Paz and included figures who had been involved in the assassinations of the Ovando and Banzer regimes.[44] The decision to eliminate Espinal, who was a highly popular figure, may well have been prompted by the preparations for the establishment of CONADE, but it is just as likely to have been made on the basis of a story run by the paper the previous week which revealed that the airforce had tortured and killed a deserter, Máximo Mamani, who presented himself at headquarters after its staff had declared that the disappearance of a number of machine-guns from its arsenal had been undertaken by 'an extremist network' under Mamani's direction.[45]

Despite the consolidation of CONADE Gueiler proved unable to hold back the *golpistas*. Indeed, it is arguable that she did not make very great efforts so to do. On 9 April the president announced that the army commander General Rocha Patiño would be replaced by her cousin García Meza, one of the most prominent members of the hardline current. It took five days for the appointment to be confirmed because although García Meza had cultivated broad support in the La Paz garrison, he was strongly opposed by Santa Cruz, where Echeverría had his own ambitions, while Oruro and Cochabamba publicly declared their 'neutrality', not least because García Meza had been army commander under Natusch and article 48 of the institution's organic law prohibited any officer from holding this post twice. The aspirant blithely dismissed this objection on the grounds that his first appointment had been 'the act of a *de facto* regime' and could not, therefore, be subject to legal or constitutional considerations. Gueiler eventually acquiesced in this piece of nonsense, proclaiming on 14 April, 'Because of his record and because of the oath he has just sworn my government and his companions in arms see in him a soldier of honour who will place all his resources and abilities at the service of the greater interests of the country, of constitutionality and the legally constituted order.'[46] General Rocha Patiño bluntly declared that Gueiler had managed to clear away the final obstacle to a coup, apparently justifying the use of the popular nickname of 'the idiot princess' for the president. A month later the reactionary but somewhat slothful Niño de Guzmán was replaced by the more thrusting Waldo Bernal as head of the airforce.

It is possible that Gueiler accepted García Meza's appointment not only because they were kin but also because he had no record of political affiliation, was not close to Banzer or Santa Cruz, and gave no indication of being overly intelligent. Whatever the case, the general did not lack persistence and immediately began to cast doubts on the

elections. Four days after his appointment García Meza returned to
the Colegio Militar to give a speech which sagged under the weight of
semi-literate phrases and all the pompous gobbledygook that so
enchants senior commanders but which was pointedly not designed to
reassure his president, the political parties, the COB, or the State
Department:

> 'the country is . . . in political chaos, an economic debacle,
> hunger, poverty aggravated by the subversive terrorism of the
> ultra-left, the pressure applied by neo-colonialism and its
> governments and the threat of a virtual dissolution of the nation
> by a possible '*nicaraguazo*' . . . the Armed Forces, the interpre-
> ters of the true desires and aspirations . . . of the real people of
> Bolivia conform to an organic and rigid political entity, with a
> *bolivianista* ideology and sense of society, which derive from the
> titular force of national existence. In the face of the failure of
> party politics the Armed Forces are impelled by their own res-
> ponsibility to reopen the periods of political space or of conflict
> for power, or rather to champion a new democracy against that
> of fraudulent elections . . .'.[47]

When pressed on this 'new democracy' ('*democracia inédita*') that he
espoused, García Meza was somewhat more coherent:

> 'Democracy hasn't yielded any positive results in this country.
> This is a young country where a bad interpretation of democracy
> has been made and this has degenerated into threats against our
> institutions and against the principle of authority. Famous
> democracy has been confused with the behaviour of libertines.
> All the institutions are in chaos.
> So, is there a democratic solution for the country?
> One cannot yet have a democracy like that. The democracy I
> am thinking (sic) about will be controlled and Bolivian. You
> can't speak about democracy while there is still extremism. The
> Armed Forces are of popular extraction. What the extremists
> want is to set us against the people from which we come. To be an
> indian is to have pride. . . . In this country nobody works, we say
> we are rich but we do nothing to get out of our situation . . . there
> are no leaders; the old ones cannot carry on any longer . . . they
> should be retired . . . I don't agree with the thinking of General

Ovando. I've read a little, yes, but I don't agree with his ideas . . . there's nothing left to nationalise in this country.'[48]

This was one of the mildest of several interviews that the new army commander gave upon taking up his post, and his public utterances revived fears of yet another coup. Reacting to these fears, the executive committee of the COB — but not CONADE — took the unprecedented step of signing a pact with the high command. This agreement, signed on 29 April by Gueiler, the high command (including García Meza) and the seven most senior members of the COB, pledged both sides to respect the constitution, enter into dialogue, and affirm 'a solemn commitment to mutual institutional respect, and to make a joint effort to sustain the democratic process, which should culminate in the elections . . . '[49] Such an agreement broke the COB's long tradition of rejecting any written pact or truce with the military, and it received harsh criticism from the left. However, the concordat soon proved to be completely useless when, within three weeks, García Meza announced that the deputies bringing treason charges against Banzer should themselves be put in front of a court martial; two days later he denied that the 'pact' with the COB was anything other than a 'dialogue'.[50] A silly little piece of paper was not going to stop any coup.

On 15 May the electoral register closed to confirm a line-up little different to that of the previous year. From February onwards the most emphatic effort to alter this situation had been made by the PS-1, which attempted to persuade the main parties of the UDP, the PRIN, and MRTK to join a united left front of workers' parties. The effort, which was not without some support beyond the ranks of the PS-1, eventually foundered on the outright antagonism of the MIR and the PCB's insistence upon a cross-class movement, support for CONADE, the primacy of change through electoral means, and the banishing of any idea of insurrectionism as a valid feature of political conduct except in some future revolutionary situation.[51] The PS-1 thus stood alone once again and could expect to pick up only a minority of the extra votes available once Lechín withdrew the PRIN slate from the contest and declared his critical support for the UDP. This slate had also included the MRTK, which now found itself obliged to continue supporting a front that it had angrily quit after suffering a number of clumsy organisational assaults by the MIR. Banzer's ticket remained intact although the ADN managers had seen fit to drop the old slogan for 'Banzer vuelve' ('Banzer returns'), thought to be more in keeping with the party's adoption of a less provocative style after the *natuschazo* and in a situation where there existed an independent *golpista* challenge inside the military. The central difference with the 1979 poll was expected to rest with the fate of the MNR, which had lost considerable popularity, less because of doubts about Paz's involvement with Natusch than for his party's introduction of the November devaluation and its almost complete identification with the weakest administration to rule Bolivia for a decade. Yet, since December the possibilities of this shift in popularity being translated into congressional seats had scarcely ever been at the forefront of political affairs simply because of the doubtfulness of the entire electoral project. Over the month leading up to the poll these doubts grew greater still as the *golpistas* increased their activity.

The final phase of preparations for and destabilisation of the poll began on 2 June, when a light plane hired by the UDP from a company owned by Arce Gómez and airforce Colonel Norberto 'Buby' Salomón crashed seconds after taking off from El Alto on a campaigning trip to the Beni by the front's senior team. Hernán Siles had been due to fly but had to drop out at the last moment to attend the funeral of a relation; the only survivor was Jaime Paz Zamora, who threw himself out of the craft as it hit the ground and exploded. Paz Zamora's critical state meant that, after an emergency operation in a La Paz clinic surrounded by *miristas* for his protection (and to which he had been obliged to travel in the LAB passenger bus because there was no ambulance at the airport), he had to be flown to the US for advanced treatment of burns, which not only restored him to health and his good looks but also put his life out of further danger. Although the crash resulted from the stalling of an engine rather than a bomb explosion, the fact that Paz Zamora's house had been bombed the day before strongly suggested sabotage. Moreover, the ownership of the aircraft cast doubts on the aviation authority's very swift pronouncement that there had been a 'technical failure' even in the minds of those citizens who were not aviation experts. Colonel Salomón experienced no difficulty in collecting the insurance.[52]

The next day CONADE declared itself in a state of emergency, less directly because of the deaths of the UDP leaders than because the Washington Post had published an article by its correspondent Charles Krause claiming that a coup had been planned for 20 May but aborted at the last moment because of lack of support amongst junior officers and NCOs. Shortly after the report was published Krause was removed from the Sheraton Hotel by men in civilian clothes and subjected to a violent interrogation by Arce, who demanded to know his sources. The new US ambassador, Marvin Weissman, had intervened to stop the rising upon being informed by the Defence Intelligence Agency that the Argentine military attaché had abruptly sent his family back home on holiday; the Argentines were by now widely recognised to be playing a leading role in the operations of Arce's unit and its unofficial affiliates. Through Weissman the Pentagon sent a telegram to García Meza advising him against any rebellion. On the 4th State Department spokesman Hodding Carter backed this up with a strong public statement in favour of the democratic process. Upon receipt of this declaration the high command immediately issued a reply that described Carter's expressions as 'a calumny' and 'insolent', declaring that, 'whatever the pretext, no country has the right to meddle in the affairs of independent and sovereign states such as ours . . . the Armed Forces of the Nation declare all those who express support for the bare-faced interventionism of the government of the United States to be TRAITORS TO THE PATRIA.'[53] This was surprisingly strong but not so different from the reaction of some Chilean and Argentine officers to the pressure applied by the Carter administration. However, on the 6th General Echeverría, commander of the second corps in Santa Cruz, declared that if Weissman did not leave the country immediately he would march his unit on La Paz to have him expelled. The next day the high command formally declared the ambassador *persona non grata*, prompting the government not to issue a contradiction and rebuke but a statement expressing its 'understanding' of the feelings that had been aroused in military circles and yet reaffirming its conviction that the elections were receiving full international support.[54] Presented with an unparalleled opportunity to steal a march on the left and demonstrate its anti-*yanqui* credentials, a group from Carlos Valverde's sector of the FSB announced that it was going on hunger strike, occupying first the Papal Nunciature and then, when the press was denied access, the lobby of congress in protest against 'imperialist intervention'. This act of principled abnegation was openly prolonged by the infusion of thick and sustaining beverages but eventually brought to a halt when a casual nocturnal visit by the press revealed that take-away chicken dinners were also on the bill of fare.

The explicit support given by Washington to the elections was construed not only by the UDP and the MNR but also by the ADN to be little less than an absolute guarantee that they would go ahead. Since November the parliamentary left had not been conspicuous for its invectives against imperialism; it now found itself outflanked by the extreme right, which was quite evidently not inveighing against '*yanqui* neo-colonialism' simply as a propaganda ploy but also because it felt sufficiently secure to issue an open challenge to its traditional patron. The strength of Argentine support played a large part in this and underscored the fallacy of simplistic views of the relationship between the metropolis and its peripheral sepoys. If there was ever any single moment when the political decision to stage a coup was signalled this was it. There was, nonetheless, a failure on the left to take sufficiently seriously the possibility of a more than momentary and inconsequential rupture between the military and the US. The POR was labelled '*golpista*' because it denounced Carter for his intervention as well as García Meza for his planned coup, and Banzer's evidently whole-hearted commitment to the electoral process was read as denying the high command the social or political base on which to stage a rebellion. García Meza and Arce Gómez were believed to represent only a small minority of the officer corps, and undue confidence was placed in CONADE, which in fact existed only on paper and was far from properly prepared.

The warning signs did not stop. On the same day as the high command issued Weissman his marching orders the president herself became the victim of a military assault. Despite her public failure to offer the most minimal resistance to the advances of the hardliners, Gueiler evidently harboured some private fears since even inside the modern and highly-fortified presidential residence at San Jorge she took the precaution of locking her bedroom door at night. It was this customary domestic act that saved her life when, at 6 a.m. on 7 June, the commander of her bodyguard, Colonel Carlos Estrada Estrada, arrived at the residence in a state of absolute inebriation, ordered the sentries to surround the building, and, armed with an automatic rifle, attempted to enter the president's room and kill her. Estrada's shouting and blows on the door gave Mrs Gueiler time to telephone for help, and his lone endeavour was brought to a swift conclusion by the president's adjutant and his staff, who overpowered and disarmed the would-be assassin without great difficulty. It was a madcap effort and hardly in the repertoire of the cool Argentine colonels advising Arce but served to underline the extreme fragility of the situation. Two days later the high command, meeting in Cochabamba, called for the postponement of the poll for at least a year because the campaign was causing disruption, worsening the economic situation, had been badly organised, and would yield a weak government.[55] This last gambit was rejected immediately by all interested parties except the president herself, who tarried two days before announcing that the election would take place on the 29th as planned; the left press depicted the Cochabamba conclave as one dedicated principally to the timing of the impending coup. Over the following days the military leadership made no further declarations except to announce that it was on the alert 'against any attempt to impose systems foreign to Bolivia', but Echeverría allowed the FSB and a group of 'nationalist' peasants to take over Santa Cruz without let or hindrance for two days, during which the prefect was badly wounded and there prevailed a state of affairs not unlike that in August 1971 until the COD and students dislodged the falangists by force of arms. In La Paz the Lido café, a favourite haunt of the left, was bombed with the loss of 2 lives, and grenades were thrown at a UDP meeting, resulting in 4 deaths and 63 people being wounded. The authorship of such acts was in little doubt, as indicated by the grim entry into the local argot of the verb *'arcecinar'*, interchangeable with *'asesinar'*.

If such activities constituted part of a carefully-graduated strategy, that strategy did not involve the interruption or halting of the election itself. The poll took place on 29 June in an orderly manner and without great problems. The processing of the results was extremely slow but it was soon clear that the UDP had won a victory which, despite a fall in its overall vote, was more decisive than that of 1979. The soundly beaten Víctor Paz did not delay in conceding defeat, although he did so in somewhat ambiguous style: 'The UDP must be made to form a government'. Banzer, who had polled well, likewise recognised the result and the ADN publicly committed itself to play the role of a responsible opposition. No party cried fraud or attempted to thwart the Siles-Paz Zamora ticket claiming the presidency. The UDP lacked an overall congressional majority but it had survived the considerable rigours of the previous year to reclaim its popular mandate. Once the vote had taken place the threat of a coup seemed to have diminished; Siles would be sworn in as president on independence day, 6 August.

There was no military outburst or signs of unusual activity following the announcement of the results on 10 July. when, on the 14th, Siles found himself in the company of the commanders of the three services as a result of a meeting arranged by Bedregal and Fellmann Velarde, who told neither side who they were going to see and were, as a result, quickly ejected, he simply stated that the UDP reserved the right to make new institutional appointments but would adhere to the armed forces' organic law. García Meza, Bernal and Terrazas responded by promising to support the constitution, but they knew that as matters stood their careers had less than three weeks to run.

In the end it was García Meza who began the coup and Arce Gomez who ensured its success. At 5 a.m. on 17 July Colonel Francisco Monroy took over Trinidad, the scene of the October 1979 coup attempt and the headquarters of the sixth division, once commanded by García Meza, who happened to be in town on that day. At 7.15 Monroy called for the overthrow of Gueiler, the annulment of the election results and the formation of a military junta. News of the rebellion reached La Paz forty minutes later but was not at first taken very seriously. At 8.30 CONADE called a meeting for 11 a.m. and at that hour the leaders of the UDP went into conference with Gueiler at the palace. There was no untoward military activity in La Paz although the Santa Cruz garrison had declared itself 'in emergency'. At 11.10 the leadership of CONADE agreed to call a general strike and blockades of all roads, issued a statement to that effect, and began to discuss a detailed plan of action. Half an hour later Arce struck, using not troops but paramilitary personnel travelling in ambulances to mask their approach. Some twenty men rushed the COB building under cover of heavy volleys of fire which lasted for twenty minutes. The FSTMB leader Gualberto Vega and Carlos Flores, a leader of the POR (Vargas), were killed immediately, the rest of the occupants surrendering once the firing stopped. As they were marched out, a member of the assault team tried to separate Marcelo Quiroga from the rest. The socialist leader refused to move and was shot on the spot. Thirty five people, including Lechín, Reyes, Liber Forti, Víctor Sossa, Noel Vázquez, and Father Julio Tumiri, were taken prisoner. Upon hearing this news, Siles, Antonio Aranibar, and Jorge Kolle, who had been at the palace, went underground, narrowly missing the assault on the palace which was conducted with equal speed and efficiency. Gueiler was immediately parted from her ministers and members of the press

Table 11

The Election of 29 June 1980

Slate	Major Parties	Candidates	Votes	Seats
UDP	MNRI MIR PCB MPLN PS-Atahuichi VO	Hernán Siles Jaime Paz	507,173	53
AMNR	MNR MNRI-1 PCML	Víctor Paz Ñuflo Chávez	263,706	40
ADN	ADN PIR MARC	Hugo Banzer Jorge Tamayo	220,309	25
PS-1	PS-1	Marcelo Quiroga José María Palacios	113,309	11
FDRNA (a)	PDC PS ALIN POR (Vargas)	Luis Adolfo Siles Benjamín Miguel	39,401	5
PRA	PRA	Walter Geuvara Arze Flavio Machicado	36,443	3
MNR-*Unido*	MNRU MIN	Guillermo Bedregal Miguel Trigo	24,452	2
FSB	FSB	Carlos Valverde Enrique Riveros	21,372	2
PRIN	PRIN MRTK POR (Combate) OST	Juan Lechín Anibal Aguilar	withdrew	
APIN-MNR (b)	MNR-*Unidad*	Roberto Jordán Pando Edmundo Roca Diez	17,150	—
MITKA-1	MITKA-1	Constantino Lima Honorato Sánchez	17,023	1
MITKA	MITKA	Luciano Tapia Medardo Velez	15,852	1

Notes: a. *Frente Democrático Revolucionario—Nueva Alternativa*
b. *Alianza de Fuerzas de la Izquierda Nacional*

Sources: Coyuntura, no. 46, 1 June 1980; *Hoy*, 22 and 24 Sept. 1982.

attending a news conference, the president being taken to Miraflores to sign her resignation while the rest were beaten up and made to lie face-down for several hours on the dung-laden floor of the stables of the nearby police barracks. Another paramilitary group took over Radio Fides under the command of Fernando 'Mosca' Monroy, who had just been released from the Panóptico by Arce. Within hours only the army's Radio Batallón Colorados was on the air and the rebels held all the city's strategic points, including the university. Only at 3 p.m. did troops take to the streets to impede mass demonstrations while the paramilitary squads conducted raids on the houses of those listed on the SIE's files abducted by Arce. CONADE's strike had come into effect but the rebellion was already consolidated. The lessons learnt from Natusch's debacle, eight months of planning, and the advice of the Argentine staff were all in evidence.

Arce Gómez's direction of affairs was total. At midday on the 18th the high command met to discuss the leadership of the movement; after five hours it had come to no conclusion. Only the intelligence chief's participation in the meeting and insistence that García Meza assume the presidency of the junta resolved the issue and enabled the three officers to take the oath decked out in their bomber jackets. Meza then went on television to label the UDP as 'Castroite', blame Gueiler's 'monetarism' for the economic chaos, and announce a dusk to dawn curfew. Over the weekend the junta issued decree law 17531 which outlawed all trade-union activity and ordered the immediate dismissal of those who did not return to work on the Monday.

The news of the assault on the COB and the swift activity of the paramilitary had a great impact on the urban population, and it was widely rumoured that Lechín, Reyes and many other COB leaders had been killed. Lechín's survival was only confirmed when he appeared on television on the 22nd in an extremely poor mental and physical state to declare, 'We can talk over our problems and ambitions some other day, but let us now avoid useless bloodshed. I repeat: I exhort all workers and *campesinos* and the people in general to abandon blockades and civil resistance.'[56] Over the next two days the strike crumbled. The effect of Lechín's broadcast, some 30 deaths, the taking of at least 500 prisoners, and the great brutality of the paramilitary squads who roamed the streets at leisure sufficed to impede any resistance of the type mounted against Natusch. Arce Gómez was appointed interior minister and Colonel Quiroga made chief of the *servicio Especial de*

Seguridad (SES), the DOP of the 1980s; from the start both men acted in the manner of their Chilean and Argentine colleagues. Within a week the only organised resistance they faced was in the mines. The democratic experiment had come to an abrupt and bloody end, finished off less by the military than by its most extreme elements, prepared to make extensive use of civilian gunmen and terror-tactics in callous and deliberate violation of human rights, unflustered by Washington's immediate severance of relations and economic boycott or the possibility of expulsion from the Andean Pact, and no less sanguine in their attitude to the cocaine mafia that was perceived to be deeply involved in the coup. From its inception the regime was condemned to the squalid criminality associated with the drug trade and repudiated from almost every quarter.

8.
THE DELINQUENT DICTATORSHIP

Several days after taking power General García Meza gave an interview to a Chilean magazine in which he stated, 'I will stay in power for twenty years, until Bolivia is reconstructed. My government has no fixed limits and in this sense I am like General Pinochet.' Given the efficiency of the coup, the extremely tight and violent control imposed in its aftermath, and the apparently comprehensive defeat of the constitutionalist camp, such a claim was treated seriously. Banzer had, after all, ruled for seven years, and García Meza had begun his rule in an equally if not more consolidated and confident manner. Yet García Meza's regime lasted one year and 18 days and was within six months wracked with contradictions, hemmed in and destabilised by external repudiation, debilitated by dissent within the military, and unable to eliminate the passive resistance that began to take an increasingly open form as the government lurched from one crisis to the next. The three short-lived administrations that followed suffered the same fate as they attempted first to sustain the project of July 1980 and then to conduct a measured retreat. By mid-1982 the endeavour to impose an organic dictatorship and eradicate all vestiges of the democratic interlude had collapsed completely.

An inebriated García Meza assisted to bed by his orderly, Sergeant Ernesto Gandarillas

The roots of the crisis that drained this militarist exercise of any potential were the same as those which had undermined constitutionalism: a severe and escalating fiscal crisis of the state inherited from Banzer and worsened by decreasing production and falling prices for the country's core exports; substantial disunity inside the dominant bloc; and an inability to complement the political defeat of the left with a complete destruction of its syndicalist foundations. However, the form taken by the political emergency between July 1980 and October 1982 was quite distinct from that which had preceded it, reflecting above all else the weakness and lack of unity inside the armed forces. It proved impossible to sustain a right-wing regime on anti-US policies for any length of time, and even after these were first tempered and then reversed the effects of a 15-month boycott imposed by Washington continued to erode legitimacy, restrict foreign assistance, and encourage internal competition. The same was true of the initial, ill-conceived assault on the Andean Pact that further blackened the regime's reputation. Furthermore, while receipts from the cocaine trade were substantial and facilitated the funding of a sizeable informal apparatus of control, the purchase of loyalty in the upper echelons of the military, and the accumulation of impressive personal fortunes, they could not compensate for the collapse of the legal economy, service the foreign debt, or finance state operations as a whole for any length of time. At its peak income from cocaine was perhaps four times greater than that from traditional exports, but a great deal of it did not return to Bolivia and much of that which did fuelled largely non-productive activity or conspicuous consumption. In some cases — the plantation zones of La Paz and Cochabamba, and the commercial entrepots of the Beni — short-term regional booms occurred, but because of its outlaw status the trade failed to revive general business confidence. While cocaine capital did not in general derive from a process of primitive accumulation, the rules of competition in this sector were loose and not unlike those of early capitalism, exaggerating the historical tendency of the Bolivian state to be a site for plunder.

The working through of this process allied to the exceptional violence, extreme capriciousness, and lack of any serious strategy or social support on the part of the García Meza government determined its downfall. During the two years of military rule there were no less than six open attempts at a coup d'etat, an even greater number of strikes than over the five previous years, and five different presidents. After

Meza himself was finally prised from power early in August 1981, a junta of commanders managed amidst constant bickering to cling to office for a month. The eventual resolution of their institutional differences in the appointment of the army commander General Celso Torrelio Villa as president proved to be highly inconclusive. Torrelio was a García Meza appointee, a front-man unable to meet the most minimal conditions for holding high office save the fact that he represented the army. His very weakness ensured the continuation of the existing structure of power and the protection of those sectors that had flourished under Meza and Arce Gómez, but it was an inadequate defence against both competitors from those factions and the more consolidated institutionalist currents regrouping inside the military. Unwilling to preside over a meaningful *apertura* and unable to contain the challenges of officers such as Faustino Rico Toro, identified both with *narcotráfico* and the extreme right wing, Torrelio simply held the fort until his presence in the palace served no useful purpose for any faction. His replacement in July 1982 by General Guido Vildoso Calderón marked a shift to a more agile and perspicacious policy of negotiation on the part of an institution that continued to inflict repression and persist in empty, stentorian claims to a mandate for power but which had been badly buffeted by working class action, weakened by sharp domestic divisions, and was clearly seeking sanctuary in the barracks. Thus, in October 1982 the armed forces handed power back to the constitutionalist camp, Hernán Siles Zuazo and the UDP retrieving the office denied them in August 1980.

This withdrawal signified a formal victory of democracy over dictatorship, was widely and enthusiastically celebrated as such, and certainly represented a shift in the balance of forces and the quality of everyday life. Nonetheless, it did not mark a new era in the country's economic fortunes and soon proved to have compelled very few alterations in the comportment of the civilian political elite. The crisis continued amidst growing popular discontent, renewed squabbling over the spoils of office, and a crippling lack of concrete policy and leadership. The considerable advantages gleaned from military exhaustion, international goodwill, and a regional retreat on the part of the forces of authoritarianism sustained the Siles administration for a number of months but could not suppress the profound conflicts within Bolivian society, still less resolve them. In so far as the brutal and provincial effort at a new *pinochetazo* had collapsed in complete ignominy certain political options were closed off, at least for a while, and another cycle of the process begun in 1952 brought to a halt; but it was a subsidiary cycle, rehearsing familiar encounters inconclusively. Thirty years after the April revolution — an event which seventy per cent of Bolivia's population in 1980 had not witnessed — its legacy remained both open and daunting.

The 'Government of National Reconstruction'

The speed with which the junta's paramilitary forces took possession of the urban centres and whittled down resistance contrasted with the extended and difficult military campaign to bring the mines under the regime's control. This took a full fortnight and although it was finally achieved with an unprecedented deployment of troops and extreme brutality, soon transpired to have been only partially successful in the sense that the miners' spirit was not broken and clandestine unions were able to reorganise, depriving the yellow union *relacionadores* of any following. Once it was clear that none of the major camps was going to heed Lechín's call for the raising of the strike, the local garrisons prepared to occupy them. There were a number of instances of paramilitary activity, but these had little effect and the mining proletariat at least had the advantage of confronting an enemy with whose methods it was fully conversant.

In the southern camps the army was initially impeded by the road blocks organised by local *campesinos*, who, in distinction from the rural population in the rest of the country, proved to be resilient in their opposition to the coup. Particularly fierce resistance was put up in the mines around Potosí, especially the Santa Ana camp, where the army was twice forced to withdraw and, when it finally made a breakthrough, found itself confronted with a human wall of women and children guarding the *sindicato* building which housed the radio. (Since the miners' radio stations were linked up from the afternoon of the 17th there was a high degree of tactical cooperation that thwarted a number of army manoeuvres). Similar scenes were enacted at Huanuni, where young conscripts were driven back with antique rifles and bombardments of dynamite, necessitating the use of the airforce to bomb the radio station and reinforce the army's siege. These raids caused much terror but had to be called off once it was clear that they risked destroying valuable plants. Huanuni held out for five days, protecting one approach to Siglo XX-Catavi and sowing considerable demoralisation amongst the troops, many of whom came from the region; there were reports of soldiers refusing to open fire and being shot by their officers. This also occurred in the assault on the northern copper mine of Corocoro, and in La Paz three truckloads of conscripts killed their officers and deserted. In Siglo the conflict took a more fluid form with skirmishing being interrupted by attempts to make a truce. Fighting took place intermittently between the evening of the 18th and late on the 23rd, when the *campesinos* withdrew and many proletarian snipers either went underground or left the district. On that day the local commander, Colonel Arrázola, signed an agreement with the union that promised certain guarantees with respect to job security and the release of prisoners. However, the agreement was considered too generous by the regime and thus immediately boken, prolonging the strike for a further week until lack of supplies, the disappearance of leading militants, and the aggregate effect of repression forced a return to work. Nonetheless, active resistance was not fully stamped out until early on 4 August when, in a final onslaught against a prolonged armed defence of the small and isolated camps of Caracoles and Viloco, inebriated troops of the Max Toledo, Tarapacá and Camacho regiments perpetrated one of the most terrible massacres in the tragic history of Bolivia's mines. So many workers were killed or wounded that replacement labour had to be brought in from distant districts. According to a letter sent on 9 August by the women of Caracoles to Archbishop Manrique of La Paz, one miner was executed by having a stick of dynamite exploded in his mouth, a number of prisoners and wounded were bayoneted to death, three women died after being raped, children were made to eat gunpowder, whipped with cables and then forced to lie on broken glass while they were marched over by soldiers. Some nine hundred people were said to have disappeared, and although the majority were later confirmed as prisoners, the level of attrition was without precedent.[1]

The ferocity of the Caracoles assault assured the cessation of armed resistance and enabled the regime to resume Comibol's operations under the supervision of new *relacionadores*, who, by decree 17545 (12 August) were designated the only legal representatives of the working class; the sole union to retain its former structure and officers was that of the transport workers, traditionally *banzerista* and already expelled from the COB. In line with the corporativist system the junta's advisers were sketching out on paper, the officially-designated representatives were pledged to a 'social pact', established by decree 17610 of 7 September, whereby harmony would henceforth exist between capital and labour on terms determined by the regime.[2] By mid-October some 1,000 *relacionadores* had received their credentials, the majority being either longstanding 'nationalists' or tame, unknown nominees (usually white-collar workers) thrust into posts for which they had little appetite but dared not refuse. A very small minority were members of the PCB or MIR who adopted the position that retention of any post was a valid tactical move (most of these were elected in military-sponsored 'open assemblies'), and a larger group was closely linked to the paramilitary squads. This latter group was instrumental in imposing the curfew, seeking out militants, imposing large fines for infractions at work, and overseeing punishment details; many junior employees made a good trade out of selling the bricks that errant workers were obliged to make to compensate for bad time-keeping or low productivity as well as 'civil crimes', such as being outside after 9 p.m. or meeting in unauthorised groups of more than five people. At no stage, however, did this regime prove capable of reducing the high level of sabotage and go-slows with which the workers responded; equally, since mining communities are very tight, over-zealous repression carried with it the threat of life-long social ostracisation and possible retribution that could without great difficulty be masked as an industrial accident. Thus, the egalitarian organism of Bolivia's mines built up a low-level antidote to the toxins introduced into its system. (When I visited Siglo XX in the last week of García Meza's rule it was not possible for a foreigner to enter the camp legally without submitting to a prolonged and frequently unpleasant interview with the local chief of police, and it was effectively impossible to stay there for more than a few hours without written authorisation. However, it was possible by dint of careful security measures and minor evasive action to attend a meeting of the clandestine *Comité de Bases*, then dominated by the POR *De Pie*, in which discussion centred on the degree of severity that *justicia proletaria* should take against paramilitary personnel, lists of whom had been drawn up.)

In the towns such a reaction was far more tentative and for a long while limited to the largest factories: Said (La Paz) and Manaco (Cochabamba). In the countryside it was even more restricted although much was done to keep independent peasant organisation alive by Genaro Flores, who continued to work in clandestinity, becoming the first *campesino* to head the national workers' movement when, by virtue of his seniority in the COB and the death, imprisonment, or exile of other national leaders, he became the *de facto* executive secretary inside the country. This position was confirmed on 16 November when Lechín and Reyes were sent into exile following the broadcast of an interview conducted by Arce Gómez, who solicitously addressed Lechín throughout as 'Don Juan' and palpably enjoyed the public degradation he was inflicting on the COB's executive secretary, who, in turn, did his reputation no good by treating his tormentor with remarkable deference while Reyes maintained a tight-lipped aloofness.[3] Arce had already demonstrated the degree to which he was prepared to take his scorn of the union movement by having the COB headquarters demolished; several days beforehand an international delegation from ORIT, visiting La Paz to hand over a donation to the families of jailed union members and to request the government to respect basic human rights, was detained by the SES, threatened with physical violence, robbed of $30,000 and personal effects, and expelled.[4] Divided between internal and external wings, with the majority of its most seasoned veterans abroad or in jail but ultimate authority resting with the internal leadership, the COB experienced grave organisational difficulties, many of which predictably concerned the management of substantial sums of money received through international solidarity. Flores himself came under great pressure to follow a pro-UDP line, a course of action he resisted unevenly until, on 21 June 1981, he was apprehended by the SES, and, in attempting to make his escape, shot down and critically wounded. Only insistent pressure from Amnesty International and the French government saved the *campesino* leader from the inevitable consequences of the *ley de fuga*, the regime eventually expelling him in a very poor physical state and too late for surgery in a Paris hospital to save him from being paralysed for the rest of his life. (In the event, the disability which confined him to a wheelchair did not impede Flores from resuming union activity and served to enhance his reputation as a courageous and committed leader).

The parties of the left were hit as hard as the unions although the PCB and the Trotskyist parties possessed sufficiently disciplined organisations to embark upon clandestine activity within a relatively short space of time. The MIR, of which only the upper echelons were organised in tight cadre-based cells, was hit particularly acutely, as was the PS-1, which suffered badly from the loss of Quiroga. Internal political resistance on the part of the UDP centred on Siles's declaration of a *Gobierno de Unidad Nacional* (GUN), established in clandestinity on 6 August, when the UDP should have assumed office. The GUN issued a number of fighting declarations but its foundation proved to be a miscalculation since it was nothing more than an organ for propaganda, and without some tangible evidence of authority its existence signified only the extent of the defeat rather than offering a rallying point for opposition. Once this was clear, Siles left the country (September) and the project was tacitly dropped although both the MNRI and the MIR continued to make occasional reference to it for nearly a year.[5] Unable to make any impact on domestic resistance, which fell largely to the clandestine unions, the leaders of the UDP threw themselves into the task of touring the chancelleries of the world and stiffening the economic blockade.

It is difficult to appreciate the nature of the García Meza regime without recognising that the form in which it imposed political control was distinct even from that of the Banzer era and on a scale that shocked and demoralised a population that was more familiar than most with the exigencies of life under the military. This was the main contribution of Arce's Argentine advisers, who were said by *Le Monde* to number more than two hundred in the period immediately after the coup. The contingent was led by Lieutenant Colonels Julio César Durand, Benjamín Cristoroforetti and Osvaldo Guarnaccia, and included figures such as Captains Miguel Angel Benazzi, Antonio Pernia ('the rat') and Schelling ('the penguin') drawn from the infamous Escuela Mecánica of the Argentine navy, a well-known torture centre. Under Argentine supervision Arce set up an apparatus for intelligence and political control operations that ran parallel to the established police structure and centred on the SES, linked to the interior ministry, and the *Comando de Operaciones Conjuntas* (COC), which was headed by hardliners like 'Tinino' Rico Toro and Rodrigo Lea Plaza, who began to build up their own paramilitary squads, often in direct competition with Arce. Some estimates put the number of paramilitary personnel as high as eleven thousand, but in all likelihood there were no more than three thousand, the majority being members of the armed forces undertaking operations in mufti. A greater number of people collaborated with this network, receiving jobs throughout the public service from which they could report on their colleagues.

Attention has, however, been focussed on the antics of a few well-known foreigners of fascist beliefs and a background in mercenary activity who, upon perceiving rewarding job opportunities in Bolivia, either emerged from the woodwork inside the country or travelled there, in many instances some time before the coup took place. Most prominent amongst these, of course, was Klaus Altmann/Barbie, the former head of the Gestapo in Lyon who had arrived in Bolivia in 1951, maintained relations with the FSB, but received his citizenship in 1957 from the Siles government and pursued an untroubled existence at least until 1971, when he was tracked down by Beate Klarsfeld. Barbie made no bones about his involvement in security operations, continued to live quite openly in his flat in the Edificio Jasmín on the Avenida 20 de Octubre, and was well protected by the high command from extradition demands by the French government. He provided a useful contact with other old nazis, such as Hans Joachim Stellfeld, a former employee of the *Kamaradenwerk* organisation who died in mysterious circumstances late in 1980, as well as established foreign mercenaries: the notorious Jean 'Black Jack' Schramme, who had made his mark in the Congo, Albert Van Ingelgom, formerly a senior official at the Auschwitz concentration camp, Roger Van Zande and his son, who worked with the SES and was known as '*El Tigre*' for his skill in extracting information by physical means. A younger group contained men like Joachim Fiebelkorn, Stefano delle Chiaie and Pier Luigi Pagliai, who had records of neo-fascist attachments, were linked to a number of terrorist operations in Europe (including the Bologna railway station bombing), and exhibited a special interest in the cocaine trade. Such specimens found themselves at ease with kindred souls like Arce, Monroy Daniel Salamanca, Guido Benavides, Carlos Mena, Freddy Quiroga and Rafael Loayza, giving rise to the observation that while the other states of the southern cone had 'Chicago boys' of the Milton Friedman school, Bolivia's belonged to the Al Capone tradition. Although he considered all members of the para-military squads to be 'comrades . . . the advanced guard of national-ism', Arce freely admitted to the presence of many foreigners in their ranks: 'They work in intelligence — foreigners are very useful in this job because it is necessary to control several frontiers — and they arrest people.'[6]

The SES and COC concerned themselves with frequent midnight raids, in which the entire contents of some households disappeared, imposing the 9 p.m. curfew with unprecedented ferocity (again, there were rich pickings in extracting bribes for releasing offenders or, if they lacked the requisite cash, satisfaction in administering beatings and hosing prisoners down while they were left outside in the freezing Andean night) as well as selective killings and far from sophisticated interrogations. Right up to the fall of the military government their presence was made conspicuous by a propensity for parking their vans at major intersections or outside public institutions, lingering with great menace and less than playful manipulation of gleaming Uzi machine-pistols. In the first days of the regime such forces were largely employed in mass round-ups of 'suspects', some five hundred people being detained in the changing rooms of the La Paz football stadium, where they were packed together for two days and nights without food or water and forced to sleep and urinate where they stood. Later, activities became more selective but affected all sectors of the population. The liberal church, for example, was harassed with great zeal, many priests being jailed and church property frequently being raided. Padre Julio Tumiri, the 69 year-old president of the Human Rights Assembly, had to be hospitalised after his interrogation by the SES. Archbishop Manrique, the septuagenarian leader of the church in La Paz who constantly denounced the excesses of the regime, was threatened on television with unspecified 'sanctions' by Arce, and, when he condemned summary executions, accused by García Meza of 'collaborating with extremists'. One senior officer who had taken up arms in defence of 'Western Christendom' drew more profound conclusions from the churchman's protest and denounced him for being 'in league with Satan'.[7]

When describing repression or the violation of human rights there is always the danger of lapsing into hectoring itemisation, which only serves to increase a reader's sense of detachment from what is perceived as a thoroughly reprehensible but regrettably common activity. However, of the scores of testimonies available I will quote just one at some length in order to give the European or North American whose life has been happily free of political terror a sense of what is indeed almost a residual condition in much of Latin America but, by the same token, a phenomenon central to the comprehension of daily life and political activity there. The writer of these lines is Filemón Escóbar, who has

been chosen not because he suffered particularly harsh treatment —
he emerged badly shaken but alive and had undergone similar experiences in the past — nor because he was (and is) a prominent political
and union activist, but because he describes the episode with some
insight and goes beyond a simple listing of physical injuries. It is worthy
of note that the events described below took place not under the rule
of García Meza and Arce Gómez but in February 1982, when General
Torrelio's regime enjoyed the recognition of the US and Great Britain
and was preparing to call elections in line with its declaration that it
had assumed power 'with the law in our hands'.

'The security apparatus is full of bestial people; they're abnormal
beings who experience extraordinary pleasure in torture. They
like to hear people moan in pain, it makes them laugh. They
handle the *picana* (electric prong) with the skill of a surgeon on
the naked body of their victim. Each charge of electricity is met
with the desperate cries of the prisoner. For the torturer it will
have only been a good surgical operation of which to be proud. If
they aren't satisfied with the statement they go back and hang up
the naked detainees and beat them with whips. They play with
the body as if playing with a baseball. Sharp blows on the legs, on
the arms and above all in the region of the kidneys until the prisoner begins to bring up blood. It will be after this treatment that
the interrogation begins. The agents believe that the victim is
sufficiently softened up. Any effort to trick or deceive means that
torture will be resumed and even more brutal. . . . The cells are
individual. No light comes in. You don't know if it is night or
day. When the number of prisoners exceeds capacity you can
find yourself joined by others. In order to save your skin it is better not to ask any questions. Silence is a form of security and hope
because there is sure to be more questioning.

'I was arrested on 2 February, and on the 3rd I was already in
La Paz. The Boeing 727's are used to transport those who are
considered "dangerous agitators". A trip accompanied by two
suitably armed agents and the wife of one of them. The idea of
escape is a surreal supposition. There is a bevy of agents at the
airport. They take the prisoner to an ambulance that instead of
carrying the infirm transports political prisoners. The vehicle has
radios linked to the headquarters, which monitor the journey.

The precision of the security apparatus has been clockwork. Nothing has been left out. The prisoner now feels the terror, which invades the whole body.

'Taking the prisoner out of the vehicle entails a complete deployment of agents. They take up different strategic positions, pointing their weapons in all directions. The door which leads to the torture chamber opens automatically. A man receives the prisoner, his expression is aggressive; he orders with a point of his finger that they put him inside. The prisoner enters the iron gates. The first phase of physical torture begins. With punches and kicks they take you to the cell, undoing the chains and the enormous padlock. From this moment the prisoner feels the closeness of death. He has heard much talk of the security forces but never took it that seriously. Now he is the principal actor. That which you are told about is never as terrible as reality seen with your own eyes. The experience being lived out is transformed into sweat, the sweat of fear. The fear will never go away; it will be your constant companion whilst you live in that obscure cell. Outside, on the concrete patio, the scene is relived: others enter to receive the same punches and kicks; the doors of the cells open and close.

'After a few minutes, before the pain of the first assault has worn off, an agent enters. They grab you by the shoulders and put a hood over your head and tie up your wrists. After a few minutes' walk a voice is heard: "You're going to tell us all you know, shit." You are roughly made to sit down. A cry of pain as you are punched in the pit of the stomach. "No more noise arsehole! Turn up the music!" Another punch; another cry of pain. "You're going to confess everything you bastard or you leave here dead. Strip him." A third round. "Look at the prick on this one", says one of the thugs. "On to the bed." The victim's body is stretched out in the same form that the Spaniards laid out Tupac Amaru to be pulled apart by four horses. "Stick the *picana* on the bastard." The torture begins in earnest. On the gums, behind the ears, on the chest, around the heart. The pain draws cries of desperation. It is impossible to keep silent. The pain is limitless; it gives you the sensation that a surgeon is cutting through living flesh. Again the voice of the thug: "put it on the bastard's prick." The pain is excruciating; you start to lose consciousness. The thugs mechanically untie the victim, make him sit up, still naked, to increase the humiliation. The interrogation begins. The victim, tortured and humiliated, responds mechanically to the questions. He is incapable of responding with reflection. Not only this, you go further: you try to please, instinctively, to satisfy the interrogators. The softening up process has worked.

'After more than three hours of beatings and questions the prisoner signs a statement, with a trembling hand held by the thug. The hood is a mute witness to the tears of pain, and to those who have inflicted it. The prisoner leaves a world of terror, worse than that in fiction. Back to the cell. But the torture might continue. The prisoner prays to God that they don't open that padlock. Your only wish is that they don't come back to drag you off. Other doors open and steps are heard. The music — they are always protest songs — cannot hide the cries of pain.'[8]

Practices of this nature were given wide publicity abroad, especially in the US, the government of which had habitually acquiesced and even offered training in such interrogation techniques. Bolivian ambassadors in Washington, Paris, Quito, Caracas, Mexico City, Brussels and London resigned their posts and denounced the new regime, some receiving death threats as a result. The Andean Pact countries, all of which were now ruled by civilian administrations, maintained a strong position against the coup, and on at least a dozen occasions over the last six months of 1980 García Meza declared either that Bolivia had withdrawn from the organisation or was 'abstaining'. The president was pointedly not invited to the meeting of Pact heads of state at Santa Marta, Colombia, on 17 December to celebrate the 200th anniversary of Bolívar's birth, and Meza duly 'refused to recognise' the meeting. Arce, who was on occasions prone to play the role of foreign minister as well as fulfilling his domestic duties, declared that the Agreement of Cartagena was not, 'a gentleman's pact, nor a trench or fortification for the reciprocal defence of the various parts. Neither is it an association for mutual influence in order to refine democratic fictions or prop up vacillating governments.'[9] Although the general consensus amongst the senior officers was to have done with the sly and effete civilians who administered the Pact and concentrate on forming a new alliance with the military regimes of the southern cone, they were persuaded out of taking precipitate action by extensive lobbying on the part of the CEPB, important members of which depended on the Pact's market and assistance, and COFADENA, which had a number of important projects at risk. During the last months of 1980 the *paceño* press was full of articles extolling the virtues of regional planning and warning against foolhardy isolationism. Equally, despite Venezuela's decision to cut $40 million of bilateral aid, the Pact itself tried to prevent a complete rupture as had occurred with Chile several years before. After this initial period of pressure, diplomatic relations were, therefore, re-established in a cool fashion, existing collaborative projects ratified, and outright condemnations dropped although the exiled leadership of the UDP was warmly welcomed and frequently given a public platform. In November the countries of the Pact sponsored an OAS motion calling for a full investigation of the violation of human rights in Bolivia.

The question of relations with Washington was far more problematic, not least because the coup had lost Bolivia around $135 million in aid as well as impeding any short-term renegotiation of the massive foreign debt. However, with the US presidential elections coming up the regime was disposed to ride out the crisis for a while, and once Reagan had won, it was convinced that the situation would soon change. On 1 December Arce claimed with confidence that Jaime Paz Zamora's lobbying of the Reagan transition team for a continuation of the boycott was in vain: 'the existing situation between Bolivia and the United States will change as from 20 January.'[10] However, the colonel did not perceive that while Reagan's interest in human rights was even more partial than that of Carter, the issue of *narcotráfico* was likely to produce the same end result, being repugnant to the moralism of the New Right and having very little to do with the cold war. Thus, once it was obvious that relations would not be resumed automatically, the regime embarked upon a very unsophisticated endeavour to curry favour in Washington by spending $250,000 for the services of a public relations expert (the gentleman in question having just completed some sterling work for the Shah of Iran), sending off 'special envoys' who upon arrival in the US caused considerable confusion by declaring themselves to be ambassadors although they lacked accreditation, and by editing out of their public pronouncements denunciations of 'imperialist blockades' or promises to 'eat potatoes' for a decade rather than submit to 'colonialist blackmail'.[11]

A month after the coup the regime was recognised by only 16 states, but amongst these were all of Latin America's military regimes, some of which directly aided Meza's rebellion and provided early and enthusiastic support. Because of the issue of an exit to the sea Chile remained somewhat aloof, but within a week of the coup the Brazilian delegate to the OAS strenuously opposed the adoption of any sanctions against the new Bolivian government by invoking the principle of non-intervention.[12] President Rafael Videla of Argentina was more forthright in outlining the reasons behind his government's support for the coup: 'What has happened in Bolivia is that of two options on the table in the neighbouring country the one that was formally correct was the assumption of power by an elected government, but for us this represented a high level of risk due to the possibility of diffusion of ideas contrary to our way of life. We have viewed the other option—the establishment of a military government—with much more sympathy because we don't want in South America what Cuba is for Central America.'[13] To back up such sentiments Videla offered a loan of $200 million, a supply of wheat, and the promise to buy natural gas at a generous price. Yet, within a matter of months the very poor state of the Argentine economy, concern over the continued isolation of the Bolivian regime, and exasperation at divisions inside its military compelled a steady process of withdrawal from wholesale economic patronage although the less overt and costly military assistance was retained. Buenos Aires continued to be the regime's most important ally throughout.

International difficulties and the advice of the Argentines that it proceed to institutionalise its rule lay behind the government's attempts to provide itself with an advisory body that might compensate for the high command's lack of political experience and oversee the elaboration of general policy and a new legal order. The *Comisión Nacional de Asesoramiento y Legislación* (CONAL), set up on 17 September 1980, was of critical importance since García Meza lacked formal support from any of the major political parties and needed the administrative skills and political 'know how' of the traditional right. CONAL provided an acceptable conduit for the collaboration of this sector without committing it to formal and public backing. The body was headed by General Juan Lechín Suárez and contained several serving and retired officers but also included figures such as Abel Ayoroa and a goodly stock of senior ADN members—Raúl Boada Rodríguez; Carlos Calvo Galindo; Guillermo Fortún Sanjinés; Jorge Tamayo

Ramos — whose entry was tacitly approved by Banzer, as well as representatives of the Santa Cruz oligarchy (Fernando Bedoya) and the FSB (Edgar Millares Reyes).[14] CONAL oversaw the restructuring of the universities (which remained closed until early 1981) by a subsidiary body known as CONRUB, proclaimed the 1967 constitution to be in force in the same manner as it had been retained by Banzer, and began to discuss the preparation of a new constitutional charter. However, by virtue both of its terms of reference and its membership the body soon manifested a number of differences of style and policy from the leaders of the regime. Together with the CEPB, CONAL supported continued membership of the Andean Pact, and it combined with the Church to veto Arce's proposed security statute that introduced the death penalty, a measure that was finally withdrawn on 19 November, this being the first tangible setback experienced by the regime as a result of differences inside the dominant bloc. As internal divisions deepened CONAL became an important mouthpiece for the civilian elite dismayed by the regime's impulsive and excessive actions, but although it could register discontent and counsel caution, it lacked any executive authority and failed to impose any meaningful restraint. Significantly, the scarcely-veiled campaign against the security statute followed the first visible signs of discontent inside the military, leading to the removal of Generals Echeverría and Vargas Salinas from their powerful provincial posts at the beginning of November. The widespread rumour that a new coup was being planned by Natusch — still without a formal appointment and known to be outraged by his treatment by the men whom he held responsible for the calamities of November 1979 — strengthened convictions that although Banzer had allowed the ADN to enter CONAL, he was encouraging his followers inside the army to put pressure on the regime and preparing the ground for an alternative administration that would inherit the gains of July but be acceptable to Washington and fully incorporate the civilian right.

Much of this discontent was caused by the intemperate activities and vociferous proclamations of Arce, who ran the regime virtually single-handed in its first months and whose independent and overbearing paramilitary forces antagonised many sectors of the officer corps. There is a scant history of the Bolivian military repudiating figures who proclaim themselves to be 'a hard man, always in the front line when there is danger', but Arce's antics became counterproductive from an institutional viewpoint when they resulted only in hardening Washington's antipathy towards the government. This was most clearly evident following the interior minister's decision to make a foreign trip between 23 November and 2 December in order to vindicate his honour and counter charges that he was involved in the cocaine trade. Accompanied by Mario Rolón Anaya of the ADN, Arce visited Washington in a private capacity to file suits for defamation against several newspapers and, most particularly, Mike Wallace, producer of a film shown on CBS's 'Sixty Minutes' documentary series which levelled a number of serious charges against the minister and bore the signs of close cooperation from the US Drug Enforcement Administration (DEA). It was also planned to hold discussions with Senator Jesse Helms and the American Legion, and place a wreath on the tomb of the Unknown Soldier in Arlington cemetery. The trip, which from the start received a great deal of publicity, produced no litigation and came to an abrupt end when Arce, refused official permission to visit Arlington, went anyway, evading the security guards to make his floral offering before being escorted away and formally requested to leave the country forthwith. He then flew to Brazil to institute legal proceedings against the magazine *Veja* for its accusations that he was involved in *narcotráfico*, but following protests from the journalists' union, the neighbouring government took the same attitude as its northern ally, and Arce was obliged to sit out the rest of his excursion closeted with 'real friends' in Paraguay. This foolish episode served more than any other single incident to relight international interest in the regime's connections with commerce in cocaine, and in all probability it proved instrumental in the decision of Reagan's transition team to continue Carter's boycott.

Coca and Cocaine

Outside the countries of the Andes people are more familiar with cocaine than with coca, the plant from which it is derived. Yet the world in which cocaine is fabricated, transported and marketed is obscure, resistant to intrusion and, as a consequence, prone to description that employs excited hyperbole and the most grotesque conspiracy theories. It is almost as if the thrill of consumption must be transferred to the conditions of production.[15] This image is not without some foundation in so far as the very illegality of cocaine has given rise to extremely unstable terms of competition which have trickled down the production process, affecting cultivation of the coca leaf to an appreciable degree. Nonetheless, one should not lose sight of the fact that cultivation of coca remains a legal and open form of agriculture that has been practised in Bolivia for many centuries. At no stage during its recent boom has cocaine simply been the concern of a few small groups of *traficantes*; its impact has registered in entire communities, directly affecting some 200,000 people whose livelihood is connected with it. For this reason it is utterly erroneous to view the trade as a discrete criminal activity determined only by the violent and esoteric customs of the mafia.

The contemporary importance of the industry—for such it is—can only be quantified in terms of estimates, but these are consistently impressive. In 1980 the narcotic trade in the US alone was valued at $50 billion; of this figure perhaps $30 billion was accounted for by commerce in cocaine, sixty per cent of which originated from Bolivian coca.[16] According to the DEA—an organisation that does precisely the reverse of enforcing drugs—some ten million people in the US consume cocaine on a regular basis and another five million have taken it at some time or another.[17] This may be an inflated figure but it is not greatly exaggerated and there clearly exists an extensive market both in Europe and the US, where, largely as a result of the Vietnam war, cocaine is no longer the preserve of the elite but a very popular albeit highly expensive item of consumption. Since Bolivia provides at least half the world's supply of coca the internal impact of this new metropolitan market has been considerable; estimates for production of coca in 1980 ran as high as 80,000 tons, those for revenue in 1981 ranging between $1.3 billion and $8 billion. The value of legal exports in 1980 was below $1 billion.[18] Since cocaine is the only major commodity marketed by a Latin American country to have risen in price over the last four years it is not surprising that some commentators began to talk of a 'new economic cycle' replacing that of tin, or that many of those who reject the form the commerce takes still perceive advantages in the new terms of trade. There is even wider resistance to the one-sided moralism of gringos who wish to destroy the *cocales* and plant coffee or citrus fruits instead, as if this were a simple case of crop rotation.

Various types of coca (*Erythroxylum coca*) have been grown and cultivated in the valleys and foothills of the Andes since well before the Spanish conquest. Evidence suggests that under the Inca empire consumption was integral to many religious ceremonies and may have been limited to the upper echelons of society. It was used as a tribute, and specific communities were charged with its cultivation. The chronicler Garcidiez, writing in 1567, reported that only indigenous priests chewed it, but it is clear that very soon after the conquest consumption became an integral part of the life of the *mitayos*, the labourers press-ganged into working in the silver mines. Some Spaniards even took up the habit but *el coqueo* had always been an indigenous custom, central not simply to labour in the mines or fields but to communal life in general. Coca is frequently exchanged between families or groups as part of *mink'a* or *ayni*, systems of reciprocal labour or favours, and still plays a very important part in ritual and recreation. It is used mostly as a stimulant at work but viewed equally widely as a medicine giving protection against the cold and dulling hunger; it also possesses the qualities of an aphrodisiac although these are less marked than in cocaine. The coca leaf is continually masticated and held in the cheek in a ball, its chemical properties being released by the addition of a small amount of alcaline substance (*llujta* or *tocra*), usually ash from vegetables. This process is known as *acullicu* and was estimated by the United Nations in 1950 to introduce between 150 and 300 milligrams of cocaine into the system daily, compared with between 50 and 150 milligrams in a single inhalation of commercial cocaine.[19]

Amado Canelas writes, without exaggeration, that, 'coca is an essential, integral factor in the life of the *campesino*; it constitutes a mediating element with the everyday supernatural, to help calm the gods and put one in favour with them.'[20] Although there is growing evidence of a generational divide in intensity of consumption, and urbanisation has to some degree reduced the practice of *coqueo*, it is still very widespread in the countryside and considered an integral part of the wage in many mines. However, the UN has persisted in its attitude — based on the 'scientific findings' of its 1949–50 research — that the *acullicu* is harmful to health (despite the fact that coca is not classed as toxic) and that it aids malnutrition and prompts 'unfavourable modifications' of an 'intellectual and moral' nature as well as a 'reduction in efficiency' of work.[21] Little or no statistical evidence can be brought to bear in substantiation of such claims, which appear to derive primarily from the received beliefs of an urban managerial stratum that might well be expected to ignore or despise the ritualistic properties of the leaf and label as liars those labourers who say they chew it to help them work, but presumably failed to consult the mine-owners who provide tons of leaf to their labour force. The medical debate over coca continues, but the UN's dogma remains and has, no doubt, played a part in encouraging eradication of plantations as a means of stemming the cocaine trade.

During the colonial epoch coca production flourished in line with the cycle of boom and slump in the silver industry but probably never exceeded 4,000 tons a year, at least a third of which was consumed in Potosí. Cultivation for the region that is now Bolivia was centred on the Yungas region of La Paz with the townships of Coripata and Chulumani being the major foci. While Chulumani was a zone dominated by indigenous communities, land round Coripata was held in hacienda. By 1870 there were no communities left in Coripata and its eighty square kilometres of rich coca land was divided between 34 private estates. The tin boom dynamised the local economy in the first decades of the century, making a fortune for José María Gamarra, 'the king of coca' who owned seven haciendas by 1928 and was the driving force behind the *Sociedad de Proprietarios de Yungas*, closely allied to the Rosca. Since the coca bushes in the steep valleys of the Yungas had a natural life of between 25 and 30 years and could be harvested three times a year there existed a ready and profitable supply for the inelastic market in the mines.[22] The agrarian reform dispossessed the big landlords, replacing them with *minifundistas* who acquired plots that were very fertile but too small to allow major commercial operations. Production certainly fell and trading often took the form of barter. However, since even at official (1982) prices a hectare of land in the Yungas will pay Bs.91,800 a year from coca against Bs.81,000 from coffee and, on a conservative estimate, the unofficial price for coca leaf is at least three times higher than that paid by the government, it is clear why production in the Yungas has been maintained and gradually expanded.[23]

Until the early 1970s the Yungas dominated production, but throughout the decade it was first challenged and then overtaken by a new zone of production: Chaparé, in the east of Cochabamba. Chaparé had always been an extremely backward area locked into a low-level subsistence agriculture that made no impact even on the regional market and barely managed to keep its population of 3,500 (1944) victualled. After the agrarian reform Chaparé was one of the zones designated for colonisation and its new pioneer smallholders soon began to experiment with different varieties of coca, experiencing most success with 'Coca Trujillo' (*Erythroxylum truxillense Rusby*). However, the local consumers, accustomed to the Yungas leaf, did not take readily to this *kochala* (literally — 'coca from Cochabamba'), prompting the search for an alternative market.

Chaparé's insertion into the cocaine market was not initiated by large landlords; in 1981 51 per cent of the 11,000 farmers working some 13,250 hectares owned plots of less than a hectare and only 14 per cent owned plots of more than two hectares.[24] However, the region possessed a number of natural advantages over the Yungas from the point of view of establishing an 'informal' market. Most important in terms of production was an average yield of 2.6 tons per hectare per year, due to the fact that the local climate and soil allows four harvests a year. This complemented an existing price advantage possessed by coca, providing an income over five times as great as that derived from rice and nearly ten times higher than that from maize, the other two staple crops. Additionally, Chaparé is a large and inaccessible region that is extremely difficult to control whereas the Yungas has very few exits — the only paved road being easily monitored by the customs post at Unduavi — and no terrain suitable for landing even light aircraft. Thus, the cocaine boom of the 1970s was fuelled principally by coca from Chaparé, which by late 1982 was fetching Bs.19,000 ($80) for a *tambor* (bale) of 58 pounds, a price that gave the region's peasant farmers a yearly income of $7,040 a hectare, roughly twenty times Bolivia's annual per capita GDP.[25] Although statistics in this sphere are notoriously unreliable and vary not just between the institutions concerned but also within them, Table Twelve indicates quite clearly the impact of increased demand upon production. It is worth bearing in mind that for the last 15 years the legal domestic demand for coca leaf has remained steady at around 4,000 metric tons, but by 1981, when overall production certainly exceeded 70,000 tons, this demand could not be met and there was a great scarcity of leaf in the markets.

The process of transforming the coca leaf into cocaine ($C_{17}H_{21}NO_4$) is neither highly sophisticated nor very costly. The leaf is placed in tubs, mixed with diluted sulphuric acid, and then trodden into a paste. Alcohol is then added to bring the alcaloids to the surface, the syrup being syphoned off and left to solidify. This substance is known

Table 12

Production of Coca

Year		Metric Tons	Source
1845		3,579	Dalence (a)
1930	Yungas	3,067	Morales (b)
1950		4,830	Censo Agropecuario
1952	Yungas	3,987	Aduana de La Paz
1958	Yungas	2,627	Aduana de La Paz
1965		5,515	INE (c)
1970		6,000	INE
1971	Chaparé	2,666	UMSS (d)
1973		9,400	INE
1975		11,800	INE
1976		14,760	INE
1977		15,600	INE
	Yungas	5,691	SIC (e)
	Chaparé	19,512	SIC
1978		18,860	INE
		15,410	PRODES (f)
		25,248	DNSP (g)
	Yungas	8,651	OCPFHC (h)
1979		22,000	INE
1980	Chaparé	58,275	SEC (i)
1981	Chaparé	64,275 est.	SEC
1982	Chaparé	82,000 est.	SEC

Notes:
a. José María Dalence, *Bosquejo Estadístico de Bolivia* (Chuquisaca 1851)
b. José Agustín Morales, *El Oro Verde de los Yungas* (La Paz 1938)
c. Instituto Nacional de Estadística
d. Universidad Mayor de San Simón, Cochabamba (1972)
e. Seminario Interamericano sobre la Coca, Lima (1980)
f. Proyecto de Desarrollo Chaparé – Yungas, Cochabamba.
g. Dirección Nacional de Sustancias Peligrosas, La Paz.
h. Oficina de Control de la Producción y Fiscalización de la Hoja de Coca, La Paz.
i. Satellite Earth Corporation, Washington (1981)

as cocaine sulphate, paste, or basic paste, and it is in this form that most cocaine is exported from Bolivia. In the next stage of the process the sulphate of cocaine is washed, sometimes in ether but more generally in acetone, which does not smell as strongly, and hydrochloric acid is added to produce chlorohydrate of cocaine ($C_{17}H_{21}NO_4HCL$). Roughly 2.5 kilos of paste will, when processed, produce one kilo of chlorohydrate of cocaine, which, when refined, will yield 800 grams of pure cocaine. With all the necessary caveats with respect to the dependability of data but using information provided by the DEA, we can say that the 200 kilos of coca leaf required to produce a kilo of basic paste would cost some $350 (1980), the sulphuric acid, alcohol, and acetone amounting to a further $100. The pay of the workers employed to tread the mass and that of the amateur chemists would not be in excess of $500 and those who transport the sulphate might receive $200, again for each kilo. On this basis the cost of a kilo of cocaine in Bolivia amounts to some $1,150.[26] Sources agree that the sale price — usually to dealers from Colombia — is approximately $5,000 a kilo. Once in Colombia the basic paste has acquired a value in the region of $11,000. After refining the same quantity of chlorohydrate of cocaine will fetch $60,000 when exported to the US. But neither the production process nor the mark-up ends here since ninety per cent pure crystal is never marketed before being adulterated either with amphetamines or fine-ground sugar or talcum. The degree of 'cutting' of the pure cocaine increases as the commodity moves down the marketing ladder; it is extremely rare to find retail crystal of more than twelve per cent purity. In this way the single kilo of ninety per cent purity becomes eight kilos of retail cocaine with a total street value of some $500,000, a considerable increase on the $12,500 required to buy the 2.5 kilos of Bolivian sulphate that forms its basis.[27] In recognition of this fact Bolivian dealers have attempted to concentrate more of the production process under their control and by 1980 were turning out limited amounts of chlorohydrate of cocaine as well as basic paste. There can be no firm guide as to the extent to which this has occurred, but it is perhaps indicative that 28 per cent of confiscated cocaine tested by the narcotics control organisations in Bolivia between 1975 and 1980 was in chlorohydrate form.[28] This fact may account for the periodic bouts of bad relations with the Colombians although the sale of inferior sulphate or independent marketing forays are more likely to be the cause.

As we have seen, narcotics did from time to time make brief appearances in Bolivian public life before the 1970s, but such cocaine production as did take place was a strictly peripheral activity that failed to attract the interest of local entrepreneurs on a significant scale. It seems likely that there was a very gradual expansion from the mid-50s although in the early 60s the Bolivian police were still sending captured substances to London for analysis, suggesting no great concern about the trade. In 1963 the UN Permanent Commission on Opiates claimed coca production had risen to 12,000 tons but the Bolivian government maintained that it stood at 3,000 and was falling. In mid-November 1970 a haul of 27 kilos of cocaine sulphate was seized by police in Oruro whilst in transit for processing in Chile, the one neighbouring country that has not been significantly involved in the trade during the boom years.[29] It is difficult to draw general conclusions from the size of the consignment or its price ($11,000 a kilo) but it is improbable that it was a solitary transaction. The thesis developed by René Bascopé is that real expansion only began with the collapse of cotton in 1975/6 and was the result of a number of exploratory studies sponsored by the Banzer regime in close alliance with the over-financed but under-productive members of the *Asociación de Productores de Algodón* (ADEPA), centred in Santa Cruz. It is inconceivable that some degree of high-level planning did not take place since, for example, sulphuric acid was needed in quantities that required a major commercial operation and some state assistance. Equally, sufficient numbers of the tighly-knit *cruceño* agro-industrial elite have subsequently been implicated in *narcotráfico* to give the lie to any notions of a completely uncoordinated build-up of isolated operations that suddenly took off after July 1980. Furthermore, the sums of money involved and the exigencies of obtaining credit, organising transport, protection, and marketing contacts outside the country preclude the possibilities of either complete ignorance on the part of the police and military or of a predominantly small farmer enterprise; almost all sources of information identify the Banco Agrícola as a key component in the rise of cocaine. However, there is as yet no firm evidence to prove a concrete policy of unqualified state backing and patronage under Banzer rather than a generally benevolent attitude, occasional assistance and direct involvement on the part of certain individuals.

Having said this, Bascopé's identification of three principal geographical axes of production that overlap in several ways but possess a number of distinct characteristics with regard to the timing of their emergence and clan membership would seem to carry weight. The first of these was firmly based on ADEPA, civilian in character and centred on the rich farming lands north of Santa Cruz, stretching from San Javier through Portachuelo to the garrison and railhead town of Montero. Bascopé lists as members of this group José Roberto Gasser, Willy Banzer Ojopi, Jose Paz and other prominent landlords. Its undisputed leader is Roberto Suárez Gómez, head of a traditional *latifundista* family and owner of extensive lands around Santa Ana de Yacuma, far to the north in the Beni. Suárez is Luis Arce Gómez's cousin and was temporarily jailed in 1976 for possession of cocaine. It would, however, be misguided to see him as some type of socially-marginalised miscreant; he is an extremely popular *patrón* in Santa Ana, liberal in his distribution of favours and contributions to local charities, and widely held to be responsible for the town's newfound wealth. A regional caudillo of the old school, Suárez is viewed as making if not a strictly legal then at least an open living from a trade that has done the area no perceptible harm thanks to *yanqui* dollars. This explains why he was able to remain at liberty for so long and even though the net was closing in around him in mid-83, he still possessed sufficient resources to impede arrest by the civilian regime for nigh-on a year.

It might be thought odd that Suárez, a man who owns land in Santa Cruz but is based in the Beni, should be so closely attached to the *cruceño* axis, but it must be borne in mind that one of the key factors in the cocaine trade is transport. This is invariably undertaken by light planes that are extremely difficult to track and can land on isolated grass strips but lack the capacity to make an uninterrupted flight from Santa Cruz to Leticia, the southern Colombian town that is the major entrepot for the trade. Santa Cruz has at least 500 airstrips but the even more isolated and unvigilated Beni possesses some 3,000. Thus, once the cocaine sulphate has been prepared in eastern Cochabamba or Santa Cruz and transported on back by the peasant *zepeadores* to a local airstrip or town, it is usually flown first to the Beni and from there out of the country, normally to Colombia but more recently to Brazil, Venezuela, Panama, Curaçao or Martinique before making the last stage of its journey into Florida, a state that has a coastline of over 1,500 kilometres and some 216 private airstrips. It is usually on the European run that individual 'messengers' are used to transport the drug on commercial flights, Madrid's Barajas airport being a favoured destination. In such cases the preferred method of transport is by swallowing plastic bags of cocaine. One 19-year-old Colombian student was detained at Bogotá airport in June 1982 in a state of high agitation and soon confessed to carrying cocaine in her stomach en route for Frankfurt; the subsequent evacuation revealed some 163 bags of the drug weighing over 500 grams. This method is, however, far from efficient and entails great risks; there have been several instances of horrible deaths occurring in airliners after stomach acids have permeated the plastic bags and released a lethal dose of cocaine into the system.

The second of Bascopé's groups is perhaps more directly concerned with transport than production since it is centred in the Beni. The membership of the San Javier—Santa Ana—Paraparau axis is more obscure than that of the first clan but evidently came together later and incorporates a greater number of military personnel since one of its original foci was the large COFADENA ranch of Paraparau. If this is the case—and there are conflicting versions as to the scope and nature of military involvement—it seems likely that there has been a close correspondence with a faction identified by Anibal Aguilar as dominating the trade in the Yapacaní zone of Chaparé under the leadership of Generals Echeverría and Bernal along with Colonel Moisés Chirique (commander of the Montero garrison) and Captain Rudy Landivar (head of Santa Cruz customs).[30] Finally, Bascopé notes a group of traditional landlords based around Vallegrande on the Santa Cruz—Cochabamba border and closely linked through kinship. This group is apparently concerned with production of basic paste and lacks its own facilities for long-range transport. Amongst it Bascopé identifies as leaders Willy Sandoval Morón, who became an adviser to Arce after July 1980, and the Eid and Franco families.[31]

In all likelihood the geographical dispersion of the cocaine trade inside the country has led to differences in style, divisions of labour, and preferences in the formation of alliances. Yet it would be wrong to conclude that each axis constitutes a distinct mafia or that there is not a high degree of interaction and collaboration as well as outright competition. The more ambitious and less reliable list of leading *traficantes* compiled by Anibal Aguilar in February 1981 also identifies three different groups—the Banzer/Gasser faction in San Javier; the 'Syrian-Lebanese group' led by the Razuk brothers, Arce, Pereda and Buby Salomón in eastern Santa Cruz; and the Echeverría/Chirique clan operating out of Yapacaní with the collaboration of Suarez. There are in each of these clans members of ADEPA that Bascopé believes belonged to the first phase of expansion. One must, therefore, remain sceptical as to precise compartmentalisation.

Although the UN and Washington had since the 1950s expressed a constant concern about the level of cocaine production in Bolivia, it was only in the mid-70s that high-level measures were taken to try to curb it. In 1976 Henry Kissinger visited Banzer in Santa Cruz, offering $2 million to train the narcotics police and up to $45 million to assist the cultivation of substitute crops. In return, the local press reported, the president was presented with a list of a hundred known traffickers and invited to show his regime's goodwill by jailing at least ten of them.[32] Neither side of the bargain was kept, but the following year Banzer did put his signature to a UN agreement to limit the coca crop and halt the drugs trade, thereby partially compensating for Bolivia's failure to ratify the similar accords of 1961 and 1971, which had been signed by no less than twenty other American states. However, in March 1979 the UN declared that the Bolivian government had done nothing to halt the growth of coca plantations and cast grave doubt on both its willingness and its ability to contain *narcotráfico*.[33]

There were further, more tangible signs of trouble at the top. In February 1973 a group of agents from the DIN and Interpol were called in to meet the chief of police, Colonel Vázquez Sempértegui, and told to stop investigating a case resulting from the seizure of ten kilos of chlorohydrate of cocaine because they had traced the cargo to Carlos Valverde, then minister of health.[34] Two years later Edwin Tapia Frontanilla, Banzer's private secretary, was arrested at Montreal airport with a consignment of cocaine. In the same operation Luis 'Chito' Valle, Banzer's son-in-law and the Bolivian consul in Montreal as well as a student at McGill university, was found in possession of the drug and discreetly asked to leave the country; two other Bolivian diplomats were condemned to five-year sentences.[35] The fact that Banzer's wife Yolanda had recently travelled on an unscheduled flight from Santa Cruz in an airforce jet to visit her son-in-law in Canada did little to distance the presidential family from such unsavoury matters. A further member of the family, Guillermo 'Willy' Banzer Abastaflor, Hugo Banzer's nephew, was later arrested in Florida for cocaine trafficking. Upon being returned to the Panóptico in La Paz he was registered as plain Guillermo Abastaflor but rapidly regained his freedom after a severe case of haemarroids was diagnosed, necessitating immediate treatment in an outside clinic, where security was a good deal more lax than the putative state of Willy's anus.[36] In the final weeks of his rule Banzer appointed his cousin Guillermo Banzer Ojopi as consul in Miami, but his designation was met with a leak from the DEA that Banzer Ojopi was involved in the cocaine trade, causing a flurry of press reports and obliging Banzer later to shift the blame for the appointment onto Pereda, a claim that was rapidly refuted with presentation of the relevant documentation.[37]

In the first months of 1980 a series of incidents highlighted both the growing audacity of the cocaine traders and their increasing vulnerability to discovery and capture. In January the narcotics division of the Santa Cruz police under the command of Major Carlos Fernández Navarro raided a hacienda in the San Javier region and seized a Colombian aircraft that had been reported making frequent flights into the area. Resisted by a large number of armed men, the police retreated to gather reinforcements. When they returned, Fernández found not the Colombian plane but a Bolivian airforce craft accompanied by an officer from the local training school who ordered the police to leave the area immediately. Fernández refused and proceeded to raid Banzer's hacienda of 'El Potrero', where a number of suitcases containing 300 kilos of cocaine sulphate were discovered along with a store of military uniforms. The next day the ex-president protested that somebody was using his property for illegal purposes.[38] In May an operation of far greater consequence organised by the DEA very nearly decapitated the Suárez network. Early in the year a DEA undercover agent, Mike Levine, made contact in Buenos Aires with Marcelo Ibañez, one of Suárez's more important assistants, and convinced him that he was looking to buy a large shipment of cocaine. Levine invited both Suárez and Ibañez to Florida to look over his facilities and 'family'. In the event, only Ibañez made the trip, being shown a colonial mansion in Fort Lauderdale, a dummy laboratory, and three suitcases containing $9 million drawn by the DEA from the Federal Reserve Bank of Miami. The money was transported to the Kendall Bank under Ibañez's observation. The Bolivian then made a radio call to Suárez to say that the North Americans would accept 500 kilos at $16,000 a kilo. The next day, 16 May, Richard Fiano, a DEA operative, three pilots and Ibañez flew to a landing strip near Lake Roguaguado in the Beni to be met by Roberto Suárez Levy, the son of the *padrino*. In the meantime Alfredo 'Cutuchi' Gutiérrez and Roberto Gasser Terrazas, two senior members of the Suárez clan, had flown to Miami, Gutiérrez telephoning Suárez to say that they were ready to embark upon the transaction. In the event, the DEA crew loaded only 854 pounds of cocaine into their Corvair 440 aircraft since they felt that any more would be dangerous. Once in the air, Fiano radioed through to Miami, and Gutiérrez and Gasser made their way to the Kendall Bank, were led down into the vaults and then arrested. The DEA's haul was the largest confiscation of cocaine ever made.[39] However, the charges against Gasser were not upheld whilst Gutiér-rez's original bail of $3 million was reduced by Judge Alcee Hastings to $1 million, which was promptly paid in notes, allowing the suspect, who is an accomplished pilot, to make his escape to Bolivia. In October 1981 the Torrelio regime handed Gutiérrez back to the US authorities as part of its campaign to regain diplomatic recognition but refused to hand Suárez over on the grounds that, 'there is no formal charge against him'[40].

Other figures were also attracting attention. Early in 1980 a plane belonging to Buby Salomón crashed in the Beni and was found to have 300 kilos of sulphate aboard; Salomón was quickly posted as military attaché in Caracas.[41] On 3 July, a fortnight before the coup, a Piper Aztec crashed at Laja, not far from El Alto, killing the three persons aboard and scattering fifty and one hundred dollar notes over the surrounding area. The plane belonged to Salomón and Arce, who immediately appeared in a helicopter and ordered the police to leave the wreck alone, tearing up their report.[42] Some of these incidents appeared in the Bolivian press but over the period leading up to the elections there was an almost deafening silence in political circles on the question of the cocaine trade. Given that the UDP had hired Arce's planes, it is not beyond the realm of possibility that this silence stemmed at least in part from ignorance of the scope of the trade, but it was clearly read by the clans as a tactical move prior to close collab-oration between a UDP government and the DEA in an extensive anti-drugs operation. Subsequent events lend some credibility to this expectation, which lay behind the strong support for the coup of 17 July from the major cocaine clans.

The terms of the clans' funding of García Meza's rebellion remain somewhat obscure. Most secondary sources state that a sum in the region of $1 million was passed to the general by Abraham Baptista, the longstanding intelligence officer employed by G-2 who was known to be an important link with the mafia. However, *Aquí*, now being produced in clandestinity, reported a month after the coup that José Paz had delivered $800,000 to General Hugo Echeverría and that an undisclosed sum received by Meza from Pedro Blayer and José Roberto Gasser, whose family had funded Banzer's 1971 rising, was separate from this.[43] This would suggest an initial division of interest that was soon mirrored in competition between the two officers, Echeverría losing out because of Arce's backing for Meza. For the first few weeks after the coup there were undoubtedly difficulties within the regime and between some of the producers. In a testimony made to Italian police in August 1982 the mercenary Elio Ciolini reported that his group was directed at the onset by Echeverría, who was paid by Suárez. One of the most prominent members of this group was Joachim Fiebelkorn , employed to enhance Suárez's security. (He appears to have been successful in this in so far as the establishment of bazooka emplacements around the Suárez airstrips reduced underhand practices by Colombian dealers.) Yet, shortly after the coup relations with Suárez cooled considerably and the imported mercenaries were placed directly under Arce's command.[44] The highly active Abraham Baptista soon fell foul of the new power structure. Less than a fortnight after the takeover a paramilitary group under his command received $6 million from some Colombians who had flown into Santa Cruz, and Baptista took this money directly to García Meza. According to some sources, the president ordered Baptista to pay $4 million into the account of his wife Olma and to hand the rest over to Arce. However, the Colombians thought that they were dealing exclusively with Arce, and when they learnt of Baptista's activity offered the minister $1 million for protection. Arce, fearing the establishment of a network outside his control, ordered Baptista out of La Paz and prevailed upon García Meza to expel him from the army. The disgraced man responded by threatening to reveal the regime's involvement in the trade, a move born of desperation, certain to deprive him of any friends, and most probably responsible for his assassination outside a pizzería in the centre of Santa Cruz on 6 October. Monique Lecerf and Francois Fallarean allege that the assassins were paid off by Echeverría, who had little to gain from Baptista's activities even though he was not on good terms with Arce.[45] The deaths of Carlos Roca, shot on his hacienda in Santa Cruz late in 1980, Colonel Emilio Arabe, a supposed member of the Vallegrande group who died when his plane exploded on take-off in 1981, and Arce's right-hand man 'Mosca' Monroy, shot in Santa Cruz on 18 June 1982, may all be ascribed with some confidence to internal feuding, which also resulted in the killing of a greater number of less important individuals as well as some Colombians.

Although these tensions were on occasions acute, they never escalated into clan warfare and were in general resolved at an institutional level. At least in the first phase of the García Meza regime Arce was able to impose an informal system of taxation that, combined with the funds from the clans, gave rise to the much publicised remark by Peter Passage of the US State Department that, 'for the first time the mafia has bought itself a government'.[46] According to the *New York Times*, General Bernal received payments of $10,000 a week for permitting transport of cocaine to take place without interference; the *Wall Street Journal* alleged that part of these sums was directed towards the purchase of fighter aircraft.[47] Bolivian sources claim that the tariff charged on a lorry loaded with 10,000 kilos of leaf yielded $5,000 for Arce, $2,375 for García Meza, and between $1,250 and $650 for various officials in the ministry of the interior, the customs, and the police. The total tax on such a cargo is said to have been Bs.300,000, which still left those engaged in transport a tidy profit margin.[48] In all probability it was through this means of charging for non-interference that the regime and certain sectors of the military were most generally involved in the trade. This is not to say that fabulous sums were not accumulated both in cash and in kind. By the time he had fallen into disgrace, Arce's registered fixed assets extended to three palatial mansions, four luxury flats in La Paz, Santa Cruz and Buenos Aires, five ranches, a milk processing plant, and a number of aircraft.[49] Early in 1981 much attention was given to a trip to Zurich made by Señora García Meza, who was said by *Der Spiegel* to have lodged $40 million in a Swiss bank account.[50] The first lady was minded on her journey by Federico Nielsen Reyes, translator of *Mein Kampf* into Spanish, erstwhile Bolivian consul in Frankfurt who sold his post to the owner of a shoe factory so that he could buy a horse to compete in the 1972 Olympic games, a prime mover of Banzer's immigration schemes, and one of García Meza's most trusted lieutenants.[51] It is possible that any moneys conveyed to Europe by Olma de García Meza contained a portion of the $5 million donated by Colonel Bo Hi Park on behalf of the religious sect led by Sun Myung Moon, who, along with the government of Taiwan, was a staunch defender of the regime.[52]

Whatever the degree of veracity in such reports, they were widespread and served to worsen the regime's already exceedingly poor reputation. It is also indicative that a great many stories stemmed from leaks made by the DEA, which continued to pursue a high-profile campaign against the Bolivian government. This had the effect of cooling relations between García Meza's administration and the other military regimes of the southern cone, particularly when Reagan continued the boycott imposed by Carter. The maintenance of this policy shook the La Paz government into the realisation that it would have to make some effort to clean up its image. A fortnight after the coup Arce had responded to Washington's accusations over cocaine with an open defiance that reflected the government's confidence both in its regional allies and a forthcoming change of attitude on the part of the US: 'Complete responsibility for the inherent problem of trade in hallucinogens and the rise in the export of drugs falls on President Carter since at the present time, having cut off aid, he is the sole author of the increase in the consumption of cocaine in the United States.'[53] In the same vein Arce publicly implied that should the US boycott continue there might be no alternative to the legalisation of cocaine inside Bolivia. A year later circumstances had changed sufficiently for him to state that *narcotráfico* constituted 'an evil that is growing day by day to the detriment of our country.'[54]

Early in 1981 García Meza began to respond to demands that some formal apparatus of control be established. On 3 April he imposed a state monopoly on purchase of the coca leaf from the growers (supreme decree 16168) in order to give greater powers to the *Consejo Nacional de Lucha Contra el Narcotráfico* (CNLCN), set up the previous month (supreme decree 18121, 11 March 1981) to supervise anti-drug operations, particularly those directed by the *Dirección Nacional de Sustancias Peligrosas* (DNSP). However, the president, now under pressure from both the military and civilian participants in the trade, could not decide if the armed forces or the police would take overall charge of the operation. On 19 May he announced that the military would withdraw from all involvement, but 48 hours later he reversed this decision.[55] One reason for this uncertainty was renewed conflict between the clans resulting from the appointment of Colonel Arturo Doria Medina to lead the CNLCN. Doria Medina was a bitter opponent of Arce's, and upon taking up his post had begun to move against his rival's interests. Moreover, when, in May 1981, the Brazilian police captured half a dozen of Arce's mercenaries operating well over the border replete with nazi insignia, heavy weapons and a goodly quantity of cocaine, Colonel David Fernández, head of the DNSP, publicly supported all the charges made against those arrested while General Edén Castillo, minister of defence, protested the innocence and good character of some of the motley crew of Italians and Germans who were going by the name of '*Los Novios de la Muerte*' ('The Grooms of Death'). In the ensuing conflict Castillo was to lose his post but the CNLCN's campaign was also restrained, Doria Medina eventually being given the less powerful but equally remunerative post of chief of the customs service.

The CNLCN was taken to be something less than a complete charade partly because of Doria Medina's appointment, which reflected if not a disposition to control the trade then at least a preparedness to clip Arce's wings, and partly because there was manifest concern amongst the officer corps that matters had got completely out of hand. But there is little evidence to suggest that real progress was made. In the first place, the organs of control were hopelessly unprepared in logistical terms. They possessed not even a single helicopter of their own and their sole means of tracking air traffic in Chaparé was one VHF radar with a range of only ten kilometres. There were no resources to match the unofficial price for leaf and insufficient manpower to cover the major cities, let alone the countryside. More importantly still, there was no political will to make a campaign work, purge a notoriously corrupt institution, or oblige other parts of the state apparatus to collaborate. Thus, while the CNLCN issued a great deal of propaganda, prepared detailed studies, and made occasional raids in which small producers were captured, the trade continued virtually as before. Early in April 1981 García Meza was obliged to admit that 140 kilos of a cargo of 150 kilos confiscated in a combined police and military raid had 'mysteriously disappeared' before it was due to be destroyed, but the president denied that the culprits could be identified or that the case indicated 'infiltration within the Armed Forces'.[56] In June the prefecture of Santa Cruz complained that over the previous 15 months none of the cocaine confiscated by the local office of narcotics had been sent as required by law to the Banco Central in La Paz, and the city's attorney announced that of the several hundred people charged with trafficking only 35 had been sent for trial.[57] Some days beforehand the military-appointed prefect had denounced the narcotics police for 'abuses, destruction of property and personal outrages, illegal raids, appropriations of money and goods.'[58] If such a style might be thought necessary in the face of resourceful and well-organised opposition, it produced signally poor results: between September 1981 and January 1982 the DNSP managed to confiscate only 132 kilos of cocaine and detain 130 people, none of them having 'managerial' status inside the industry.[59] Even by March 1982, when the CNLCN was cooperating with the DEA after a fashion, it was still possible for Colonel Angel García Ricaldi to continue in his post having been caught red-handed in command of a convoy of lorries transporting leaf to a processing plant.[60]

The shift to formal cooperation with the DEA was evident over the last months of 1981 and early 1982; it was effectively sealed in June 1982, when the US embassy formally approved the CNLCN's plan to destroy coca plantations within a matter of six months. This realignment followed the fall of García Meza and Arce Gómez and corresponded to the need of the Torrelio government to reach a *rapprochement* with Washington in order to tend to the state of virtual bankruptcy that prevailed in the formal economy. However, inside Bolivia it resolved few problems. On 23 April 1982, the largest anti-cocaine operation ever undertaken in the country was staged with combined military and police units under the direction of the CNLCN mounting raids on small factories and plantations between Santa Cruz and Cochabamba, concentrating particularly on the Yapacaní region around the river Ichilo. Some four tons of cocaine sulphate was captured, the usual assortment of lowly *zepeadores*, planters and attendants taken prisoner, and ninety hectares of coca bushes destroyed. It was an operation designed to impress, and it succeeded, but less because it struck a blow at the 'big fish' than because some two thirds of the area in coca had been destroyed by the use of the powerful herbicide 2-4-D under the direction of a North American expert, Frank Tachierley. The CNLCN's protestations that 2-4-D had been proved scientifically to be safe failed to curb complaints that, like Agent Orange and 2-4-5T, it contained triclofenoxiatic acid and therefore dioxin, an extraordinarily potent poison.[61] The use of such a substance is illegal under Bolivian law, but very possibly it was as much the cost of destruction by 2-4-D, roughly $2,000 a hectare, as popular protest that stopped its use, for the time being. This episode revitalised fears about the US embassy's zealous interest in destroying plantations and with them the livelihood of thousands of peasants. The campaigns on both sides were to escalate over the following year and continue beyond the fall of the dictatorship.

Retrenchment versus Retreat

The decomposition of García Meza's regime that accelerated from the start of 1981 was always underpinned and sometimes directly provoked by the cocaine problem. But it also resulted in no uncertain terms from more familiar factors: working-class resistance, regional discontent, a generalised sentiment of anti-militarism, and seemingly endless downward spiral of the economy.

Having instituted the apparatus for control of the labour movement in its first phase, the regime began late in 1980 to prepare the ground for full negotiations with the IMF, which had continued to monitor the economic crisis and ensure that basic debt repayments were covered or rolled over in an orderly fashion but — aside from more directly political considerations — clearly required evidence of extreme fiscal sobriety if it was going to negotiate new loans. At the same time the government urgently required greater revenue, which meant a reduction of price subsidies and social expenditure. These were the two central objectives of the regime's economic package of 9 January 1981, which did not include the much-feared devaluation but froze all wages, reduced price subsidies on a broad range of commodities, and decreased the state's social security commitment from 50 to 33 per cent with the difference being made up equally by the worker and the employers. Since the ten decrees that comprised this budget increased the price of kerosene, petrol, electricity, bread, milk, sugar and butter it had a severe inflationary impact right at the heart of the popular economy. The immediate rise in the cost of living was over 35 per cent but this was soon increased by the effects of speculation and higher transport costs. The state recouped funds worth approximately $200 million a year but succeeded in pushing local interest rates up to 32 per cent, which greatly antagonised small businesses as well as powerful lobbies like the ANMM, which announced that the costs of production in the private mining sector would rise by $14 million at a time when overall losses were $39 million, the price of tin falling, and the US about to release further buffer stocks.[62] Since the CEPB was controlled by *mecistas* no formal complaint was issued on behalf of private enterprise but the signs of tension were visible and support for the regime in this sector fell off rapidly. The response from the working class was sufficiently strong to confirm the government's apprehension with respect to a devaluation and to emphasise the fact that the COB was still out there and able to gain broad support for a strike call even under the most taxing circumstances. On the 11th the urban sector, including the pro-government transport workers, came out on a 48-hour stoppage; the next day the miners ceased work for the same space of time. Although there was a good deal of localised harassment, the regime desisted from inflicting a new bout of general repression and contented itself with a condemnation of the strike as illegal and subversive in the knowledge that the workers' movement still lacked the economic strength or political resources for extended industrial action.

It was to discuss the results of the strike that the internal leadership of the MIR held a meeting in a house on Calle Harrington, La Paz, on the afternoon of 15 January. Informed of this, Arce staged a raid that was very similar to those of the previous July and involved some two hundred SES agents. The minister later announced that eight members of the party had been killed in an exchange of fire, but word soon got out that the *miristas* had surrendered without resistance, were cruelly tortured *in situ*, and then shot; only the UDP deputy Gloria Ardaya was spared, having been forced to witness the agony of her comrades. At a stroke the MIR lost some of its most talented leaders, including the Siglo XX leader Artemio Camargo, the economist Ramiro Velasco and student leader Gonzalo Barrón. Another that died was José Luis Suárez Guzmán, the son of a prominent retired general who immediately launched a necessarily subdued but extremely potent campaign of protest over the killings. This soon picked up much support since the death of the young politicians had produced a sense of outrage inside the capital's middle class perhaps unparalleled since 1944, when officers belonging to Radepa undertook a similar coolly-prepared liquidation of members of the political elite.[63] Arce remained unrepentant but he had overstepped the mark; the execution of the MIR leaders could not be justified in terms of the state of war that was invoked at the time of the coup, was widely recognised to have been assassination in cold blood, and did nothing to ease tension with the US. Two days later García Meza had a meeting with Banzer at which the issue of Arce's excesses must have been discussed during negotiations over a possible alliance to prop up the isolated regime. No agreement was reached.

A fortnight later Arce turned his attentions to the *Comité Pro-Santa Cruz*, control of which had been wrested from one of his nominees in the struggle to halt the building of a huge new sugar mill at San Buenaventura in the department of La Paz. This was an issue that united the *cruceño* oligarchy, which was already operating its mills well below capacity and resisted the establishment of a new 'pole of development' for agro-industry outside the region to such a degree that even the pro-government leaders of the *Comité* became distinctly vacillating in their defence of the project, surrendering without a great fight to the largely *banzerista* opposition. In an ill-judged administrative move to rectify this situation, Arce announced the establishment of a *Comité Cívica Nacional* (CCN), which would group all the regional civic committees under central government supervision.[64] The Santa Cruz committee immediately declared a 24-hour strike throughout the department in defence of its autonomy and against San Buenaventura. This measure met with widespread support and the tacit approval of the police and garrison—a strong warning to García Meza and a major blow to Arce's prestige and power. The next day the regime dropped its scheme for the CCN. A week later, 18 February, control of the DNSP was transferred to the military, falling into the hands of Arce's opponents, and on the 24th, under considerable domestic and external pressure, García Meza finally fired his minister as well as Colonel Ariel Coca, the education minister who had also been publicly linked to the cocaine trade. A number of sources agree on the story that a few days after being sacked, Arce held a meeting with leading traffickers in the house of Sonia and Pachi Atalá where he confirmed that they still enjoyed García Meza's support but for reasons of state it had been necessary to make some formal changes, and that henceforth they should shift their operations away from Cochabamba and Santa Cruz to the Beni in order to facilitate greater security against unavoidable anti-cocaine operations.[65] Arce still retained effective control of the SES and remained in power behind the throne, but his removal from office marked the first step in the regime's progressive loss of authority. Santa Cruz now became the major centre of opposition, a fact that was reflected in the appointment of no less than eleven commanders to its garrison in the space of 15 months.

Arce's fall from office opened a period of rapid political manoeuvre and extreme confusion inside the ruling class. In the first instance this focussed on Banzer, who days after the cabinet change failed to challenge the acceptance of senior government posts by ADN members

Mario Rolán Anaya and Jorge Tamayo Ramos as part of an apparent deal for the removal of Arce. A week later Alberto Violand, a leading *banzerista*, replaced the government's Marcelo Pérez as head of the CEPB. Yet Banzer desisted from offering open support, and on 6 March flew to Washington for what was considered to be a crucial exchange of views with the new Reagan administration. That day Arce was appointed to be director of the Colegio Militar. On the 16th Banzer returned to declare that the military ought to consider undertaking political reforms to prepare the way to elections, thereby signalling the need to make further changes before Washington would countenance reopening relations and that he himself would keep his distance from the regime. The next day the cadets of the Colegio took over their institution and declared themselves in rebellion, their principal demand being the removal of Arce. This move was partly prompted by the damage done to the *amour propre* of the cadets by Arce's use of the academy to train his paramilitary squads, but it soon became clear that the main reason was his connection with cocaine, which had been made a burning issue for the officer corps as a result of the distribution throughout the country's garrisons of an inordinately large number of video cassettes of the 'Sixty Minutes' programme. Many officers were obviously unmoved by Colonel Salomón's charge that producer Mike Wallace was 'on the payroll of the Soviet Bloc and the international left', and it must have been particularly galling for young men in the midst of a relentless process of indoctrination and lacking experience of the outside world to witness their commander being accused before the world of flagrantly transgressing for personal ends the moral code in which they were being so sternly tutored. Although a number of retired officers voiced their support for the rising and Doria Medina pointedly refused Arce's request that he turn the Tarapacá on the cadets, the rebellion appeared not to have been carefully planned and lacked a sufficiently focussed political dimension to spread. Isolated in suburban Irpavi, the cadets were obliged to relent, and the entire senior year of *brigadieres* was cashiered. García Meza's regime had not been greatly endangered but the sight of a complete generation of future officers being sacked for defending the honour of their academy did not please the institution as a whole, obliging Meza to remove Arce once again and send him on a 'study trip' to Taiwan until tempers cooled.

Despite the fact that the cadets' rebellion was primarily an institutional affair, the government held Banzer responsible, and for the first time encouraged political attacks on the ex-president by its supporters. On 27 March the ADN responded by pulling its members out of CONAL and threatening a complete break. As a result, García Meza travelled to Santa Cruz to negotiate again with Banzer but without success. On 13 April the ADN formally withdrew all support from the regime and broke with Rolón Anaya and Tamayo, who preferred to remain comfortably ensconced in high office. On the 19th both Banzer and Natusch were placed under house arrest for allegedly planning a coup. The regime was now at loggerheads with both the acknowledged leader of 'nationalism' and an officer who still enjoyed considerable support and respect inside the armed forces as a result of his conduct in November 1979, which was viewed as a viable and honourable exercise that went wrong for reasons beyond his control.

The next challenge to the regime was not slow to emerge, but it came from an unexpected quarter and took a rather bizarre form. Early on 2 May Carlos Valverde and an FSB 'guerrilla' occupied the Tita oil refinery outside Santa Cruz and threatened to blow it up if García Meza did not resign within 48 hours because he 'only pretends to fight the traffic in drugs in order to cover up the country's grave economic and political problems and to achieve North American recognition'.[66] Although the FSB had played a prominent part in the process of destabilisation leading up to the 1980 coup, it had not won many favours thereafter and was without doubt influenced by the shift in the balance of forces in Santa Cruz. Within a week of García Meza's failure to reach agreement with Banzer the falangists had read the situation sufficiently astutely to demand the establishment of a constituent assembly. This was scarcely consistent with the party's past record and, in view of the 'adoption of the armed struggle' less than a month later, clearly intended only as a ceremonial challenge. Once Valverde, seasoned in holiday guerrillaism, had achieved his primary objective, there ensued something of an *opera bouffe* with the prefect of Santa Cruz, Valverde's old ally Oscar Román Vaca, denouncing the occupation as 'a cowardly act undertaken by a schizophrenic terrorist who without doubt believes that he is Robin Hood'. For his part, García Meza replied to the charges against him by claiming that Valverde was funded 'with money that could belong to five fugitives from justice, accused of the crime of *narcotráfico*'.[67] The episode took a less comic turn when the eighth division was ordered to repossess the refinery under the command of Colonel Gary Prado, to whom García Meza had in desperation given this key post despite his *institucionalista* ties in an effort to mollify the city's elite, of which the Prado family was a firm member, and a restless garrison, in need of a prestigious leader to keep it in line. Prado's troops retook Tita without resistance, but while their commander was in discussion with Valverde a shot was 'accidentally' fired by one of the colonel's subordinates, gravely wounding him in the spine.[68] Prado was immediately transferred to a hospital in the city but both his family and the US embassy, suspecting foul play and fearing a further attempt to settle old scores in the manner of the Selich, Zenteno and Torres killings, succeeded in obliging the reluctant regime to release the wounded officer into the care of the USAF, which had a plane standing by to take him to the Walter Reed military hospital. Matters had come to such a pass that the embassy had to threaten further delays in re-establishing diplomatic relations before the invalid officer was allowed free. Prado's absence took a major challenger out of the field, but he made a very speedy recovery and although permanently paralysed, refused, like his counterpart Genaro Flores, to let a disability impede his activity, returning to retrieve his command after the fall of the military government as a kind of Andean Millán Astray.

By mid-May allegations of incompetence, malfeasance and sundry other illegal practices against the junta extended well beyond the cocaine question and contributed to a general air of corruption at the top. At one extreme Foreign Minister Rolón Anaya was implicated in an affair by which $87,000 was drawn from the Banco Central in order to buy from East Germany a glass model of a cow for the university in Trinidad, which had not requested such a teaching aid and presumably received no part of the very substantial 'commission' clearly incorporated into the price.[69] More importantly, the terms of the purchase of wheat from Argentina transpired to be a good deal less generous than those publicised shortly after the coup. At the end of September 1980 the purchase price of an order of 235,000 tons was revealed to be $275 per ton, $55 dearer than originally agreed and $107 per ton more expensive than (admittedly inferior) Bolivian wheat. Moreover, the contract gave full rights of transport to an Argentine shipping firm, which lethargically moved the cargo by sea to the Chilean port of Antofagasta, where Bolivia possessed insufficient storage facilities for such a huge quantity. The result was that when it finally arrived at La Paz, the shipment was found to contain millions of toadstools and was largely unusable.[70] Early in 1981 the junta authorised another contract with an Argentine firm (Nidera Handels Co., by decree 18233) for the purchase of 80,000 tons of low quality wheat at a total price of $26,817,000, or $335 per ton. This was considerably higher than the market rate of $260 for a ton of 'Hard Winter 2', a superior grain that is almost always used for human consumption. The commission on this transaction was alleged to be $6 million.[71] However, the most damaging political scandal was caused by the revelation on 6 May 1981 by the Santa Cruz daily *El Deber* that on 8 October 1980 the junta had signed a 'private document' with a firm known as 'Rumy Ltd.' for the exploitation of semi-precious stones in the region of La Gaiba, on the border with Brazil. By the terms of this confidential contract the three members of the junta — García Meza, Bernal, Terrazas — would receive fifty per cent of all sales.[72] Such a deal was, of course, illegal on a score of counts and particularly infuriated elements of the officer corps because the land being prospected belonged to COFADENA. A number of half-hearted disclaimers were issued but *El Deber*'s information was too precise for the generals to escape the backlash, the incident giving rise to a popular joke that the old Inca catechism of '*Ama Kella, Ama Llulla, Ama Sua*' (Do not be lazy, Do not lie, Do not steal) had mutated into '*Ama Coca, Ama Tista, Ama Iami*' (Love Coca, Amethyst, To Miami).

The La Gaiba affair was invoked by the author of the next rebellion against the regime, Lieutenant Colonel Emilio Lanza, commander of CITE. Five days after the contract was publicised Lanza stormed out of a meeting of senior officers of the Cochabamba garrison at which he had angrily demanded action against García Meza, and led his troops into the city. There was a momentary crisis but Colonel Turdera, the firm loyalist who commanded the seventh division, managed to overwhelm the CITE and force Lanza into hiding. However, in Santa Cruz units of the eighth division prevented the SES from apprehending Banzer, and while Lanza had broken the elementary ground rules of *golpismo* by launching a rising without any semblance of prior conspiracy, it was plain that matters were coming to a head. The next day Natusch was arrested and exiled to Peru and Banzer flew off to Buenos Aires. At the same time the MIR, judging the moment to be propitious for a major political initiative, broke definitively with its old anti-militarism in calling for a movement of 'national convergence' that would contain both military and civilian members and be dedicated exclusively to the overthrow of García Meza, with the strong implication that this would be achieved by a coup d'etat.[73] This proposition caused an outcry amongst the left in general and the UDP in particular, Siles joining the PCB in expressing incredulity.[74] Nonetheless, Jaime Paz Zamora and his aides steadfastly defended their position that what was occurring was not an internecine feud between *gorilas* but an entire transformation of the military mentality as a result of recent experiences, and that this mentality provided the basis for an enduring collaboration with the popular forces.[75] The leadership of the MIR had moved a long way from the basic beliefs of 1971, and this was to cause appreciable discontent amongst sectors of the rank and file, many of whom were too young to appreciate the sobering effects of a decade of opposition upon a generation of highly educated middle-class radicals who saw themselves as the new MNR and were in near-despair over the lack of opportunity to prove it.

Although the MIR proposal represented a significant tactical shift by the social democratic current, it had little or no immediate influence upon activity in the military sphere which now began to career completely out of control. Exactly a fortnight after his abortive *levantamiento* the ebullient Lanza, who had been dodging the SES and the intelligence section of his own division, succeeded in entering CITE's barracks and persuading his colleagues to attempt another rising. Again the paratroopers invested the city and again they were dislodged after a few hours, this time with Lanza being captured and exiled without delay. The second insurrection seemed to be a thoroughly lunatic move, but it succeeded in forcing Meza to cede critical ground to officers who did not belong to his clique, opposed Arce, and sought a major reversal of domestic and international policy. On 26 May, the day after Lanza's second rebellion, General Humberto Cayoja Riart and Colonel Lucio Añez Rivera, a supporter of Natusch associated with the *Karachipampas*, were installed as commander and chief of staff of the army. Bernal, who was now obviously fostering his own ambitions and taking advantage of Arce's absence to distance himself from García Meza, managed to retain control of the FAB, but on 28 May the navy called for the removal of the president, and on the 29th forced the resignation of Terrazas in favour of Captain Oscar Pammo.

The Cayoja-Añez faction did not stand on ceremony; at the same time as Banzer pronounced that García Meza was alone responsible for La Gaiba the new high command went into a conclave to discuss the question of the presidency, which formally required institutional ratification before independence day, 6 August. The result of this meeting on 5 June was 14 votes for García Meza's resignation, 2 against, and 2 abstentions. The president then formally announced that he would be standing down, leaving the high command to designate his successor.[76] A major breakthrough appeared to have been made, but it was far from irreversible since Meza still retained the support of a powerful group of field commanders who did not sit on the high command, the cocaine clans, and the paramilitary apparatus. Matters were made more critical by the declaration of the IMF on 16 June that it would not embark upon negotiations until the succession issue had been fully resolved; the State Department took the same position. On 21 June Añez and a group of senior staff officers made an apparently routine visit to Panama at the invitation of Torrijos, but it was anticipated that they would call at the headquarters of US Southern Command in the Canal Zone. Since Paz Zamora was at the time living in Panama City it was rumoured that the MIR proposal had finally attracted military interest and that discussions over an alliance were underway. This was fervently denied on both sides, and since Paz quickly left the country it seems most likely that Añez was simply concerned to iron out details with the Pentagon. All the same, on his return to La Paz the chief of staff confirmed that the military would preside over a 'national agreement' between workers, employers, and 'political parties which are not financed from abroad'; he also called for a 'real democracy', in which 'we rid ourselves of the leaders who think as if it were thirty years ago. We are with those who live in the realities of 1981 and think of the century which approaches.'[77] Two days later, 27 June, Añez and Cayoja attempted to pre-empt García Meza's mounting counter-attack by staging a coup. Once Doria Medina's tanks had entered the city this seemed to have been successful, but after an hour of uncertainty the bulk of the units pledged to the rising withdrew, their commanders—Doria Medina, Alberto Gribowsky, and Faustino Rico Toro—deciding at the last moment to reconfirm their backing for the president. This extraordinary about-turn which ran against all political logic was only later explained by the publication of a letter sent by García Meza to the new Interior Minister, General Celso Torrelio, requesting him to pay out $2,180,000 to 26 officers as a 'reward for loyalty'. Doria Medina and

Gribowsky were to receive $100,000 each, the more dangerous Rico Toro being allocated $200,000.[78] Cayoja and Añez were initially to be charged with treason before a court martial, but when the garrisons protested at this, they were sent into exile along with their accomplices in the EMG, Mario Oxa, Rolando Saravia, and Simón Sejas. Once again a bid to oust Meza had failed, this time in the face of a volley of dollars. The president's survival had entailed the expulsion of almost all of Banzer's and Natusch's most powerful allies as well as the *Karachipampas*, and although these figures might fulminate against the regime and their turncoat colleagues from exile, the command of the armed forces was now controlled by men who had no clear option other than stick with Meza until the end.

On 10 July the embattled president sought to consolidate his position by holding a mass rally in La Paz. This was a typical affair, attended by some 10,000 public employees 'invited' by their superiors to show up during working hours, 'nationalist' peasant groups, and a lumpen periphery marshalled by SES agents, who, instructed that this was an opportunity for them as well as García Meza to prorogue, led chants of 'Stay', 'Now or Never', and 'Make up your mind'. Some peasant leaders even threatened to blockade the roads until the president was ratified. García Meza, passive and smiling, desisted from making a long speech, declaring, 'Fine. Since you have already decided I will stay and that's that.'[79] This engaging piece of repertory by 'the crocodile' fooled nobody. Meza himself announced that the country was 'in a state of civil war', faced a further 24-hour strike by Santa Cruz, another in Huanuni in demand for the restitution of union rights, and was told by CONAL that it had no powers to reform the constitution or establish the bases for a new one, thereby effectively declaring itself redundant. Having already used his powers under the agrarian reform to donate his wife 6,592 hectares of prime land in Santa Cruz, the president took the prescient move of signing an unpublished decree that increased the pension of ex-presidents to Bs.50,000 ($2,000) a month for life.[80]

Early in the morning of 27 July the population of La Paz was awakened by the sound of a squadron of GAC fighters roaring up the valley from Calacoto and Obrajes towards the city, machine-gunning the barracks and presidential residence at San Jorge. This, it seemed, would be the final move, fought out in earnest. But it was yet another bluff, the ammunition blank, and the intention simply to intimidate and confuse. The airforce high command later announced that it was an ordinary exercise, but such manoeuvres are always preceeded by public warnings. As if it were possible, confusion and tension increased further still. Bolivia appeared to have lost all semblance of government, the effective apparatus of the state being reduced to the SES, which patrolled the streets while the economy slowed to a halt and the military tore itself apart.

The war of nerves finally broke early on 3 August, when the Rangers and the eighth division took control of Santa Cruz without resistance, in a manner that suggested careful planning, and with fulsome local support. At 7.30 a.m. the city's radios announced that Generals Natusch and Añez were the leaders of the '*Movimiento de Dignidad Nacional*', which demanded the immediate removal of Meza, restitution of democratic rights, an authentic campaign against cocaine, reincorporation of all officers purged since July 1980, and the military election of a new president pending fresh general elections. Within a matter of hours the rebellion received the support of the major garrisons in the eastern departments as well as those of Potosí and Tarija. The naval base at Tiquina also backed the rising and a unit of naval commandos temporarily put the power station serving loyalist Cochabamba out of action. Ex-presidents Luis Adolfo Siles and Hugo Banzer broadcast in support of the rebels, the MIR also lent its backing although this was less open and denied by the rebel leaders. Gonzalo Guzmán, a *mirista* in the leadership of the COB, issued a strike call that was implicitly in support of the coup, but this was replaced in a short space of time by a new document backed by the entire union leadership which made it clear that the call for a general strike was independent of any military faction and directed towards obtaining fundamental liberties; the strike was to be indefinite. The day ended with battle lines drawn. On the 4th the main mines ceased to work and the large factories followed suit. A delegation of senior officers was sent to Santa Cruz to parley but got nowhere. Later several plane-loads of troops were ordered to make a surprise attack on the rebels but simply changed sides upon landing. At midday García Meza was informed that six of the country's nine garrisons required his resignation; at 7 p.m. he handed power over to the junta, now comprising Bernal, Pammo and Torrelio, the new army commander. His final words: 'General García Meza is no coward and everyone knows that, but before pride, before vanity there is the Patria, and for this reason I have decided to give up the presidency . . .'.[81]

The final ousting of Meza was a major achievement, but it did not satisfy the rebels. They wanted a completely new line-up at the top and were accumulating a powerful force of some 4,000 men to impose it. On the other hand, the removal of the president assuaged many neutral unit commanders who were deeply concerned at preparations for outright conflict that were more advanced than at any time since 1952. Añez and Natusch, outwitted before, remained implacable while the SES and hardliners refused to allow the vacillating commanders to give way. Over the next two days the general strike took root, fuel supplies to La Paz were cut off, and the city's markets and shops were emptied of foodstuffs. The Bolivian armed forces had driven themselves into a stalemate; two armies faced each other, both with their own lines of command, claims to office, and sources of political support. There was minimal movement and an eery silence in the streets of La Paz; no popular insurrection was in the offing, but the masses were waiting in the wings.

This deadlock was broken not by force of arms but through the 'good services' of the military's erstwhile ally and the only national institution bar the COB to have retained a degree of unity and organisation over the previous year: the Church. On the 6th Monsegnor Genaro Prata embarked upon the task of cajoling the two sides into fraternity. Yet, the eventual collapse of the revolt on the 8th was due less to ecclesiastical diplomacy than to the fact that once it had enticed Natusch into talks in La Paz he gave up his cause almost immediately and for no apparent reason other than the junta's agreement to reincorporate all those who had previously lost their posts. Rumours of yet another lucrative offer abounded, Añez denounced his colleague and refused to ratify the accord, but Natusch's announcement that the 'natural chain of command' had been re-established took the wind out of the rebels' sails, and after nine days they reluctantly gave way. The maverick turncoat declared that he had retired from the army and retreated to his hacienda, the Santa Cruz force was disbanded to await reappointment, and the junta was confirmed in office, the ungainly Torrelio falling over as he entered the cathedral for a celebratory *Te Deum*.

The appointment of the junta solved nothing. Neither Washington nor the IMF would recognise it, stating that it represented no change from the previous regime and was incapable of establishing a stable government. García Meza stayed put in the presidential residence with the excuse that he couldn't find suitable alternative accommodation. Arce and Rico Toro menaced the commanders from the right, the *cruceño* rebels continued to agitate for change, and Banzer refused to cooperate. The killing of a PCB union leader in Siglo XX by the SES provoked a five-day strike that was allowed to run its course and further increased the confidence of the labour movement. The only tangible act of government undertaken by the junta members was to declare that each of them was president individually as well as collectively, a proclamation that appeared to have more to do with their sponsor's revised retirement plans than any fine constitutional issue. Buying off Natusch had brought precious little relief. On 29 August, three weeks after the junta had come to power, most of the military members of CONAL issued a statement calling for a single president and then resigned. This demand was repeated by the garrisons, which by now had been brought to the understanding that US recognition was central to the resolution of the extended crisis. Once again the question of power had to be confronted, but after the traumas of the beginning of the month before there was a discernible effort to act with celerity. This time rivalry took the form of inter-service claims, with Bernal making a strong bid on behalf of the FAB and himself, and then, when this option was vetoed by the army, proposing the now retired Julio Sanjinés Goitia as a respectable figure with strong US connections. However, the García Meza clan put all its weight behind Torrelio, who was the least able of the trio running the country but, unlike his colleagues, not connected with any major scandal, and, having been promoted twice within the space of a year, the most beholden to the old regime for his newfound status.

The Torrelio government was not unlike the man: it wanted to be one thing but found itself constantly obliged to be another. Throughout its ten month existence the leading figures of the administration were drawn overwhelmingly from García Meza's supporters, although once Banzer offered his measured support the quality—if not the politics—of its senior staff improved somewhat. In a sense the regime was the least offensive that the authors of the 1980 coup could put together to protect their flanks in retreat, but it was still resolutely *continuista*. García Meza and Arce Gómez adopted a lower profile, their places being taken by Rico Toro and Lea Plaza, who, along with the new Interior Minister Colonel Rómulo Mercado, were said to constitute the leadership of a shadowy military lodge known as 'The Black

Eagles'. The SES was formally abolished but in practice simply underwent a change of name, becoming the *Dirección de Inteligencia del
Estado* (DIE). As we have seen from the experience of Filemón Escóbar,
there was no notable refinement of its activities. Indeed, since open
military conflict had already been taken as far as possible outside of
the complete rupture of the institution the DIE's role in controlling the
institucionalista current took on greater importance. In October it
kidnapped Añez's daughter and arrested Oxa; in November an attempt
was made on the life of General Aguila Terán; in February 1982 the
homes of both Añez and Padilla, who had assumed the role of senior
military spokesman for a return to sobriety and the barracks, were
badly damaged in bomb attacks; and as late as March, when the
government had already declared that elections would be held and
then brought them forward from 1984 to 1983, sorties by DIE agents
forced Generals Terrazas and Padilla to go underground. Such activity constituted a permanent reminder that whatever good intentions
were voiced by the regime the Arce apparatus remained intact. Torrelio's administration may well have been the least offensive the likes
of García Meza could put together, but that still made it deeply repugnant to the vast majority of the population.

Yet it was politically impossible for the new government to avoid some
kind of gesture towards an *apertura*. While its military leaders were
deeply suspicious of this and clung at every opportunity to retrenchment, the members of the ADN and MNR drafted into the cabinet perceived that the regime's fragility lay in its immobility and urged a
speedy truce with Washington. Thus, the government found it
acceptable to describe itself as transitional. Once this was clear, both
the US and the major European states, aware that prolonging isolation
would be highly dangerous, finally granted recognition. A new British
ambassador presented his credentials early in October, to be followed a
month later by Edwin Corr, a specialist in drug control operations
drafted in from the US embassy in Lima. This gave the regime a modicum of stability but also enabled groups like the CEPB to voice more
openly their demands for demilitarisation.

At every stage the Torrelio government had to be forced to yield
ground. Its block on reform, refusal to grant even a limited amnesty,
maintenance of troops in the mines, and strict regulation of the curfew were initially considered outside the field of negotiation. This had
the effect of shifting the axis of conflict away from the military sphere

and back to more familiar encounters with the working class, which, between November 1981 and February 1982 broke the back of the labour policy introduced in July 1980 in a series of uneven but largely successful strikes and mobilisations. Huanuni played the vanguard role in this, coming out on strike on 12 November for the right to independent unions, increased wages and an amnesty. After several days of uncertainty the regime decided to take a hard line and had the camp occupied on the 18th. This only succeeded in provoking solidarity stoppages in the other mines as well as sparking off a hunger strike staged by women in La Paz. Faced with a scenario that was very akin to that which had driven Banzer into retreat, the government opted for negotiations on the 24th. However, it still could not overcome its basic instincts, and by 12 December no agreement had been reached on any of the issues at stake. On the 17th Huanuni returned to its strike and once again this spread through the industrial sector. By this stage more than 1,000 people were on hunger strike. Two days later Torrelio gave way, agreeing to recognise independent plant unions within three months and promising to legalise the COB within a year. These concessions were strenuously opposed by the hardliners, but once they had managed to veto the amnesty Torrelio was allowed some more time at the top.

The bemused general also had to face the economic crisis since he had officially given himself two years in power and something patently had to be done. After 18 months of the IMF's boycott, carefree military spending, incompetent and corrupt financial management, the foreign debt crisis had acquired unprecedented proportions. By the end of 1981 the Banco Central had only $1 million of disposable reserves in its vaults. Furthermore, over the previous year the price of tin had fallen by over 18 per cent and Comibol's deficit stood at $313.5 million. Technically the Bolivian economy was bankrupt, in practice its current account was kept marginally afloat by revenues from cocaine, but the legal economy had been driven into a process of contraction from its previous parlous state. In 1980 the overall growth figure was 0.9 per cent compared with 2.0 per cent in 1979; this figure represented a reduction of the country's per capita GDP of 1.8 per cent.[82] Having been frightened by the pre-Christmas strikes, the regime decided to graduate its treatment, first further reducing subsidies, readjusting prices and taxes (5 February) and then moving (23 March) to release the peso from its fixed exchange rate of 44 to the dollar to float to its 'natural level'.[83] There was no simultaneous wage freeze but this was academic since once free-market transactions were officially permitted (there was already a flourishing 'parallel market' centred on the Avenida Camacho in La Paz) inflation soared out of reach. Within six months the peso had reached 400 to the dollar, speculation was rife, basic commodities scarce, and inflation agreed by senior bank officials to be well over 300 per cent. On the occasion of both stages of this deregulation of the economy the COB staged 48-hour general strikes which received full backing at national level. Neither had any impact on government policy, but they confirmed and encouraged union reorganisation as well as expressing popular anger at the state of the economy. Six union demonstrators were shot dead in Cochabamba at the end of March in a sharp warning of the risks involved in this, but the regime was obliged to permit a May Day march. This was attended by 40,000 people and was viewed as a landmark in the restoration of the COB's position even if the military could not bring itself to make formal recognition of this. Union and political leaders began to return to the country but took care to conduct their activities with great caution. Autonomy was restored in the universities after a bitter struggle by the students, but again the paramilitary groups continued to be vigilant and often intervened in campus affairs. As late as mid-May Torrelio failed to get permission from the high command to grant an amnesty, but over the following month pressure built up from below to such an extent that it had to be conceded. The resignation of the director of the Banco Central—due, he said, to being forced to pay García Meza $50,000 at Bs.25 to the dollar for expenses on a trip to Taiwan—steady harrying from Washington, and disturbing incidents such as the appearance of an advertisement in *Presencia* on behalf of a previously unknown company, 'Para Mi Ltd.' listing 163 'debtors' who should pay off the sums they owed to the central office in Buenos Aires, combined to convince the high command that it would have to accelerate the pace of withdrawal whilst it still possessed some control over it.

This provoked the final show-down with the *mecista* bloc. In mid-July Rico Toro made an open bid to replace Torrelio by declaring that the president no longer enjoyed the confidence of the armed forces whereas he did. This last-ditch challenge was conducted with extraordinary bravado and plunged the military into another sharp crisis, but it came too late both for the delinquent right and the desperately ambitious Rico Toro. Agreeing that Torrelio had indeed nothing left to offer, the generals decided both to replace him and marginalise Rico Toro. They chose the chief of operations at the time of the 1980 coup, General Guido Vildoso Calderón, who assumed the presidency on 21 July. Although no less connected with the previous regime than Torrelio, Vildoso was a soft-spoken and smiling officer who had no need to prove his conservative credentials — as evidenced by the fact that the first visitor to the Quemado was Klaus Barbie — but possessed the skill and temperament to oversee the completion of the *apertura*.

His brief upon taking office was to direct the process of withdrawal up to the elections of mid-1983, but such an objective was soon made untenable by a renewed phase of popular mobilisation, which now took the form of a struggle for immediate restitution of democratic rule. All the political parties from the FSB to the PS-1 were agreed upon the necessity of a return to parliamentarianism, but there existed critical differences of opinion with respect to the pace and form that this should take. The right, perceiving the necessity of accepting the UDP administration as well as the advantages of its congressional majority and a quick solution, argued for a simple assumption of office by the legislature elected in June 1980. The MIR also backed this proposal, declaring that speed was of the essence and that the UDP could do nothing less than assume its existing mandate. However, the rest of the UDP remained suspicious both of the machinations of the right and the goodwill of the Vildoso regime, preferring to back a new poll later in 1982 which, it expected, would gain the front a clear parliamentary majority as well as presidential power. This also became the COB's policy, derived largely from discussion at the FSTMB's nineteenth congress at Huanuni, where the PCB demonstrated its traditional organisational prowess but once again antagonised independent delegates with its overbearing behaviour although it held back from pursuing a resolutely pro-UDP line, partly because of the experience of Telamayu and partly because the UDP was itself split over tactics.

In the event, popular impatience decided the issue in favour of an immediate hand-over to the 1980 congress. Siles managed this situation with great tactical skill. Holding court in Lima, he issued frequent communiqués in denunciation of the regime's lack of good faith, and persistently rejected the MIR's pleas that he return to La Paz, first on the

Above, from left to right The 1980 Junta: Waldo Bernal, Luis García Meza and Ramiro Terrazas. *Below* Colonel Luis Arce Gómez with Juan Lechín and Simón Reyes, November 1980

16·11·80 D

dirigent... ...ndicales, d... ...na conferencia de prensa ... ...mintieron las ver-

Above The junta of August 1981 (from left to right); Celso Torrelio, Waldo Bernal and Oscar Pammo. *Below right* President for the third time: Hernán Siles Zuazo, October 1982. *Below left* Genaro Flores

grounds that he had no guarantees for his personal safety and then, when these were offered, because the regime could not control the paramilitary forces, which would lose no opportunity to kill him. This waiting game soon became the main item of political news, overshadowing the high command's frequent meetings to decide what course of action it should follow. Combined with the gravity of the economic situation, which provoked a string of transport strikes and wildcat stoppages in almost every sector, pressure for an immediate military withdrawal became irresistible. In the first week of September students blocked the streets of La Paz on every day, isolated paramilitary personnel were attacked — and on one occasion nearly lynched in the manner of Villarroel — the riot police cowed into allowing demonstrators to enter the Plaza Murillo to chant insults against the armed forces, and military vehicles commandeered and burnt. On 7 September the MIR held its own 'hunger march', attracting a crowd of tens of thousands, some of whom went on to attack public buildings. A week later the COB, now persuaded that the reinstatement of the 1980 congress was the most viable way forward, called a mass march for the 17th to be followed by a general strike until the army handed over power. The march was impressive even by the COB's standards of mass mobilisation; it congregated some 100,000 people in a potent protest that echoed off the walls of the capital for six hours, drove the paramilitary squads from the streets, and combined an effusion of anger pent up for over two years with vociferous demands for wholesale social change. Lechín, pleading illness, did not speak, the greatest applause being given to Genaro Flores and Filemón Escóbar, who was simply a delegate from Siglo XX but, in line with his position that the UDP should be made at all costs to govern to force its contradictions into the open, had pushed harder than many leaders of the front itself for its entry into government.

If there had ever been any lingering doubts in the minds of the generals the COB march and strike call dispelled them. Later that day congress was formally convoked for 5 October. At 8.25 p.m. on the 5th parliament provided the exchange of power with legal force by voting overwhelmingly that Siles and Paz Zamora be installed as president and vice-president. The inauguration took place on the 10th in the presence of a multitude of foreign dignitaries and with the crowds in the Plaza Murillo keeping up a constant barrage of insults against the troops participating in the ceremony; Siles had to implore them to 'be kind' to Vildoso, who had conducted the hand-over with unusual grace while his colleagues hurriedly cleared their desks — in some cases completely, and with good reason — and made for home. Another cycle in the process begun thirty years before had been turned; the man who addressed the crowds from the Palacio Quemado in the afternoon of 10 October 1982 was the same one who had done so in the morning of 11 April 1952. This gave the event a strong historical aura that its participants celebrated to the full, but history is neither rectilinear nor symmetrical, her appearance being as deceitful as it is deceptive. Democracy had triumphed but was known to have feet of clay, the armed forces had withdrawn but remained intact, the *narcotráficantes* were vilified by all and sundry but continued to ply their trade unhampered, the people celebrated the recuperation of their rights and liberties but now needed to use them to overcome their poverty, the US promised support and encouragement but was engaged in an escalating global campaign against the Soviet Union in particular and the left in general that would permit no deviation from the capitalist path, and a strictly administered capitalist path at that. The celebrations of the end of an era were, in fact, festivities to mark the opening of a new phase of a familiar contest, the terms of which had become more not less critical.

Afterword

The first six months of the Siles administration brought few surprises. Those that there were consisted, for the most part, in skimming off the scum that had settled on Bolivia over the previous years, attracting much attention in Europe, whence these criminal elements originated. On the day of the hand-over agents of the CIA/DEA and the Italian secret police shot and gravely wounded Pier Luigi Pagliai, a mercenary employed by Arce and who was wanted for terrorist crimes in Italy. After much confusion that entailed an Alitalia DC-10 supposedly suffering from engine trouble hopping between La Paz and Santa Cruz, Edwin Corr stumped up to El Alto with the $11,000 required by the airport authorities to allow the plane and its mortally wounded passenger to leave the country. Some weeks later the Interior Minister, Mario Roncal, staged his own deft security operation, arresting Barbie for a minor case of debt and then, when the matter seemed resolved, complying with the Mitterrand government's extradition request by smuggling the prisoner out of the country on a special TAM flight to Cayenne, Guyane, whence the former Gestapo chief flew into the limelight. The affair brought some peripheral attention to the plight of the country but media interest centred on Barbie's initial victims (who were undeniably greater in number) and his post-war collaboration with the US secret service. Siles's subsequent visit to Paris was the occasion of much mutual congratulation but raised little economic aid, with a goodly proportion of that which was forthcoming being allocated for the completion of the military hospital.

Command of the military was taken over by the portly Simón Sejas who, assisted by Añez, Prado, Arsenio González and other *institucionalistas*, made a number of limited but emphatic moves against the old cabal. García Meza, Arce, and Freddy Quiroga all slipped across the border into Argentina, where they were given political asylum and told to keep out of sight. This, however, did not impede Arce from intervening in press conferences with his habitual candour. The object of one assassination attempt, he was soon an acute embarrassment to his hosts, who were requested by both Bolivia and the US to hand him over to face a multitude of criminal and civil charges. Other figures—Lea Plaza, Rico Toro, Salomón—attempted to put up some form of legal defence but were rapidly discharged along with some thirty officers implicated in the cocaine trade. On the other hand, anti-cocaine operations languished as before, the civilian government lacking the financial resources or political will to put its fighting talk into actions. Confronted with popular opposition to US schemes for the destruction of the *cocales*, it stalled on the issue and failed to produce any alternative.

On the economic front the UDP's call for 'a hundred days of sacrifice' yielded few positive results aside from the cancellation of the costly US soap opera 'Dallas'. The administration relied too heavily on popular goodwill to fritter everything away in a hasty devaluation. The MIR, which had inherited the key ministry of finance, leant on the skills of the talented economists in its periphery to undertake a 'dedollarisation' of the economy and restore fixed exchange rates. This introduced an element of order into the crisis but was quite insufficient as a basis for lasting recovery; the parallel free market in the dollar continued to flourish, inflation surpassed the 500 per cent mark, and ritual speculation and scarcity returned to the markets. Negotiations with the IMF were protracted and unrewarding. The economic state of the country had become even worse than that in 1956 but the same remedies could not be applied without the risk of destroying the entire democratic experiment.

The tensions inside the UDP that had been visible since its inception broke into the open within twelve weeks, the MIR quitting the government in January because, it alleged, there was insufficient persecution of the paramilitary and Siles was being controlled by a 'palace clique' of the MNRI. Others responded that the party was simply seeking to expand its six seats in the cabinet, which were now filled by independents, many of whom had served under Torres. The MIR's boisterous and ill-considered departure lost it much public support and left Jaime Paz Zamora in the anomalous position of being vice-president in a government no longer supported by his party, which sided increasingly with the right in congress to impeach a number of MNRI ministers. The MNRI itself split into at least three identifiable factions, gravely weakening the presidency and depriving it of all possibility of taking its hazy programme through parliament. Equally, the position of the UDP's third main member, the PCB, was put in extreme jeopardy when, in April 1983, a strike by Comibol's administrative staff prompted the FSTMB to take direct control of the nationalised mining sector against the wishes of the PCB-controlled ministries of mines and labour. In the extended sparring that followed the party found itself badly divided with many union militants, such as Simón Reyes, obliged to take up positions as union-appointed worker directors of Comibol. This brought the issue of workers' control to the forefront of political debate, the COB demanding that it be implemented with full powers of veto while Siles, also reliving the exchanges of the 1950s, insisted that there be parity between labour and management. The MIR was reluctant to pronounce on the issue, the MNRI divided over it, the PCB in theory for but in practice against, the military defeaningly silent. In the end, the FSTMB did win a majority on the Comibol board, but at the time of writing it is far from clear whether this would provide the basis for an authentic workers' control or simply signified a further variation of cooptation *in extremis*. Paz and Banzer began to intervene from the sidelines in a manner that was disturbingly familiar. Congress and the political parties in it were looked upon with increasing popular derision, their antics attracting dangerously little interest from the point of view of maintaining the parliamentary system. Outside the mines the issue of workers' control enjoyed broad support but not enthusiastic backing although the COB was now demanding its adoption throughout the economy; political mobilisation remained constrained by the fight for economic survival.

This was most acute in the countryside, where the effects of the freak climatic conditions known as '*El Niño*' brought storms and destructive floods to Santa Cruz and a drought the like of which had not been seen for a century to the *altiplano*. Potosí suffered most heavily, with water having to be shipped in by train and thousands of *campesinos* migrating to La Paz to seek charity, but the economic consequences for highland agriculture as a whole were calamitous. It was not simply that one harvest had been destroyed but that many lands would prove incapable of yielding crops for many years. This natural disaster was a particularly cruel blow both to the population and to the prospects of parliamentary democracy, but the state of its victims and the manner in which their plight was treated by the government underscored the fact that over thirty years some things had not changed at all in Bolivia whatever the institutional provenance or political complexion of its rulers.

We have here been concerned primarily with providing a narrative account of these thirty years, but if any feature of this account is worthy of more extended consideration it would be less that the revolution of 1952 was comprehensively ambushed first by the MNR and then by the military to condemn the country to continued backwardness in a process of combined and uneven development, than that of all the post-World War Two political revolutions which failed to achieve the abolition of capitalism that in Bolivia exhibited the highest degree of proletarian politicisation within a broad Leninist idiom and the most consistent resurgence of mass mobilisation. The country remains one of the weakest links in the over-stressed international capitalist chain both through the abject poverty of its people and through the extreme difficulties in containing their reaction to this. If, for this reason, Bolivia has become a byword for sheer political anarchy in certain circles, it is by the same token the site of high expectations in others. Our contention that neither the UDP administration nor any reformist government can bear the strain for any length of time is, in view of the political trajectory outlined above, far from adventurous. The fear that this will only lead to a reimposition of a brutal military mandate clearly cannot be discounted. But what is certain is that a further alternative — a mass political movement for socialism — has acquired exceptionally strong roots and remains a vital possibility. Nowhere else in Latin America, perhaps the world, can one so readily perceive such an outcome flowing from the process of national liberation. The second Bolivian revolution has already inherited a powerful legacy from the first, but if like its predecessor it begins as a lonely struggle fought out on the heights of the world, it will not be ignored for long.

Notes

Chapter One

1 Detailed descriptions of the events of April 1952 may be found in Luis Peñaloza, *Historia del Movimiento Nacionalista Revolucionario 1941–1952* (La Paz 1963) pp.263 ff.; Hugo Roberts B., *La Revolución del 9 de Abril* (La Paz 1971); General Antonio Seleme Vargas, *Mi Actuación en la Junta Militar de Gobierno con el Pronunciamiento Revolucionario del 9 de Abril de 1952* (La Paz 1969) and in the anniversary edition of *La Nación*, La Paz, 9 April 1962.

2 James W. Wilkie, *The Bolivian Revolution and US Aid since 1952* (Los Angeles 1969) p.29.

3 Asthenio Averanga Mollinedo, *Aspectos Generales de la Población Boliviana (La Paz 1956);* Herbert S. Klein, *Parties and Political Change in Bolivia, 1880–1952* (Cambridge 1969) pp.392–393; CEPAL, *El Desarrollo Económico de Bolivia* (Mexico 1958).

4 For general studies of the tin industry see Walter Gómez, *La Minería en el Desarrollo Económico de Boliva 1900–1970* (La Paz 1978); Sergio Almaraz, *El Poder y la Caida* (La Paz 1966); Juan Albarracín Millán, *El Poder Minero* (La Paz 1972) and Eduardo Arze Cuadros, *La Economía de Bolivia* (La Paz 1979).

5 Laurence Whitehead, *'Desarrollo hacia Afuera—El Caso de Bolivia'* (Mimeo, Oxford 1975). For detailed figures on production, see Peter J. Bakewell, 'Registered Silver Production in Potosi, 1550–1735' *(Jahrbuch für Geschichte von Staat, Wirtschaft und Gesellschaft Lateinamerikas,* 12, 1975); Adolf Soetbeer, *Edelmetallproduktion und Wertverhältnis zwischen Gold und Silber seit der Entdeckung Amerikas bis zur Gegenwart* (Gotha 1879); Pierre Vilar, *A History of Gold and Money, 1450–1920* (London 1976). A concise survey of the colonial period in English is given in Herbert S. Klein, *Bolivia. The Evolution of a Multi-Ethnic Society* (New York 1982). For detailed histories of Potosí, see Bartolomé Arzans de Orsua y Vela, *Historia de la Villa Imperial de Potosí,* ed. Lewis Hanke and Gunnar Mendoza 3 vols (Providence, R.I. 1965) and Luis Capoche, *Relación General de la Villa Imperial de Potosí* (Madrid 1959).

6 The best survey of nineteenth century silver mining is Antonia Mitre, *Los Patriacas de la Plata* (Lima 1981).

7 Charles F. Geddes, *Patiño: The Tin King* (London 1972).

8 Almaraz, *Poder y Caida,* pp.47 ff.

9 Afonso Crespo, *Los Aramayo de Chichas* (Barcelona 1981).

10 Compagnie Aramayo de Mines de Bolivie S.A., *Sinopsis de su Economía en el Ultimo Quinquenio, 1944–1948* (La Paz 1949); *El Caso Aramayo* (La Paz 1969).

11 Kathryn Ross, *Bolivia and the War Effort: An Economic History of 1939–45 in the Context of Allied Tin Procurement Policy* (Unpublished B. Phil, University of Oxford 1977).

12 *Financial Times,* 5 March 1951, quoted in Laurence Whitehead, *The United States and Bolivia. A Case of Neo-Colonialism* (Watlington 1969) p.6.

13 *Report of Joint US-Bolivian Commission of Labour Experts* (La Paz 1943) pp.2 ff.

14 Servicio de Publicidad y Orientación Popular del MNR, *Víctor Paz Estenssoro y la*

Masacre de Catavi (La Paz 1943) p.14; Sindicato Mixto de Catavi, 'Pliego de Peticiones' (15 October 1946), Archive of papers belonging to Fernando Bravo. I am very grateful to Alberto Aguilar Morales for allowing me to consult these papers. These rates are for Patiño mines. Hochschild paid equally low wages whilst Aramayo's were only marginally higher. Gómez estimates that in 1926 labour costs were not greater than 13 per cent of production costs, p.48. Much useful data on the Rosca is given in Ricardo Anaya, *Nacionalización de las Minas de Bolivia* (Cochabamba 1952).

15 *La Calle*, La Paz, 20 April 1944.

16 Luis Mealla Caso, *Consideraciones sobre la Vida de los Obreros Mineros de Bolivia* (Cochabamba 1945).

17 Gumercindo Rivera, *La Masacre de Uncía* (Oruro 1967); Guillermo Lora, *A History of the Bolivian Labour Movement* ed. Laurence Whitehead (Cambridge 1977) pp.216 ff. (This volume is a severely edited translation of Lora's monumental six-volume work *Historia del Movimiento Obrero Boliviano* (La Paz 1966–80), parts of which are now difficult to obtain. When possible, reference will be made to the English edition.) Agustín Barcelli, *Medio Siglo de Luchas Sindicales Revolucionarias en Bolivia* (La Paz 1956) pp.108–111; 161–164; Juan Manuel Bálcazar, *Los Problemas Sociales en Bolivia* (La Paz 1947).

18 Asociacíon Nacional de Mineros Medianos, *Informe Presentado por el Directorio de la ANMM a la Junta General Ordinaria Correspondiente a la Gestión 1947–48* (La Paz 1948) p.39.

19 René López Murillo, *Los Restaurados* (La Paz 1966) p.62.

20 Espy to Washington, No.548, 14 Sept. 1949.

21 Flack to Washington, No.1045, 3 March 1947.

22 Lora, *A History*, pp.246–252.

23 James Kohl, *The Role of the Peasant in the Bolivian Revolutionary Cycle, 1952–1964* (Unpublished Ph.D., University of New Mexico 1969) p.50; William S. Stokes, 'The "Revolución Nacional" and the MNR in Bolivia' (*Inter-American Economic Affairs*, XII, Sept. 1959); David Weeks, 'Land Tenure in Bolivia' (*Journal of Land and Public Utility Economics*, XXV, Jan. 1950).

24 A thesis maintained by William E. Carter, *Aymara Communities and the Bolivian Agrarian Reform* (Gainesville 1964).

25 Kohl, pp.41–42; Amado Canelas, *Mito y Realidad de la Reforma Agraria* (La Paz 1966) p.98.

26 Rafael Reyeros, *El Pongueaje* (La Paz 1949) pp.141–142. An excellent overview of the pre-revolutionary peasantry is given in Andrew Pearse, *The Latin American Peasant* (London 1977) pp.119–162.

27 Cottrell to Washington, No.967, 26 Jan. 1926.

28 Quoted in Jorge Dandler Hanhart, *Local Group, Community and Nation: A Study of Changing Structure in Ucureña, Bolivia, 1935–52* (Unpublished M.A., University of Wisconsin 1967) p.38.

29 *Los Tiempos*, Cochabamba, 23 May 1945.

30 Sociedad Rural Boliviana, *El Ataque Comunista del PIR a la Democracia y a la Agricultura* (La Paz 1949) p.iv.

31 For example, *El Diario* and *La Noche*, La Paz, 5 June 1947.

32 José María Dalence, *Bosquejo Estadístico de Bolivia* (Sucre 1851); *Censo Nacional de Población* (La Paz 1950); *Censo Nacional de Población y Vivienda* (La Paz 1976).

33 Gosling to London, No.21, April 1914, FO 371/1914. In 1928 Ambassador Mitchell reported of President Siles that he was 'both weak and false—his code of honour is far below that of a Chinaman.' FO 371/13466.

34 Bautista Saavedra, *El Ayllu—Proceso Mohoza* (La Paz 1971).

35 Mitchell to London, No.12, 13 Sept. 1927, FO 371/11963.

36 Cottrell to Washington, No.1366, 27 Aug. 1927.

37 Laurence Whitehead, 'El Impacto de la Gran Depresión en Bolivia' (*Desarrollo Económico*, No.45, Vol.12, April-June 1972).

38 The literature on the Chaco War is positively daunting in size and often extremely detailed in character. There is still only one full and dependable study in English, David H. Zook, *The Conduct of the Chaco War* (Gainesville 1960). I have tried to provide a concise and sensitive description in the final chapter of my *Politics of the Bolivian Army; Institutional Development 1879–1935* (Unpublished D.Phil, University of Oxford 1979) pp.216–285. The best overall study from the Bolivian side, although it should be read with a sharp eye for ideological intrusions, is Roberto Querejazu, *Masamaclay* (La Paz 1965). The standard military work is by the Chilean Aquiles Vergara Vicuña, *La Guerra del Chaco* 7 vols (La Paz 1940–44), the corresponding work from the Paraguayan side being Carlos José Fernández, *La Guerra del Chaco* 3 vols (Buenos Aires and Asunción 1956–67). Klein, *Parties*, pp.160–198, gives a vivid sketch but is much more detailed and useful on the post-war regimes, of which his account remains the best.

39 Quoted in Marcos Domic, *Ideología y Mito: Los Orígenes del Fascismo Boliviano* (La Paz 1978) p.201. For the FSB's own vision of its development, see Enrique Achá Alvarez and Mario H. Ramos y Ramos, *Unzaga: Martir de America* (Buenos Aires 1960) and Mario Gutiérrez, *Memorias* (La Paz 1979).

40 *Movimiento Nacionalista Revolucionario* (La Paz 1942). For a survey of the early leadership of the MNR, see Christopher Mitchell, *The Legacy of Populism in Bolivia* (New York 1977).

41 Willard Galbraith, 'Report on Political Parties and Aggroupments in Bolivia', enclosed in Flack to Washington, No.619, 21 Nov. 1946.

42 José Antonio Arze's massive *Sociología Marxista* (Oruro 1963) is representative of his theoretical approach. The original PIR programme is reprinted in *El PIR y Desarrollo Nacional. Soluciones para los Problemas Nacionales* (La Paz 1961).

43 For a close and critical analysis of the early years of the POR by one of its militants, see Guillermo Lora, *Contribución a la Historia Política de Bolivia* Vol.1 (La Paz 1978). The positions of the party in its first phase are given in *Boletín de Información* (La Paz 1939).

44 The Villarroel regime is surveyed from different positions in Augusto Céspedes, *El Presidente Colgado* (Buenos Aires 1975); José Antonio Arze, *Bolivia bajo el Terrorismo Nazifascista* (Lima 1945); Pedro Zilveti Arce, *Bajo el Signo de la Barbarie* (Santiago 1946); René González Torres and Luis Iriarte Ontiveros, *Villarroel y el Atisbo de la Revolución Nacional* (La Paz 1983).

45 For this important episode, see Alfonso Finot, *Así Cayó Villarroel* (La Paz 1966); Germán G. Villamor, *Historia de la Revolución Popular del 21 de Julio de 1946* 2 vols (La Paz 1946). On 25 July the US ambassador sent Washington his 'Diary of a Successful Revolution', describing it as 'a very popular revolution in every sense of the word . . . this may prove to be the first democratic government in Bolivia's history . . . an irreparable blow to the formation of the anti-US bloc so dear to Perón's heart.' Flack, 25 July 1946.

46 The broad political characteristics of this period are ably summarised in Manuel Frontaura Argandona, *La Revolución Boliviana* (La Paz 1974).

47 Dandler, *passim.*; Antonio Mamani Alvarez, 'Llamado a los Indios Bolivianos' ed. James Johl (*Journal of Peasant Studies*, Vol.4, No.4, July 1977).

48 At least eighty officers were purged in the year after the revolution, many maintaining contact with their colleagues from hiding or exile. The strength of feeling of this group can be gleaned from a typical letter sent by a field officer to the new president of the military court: 'You, Bretel, are an imbecile who has grown old in the army

watching your stars and salary increase with great regularity...' Captain Carmelo Cuellar Jimenez, *Dos Anatemas contra la Villanía (Buenos Aires 1948)*. For RADEPA, see Col. Francisco Barrero, *RADEPA y la Revolución Nacional* (La Paz 1976).

49 Peñaloza gives the fullest account of MNR activities during the *sexenio*. Lora, *A History*, and Barcelli outline the principal developments in the labour movement.

Chapter Two

1 *El Diario*, 11 April 1952.

2 *Reflexiones cerca de la Unidad del MNR (La Paz 1955) p.16.*

3 *El Diario*, 16 April 1952.

4 Ibid., 17 April 1952.

5 Lora gives his view on Lechín's background and early activities in *A History*, pp.297–301; Barcelli, *Medio Siglo*, presents a more favourable evaluation.

6 *El Diario*, 20 April 1952.

7 Ibid., 22 Aug. 1952.

8 Central Obrera Boliviana, *Cartilla de Organización* (La Paz 1954) p.4.

9 Lora, *A History*, p.284.

10 Jorge Claros Lafuente, *Frente de Liberación Nacional* (Cochabamba 1953) pp.3; 6.

11 Pierre Scali, *La Revolution Bolivienne (1952–54)* (Paris 1954) p.36.

12 Quoted in Lidia Gueiler, *La Mujer y la Revolución* (La Paz 1959) pp.119–121. An edited English translation is given in James Malloy, *Bolivia: The Uncompleted Revolution* (Pittsburgh 1970) pp.224–225.

13 *El Diario*, 19 Sept. 1952.

14 Gueiler, p.125. See also Lora, *A History*, p.282, for further comments by the author of this piece, Alfredo Candia.

15 See Siles's comments to the *New York Times*, 19 April 1952.

16 See, for example, *El Diario*, 23 May 1952.

17 Ibid., 5 Sept. 1952.

18 Ibid., 28 May 1952.

19 Ibid., 5 June 1952.

20 Ibid., 16 Sept. 1952.

21 For an extremely clumsy but generally informative discussion of democratic forms in Latin America, Göran Therborn, 'The Travail of Latin American Democracy' (*New Left Review*, Nos.113–114, Jan.–April 1979).

22 Guillermo Lora, *La Ausencia de la Gran Novela Minera* (La Paz 1979).

23 Guillermo Lora, *Miguel Alandia* (La Paz 1978).

24 A full account of the MNR women's struggle is given in Gueiler.

25 *El Diario*, 5 Oct. 1952.

26 Víctor Andrade, *La Revolución Boliviana y los Estados Unidos 1944–1962* (La Paz 1979). Significantly, this book first appeared in English.

27 *El Diario*, 20 April 1952.

28 *American Metals Market*, 2 April 1952.

29 *Time*, 5 May 1952.

30 *El Diario*, 3 May 1952.

31 Guillermo Lora, *La Revolución Boliviana* (La Paz 1964) pp.117–127.

32 *El Diario*, 24 Oct. 1952.

33 Quoted in Robert Alexander, *The Bolivian National Revolution* (New Brunswick 1958) p.103.

34 *Al Año de la Nacionalización de las Minas* (La Paz 1953).

35 Ford, Bacon and Davis report on Comibol cited in René Ruíz González, *La Administración Empírica de las Minas Nacionalizadas* (2nd. edn, La Paz 1980) p.190.

36 Gómez, pp.24; 229.

37 Thorn, 'The Economic Transformation', in James Malloy and Richard Thorn (eds), *Beyond the Revolution. Bolivia since 1952* (Pittsburgh 1971) p.173. Thorn bases his assertion on unreliable figures given in the US Army Handbook and a narrow reading of Ruíz González, who substantially qualifies the depiction of an overall fall in productivity.

38 Sinforoso Cabrera R., *Informe de Labores* (La Paz 1960); Amado Canelas, *Mito y Realidad de la Corporación Minera de Bolivia* (La Paz 1966) p.43.

39 Laurence Whitehead, 'Los Trabajadores Mineros de Bolivia: Sus Tradiciones y Perspectivas Políticas' (Paper given to the Simposio sobre Bolivia, Instituto de Estudios Peruanos, Lima 1976).

40 For a summary, see Ruíz González, pp.169–172.

41 Thorn, p.174; George Jackson Eder, *Inflation and Development in Latin America: A Case Study of Inflation and Development in Bolivia* (Ann Arbor 1969) p.118. This criticism is also supported from an entirely different position by a leading Trotskyist FSTMB militant, Filemón Escobar, *Testimonio de un Obrero* (manuscript, 1967–79) p.43.

42 *El Catolicismo Frente al Falange Fascista* (La Paz 1953) pp.4–5.

43 Carlos Velarde, *El Nacionalismo y la Acción Demagógica y Proimperialista del Trotzkismo* (La Paz 1953). For an attack from the party's centre-left, see René Zavaleta Mercado, *El Asalto Porista* (La Paz 1959).

44 Lora, *A History*, p.289, is quite clear on the use made of the PCB, an interpretation borne out by press reports of the COB debates.

45 *El Diario*, 6 June 1952.

46 Ibid., 2 August 1952.

47 Ibid., 18 June 1952.

48 Klein, *Evolution*, p.233. For a marvellous study of the French case, see Georges Lefebvre, *The Great Fear of 1789, Rural Panic in Revolutionary France* (London 1973).

49 *El Diario*, 10 Nov.; 20 Nov. 1952.

50 *La Patria*, Oruro, 19 June 1952.

51 *El País*, Cochabamba, 10 Dec. 1952, quoted in Kohl, p.68.

52 *El Diario*, 2 July; 3 July 1953.

53 Ibid., 22 Nov. 1952.

54 J. Blanco, *Antonio Alvarez Mamani, Historia de un Dirigente Campesino* (La Paz 1969).

55 *El Diario*, 18 March; 30 March 1953.

56 Ibid., 14 June 1952.

57 Ibid., 2 Feb.; 3 Feb. 1953. A very detailed but equally partisan narrative of peasant mobilisation and unionisation in the first years of the revolution is given in Luis Antezana Ergueta, *La Revolución Campesina en Bolivia* (La Paz 1982).

58 These objectives are discussed in Carter, 'Revolution and the Agrarian Sector', in Malloy and Thorn, pp.243 ff.

59 Carter, p.246.

60 Kohl, p.116.

61 Amado Canelas, *Mito y Realidad de la Reforma Agraria* (La Paz 1966) pp.217 ff.

62 *El Diario*, 3 August 1953.

63 Central Obrera Boliviana, *Primer Congreso Nacional de Trabajadores: Discursos* (La Paz 1954) p.13.

64 COB, *Cartilla*, p.9.

65 Central Obrera Boliviana, *Programa Ideológico y Estatutos de la* COB (La Paz 1954) p.22.
66 Ibid., pp.13–14.
67 *El Diario*, 9 Jan. 1953.
68 COB *Programa Ideológico*, pp.4–5.
69 The history of the split is detailed and highly contentious. One forceful viewpoint which criticises both sides harshly is give in Liborio Justo (Quebracho), *Bolivia: La Revolución Derrotada* (Buenos Aires 1971). Lora's version is outlined at length in *Contribución*, II, pp.255–307. I will discuss this issue at greater length in a forthcoming study.
70 Mitchell, p.43.
71 *El Diario*, 10 Oct. 1956.
72 PIR, *Soluciones Nacionales*, p.74.

Chapter Three

1 Sergio Almaraz, *Requiem para una República* (La Paz 1980) p.17.
2 See, for example, Nicos Poulantzas, *Political Power and Social Classes* (London 1973).
3 Wilkie, pp.13; 48.
4 Eder, p.590.
5 Ibid., p.241. This and other statements below are quoted in a particularly sharp and useful survey of the mission's work by Laurence Whitehead, *The United States and Bolivia. A Case of Neocolonialism* (Watlington 1969).
6 Eder, pp.603; 195.
7 Ibid., p.164.
8 Ibid.
9 Ibid., p.274.
10 Ibid., p.498.
11 The full decree is outlined in ibid., pp.269–273.
12 Guillermo Lora, *La Estabilización: Una Impostura* (La Paz 1959) p.27. The plan and its effects are closely considered in Paul Cammack, *The Politics of Stabilisation. The Bolivian Stabilisation Plan of 1956* (Unpublished B.Phil, University of Oxford 1976).
13 Cornelius H. Zondag, *The Bolivian Economy, 1952–1965* (New York 1966) p.161.
14 Eder, p.138. For further quotes, see Lora, *A History*, p.305.
15 For full details of the congress, see Lora, *A History*, pp.307–308.
16 Ibid., p.309.
17 Information given to Jorge Dandler Hanhart and cited in Laurence Whitehead, *The Mineworkers' Federation* (unpublished ms.) p.118A.
18 Ibid., which contains a full discussion of these themes.
19 Ibid., pp.95 ff.
20 Zondag, p.135.
21 Arze Cuadros, pp.268–269.
22 The *cruceño* pattern of politics is outlined in Laurence Whitehead, 'National Power and Local Power: The Case of Santa Cruz de la Sierra, Bolivia' in Francine Rabinovitz and Felicity Trueblood (eds) *Latin American Urban Research* Vol. 3 (Beverly Hills 1973). Sandóval gives his own version in an as yet unpublished text, *Bolivia: Revolución y Contra-revolución en el Oriente, 1952–1964*. I am indebted to José Luis Roca for showing me a copy of these memoirs.
23 *La Crónica*, Santa Cruz, 31 May 1961.

24 *El Diario*, 9 April 1953.

25 For some idea of the complexities of this case, see Javier Albó and Olivia Harris, *Monteras y Guardatojos* (Cuaderno de CIPCA, no.7, La Paz 1976).

26 Partido Comunista de Bolivia, *Segundo Congreso* (La Paz 1964) pp.8–9.

27 Hernán Siles Zuazo, *Mensaje-Informe dirigido a la VIII Convención del MNR* (La Paz 1960) p.6.

28 Víctor Paz Estenssoro, *La Revolución Seguirá Adelante* (La Paz 1960) p.29.

29 Víctor Paz Estenssoro, *La Revolución Boliviana* (La Paz 1964) p.30.

30 Federico Fortún Sanjinés, *Tercera Etapa de la Revolución Nacional* (La Paz 1964) pp.12; 13; 24.

31 *Visita del Presidente Víctor Paz Estenssoro a los Estados Unidos* (La Paz 1963) p.13. Paz once referred to the US assistant secretary of state as 'Compañero Henry Holland', a remark the left never allowed him to forget.

32 Quoted in 'XI Congreso Nacional de la FSTMB', *Control Obrero*, La Paz, June 1961.

33 Guillermo Bedregal, *El Convenio Internacional del Estaño* (La Paz 1961); *Recuperación de la Minería Nacionalizada* (La Paz 1961).

34 Filemón Escóbar, *Testimonio*, pp.60–61.

35 On the smelter issue, see Almaraz, *Requiem*, pp.41 ff.; Universidad Técnica de Oruro, *El Deber de la Hora: Hay que Derrotar el Atraso Instalando Hornos de Fundición* (Oruro 1963); Augusto Céspedes, *Fundición de Estaño en Bolivia* (La Paz 1962). In 1964 the MNR argued that a smelter was not an absolute priority, MNR *Programa de Gobierno 1964–1968* (La Paz 1964) p.11.

36 The campaign waged by President Hernando Siles against Abdón Saavedra in 1926 was something of a *cause celebre* in national political life. Saavedra had antagonised many with his ostentatious personal enrichment under the previous regime, that of his brother Bautista. Prior to his return from a long trip abroad La Paz was plastered with posters bearing just one word—'opio', while the students held a mock funeral ceremony for the vice-president. Seldom, anywhere in the world, has this office controlled much power, but equally seldom has it been so discredited that the government newspaper could depict it in the terms adopted by *La Razón* in late November 1926: 'Vice-president Saavedra walked around the plaza yesterday, alone. After he had completed a circuit, three benches and a portion of the national monument were missing'.

37 *Tesis de Telemayu. Carta del Sindicalismo Revolucionario* (La Paz 1960).

38 Bedregal, *Recuperación*, pp.19; 20; Amado Canelas, *Historia de una Frustración* (La Paz 1963) pp.177–178.

39 Quoted in Whitehead, *The Mineworkers*, pp.123–124.

40 Escóbar's autobiography, *Mi Vida*, is reprinted in *Venceremos*, La Paz, Aug. 1967.

41 For details, see Almaraz, *Requiem*, pp.54 ff.

42 Incidents cited by the polemical but always scrupulous Almaraz, ibid., p.33. Although the staff appointed to the US embassy in the 1950s were generally of a rather dour and orderly disposition, the La Paz posting had in the past thrown up its share of indiscretions. In February 1922 the British ambassador noted of his new US colleague's wife, 'Mrs Cottrell is young and pretty, but inexperienced and much divided between the desire to do right and to amuse herself'. Six years later la Cottrell had obviously made her choice: 'Mr and Mrs Cottrell departed for good in the early part of 1928 and few went to the station to bid them farewell. Mr Cottrell will not return, but Mrs Cottrell will shortly be seen again in La Paz, as the wife of someone else, with whom her name was intimately connected during the lapses of her official husband into his spells of insobriety. Mr David Kaufmann arrived in May to take Mr Cottrell's place . . . Mr Kaufman is an Israelite and reputed to be a millionaire; he certainly spends his money

right generously and often keeps open house . . . Bolivians are beginning to make fun of him . . . (and) it has been indicated to him in a friendly spirit that if he expects to reap any thankfulness from these people he is sowing seed on sterile ground.' O'Reilly, No.21, 2 Feb. 1922, FO 371/7182; Mitchell, No.6, 3 Dec. 1928, FO 371/13456.

43 Almaraz, *Requiem*, p.20. The liberal US political scientist Cole Blasier has also identified an ascendancy of the military/intelligence staff in the La Paz embassy, Malloy and Thorn, p.98.

44 Willard F. Barber and C. Neale Rolling, *Internal Security and Civic Action in Latin America* (Columbus Ohio 1966); W.H. Brill, *Military Civic Action in Bolivia* (Unpublished Ph.D., University of Pennsylvania 1965); Charles D. Corbett, *The Latin American Military as a Sociopolitical Force: Case Studies of Bolivia and Argentina* (Miami 1972).

45 *El Diario*, 27 Sept. 1963.

46 Luis Antezana, *Hernán Siles Zuazo: El Estratega y la Contrarrevolución* (La Paz 1979) p.147. For further discussion of the incident, see W.H. Brill, *Military Intervention in Bolivia: The Overthrow of Paz Estenssoro and the MNR* (Washington 1967).

47 See, for example, its defeated resolution on this point at Colquiri, cited at length in Lora, *A History*, p.326.

48 For the PCB position on the eve of the coup, see *Unidad Popular y Antiimperialista* (La Paz, October 1964).

49 *La Patria*, Oruro, 27 Oct. 1964.

50 Antezana, *Siles Zuazo*, p.166.

Chapter Four

1 *El Diario*, 8 Nov. 1964.

2 *La Patria*, 13 Nov. 1964.

3 Ibid., 22 Nov. 1964.

4 The role of the restaurant workers can at times be key since the main meal in Bolivia is lunch (*almuerzo*), lasting two hours and very often taken in town, where there are numerous popular eating houses. There have been several attempts — often motivated by transport strikes — to institute a continuous eight-hour working day but these have never met with any success.

5 Jefatura de las Fuerzas Armadas, *Morir antes que Esclavos Vivir* (La Paz 1965) p.6.

6 *Presencia*, 24 May 1965.

7 June Nash, *We Eat the Mines and the Mines Eat Us. Dependency and Exploitation in Bolivian Tin Mines* (New York 1979) p.281.

8 *Presencia*, 10 Sept. 1965.

9 Lora, *A History*, pp.351–356.

10 See, for example, Comisión Investigadora Nacional, *Daños y Costos del Sindicalismo a Comibol* (La Paz 1965). Comibol's operating costs in May and October 1965 are broken down in Hans-Jurgen Puhle, *Tradición y Política de Reformas en Bolivia* (Santiago 1972) p.141.

11 Lora, *El Proletariado en el Proceso Político 1952–1980* (La Paz 1981), pp.60–61.

12 Generales Ovando y Barrientos, *Mensaje a Los Trabajadores de las Minas* (La Paz 1965) pp.4–6.

13 Outlines of these two concessions are given by Mariano Baptista and Sergio Almaraz in *Guerrillas y Generales sobre Bolivia* (Buenos Aires 1968) and José Luis Alcazar and José Baldivia, *Bolivia: Otra Lección para América* (Mexico 1973).

14 For an overview of the oil industry see Sergio Almaraz, *Petroleo en Bolivia* (La

Paz 1969); Enrique Mariaca, *Mito y Realidad del Petroleo Boliviano* (La Paz 1966); Jorge Fernando Soliz, *Tema: El Petroleo* (La Paz 1976); Marcelo Quiroga Santa Cruz, *Oleocracia o Patria* (Mexico 1982).

15 Nash, p.233; *Espártaco* (La Paz), no.7, June 1964, pp.24–27.

16 It is instructive to compare the pay of army officers and teachers under the Barrientos regime:

Salary (monthly, US$)

Teachers		Officers	
1st. Grade	69	General	416
2nd.	61	Colonel	352
3rd.	55	Lt. Colonel	323
4th	50	Major	295
5th.	45	Captain	267
No category	38	Lieutenant	241
		Sublieutenant	216

17 Quoted in Mitchell, p.98.

18 Régis Debray, *Ché's Guerrilla War* (London 1975). Other sources on the campaign used in this account include Rubén Vázquez Díaz, *Bolivia a la Hora del Ché* (Mexico 1976); Daniel James, ed., *The Complete Bolivian Diaries of Ché Guevara and Other Captured Documents* (London 1968); Richardo Rojo, *My Friend Ché* (New York 1968); Luis J. González and Gustavo A. Sánchez, *The Great Rebel. Ché Guevara in Bolivia* (New York 1969); Luis Suárez, *Entre el Fusil y la Palabra* (Mexico 1980); Richard Gott, *Rural Guerrillas in Latin America* (London 1973).

19 'It is also the only country where the revolution might take the classic Bolshevik form — witness the proletarian insurrection of 1952 on the basis of 'soviets', which 'exploded' the state apparatus by means of a short and decisive armed struggle. The theory of the *foco* is thus in Bolivia for reasons of historical formation which are unique in Latin America, if not inadequate, at any rate secondary.' Regis Debray 'Castroism: the Long March in Latin America' in *Strategy for Revolution* (London 1970) p.38.

20 For the conduct of these campaigns, see Gott. For discussion of the *foco*, Leo Huberman and Paul M. Sweezy, *Régis Debray and the Latin American Revolution* (New York 1969).

21 *Ché's Guerrilla War*, p.37. Lora's version of this event is given in *Proletariado*, pp.167–170.

22 *Bolivian Diaries*, p.274.

23 *Ché's Guerrilla War*, p.73.

24 Ibid., p.94.

25 Ibid., pp.88; 90; 92; 122.

26 The full message is cited in Gott, pp.501–502, and was printed in *El Diario*, 31 Oct. 1967.

27 *Bolivian Diaries*, pp.95–96.

28 See interviews with Kolle reprinted in Gott, pp.537–539, and Vásquez Díaz, pp.152–158.

29 *Ché's Guerrilla War*, pp.105; 139.

30 'Las Divergencias del P.C. Boliviano con Che Guevara', *Punto Final*, no. 49, Feb. 1968, partially reprinted in Gott, pp.504–513.

31 Gott, p.476.

32 *Bolivian Diaries*, p.151.

33 Vázquez Díaz, pp.56; 98; 111.

34 Ibid., p.94.
35 *Ché's Guerrilla War*, p.114.
36 Vázquez Díaz, p.14. Accounts of the massacre can be found in Lora, *A History*, pp.345–351, and Simón Reyes, 'La Masacre de San Juan' in *Guerrillas y Generales*, pp.167–186.
37 González and Sánchez Salazar, p.179.
38 Both speeches are reprinted in *On Trial* (London 1968).
39 Vázquez Díaz, p.215.
40 Arguedas named the CIA chiefs in La Paz as Larry Sternfeld and John S. Tilton as well as listing agents such as Nicholas Leondiris, Hugo Murray, Gabriel García García, Mario González and N. Hernández. Zenteno stressed the important part played in the Ñancahuazú campaign by the intelligence coordinator in Santa Cruz, Willy Culeghan, Ramos and González. Suárez, pp.195–208. Many testimonies are given in full along with a number of interviews in Gregorio Selser, *La CIA en Bolivia* (Buenos Aires 1970).
41 *Presencia*, 3 Aug. 1967.
42 'The matter is very straight forward: I am a national leftist, anarcho-militarist, which is to say, social-nationalist, anti-marxist pro-rightist, which ought not to be confused with national socialism or popular anti-civilism. I am a type of neo-socialist anti-Russian, almost Titoist, but anti-imperialist and pro-American without having anything to do with the *poristas* of González and viewing with greater sympathy the political movements which combat Trotskyism without falling into liberalism but always marching alongside the underdeveloped peoples which suffer backwardness because of military dictatorships . . . .' Quoted in Mariano Baptista Gumucio, *Historia Contemporanea de Bolivia* (La Paz 1976) p.256. For a succinct description of Barrientos as well as the principal actions of his government, see Raúl Peña Bravo, *Hechos y Dichos del Gral. Barrientos* (La Paz 1982) or — but only for those with a very stern constitution — the truly awful hagiography penned at great expense by Fernando Diez de Medina, *El General del Pueblo* (La Paz 1972).

Chapter Five

1 'Mandato Revolucionario de las Fuerzas Armadas de la Nación' in *Documentos Fundamentales de la Revolución* (La Paz 1970) p.10.
2 Ibid., pp.10–11.
3 Ibid., pp.12–13.
4 Quoted in *El Pensamiento Político Boliviano después de la Nacionalización del Petroleo* (Cochabamba 1970) p.80.
5 Ibid., p.90.
6 *New York Times*, 30 Sept. 1969.
7 *Pensamiento Político*, p.205.
8 Following the 1964 coup it was noted that officers sent to fill diplomatic posts were frequently unable to handle routine transmission of telex messages. Under Barrientos very few army officers occupied posts that were intellectually taxing or required a modicum of planning and discussion of policy rather than simple office maintenance. One important exception was General Juan Lechín Suárez, *gerente* of Comibol, who soon acquired the respect of foreign firms who dealt with him and joined colonel Julio Sanjinés in the military's small club of '*técnicos*'. Ovando's regime began a process of greater technical training that was to be furthered under Banzer although it should be borne in mind that it was still a very small minority that wanted to take this course or indeed proved capable of availing themselves of the few possibilities on offer.
9 *El Diario*, 28 Sept. 1969.

10 Alcazar and Baldivia, pp.53–54.

11 *Documentos*, pp.29–35.

12 On 26 September the leadership of the COB, still formally illegal, sent Ovando a letter, stating that, 'For the trade union movement the integrated revolution, a profound change in structures, economic nationalism and the liberation of the country means expulsion of the imperialism of the monopolies, defence of the public sector, the removal of the economic power of *patiñismo* and the sepoy capitalist oligarchy. The intervention of the masses is essential . . . We are faced with an alternative: either the army is captured and deviated by fascists and reactionary forces . . . or it is led by healthy nationalist forces, identified with the people and following the path of a true revolution.' *Pensamiento Político*, p.234.

13 *El Diario*, 20 Oct. 1969; *Presencia*, 6 March 1970.

14 *Documentos*, pp.40–48.

15 *El General Torres Habla a Bolivia* (Buenos Aires 1973) pp.15–29.

16 For Ramos's ideas, see *Pensamiento Político*, pp.15–48.

17 Ibid., pp.158–159.

18 Lora, *Contribución*, II, pp.445–448; *Masas*, no.362, Oct. 1969. The POR (Lora) was not invited to participate in the forum from which the speeches collected in *Pensamiento Político* are drawn. The POR that appears there is that led by Amadeo Vargas and affiliated to the section of the Fourth International led by the Argentine Posadas. At the time the *posadistas* had some influence in student circles but although they provided full support for Torres, they were soon to be reduced to a pamphlet-producing sect like their parent international.

19 Régis Debray, *Prison Writings* (London 1973) pp.11; 15.

20 *Pensamiento Político*, pp.120; 126; 133.

21 Since the PDCR did not admit to close relations with the ELN it was not able to pursue the militarist line with all the force many of its members wished. The speech by Jorge Rios Dalenz reprinted in *Pensamiento Político*, pp.165–194, gives what might be called the PDCR's 'minimum programme'.

22 Baptista, *Historia Contemporanea*, p.282; Lora, *Contribución*, II, p.451; interview with Víctor López, La Paz, 11 Sept. 1982.

23 *Jornada*, La Paz, 11 May 1970.

24 *Tesis Política de la COB* (La Paz, 6 May 1970), Section Two, paragraph four.

25 Ibid., Section Five, paragraph four. Paragraphs two and three of this section are by the POR, the fourth by the PCB, and the fifth and sixth by the POR. For a discussion of this question from a Trotskyist position, see the introduction by Francois and Catherine Chesnais to Guillermo Lora, *Bolivie: De la Naissance du POR a l'Assemblée Populaire* (Paris 1972) p.LXXXI.

26 Lora, *Contribución*, II, p.453. This issue soon made Lora—himself scarcely gentle in political debate—the victim of all the vitriol the Trotskyist movement is capable of generating because of his 'capitulation to Stalinism'. His principal accusers, the International Committee of the Fourth International, led by Gerry Healy of the British Socialist Labour League (later Workers' Revolutionary Party), demonstrated neither knowledge of the concrete situation nor any proclivity to discuss the issue in a constructive manner. For their sectarian views, see *Trotskyism versus Revisionism* (London 1975) p.39–42. Another, irredeemably absurd sect known as the Spartacist League—distinguished by its description of the population of Afghanistan as 'goat-fuckers' and its 'revolutionary' call for the Soviet invasion of Poland—went so far as to invoke support for the thesis as one reason why Lora had 'blood on his hands' as a result of Banzer's 1971 coup. Such excrescences are of absolutely no interest whatsoever except as an indication of the manifest importance of—and great heat generated by—the POR inside the often desperate circles of international Trotskyism.

27 The central elements of the *Plataforma de Lucha* were: unity around the leadership of the COB and FSTMB; a workers' government and the establishment of socialism; expulsion of the US military mission, CIA and Peace Corps; the creation of a revolutionary anti-imperialist front; full democratic liberties; return of all union radio stations; cooperativisation of the press; wage increases to pre-May 1965 levels; full reinstatement of those sacked for union or political activity; *control obrero* with powers of veto; socialisation of medicine and the university; nationalisation without compensation of private mines; state monopoly on petrol and gas; radicalisation of the agrarian reform; university autonomy; support for the struggles in Vietnam and Cambodia; diplomatic relations with Cuba.

28 Baptista, *Historia Contemporanea*, p.289, defends the officers from this accusation but in the light of the subsequent activity of both Arce Gómez and Loayza the author may wish to revise his opinion even though he was a member of the Ovando government.

29 One anecdote in the 1970s had a Chilean officer asking his Bolivian counterpart why the country possessed admirals when it had no sea, to which the reply was, 'But we have always wondered why you have a ministry of justice'. In 1980 the navy numbered 2,000 men, the airforce 4,000 and the army 18,000. The navy does have a very limited political voice in times of crisis, largely by virtue of having a garrison at the port of Tiquina, on Lake Titicaca not far from La Paz. For many of the riparian communities in Beni and Pando, which can only be crossed by river or air, its personnel are the most important representatives of the state. The navy possesses one sea-going vessel, *Libertador Bolívar*, donated by the Venezuelan president Carlos Andrés Pérez and normally docked at Rosario on the River Plate in Argentina. Early in 1978 a radio link-up enabled instructions from the ship's bridge to be broadcast inside the country; in the main plaza in Sucre, at least, this drew a discernable response from people who had never enjoyed rights to the sea and, in all likelihood, had never seen it.

30 Hugo Assmann, *Teoponte. Una Experiencia Guerrillera* (Oruro 1971) p.30.

31 Ibid., p.27.

32 Debray, *Prison Writings*, p.75.

33 Assmann, p.37.

34 Alcazar and Baldivia, pp.69–72.

35 This account is drawn mainly from *El Diario*. Detailed accounts of this confused period can be found in Isaac Sandoval Rodríguez, *Culminación y Ruptura del Modelo Nacional-Revolucionario. Torres en el Escenario Político Boliviano* (La Paz 1979) pp.63–76; Jorge Gallardo Lozada, *De Torres a Banzer. Diez Meses de Emergencia en Bolivia* (Buenos Aires 1972) pp.125–148; Alcazar and Baldivia, pp.93–97.

36 Baptista, *Historia Contemporanea*, p.283; Lora, *Proletariado*, p.216; Gallardo, p.259. The principal leaders of FARO were Alberto Jara; Sinforoso Cabrera; Alberto López; José María Palacios; Alberto López; and Gullermo Aponte, who served as minister of health until March 1971.

37 *El Diario*, 9 Oct. 1970, gives the names. Gallardo, p.154, complains about this 'lack of seriousness', and Sandoval, later a minister, criticises the debates as 'anodyne', p.82.

38 Alcazar and Baldivia, pp.97–98. Further details are given in Lora, *Contribución*, II, p.468, and Chantal Coppy and Henry Hassan, *Bolivie 1971: l'Assemblée Populaire* (unpublished thesis, University of Grenoble 1973) p.62, a work that bears the political imprint of its supervisor Pierre Broué, a leading member of the *Organisation Communiste Internationale*, to which the POR was at the time affiliated.

39 *El Diario*, 9 Oct. 1970.

40 Ibid. For the demands, see note 27 above. This document was signed by the COB,

all the major unions, the students, and the MNR (Hernán Siles Zuazo and Ñuflo Chávez), PRIN, PCB, POR (Lora), PCML, PDCR, *Movimiento Revolucionario Espártaco*, FARO.

41 Sandoval, p.76.

42 Ibid., pp.85–86.

43 The total wage bill in 1970 was Bs. 10.5 million against Bs. 14.2 million in 1965, but a further Bs. 2 million in reduced social security payments should be added to this figure. Details are given in ibid., p.109.

44 Diary of a student working in Siglo XX, quoted in Whitehead, 'Los Trabajadores Mineros', p.22.

45 *Presencia*, 20 Nov.; 23 Nov. 1970.

46 *Torres: Presidente de los Mineros* (La Paz 1970) p.11.

47 *El Diario*, 11 Dec. 1970.

48 Ibid., 24 Nov. 1970.

49 *Presencia*, 9 Jan. 1971.

50 *El Diario*, 10 Dec. 1970.

51 The main rebels were Banzer; Valencia; Mario Adett Zamora; Humberto Cayoja; Jorge Echazú; Rolando Saravia; Norberto Salomón; Carlos Fernández.

52 *Presencia*, 12 Jan. 1971; Sandoval, p.93.

53 *Business Week*, 10 July 1971. See also *El Diario*, 27 June 1971; Sandoval, p.94.

54 Gallardo, p.306.

55 *Presencia*, 27 Jan. 1971.

56 Ibid., 4 April 1971.

57 Ibid., 17 Feb.; 6 March; 11 March 1971.

58 Ibid., 15 Feb.; 29 March 1971.

59 Gallardo, p.307; Baptista, *Historia Contemporanea*, p.299; *Presencia*, 27 Jan. 1971.

60 *Presencia*, 27 March; 10 March; 29 Jan. 1971.

61 Ibid., 7 Feb. 1971.

62 Ibid., 12 June; 18 June 1971.

63 *El Diario*, 3 June 1971.

64 Ibid., 16 Nov. 1970; *Masas*, no. 386, 15 Feb. 1971.

65 Partido Comunista de Bolivia, *III Congreso Nacional. Documentos* (La Paz 1971) pp.51; 52; 57.

66 See, for example, Baptista, *Historia Contemporanea*, p.297; Klein, *Evolution*, pp.252–253.

67 Full discussion of the character of the Assembly is given in René Zavaleta Mercado, *El Poder Dual en America Latina* (Mexico 1974), part of which is translated in 'Bolivia — Military Nationalism and the People's Assembly' (*New Left Review*, no.73, May–June 1971); Guillermo Lora, *Bolivia: De la Asamblea Popular al Golpe Fascista* (Buenos Aires 1972).

68 The membership of the Assembly was dominated by the FSTMB (38 delegates), the factory workers (24), railwaymen (17), construction workers (13) and oil workers (12). The COB and CODs had 19 delegates. The middle class contingent had large student and transport representations (nine delegates each) as well as a broad spread of white-collar workers, ranging from cinema employees to artists and health and bank workers. The *Bloque Independiente* controlled 18 of the 23 peasant delegates. Eventually the PS, POR (González) and POR (Vargas) were to take up the political seats originally allocated to the MNR. The MIR had no official delegates, two places being taken by the PDCR and one by *Espártaco*.

69 This point is discussed by Zavaleta, *Poder Dual*, p.108, where he also indicates that although the MNR had no influence, the Assembly was largely dominated by

syndicalist objectives. Zavaleta was a delegate in the informal MIR group and particularly critical of the leading part played by the PCB and POR, against which his book is a powerful but highly sectarian polemic.

70 *Presencia*, 26 Jan. 1971; Suárez, *Entre el Fusil y la Palabra*, p.230. According to Torres, Paz offered him MNR support in exchange for a promise to hold elections.

71 There is no authoritative study of the *Asamblea Popular*, which did not have the resources to provide for reproduction of its debates outside press coverage, which was quite extensive. The following succinct description is based on reports in *El Diario* and *Presencia*, discussions with participants of various political allegiances, typewritten copies of resolutions and reports, and the first-hand notes kindly lent to me by Laurence Whitehead, who attended the last three days of debate.

72 *El Diario*, 26 June 1971.

73 Ibid., 27 June 1971.

74 Ibid., 25 June 1971.

75 Ibid., 1 July 1971.

76 Ibid.

77 The regime's response to the Assembly is outlined in Hugo Tores Goitia, *El Gobierno Revolucionario y la Asamblea Popular* (La Paz 1971).

78 *Presencia*, 20 June 1971.

79 Ramiro Sánchez, *Brazil en Bolivia: Lecciones de un Golpe Militar* (Santiago 1972) p.12.

80 Ibid., p.27.

81 *El Diario*, 27 July; 28 July 1971.

82 The manifesto is reprinted along with other important documents from this period in *Bolivia; El Retorno del Fascismo* (*Cuadernos de Marcha*, Montevideo, no.51, July 1971). (In fact, this issue must have been issued later than 18 August but it carries July on its cover.)

83 Alcazar and Baldivia, p.158.

84 'Monitor' (Stoffregen-Böller and Gisela Vollmer-Koenig), 28 Feb. 1972. As well as confirming the fears of a full nationalisation of coffee and sugar, the participants emphasised concern about a radicalisation of the agrarian reform. One entrepreneur, Kyllman, assessed financial support for the coup from the German business community at $20,000 in Santa Cruz and $10,000 in Cochabamba; much more was collected under the supervision of Bernhard Elsner in La Paz. Selected transcripts from this programme are reprinted in Marcelo Quiroga Santa Cruz, *Bolivia Recupera la Palabra. Juicio a la Dictadura* (La Paz 1982) pp.66–69. According to the *Cámara de Comercio Boliviano-Alemán de La Paz*, German companies controlled 30 per cent of national private commerce, *Aquí*, La Paz, no.18, 14–20 July 1979. For further details, see *Stern*, Nov. 1972.

85 Sánchez, pp.13–15.

86 *La Crónica*, 21 August 1971.

87 'According to an eye-witness, Colonel Selich gave the order to kill all the prisoners with these words. "I don't want prisoners or wounded". This set off the most excited groups, which opened the assault on the university building by blowing down the doors with grenades . . . We heard, "Kill them", "No red dog alive" . . . The only thing we did was to throw ourselves to the ground.' Central Obrera Boliviana, *Informe: Violación de los Derechos Humanos en Bolivia* (La Paz 1976) pp.126–127. 'So great was the bestiality exhibited in his punitive actions by this dapper, sickly and neurotic *gorila*, one hundred per cent *gorila*, that the *Cristiana Asociación de Damas Paceñas* felt obliged to decorate him.' Lora, *Proletariado*, p.295.

88 David Padilla, *Decisiones y Recuerdos de un General* (La Paz 1980) pp.81–82.

89 *Cuadernos de Marcha*, p.89.

90 Gallardo, p.365.

91 Lora, *Proletariado*, p.271.
92 *Washington Star*, 23 Aug. 1971; *El Diario*, 18 Aug. 1971.
93 *El Comercio*, Lima, 21 Aug. 1971.

Chapter Six

1 *El Diario*, 31 Aug. 1971.
2 *New York Times*, 2 Sept. 1971.
3 *Washington Star*, 24 Aug. 1971.
4 'Bolivia: The War Goes On' (*Nacla's Latin American and Empire Report*, Vol. VIII, no.2, Feb. 1974) p.30.
5 *Latin America*, London, 15 June 1973.
6 *Nacla*, pp.27—29.
7 US Senate, Committee on Appropriations, *Foreign Assistance and Related Programmes, Appropriations FY 1973* (92nd Congress, 2nd Session, Washington D.C. 1972) p.928.
8 See, for example, *Newsweek*, 20 Aug. 1973.
9 Opposition was by no means limited to the left, but the most telling critique was levelled by Marcelo Quiroga Santa Cruz in his book *El Saqueo de Bolivia* (Buenos Aires 1973), some of the findings of which are expanded in the posthumously published *Oleocracia o Patria* (Mexico 1982).
10 Quoted in Quiroga, *Juicio*, p.77.
11 Ibid., pp.76—77.
12 *Hoy*, La Paz, 18 March 1972.
13 Russell Tribunal, *Repression in Latin America* (London 1975) pp.136—137. This English version does not reproduce the lengthy testimony presented by Jaime Paz Zamora which was published separately by the MIR: *Bolivia: Informe-Denuncia* (Brussels 1975).
14 *El Diario*, 10 Nov. 1971.
15 CEP, *Bolivia 1971—76. Pueblo, Estado, Iglesia* (Lima 1976) p.29.
16 The case is described in detail in *Repression*, pp.138—139; Quiroga, *Juicio*, pp.55 ff.; Lora, *Proletariado*, pp.299—305.
17 Asociación Pro-Derechos Humanos, *Bolivia 1971—1977. El Gobierno de Banzer y la Violación de los Derechos Humanos* (Madrid 1977) passim.; Mariano Baptista, ed., *Porqué se van los hijos de Bolivia?* (La Paz 1975).
18 *El Delito de Ser Periodista. La Libertad de Prensa en Bolivia. Documentos y Testimonios, 1971—1977* (La Paz? 1977) pp.12—14.
19 Facts on File, *Latin America 1973* (New York 1974) p.52.
20 Facts on File, *Latin America 1974* (New York 1975) p.50.
21 Pablo Ramos Sánchez, *Siete Años de Economía Boliviana* (La Paz 1980) p.180; IEPALA, *Páginas Sindicales: Bolivia* (Madrid 1979) p.10.
22 *Le Monde*, 1 Nov. 1972; *Suddeutsche Zeitung*, 2 Nov. 1972.
23 Lora, *Proletariado*, pp.453—459; Ramos, *Siete Años*, p.184; *Pueblo, Estado, Iglesia*, p.99.
24 Ramos, *Siete Años*, pp.181—182; Lora, *Proletariado*, p.461—462; *Pueblo, Estado, Iglesia*, p.99 give slightly different calculations.
25 The fullest account is Comisión de Justicia y Paz, *La Masacre del Valle* (La Paz 1975). Others are given in *Pueblo, Estado, Iglesia*, pp.114—120; MIR, *La Masacre Campesina. Cochabamba, Enero 1974* (La Paz 1974).
26 *Presencia*, 1 Feb. 1974.
27 IPE, La Paz, 13 Oct. 1973, quoted in Mitchell, p.127.

364

28 Fausto Reinaga, *Manifiesto del Partido Indio de Bolivia* (La Paz 1970) p.106.

29 Julio Tumiri Apaza, 'The Liberation of the Indian in Kollasuyo (Bolivia)' in *The Indian Liberation and Social Rights Movement in Kollasuyo (Bolivia)* (Copenhagen 1978) pp.1–15. MINK'A also sponsored the publication of perhaps the fullest and most trenchant study of indian oppression: Wankar (Ramiro Reinaga Burgoa), *Tawantin-suyo. Cinco Siglos de Guerra Qheswaymara contra España* (Chukiapu 1978).

30 *Criterio*, La Paz, 10 March 1983. The policies of Julio Tumiri's wing of MITKA are outlined in *Pueblo Indio*, Lima, theoretical journal of the *Consejo Indio de Sud América* (CISA).

31 Many of these are reproduced in *Pueblo, Estado, Iglesia*.

32 Ibid., p.19.

33 Quoted from original documents in Penny Lernoux, *Cry of the People* (London 1982) p.143.

34 *Presencia*, 15 Jan. 1974.

35 I am grateful to Colonel Arsenio González for discussing the aims of the movement with me. Over the next three years what became known as the '*movimiento gen-eracional*' issued a number of documents, arguing for economic diversification, concentration on infrastructural development, limits on foreign capital, and income redistribution. Its slogan was, '*De incapaces, traidores y cobardes libertemos a este Pueblo*'. 'Objetivos Nacionales del EMG de la Oficialidad Jóven (mimeo, Aug. 1976); 'Bases de una Doctrina Militar para un país subdesarrollado' (mimeo, Aug. 1976).

36 The main articles of decrees 11947 and 11948 are cited at some length in Quiroga, *Juicio*, pp.30–36.

37 J.M. De la Cueva, *Bolivia: Imperialismo y Oligarquía* (La Paz 1983) p.68.

38 Ramos, *Siete Años*, pp.159; 163; 166.

39 De la Cueva, pp.71–72; Ramos, *Siete Años*, p.54.

40 Ramos, *Siete Años*, p.125.

41 Ibid., p.203.

42 MIR, *La Gran Mentira. Informe sobre la Situación Económica del País en 1976* (La Paz 1976) p.4.

43 Ramos, *Siete Años*, p.215.

44 Ibid., p.229.

45 René Bascopé Aspiazu, *La Veta Blanca. Coca y Cocaina en Bolivia* (La Paz 1982) pp.56; 67.

46 Arze Cuadros, p.280.

47 Most of the data in this paragraph is drawn from George Philip, 'YPFB and the Development of Oil in Bolivia' (mimeo, London 1979).

48 Carlos F. Toranzo Roca, 'Banzerato: Un Nuevo Modelo de Acumulación?' (*Cuadernos de Marcha*, Mexico, Sept.–Oct. 1979) p.72.

49 *Latin America*, 5 Jan. 1979; Quiroga, *Juicio*, p.103.

50 Ramos, *Siete Años*, pp.140; 142.

51 *Anuario Estadístico 1977* (La Paz 1978).

52 Toranzo, p.70; MIR, *Las Empresas Multinacionales en Bolivia* (La Paz 1975) p.25; De la Cueva, pp.172–173.

53 Ramos, *Siete Años*, p.117; Toranzo, p.73.

54 Ramos, *Siete Años*, pp.119–120.

55 Ibid., p.218.

56 Ibid., p.98.

57 Ibid., pp.256–258. *Páginas Sindicales*, p.53, gives a probably exaggerated depiction of the fall in real wages. See also Yvon Le Bot, 'Bolivie: les militaires, l'Etat, la dépendence; une décennie de pillage' (*Amerique Latine*, Paris, no.3, July–Sept. 1980); Asamblea Permanente de Derechos Humanos de Bolivia, *Estudio sobre el Valor Adquisitivo del Salario de los Mineros* (La Paz 1978) pp.21–22.

58 *Presencia*, 24 Dec. 1976; CALA, 'Bolivia: Background to the Presidential Elections' (London 1978) p.13.

59 World Bank, *Annual Report 1976* (New York 1976); *Bolivia, Report of an NUM Delegation in July 1979* (London 1979) p.14.

60 United Nations, *Concise Report on the World Population Situation 1981* (New York 1982).

61 Instituto Nacional de Estadística, *Bolivia en Cifras 1980* (La Paz 1981) p.57.

62 Ibid., p.53; World Health Organisation, quoted in CALA, p.15.

63 For the PCB's attacks, see Carlos Soria Galvarro, *Con la Revolución en las Venas. Los Mineros de Siglo XX en la Resistencia Antifascista* (La Paz 1980) p.103.

64 *Le Monde*, 11 May 1976.

65 For details of Torres's exile and death, see the interview with Emma Obleas in Suárez, *Entre la Palabra y el Fusil*, pp.234–241.

66 For Domitila's vivid description of the strike, *Let Me Speak!* (London 1979) pp.214 ff. There is also a good account in the biography of one of its leaders: Juan Del Granado, *Artemio Camargo* (La Paz 1983) pp.101–123.

67 *Ercilla*, Santiago, 25 Sept. 1975.

68 Note no.68110875, 12 Dec. 1975, quoted in Quiroga, *Juicio*, p.87.

69 *Presencia*, 2 Sept. 1975.

70 The fullest survey of the documents and press items on this issue is given in *Documents on Colonialist Export from South Africa to South America* (Department of Peace and Conflict Research, Uppsala University, June 1977).

71 *Presencia*, 31 Sept. 1977.

72 Quoted in Asamblea Permanente de Derechos Humanos de Bolivia, *El Fraude Electoral: Un Atentado contra la Voluntad Popular* (La Paz 1979) p.31.

73 *Latin America Political Report*, London, 10 Feb. 1978.

74 The full list is given in *El Fraude*, pp.95–97.

75 Asamblea Permanente de Derechos Humanos de Bolivia, *La Huelga de Hambre* (La Paz 1978) p.19.

76 *El Fraude*, p.22.

77 Ibid., pp.35–40; *Presencia*, 20 June 1978.

78 *El Fraude*, pp.58–62.

79 Ibid., pp.72–74.

80 Ibid., p.76. A detailed account of the operation of electoral fraud in the countryside is given in Carmen Alcoreza and Javier Albó, *1978: El Nuevo Campesinado ante el Fraude* (La Paz 1979).

Chapter Seven

1 *Latin America Political Report*, 28 July 1978.

2 *Washington Post*, 23 July 1978.

3 *Latin America Political Report*, 11 Aug. 1978.

4 Padilla had graduated in 1948 and opposed the April rising but his bitter memories of the experience resulted just as much from the poor comportment of his peers as from the anti-militarism of the revolution. One figure whom he thoroughly despised for cowardice was Armando Reyes Villa, then a sublieutenant but in 1978 a general and shortly to become a leading figure of the *golpista* current. In his memoirs Padilla recounts that the November 1978 coup owed much to the army's reluctance to confront the UDP on the streets, drawing many 'agnostics' behind the *Karachipampas. Decisiones y Recuerdos*, pp.128–136.

5 *Presencia*, 25 Nov. 1978.

6 *Aquí*, 14–20 July 1979.

7 Ibid., 5–12 May 1979.

8 Ibid.; *Unidad*, no.489, May 1979. The representation of political parties on the 34-strong COB executive was: PCB—7; PRIN—6; MNRI—5; MIR—5; POR *De Pie*—1; *Vanguardia Obrera*—2; *Octubre*—1; MRTK—1; PS-1–1; independents—5. *Documentos y Resoluciones del V Congreso de la COB (La Paz 1979) p.19.*

9 *Aquí*, 19–25 May 1979. The change in Peking's policy following Mao's death had an appreciable impact on the pro-Chinese parties in Latin America, particularly in Peru, the bastion of Maoism in the region. Behind the slogans of 'Death to Deng Xiao Ping! Long Live the Gang of Four!' that appeared on the buildings of the Peruvian town of Ayacucho lay the emergent force of *Sendero Luminoso*, which from 1978 was to build up a guerrilla campaign of substantial proportion despite the antipathy of the rest of the left, fierce repression, and a remarkably extravagant campaign of lies and false accusations in the Lima press that was translated to the western liberal press almost intact and with very little questioning until the killing of eight journalists in 1982 by forces linked to the army. Bolivian Maoism had no capacity to stage such a campaign but although nobody in Bolivia had written a thesis on 'The Kantian Theory of Space', as had Abimäel Guzmán, the chieftan of *Sendero*, the pro-Chinese forces were not dissimilar to their Peruvian comrades in their dependence upon the petty bourgeois intelligentsia as leading cadres.

10 Ibid.

11 The PCB was in the UDP in order 'to obtain the real democratisation of the country, close the door on fascist reaction, and to achieve a representative government at the service of national interests.' *Unidad*, no.493, Aug. 1979. For further comments, see PCB, *IV Congreso* (La Paz 1980); *Unidad*, no.489, May 1979; *Aquí*, 23–29 June 1979.

12 *Aquí*, 19–25 May 1979.

13 *Latin America Political Report*, 25 May 1979; 8 June 1979.

14 Quiroga, *Juicio*, passim. The major points are summarised in Gregorio Selser, *Bolivia: El Cuartelazo de los Cocadolares* (Mexico 1982) pp.27–29.

15 The main points of the debate are contained in Germán Vargas Martínez, *Responsibilidad, Juicio o Sainete?* (La Paz 1982).

16 *Aquí*, 13–20 Oct. 1979.

17 Before the elections the UDP published as an advertisement in the national press its open letter to the chief of staff, General Víctor Castillo, asking for guarantees and desistence from destabilisation, and reminding the military that all members of the UDP were nationalists and some were members of the armed forces, *Presencia*, 11 June 1979. The position of the PCB was that, 'the Armed Forces are for the defence of the Nation. They can and ought to participate with the people in economic and social development, in line with the legal norms and regulations of the military institution. We reject attempts to separate them from the people and recognise their right to their own preoccupations and requirements.' *Aquí*, 23–29 June 1979. Earlier, Oscar Eid of the MIR had stepped very carefully around the question of military occupation of the mines: 'We believe this problem ought to be seen from different angles, we do not think that the presence of the armed forces should entail persecution in any part of the national territory...' Ibid., 31 March–6 April 1979.

18 For details, see *Aquí*, 27 Oct.–2 Nov. 1979.

19 For the essence of the UDP strategy, see MNRI, *Programa del Gobierno 1979–83* (La Paz 1979), and *Programa del Movimiento de Izquierda Revolucionaria* (La Paz 1979), both works of dazzling imprecision.

20 Bedregal's *Los Militares en Bolivia* (La Paz 1971) included this passage: 'Ambition and opportunism convert politics into an accumulation of dissensions, intrigues and vicious circles which result unerringly in military *caudillismo*, which,

mutatis mutandis, acquires the old habits of despoilment. This is a militarism of a provincial, parochial and thoroughly discredited character. It does not seek *la gloire militaire* or foreign conquest, but civil war, the blind struggle for power, the opportunity to oppress and exploit the civil population.' In the wake of his experience with Natusch Bedregal did not retire from politics but gave himself time to complete a rambling, jargon-laden but interesting volume on national politics since 1952: *El Poder en La Revolución Nacional* (La Paz 1982).

21 This question is considered in depth in *Golpe*, La Paz, 19 June 1980, which generally comes down in favour of Paz's disclaimers.

22 *Aquí*, 24–30 Nov. 1979. The following account is drawn largely from *Aquí* and *Coyuntura*, nos 33 and 34.

23 Asamblea Permanente de Derechos Humanos de Bolivia, *La Masacre de Todos Santos* (La Paz 1980) provides full details and a series of vivid photos.

24 *Aquí*, 17–23 Nov. 1979; *Presencia*, 9 Nov. 1979; *Unidad*, no.496, Nov. 1979. A full but very partisan account of this bizarre episode is given in *Esto Es*, La Paz, 21 Sept. 1982, which suggests that because Jorge Kolle Cueto was absent in Lima for the first week of the regime the PCB line became more opportunist under the leadership of Marcos Domic. Nevertheless, the article also quotes Kolle as saying that Natusch could have implemented the COB's economic plan because he had expectations of financial aid from the Arab world.

25 Pablo Ramos, *Antecedentes y Mecánica del Golpe del 17 de Julio de 1980* (Mexico 1981) p.6. In the middle of the Natusch coup Ramos wrote a discursive political essay that was more sympathetic to parliament but still pointed to its diminishing stock with the independent left, *Democracia Boliviana: Sus Defensores y Sus Enemigos* (La Paz 1979). Guillermo Lora's analysis was concentrated much more directly on the COB leadership, which, he argued, had effectively thwarted the possibilities of an insurrectionary moment by holding back the strike and acceding to negotiations, *Enseñanzas de la Semana Trágica* (La Paz 1979).

26 *Coyuntura*, no.34, 1 Dec. 1979; *Aquí*, 24–30 Nov. 1979.

27 Arce Gómez's background remains somewhat obscure, but some details are given in *Crónicas*, La Paz, April 1983, and *Bolivia-Información y Análisis*, Quito, no.1, Nov. 1980.

28 *Coyuntura*, no.34, 1 Dec. 1979.

29 *Presencia*, 12 Jan. 1980.

30 *Aquí*, 22 Dec. 1979–4 Jan. 1980.

31 For details of the measures and the IMF operation in Bolivia, see *Coyuntura*, nos. 36 and 37, 1–15 Jan. 1980.

32 Ibid., no.35, 15 Dec. 1979.

33 *Aquí*, 12–18 April 1980.

34 Ibid.

35 Ibid.

36 *Coyuntura*, no.43, 15 April 1980.

37 Ibid., no.42, 1 April 1980.

38 Ibid., no.38, 1 Feb. 1980.

39 *El Diario*, 27 Jan. 1980.

40 *Coyuntura*, no.39, 15 Feb. 1980.

41 Selser, p.44.

42 For details, see *Coyuntura*, no.41, 15 March 1980; no.43, 15 April 1980.

43 For the PS-1's position, see *Aquí*, 10–16 May 1980. The party came in for particularly heavy criticism from the POR, which maintained its critique of parliamentarianism throughout this period: Guillermo Lora, *El PS-1 Responde a la Ideología Burguesa* (La Paz 1979) and *Los Electoreros sirven a la Burguesía: La Inviabilidad de la Democracia* (La Paz 1980).

44 *Aquí*, 5–11 April 1980. A selection of Espinal's writings and an account of his life are given in *Luis Espinal: El Grito de un Pueblo* (Lima 1981).

45 Ibid., 1–8 March 1980.

46 *Coyuntura*, no.44, 1 May 1980.

47 *El Diario*, 16 April 1980.

48 *Apertura*, La Paz, no.1, 30 April–6 May 1980.

49 *Coyuntura*, no.44, 1 May 1980.

50 Ibid., no.46, 1 June 1980.

51 For the history of the PS-1's proposals, see ibid.; *Manaña el Pueblo*, La Paz, no.1, June 1980. For the PCB's response: *Aquí*, 7–13 June 1980.

52 *Golpe*, 5–11 June 1980; *Esto Es*, no.2, 28 Sept. 1982.

53 *Presencia*, 5 June 1980.

54 Ibid., 8 June 1980.

55 *Coyuntura*, no.47, 15 June 1980.

56 Full details of the coup are given in *Bolivia: Información y Análisis*, no.1, Nov. 1980; PADI, *Los Cien Primeros Días de Una Larga Noche* (Quito 1981); PADI, *Cronología de una Dictadura* (Quito 1982); POR, *Testimonios de Represión* (La Paz 1981); Latin America Bureau, *Bolivia: Coup d'Etat* (London 1980).

Chapter Eight

1 This letter is reprinted in *La Heróica Resistencia de los Mineros de Bolivia* (Lima 1981), which contains a detailed description as well as many vivid photos of the defence of the mines. See also PADI, *Cronología*, which reproduces the events of the García Meza regime on a day-by-day basis over 500 pages; *Los Cien Primeros Días*, pp.63–83; Del Granado, *Artemio Camargo*, pp.333–371; Donato Torrico, *Crónica del Abortamiento de la Democracia* (La Paz 1980).

2 *Presencia*, 22 July; 13 Aug.; 8 Sept. 1980.

3 Highlights of the programme are reprinted in *El Diario*, 16 Nov. 1980.

4 *El Día*, Mexico, 29 Sept. 1980.

5 The original decrees of the GUN are reprinted in *Bolivia: Información y Análisis*, no.1, No. 1980.

6 *Presencia*. 28 Feb. 1981; EFE, Buenos Aires, 27 Oct. 1980.

7 Full details and many testimonies of repression are given in *Los Cien Primeros Días* and POR, *Testimonios de Represión* (La Paz 1980).

8 Unpublished manuscript, Sept. 1982. Escóbar was detained for 22 days before being exiled to Spain.

9 *Bolivia: Información y Análisis*, no.2, Dec. 1980, p.2.

10 Ibid., p.11.

11 Ibid., no.4, Feb. 1981; Selser, p.197.

12 Selser, p.77.

13 *Clarín*, Buenos Aires, 6 Aug, 1980.

14 *Bolivia: Información y Análisis*, no.1, Nov. 1980.

15 This might be understood to be a very special variant of that general misconception of production when it is viewed purely in terms of appearances, a misconception that Marx endeavoured to rectify in *Capital*, where he enjoins the reader to 'take leave for a time of this noisy sphere, where everything takes place on the surface and in the view of all men, and follow (Mr Moneybags and the possessor of labour power) into the hidden abode of production, on whose threshold there stares us in the face "No admittance except on business."' Karl Marx, *Capital* (London 1974) I, p.172. I am indebted to Victoria Principal for drawing my attention to this reference.

16 *Narcotráfico y Política* (Madrid 1982) p.13. This text published by IEPALA is not written, as it claims, by the London-based Latin America Bureau but combines the efforts of Bolivians with foreign observers. It gives few sources for its information, but when I have cited it I have cross-checked the reliability of the data as far as it is possible to do. In my view the book is generally reliable but rather sensationalist. It is effectively impossible to give much information collected on this subject verifiable sources. Only the naive or the exceedingly stupid would engage in such an enterprise.

17 *Time*, 6 July 1981.

18 René Bascopé Aspiazu, *La Veta Blanca. Coca y Cocaina en Bolivia* (La Paz 1982) p.109; Amado Canelas Orellana and Juan Carlos Canelas Zannier, *Bolivia: Coca, Cocaina* (Cochabamba 1983) p.364; *New York Times*, 6 Aug. 1982. The books by Bascopé and Canelas and his son are the most thoughtful and suggestive on the subject to appear to date although Bascopé tends to exaggerate the degree to which the cocaine trade emerged as a consciously planned activity and the Canelas volume is much too kind to the military regimes of this time, possibly because the authors were employees of the CNLCN. The IMF estimate for 1980 export earnings was $49 million, *Hoy*, 22 Sept. 1982.

19 For detailed discussion of these properties and their social consequences see William E. Carter ed., *Ensayos Científicos sobre la Coca* (La Paz 1983); Antonil, *Mama Coca* (London 1978); William E. Carter, Mauricio Mamani, José V. Morales and Philip Parkerson, *Coca en Bolivia* (La Paz 1980); W. Golden Mortimer, *The History of Coca* (San Francisco 1974).

20 Canelas, p.95.

21 Cited in *Narcotráfico y Política*, pp.28–29.

22 José Agustín Morales, *Monografía de las Provincias de Nor y Sur Yungas, La Paz* (La Paz 1929); Humberto Fossati, *Monografía de Nor y Sur Yungas* (La Paz 1948); Javier Albó, *El Mundo de la Coca en Coripata, Bolivia* (La Paz 1978).

23 Canelas, p.242. Calculation of these matters is complicated by the fact that coca is marketed by the drum (*tambor*), which weighs approximately 23 kilos in La Paz and 29 kilos in Cochabamba, or by the basket (*cesta*), weighing 30 pounds in La Paz and 18.5 pounds in Cochabamba. These differences do not appear to have been taken into account by the authors of *Narcotráfico y Política*.

24 PRODES, cited in Canelas, p.226.

25 Ibid., p.412.

26 Bascopé, p.40.

27 Ibid., pp.40–41; *Narcotráfico y Política*, p.140; *Time*, 6 July 1981.

28 Canelas, p.358.

29 *El Diario*, 19 Nov. 1970.

30 Bascopé, p.90; *Marka*, Lima, 5 March 1981.

31 Bascopé, p.93.

32 Canelas, p.130.

33 *Latin America Political Report*, 2 March 1979.

34 Bascopé, pp.57–58.

35 Monique Leclerc and Francois Fallarean, 'Narcotráfico; Orígen y Base de la Dictadura Boliviana', *Excelsior*, Mexico, 7 April 1981; Selser, pp.135–136.

36 *Isto E*, Rio de Janeiro, Dec. 1981.

37 *Presencia*, 23 Sept. 1981.

38 *Marka*, 28 Aug. 1980; *Excelsior*, 7 April 1981; *Narcotráfico y Política*, pp.55–56.

39 *Miami Herald*, 14 Oct. 1980.

40 Ibid., 16 May 1981; *Presencia*, 23 Jan. 1982.

41 *Excelsior*, 7 April 1981.

42 *Veja*, Sao Paulo, 8 Oct. 1980.
43 *Aquí*, edición clandestina no.4, Aug. 1980.
44 *Panorama*, Rome, 20 Sept.; 27 Sept. 1982.
45 *Excelsior*, 7 April 1981; *Narcotráfico y Política*, p.72.
46 *El Heraldo*, Mexico, 14 Aug. 1980.
47 *New York Times*, 31 Aug. 1980; *Wall Street Journal*, 8 May 1981.
48 *Narcotráfico y Política*, p.71.
49 *Aquí*, 9 April 1983.
50 *Der Spiegel*, 5 Feb. 1981.
51 *Excelsior*, 10 April 1981.
52 *Los Tiempos*, 4 Sept. 1981.
53 *Ultima Hora*, 30 July 1980.
54 Selser, p.166.
55 *Presencia*, 20 May; 22 May 1981.
56 Selser, p.202.
57 *El Mundo*, Santa Cruz, 24 June 1981.
58 *Presencia*, 21 June 1981.
59 Canelas, p.164.
60 Bascopé, p.102.
61 Canelas, pp.275−278; *Narcotráfico y Política*, pp.155−157.
62 For details see *Bolivia: Información y Análisis*, no.3, Jan. 1981.
63 *Cronología*, pp.289−292, gives the most dispassionate of the many accounts of this incident.
64 For details of the Santa Cruz conflict see *Bolivia: Información y Análisis*, no.2, Dec. 1980; no.3, Jan. 1981; no.4, Feb. 1981.
65 *Narcotráfico y Política*, p.80; *Excelsior*, 10 April 1981.
66 *El Mundo*, 3 May 1981.
67 Ibid.
68 Valverde's detailed account appears in *Criterio*, no.21, 18 April 1983. In an earlier interview Prado avoided discussing the affair and spoke principally of the army's role in consolidating democracy, ibid., no.19, 10 March 1983.
69 Selser, pp.257−258.
70 *Presencia*, 22 Sept. 1980; 24 June 1981.
71 *Aquí*, July 1981.
72 *El Deber*, Santa Cruz, 6 May 1981.
73 *Bolivia Libre*, no.54, May 1981.
74 *Compañero*, La Paz, June 1981; *El Día*, 20 June 1981.
75 The extensive discussion between Paz Zamora and a very sceptical Gregorio Selser on this issue was published in *El Día*, 31 May; 7 June; 14 June 1981.
76 *Hoy*, 6 June 1981.
77 *Presencia*, 26 June 1981.
78 I possess a photocopy of this document which is, unfortunately, of too poor a quality to be reproduced here. The letter is dated 1 June, three weeks before the rising, but it is possible that disbursement of such funds took some time and may have even taken place in an impromptu fashion once the coup was underway. The letter mentions one officer — Colonel Tito Justiniano — twice, suggesting that it did not pass through the palace's normal bureaucratic channels. Apart from Rico Toro and Rodrigo Leo Plaza, who were to receive $200,000, the officers named are: General Carlos Turdera; Colonels Tito Justiniano; Alberto Gribowsky; Arturo Doria Medina; Jorge Moreira; Luis Cordeiro; Rómulo Mercado; Luis Kuramoto; José Quirós; Rolando Arzabe; José Miguel Padilla; Oscar Angulo; Guido Vildoso; and Captain Luis Cossio to receive $100,000 each. Additionally, Colonels Aroldo Pinto; Raúl González; Yamil Taja;

Walter Seleme; Moisés Chirique; and Javier Rodríguez to receive $50,000 each along with $30,000 for Captain Roberto Nielsen Reyes. Some officers have subsequently denied receiving any money.

79 *Presencia*, 11 July 1981.

80 Resolución Suprema 195154, 14 May 1981; *Presencia*, 15 Sept. 1981.

81 *Presencia*, 5 Aug. 1981.

82 *Bolivia: Información y Análisis*, no.8, June 1981; no.9, July 1981.

83 For details see Marcelo Calderón Saravia ed., *El Paquete Económico del Gobierno Torrelio* (La Paz 1982).

Glossary

ADN	Acción Democrática Nacionalista
ALIN	Alianza de Izquierda Nacional
ANMM	Asociación de Mineros Medianos
APDHB	Asociación Permanente de Derechos Humanos de Bolivia
APIN	Alianza Popular de Integración Nacional
BAMIN	Banco Minero
CBF	Corporación Boliviana de Fomento
CEPAL	Comisión Económica Para América Latina
CIPCA	Centro de Investigación y Promoción Campesina
CITE	Comando de Instrucción de Tropas Especiales
CNSS	Caja Nacional de Seguridad Social
CNTCB	Confederación Nacional de Trabajadores Campesinos de Bolivia
COB	Central Obrera Boliviana
COBUR	Central Obrera Boliviana de Unidad Revolucionaria
COD	Central Obrera Departmental
COFADENA	Corporación de las Fuerzas Armadas para el Desarrollo Nacional
COMIBOL	Corporación Minera de Bolivia
CONADE	Comité Nacional de Defensa de la Democracia
CSUTCB	Confederación Sindical Unica de Trabajadores Campesinos de Bolivia
CUB	Confederación Universitaria Boliviana
DEA	Drugs Enforcement Administration
DIE	Dirección de Inteligencia del Estado
DIC	Departamento de Investigación Criminal
DIN	Departamento de Investigación Nacional
DOP	Departamento de Orden Político
ELN	Ejército de Liberación Nacional
EMG	Estado Mayor General
ENAF	Empresa Nacional de Fundiciones
FAB	Fuerza Aerea de Bolivia
FARO	Frente de Acción Revolucionaria Obrera
FDRNA	Frente Democrático Revolucionario Nueva Alternativa
FPN	Frente Popular Nacionalista
FRA	Frente Revolucionario Anti-imperialista

FRI	Frente Revolucionario de la Izquierda
FSB	Falange Socialista Boliviana
FSTMB	Federación Sindical de Trabajadores Mineros de Bolivia
FUL	Federación Universitaria Local
FURMOD	Fuerzas Unidas para la Represión y el Mantenimiento del Orden y el Desarrollo
GAC	Grup Aéreo de Caza
GRO	Grupo Revolucionario Octubre
ISAL	Iglesia y Sociedad en América Latina
LAB	Lloyd Aéreo Boliviano
MACA	Ministerio de Asuntos Campesinos
MIR	Movimiento de la Izquierda Revolucionaria
MITKA	Movimiento Indio Tupac Katari
MLN	Movimiento de Liberación Nacional
MNR	Movimiento Nacionalista Revolucionario
MPLN	Movimiento Popular de Liberación Nacional
MRTK	Movimiento Revolucionario Tupac Katari
OST	Organización Socialista de los Trabajadores
PCB	Partido Comunista de Bolivia
PCML	Partido Comunista Marxista Leninista
PDC	Partido Demócrata Cristiano
PDCR	Partido Demócrata Cristiano Revolucionario
PIB	Partido Indio de Bolivia
PIR	Partido de la Izquierda Revolucionaria
POR	Partido Obrero Revolucionario
PRA	Partido Revolucionario Auténtico
PRIN	Partido Revolucionario de la Izquierda Nacional
PRTB	Partido Revolucionario de los Trabajadores de Bolivia
PS	Partido Socialista
PSC	Partido Social Cristiano
PS-1	Partido Socialista Uno
RADEPA	Razón de Patria
SES	Servicio Especial de Seguridad
TAM	Transportes Aéreos Militares
UCAPO	Unión de Campesinos Pobres
UDP	Unión Democrática y Popular
UMBO	Unión de Mujeres de Bolivia
UMSA	Universidad Mayor de San Andrés
UMSS	Universidad Mayor de San Simón
UNP	Unión Nacionalista del Pueblo
VO	Vanguardia Obrera
YPFB	Yacimientos Petrolíferos Fiscales Bolivianos

Index

380